| DATE DUE | | | |
|---|---|---|---|
| | | | |
| | | | |
| | | | |
| | | | |
| | | | |
| | | | |
| | | | |
| | | | |
| | | | |
| | | | |
| | | | |
| | | | |
| | | | |

*Change in the Amazon Basin*
*Volume II:*

# The frontier after a decade of colonisation

*Symposium held at*
*the 44th International Congress of*
*Americanists, Manchester*
*6–10 September 1982*

CHANGE IN THE AMAZON BASIN
VOLUME II:

# The frontier after a decade of colonisation

EDITED BY JOHN HEMMING,
Director and Secretary,
Royal Geographical Society, London

Manchester University Press

Published by Manchester University Press
Oxford Road, Manchester M13 9PL
*and* 51 Washington Street, Dover
New Hampshire 03820, USA

*British Library cataloguing in publication data*

Change in the Amazon basin.
  Vol. 2: The frontier after a decade of colonisation
  1. Amazon River Valley—Social conditions
  2. Brazil—Social conditions—1945–
  I. International Congress of Americanists
  (*44th : 1982 : Manchester*) II. Hemming,
  John, 19— –
  981'.1        HN290.A4

*Library of Congress cataloging in publication data*
Main entry under title:

Change in the Amazon basin.

    Organized by the Royal Geographical Society.
    Includes bibliographies and indexes.
    Contents: v. 1. Man's impact on forests and rivers—
v. 2. The frontier after a decade of colonisation.
    1. Land settlement—Amazon River Region—Congresses
2. Agricultural colonies—Amazon River Region—Congresses. 3. Amazon River Region—Population—Congresses. 4. Man—Influence on nature—Amazon River Region—Congresses. 5. Indians of South America—Amazon River Region—Congresses. 6. Deforestation—Amazon River Region—Congresses. I. Hemming, John, 1935–  . II. International Congress of Americanists (44th : 1982 : Manchester, Greater Manchester) III. Royal Geographical Society.
HD499.A45C47    1985          330.981'1          85–873

ISBN 0–7190–0967–7 (v. 1)
ISBN 0–7190–0968–5 (v. 2)

Photoset in Great Britain
by Northern Phototypesetting Co, Bolton
Printed in Great Britain
by Unwin Brothers Ltd
The Gresham Press
Old Woking, Surrey
A member of the Martins Printing Group

# Contents

# List of contributors

ROSA ACEVEDO MARIN
Paris

SAMUEL BENCHIMOL
Professor of Introduction to the Amazon, University of Amazonas,
Manaus

FR JUAN BOTTASSO
Mundo Shuar, Quito

STEPHEN G. BUNKER
Department of Sociology, Johns Hopkins University, Baltimore

RICHARD CHASE SMITH
Cultural Survival Institute, Harvard University, Cambridge, Mass.

JANET M. CHERNELA
Department of Anthropology, Columbia University, New York

ALBERTO CHIRIF
Lima

J. COLIN CROSSLEY
Department of Geography, University of Leicester

PETER A. FURLEY
Department of Geography, University of Edinburgh

LOURDES GONÇALVES FURTADO
Museu Paraense Emilio Goeldi, Belém

JEAN HÉBETTE
Paris

REBECCA HOLMES
Maraven Oil Co., Caracas

JOHAN M. G. KLEINPENNING AND SJOUKJE VOLBEDA
Geography and Physical Planning Department, Catholic University of
Nijmegen, The Netherlands

LAERCIO L. LEITE
University of Brasília

DARREL MILLER
Department of Anthropology, College at Brockport, State University of
New York

EMILIO F. MORAN
Department of Anthropology, Indiana University

L. J. A. MOUGEOT
Nucleus of Higher Amazon Studies, Federal University of Pará, Belém

STEPHEN NUGENT
Department of Anthropology, University College London and University
of London Goldsmiths' College

MARIANNE SCHMINK
Center for Latin American Studies, University of Florida, Gainesville

JANET TOWNSEND
Department of Geography, University of Durham

JORGE E. UQUILLAS
Quito

ALONSO ZARZAR
Cambridge University

# Acronyms

| | |
|---|---|
| ABA | Associação Brasileira de Antropologia (Brazilian Association of Anthropologists) |
| BID | Banco Interamericano de Desarrollo (Interamerican Development Bank) |
| BNH | Banco Nacional da Habitação |
| CAPEMI | Caixa de Peculio dos Militares (Military Pension Fund) |
| CIAT | Centro Internacional de Agricultura Tropical (International Centre for Tropical Agriculture, Cali, Colombia) |
| CIU | Comité de Iglesias Unidas (Bolivia) |
| CLAG | Conference of Latin American Geographers |
| CNPq | Conselho Nacional de Desenvolvimento Científico e Tecnológico (National Council for Scientific and Technological Development) |
| CVRD | Companhia Vale do Rio Doce (Rio Doce Valley Corporation) |
| DNER | Departamento Nacional de Estradas e Rodagem (National Highways Department) |
| Eletronorte | Centrais Eletricas do Norte do Brasil (North Brazil Electricity Board) |
| EMBRAPA | Empresa Brasileira de Pesquisa Agropecuária (Brazilian Agricultural Research Institute, Ministry of Agriculture) |
| FIBGE | Fundação IBGE (Brazilian Geographical Institute) |
| FUNAI | Fundação Nacional do Indio (National Indian Foundation; Ministry of Interior) |
| GEAMAM | Grupo de Estudos e Assessoramento do Meio Ambiente (Environmental Study and Assessment Group of CVRD) |
| IBDF | Instituto Brasileiro do Desenvolvimento Florestal (Brazilian Institute for Forest Development; Ministry of Agriculture) |
| IBGE | Instituto Brasileiro de Geografia e Estatística (Brazilian Institute of Geography and Statistics) |
| IBRD | International Bank for Reconstruction and Development (World Bank) |
| IERAC | Instituto Ecuatoriano de Reforma Agraria y Colonización |
| IFC | International Finance Corporation (World Bank affiliate investing in the private sector) |

| | |
|---|---|
| ILV | Instituto Linguístico del Verano |
| INC | Instituto Nacional de Colonizacion (Bolivia) |
| INCRA | Instituto Nacional de Colonização e Reforma Agraria (National Institute for Colonisation and Agrarian Reform) |
| INCRAE | Instituto Nacional de Colonización del Región Amazonica del Ecuador |
| INPA | Instituto Nacional de Pesquisas da Amazônia (National Institute for Amazonian Research; of CNDCT) |
| INPES | Instituto de Pesquisas (Brazil) |
| IPEA | Instituto de Planejamento Econômico e Social (Institute of Economic Planning) |
| IPLAN | Instituto de Planejamento (Brazil) |
| IVIC | Instituto Venezolano de Investigaciones Cientificas |
| KfW | Kreditanstalt für Wiederaufbau (West German Reconstruction Bank) |
| MINTER | Ministério do Interior (Brazil) |
| NAEA | Núcleo do Altos Estudos Amazónicos (Belém, Brazil) |
| Polonoroeste | Programa Integrado de Desenvolvimento do Noroeste do Brasil (Northwest Region Integrated Development Programme) |
| SEMA | Secretaria Especial do Meio Ambiente (Special Environmental Secretariat, Ministry of Interior) |
| SEPLAN | Secretaria de Planejamento da Presidência da República (Brazil) |
| SUDAM | Superintendência de Desenvolvimento da Amazônia (Amazonian Development Superintendency) |
| SUDECO | Superintendência do Desenvolvimento da Região Centro-Oeste (Superintendency for the Development of the Centre-West Region) |
| SUDENE | Superintendência do Desenvolvimento do Nordeste (Superintendency for the Development of the Northeast) |
| UFPa | Universidade Federal do Pará (Belém, Brazil) |

# Introduction

When Professor Emilio Moran chaired the first session of the symposium 'Change in the Amazon Basin' he announced that he was opening the largest conference ever organised about the world's largest river. The symposium was staged by the Royal Geographical Society as its contribution to the 44th International Congress of Americanists in Manchester, 6–10 September 1982. Thirty-five papers were presented at this symposium and they are published in two volumes. Restrictions of space have made it necessary to publish eight of these papers in summary only.

This volume *The Frontier after a Decade of Colonisation* looks at the results of Brazil's Programme of National Integration, launched with the start of the Transamazon Highway in late 1970, and similar colonisation schemes in other Amazon countries. It has analyses of demographic change, case histories of frontier communities, appraisal of government development agencies, and studies of native societies' problems of acculturation and nutrition.

The companion volume *Man's Impact on Forests and Rivers* deals with giant projects, with physical geographical aspects of change, and with indigenous use of the tropical rainforest environment. There are summaries of papers on historical themes and on Indian acculturation.

## Colonisation case studies

Many papers were concerned with reactions of individual settlers to the expanding frontiers. Janet Townsend showed how Colombian peasant-farmers overcame the wet and dry seasons in their agricultural year. Other delegates felt that this seasonality deserved further study: it could yield important lessons for frontier planning agencies. She also illustrated conflicts between capitalist agencies and settlers and the problems the peasant-farmers have to surmount to obtain credit and remain financially solvent.

A theme emerged from the papers of Townsend, Emilio Moran, Darrell Posey and Lourdes Furtado: that long-established Amazon farmers or *caboclos* were more successful than colonists introduced in new government-aided programmes. Moran told how *caboclos* near Altamira knew far more about land fertility and water availability than youthful agency administrators with good technical education. Furtado had analysed fish catches in northeast Pará and showed that skilled traditional fishermen consistently outperformed state-aided projects and newcomers.

Stephen Nugent described his research among settlers near Santarém do Pará. He sought to show negative effects of foreign aid and US aid in particular on

Amazonia. He commented that aid donors may have intended that colonists should fail in order to open up attractive investment opportunities. This argument was disputed by many delegates in the discussion period. They pointed out that US aid for Amazon colonisation had ceased long before the period under discussion. It was agreed that foreign aid could not be held responsible for failures in the Brazilian road-building programme and attendant settlement schemes.

A number of other papers focused on individual colonisation schemes. Jean Hébette and Rosa Acevedo argued that the Brazilian agency INCRA (*Instituto Nacional de Colonização e Reforma Agraria*) pursued a policy that favoured the concentration of land among mining companies, property developers and large traditional farmers, at the expense of small colonists, Indians and squatters. It did this by the distribution of plots, of credit and of technical assistance. These authors had studied the colony of Ariquêmes in the new state of Rondônia. Dr Peter Furley described a similar new settlement at Ouro Prêto in the same state. He was disappointed by the results of this scheme. Even though it was located on some of the most fertile soil in the region, it was not prospering. This was not due to any social manipulation by INCRA, and the success or failure of individual settlers did not even relate to the relative fertility of their individual soils.

Stephen Bunker attacked INCRA's aggressive promotion of 'southeastern' crops such as rice, beans and corn and its neglect of traditional Amazon foods such as manioc, bananas, game and fish. Its employees found the *várzea* floodplain frightening, and they ignored slash-and-burn farming techniques that were both ecologically sound and agriculturally productive. There was much inter-agency rivalry and misunderstanding. Agency demands for documents militated against the peasant class.

There was a valuable discussion on the merits of the staff of INCRA and other similar colonisation agencies. They were generally thought to be well intentioned and to believe in what they were doing. INCRA's own staff members often blamed the agency for excessive bureaucracy and for failure to support them with sufficient funds. Delegates felt that INCRA's young experts were generally ill-prepared and suffered from origins in cities or far more developed parts of southeast Brazil. They were consequently out of touch with the settlers they were supposed to help. Their procedures were usually inappropriate to frontier conditions and they failed to learn from *caboclos* who had long been established there. The career structure of INCRA was also criticised. Its personnel had little incentive, and the most talented were removed from field jobs to work in overmanned head offices.

In neighbouring Bolivia, Dr Colin Crossley had been impressed by many aspects of the new colonies of Piray and San Julián, created in virgin land north of Santa Cruz on the headwaters of the Madeira-Mamoré. These colonies were started by an interdenominational church committee and were then transferred to the Bolivian National Institute of Colonisation. The schemes had benefitted from foreign aid from several countries. They attracted ambitious colonists from highland Bolivia.

Although there had been much turnover in settlers, individual abandoned plots tended to be acquired by neighbouring settlers or by newcomers. There was definitely not a move towards ownership by large farms or commercial enterprises. These colonies consciously sought to imitate the American Frontier, and the colonists aspired to get rich. They found that shifting cultivation was desirable, with about a tenth of each 50–ha plot being farmed at any time. The insuperable problem was overproduction of basic crops and a chronic shortage of customers. As a result, plots in the colonies were yielding farmers incomes as small as the wages of urban manual labourers.

Two delegates studied unusual and independent social groups: the *garimpeiro* mineral prospectors; and the social elite of a growing Amazon town. Dr Marianne Schmink found the *garimpeiros* of southern Pará to be fiercely proud, independent, flamboyantly generous when lucky, and doggedly persistent in their mining toil. A recent gold rush at Serra Pelada had attracted 25 000 prospectors, only a quarter of whom were professional *garimpeiros*. The government had difficulty controlling these individualists and transferring their workings to large mining companies. Professor Darrel Miller demonstrated how the traditional landed gentry of Itaituba on the Tapajós was being replaced by a new elite of army officers, civil servants, and entrepreneurs who took advantage of new communications and financial systems.

## Demographic

Professor Luc Mougeot argued that one result of recent government intervention had been a reshuffling of population within the region. There is a trend to migrate to medium-sized towns. Places that were once 'promised lands' are being deserted in intra-regional migrations, and some remote parts of northern Amazonas are being depopulated. He had interviewed settlers at four booming towns along new highways: Conceição do Araguaia, Marabá, Altamira and Humaitá. His work showed that rural settlers migrated for survival, moving very frequently, although for short distances, in search of precarious employment and social improvement. Some poor rural workers had been clever in imitating INCRA plot layouts and procedures, in order to gain land titles. Professor Benchimol pointed out that a new government policy was to enhance and modernise isolated small towns along the main rivers, away from cattle ranches on new roads on the *terra firme*.

A meticulous analysis of the last three 10-yearly censuses by Professor Jan Kleinpenning showed that by far the greater part of the population increase of 'Amazônia Legal' was in Mato Grosso, Goiás and western Maranhão. This was clearly the result of their better communications to the big markets of southeast Brazil and the Atlantic seaboard states. There was thus a densely populated frontier pushing inland. The government should concentrate its planning effort on these fast-growing regions rather than the more glamorous and environmentally destructive colonisation schemes of the remote frontier and the new penetration roads. Professor Benchimol confirmed these findings. Apart from Maranhão

(Amazonia's 'rice-basket') and lands near the southeast, the most dramatic population growth in Amazonia was around the city of Manaus.

## Acculturation

Three papers focused on political problems of indigenous groups at the Andean edge of the Amazon Basin. Alonso Zarzar described traditional intertribal exchanges and hostility between groups on the Urubamba and Ucayali. Political hierarchies and tribal territories are being shattered by acculturation and by government colonisation schemes. Alberto Chirif outlined how successive Peruvian governments have tried to invade tribal lands. This process has intensified with new penetration roads, settlements, 'special projects', and legislation that threatens Indians' territorial rights. Dr Chase Smith gave an eloquent illustration of what was happening to the Amuesha through such a project. Most Amuesha communities will be left with lands far too small for their subsistence or survival, and with no hope for future economic development. This example was so serious that it gave rise to a series of resolutions about native communites' lands, that the Symposium delegates agreed to direct to the Peruvian government.

Father Bottasso, a Salesian missionary working for Ecuador's Shuar (Jívaro), admitted that during past centuries missionaries have often been instruments of colonialist policies. The Shuar resisted, consistently and successfully. Some missionary policies are now changing dramatically, away from religious conversion and social acculturation. Rebecca Holmes described nutritional studies by medical missionaries among the Venezuelan Yanomami. Although Indian children were smaller and appeared to have weaker diets than 'civilised' counterparts, they in fact consume more protein and grow into stronger adults (on a weight/height ratio) who are successful in resisting intestinal parasites. Also in the upper Río Negro, Dr Chernela told how one Uanano village on the Uaupés had successfully resisted an attempt by Salesian missionaries to change its traditional system of chieftainship.

The Amazon Basin occupies roughly half the South American continent, and the Amazon is easily the world's largest river. Its basin contains over 60 per cent of surviving tropical rainforests. Within the wilderness and the vast network of Amazonian rivers is a richer diversity of species of flora and fauna than in any other region on earth. The Amazon Basin is suffering more violent and lasting change in the present decade than at any time in its history. Change of this magnitude to such an important but sensitive region is of acute concern, not only to the countries of South America, but to all mankind.

The impetus for the present onslaught is to enrich the Amazonian countries. It was hoped that Amazonia could help to feed and house the poor of these Third World countries. The attempt to colonise the Amazon frontiers is one of the most ambitious settlement programmes of recent times. It was launched into a region whose tribal societies are successfully adapted their difficult environment, but who are very vulnerable to violent acculturation. For these reasons, the Amazonian settlement experiments provide important lessons in both development and ethnographic studies.

John Hemming
Director and Secretary
Royal Geographical Society
London

# 1  Recent changes in population size and distribution in the Amazon region of Brazil

JOHAN M. G. KLEINPENNING and
SJOUKJE VOLBEDA

This contribution deals with recent changes in population size and distribution in the Amazon region of Brazil and considers them in relation to the measures which have been taken by the Brazilian government, particularly since the mid-1960s, to integrate Amazônia more into the national economy and society.

## The development measures after 1960

Although the Superintendência do Plano de Valorização Económica da Amazônia (SPVEA) was created in 1953 to develop the Amazon region and 3% of federal revenues were even set aside for the purpose under a provision of the 1946 constitution, through various circumstances no significant results were achieved. During the 1960s and '70s, however, there was not only a renewed interest in the Amazon region, but this interest also led to a number of specific government measures, some of which may even by characterised as spectacular. Briefly summarised, the following events from the past two decades appear to be the most significant:

1 In 1960 a road link was completed between Brasília and Belém (Figure 1).
2 In 1964 Brazil came under a military regime which has as one of its principal aims the encouragement of rapid economic growth and which also intends to let the Amazon region make a substantial contribution to that growth.
3 In 1965 a second very important road link was completed, namely that between Cuiabá and Pôrto Velho, thus enabling Rondônia to be reached overland from the southeast.
4 In 1966, in pursuit of the government policy described under 2 above, the Superintendência do Desenvolvimento da Amazônia (SUDAM) was established as a successor to the SPVEA and given the task as a regional organisation of stimulating the progress of the Amazon region and coordinating the consequent measures to be taken by the various official bodies, as well as the activities of private entrepreneurs. One of the most important activities of the SUDAM was the encouragement and supervision of private investments facilitated by the

various tax concessions in Amazônia (Figure 2).

5 In 1967 a free trade zone was created for Manaus and its environs.

6 In 1970 it was decided to build the Transamazônica (Transamazon Highway), the first stretch of which (Estreito–Itaituba) was completed in 1972 and a second section (Itaituba–Humaitá) in 1974. This highway linked the southern part of the Amazon region with the Northeast of Brazil. Partly as a result of the extreme droughts which afflicted the northeast in 1970 a programme of social colonisation was launched, within the framework of which the government aimed to provide a new livelihood in the Amazon region for at least 100 000 families within five years. The majority of the colonists were to come from the Northeast. Although these ambitious aims were not realised for various reasons, the completion of the Transamazônica did make possible a considerable stream of spontaneous colonisation. This incidentally also occurred after the completion of other highways (see Figure 1).

7 A number of smaller road links were also completed within the framework of the efforts to achieve further economic development and integration of the Amazon region. These included the roads between Manaus and Boa Vista and Manaus and Pôrto Velho. Among the larger roads special mention should be made of the link between Cuiabá and Santarém, completed in 1976.

8 In the Second Development Plan, covering the period 1975–9 the policy was modified. There had been much criticism of the social colonisation programme for the Northeast and the results of it had been rather disappointing. This led the Brazilian government, which wished to see quick results, to place the emphasis entirely on rapid economic growth and to encourage large-scale cattle farming, arable farming, mining and forestry through the agency of major private entrepreneurs. The government assumed responsibility for the necessary infrastructure, which was concentrated in fifteen '*polos*' ('Programa de Polos Agropecuários e Agrominerais da Amazônia' – POLAMAZONIA). The intention was that private investment should also be concentrated in these '*polos*', in so far as it was not concentrated there already (Figure 3).

9 The Third Development Plan, launched in 1979, aimed essentially at a continuation of the course adopted in 1975.

## Aim of the analysis

It will be clear that this policy for the Amazon region could considerably influence future population trends. The aim of the following sections, therefore, is to examine to what extent this was the case during the period 1960–80. Not all demographic aspects are considered in the analysis, which is limited mainly to *changes in the total population* of Amazônia and its subregions and to *changes in population distribution*, including those in rural and urban areas. More specifically, this means that attention is paid to the following questions:

1 What changes have occurred in the population growth of Amazônia and what

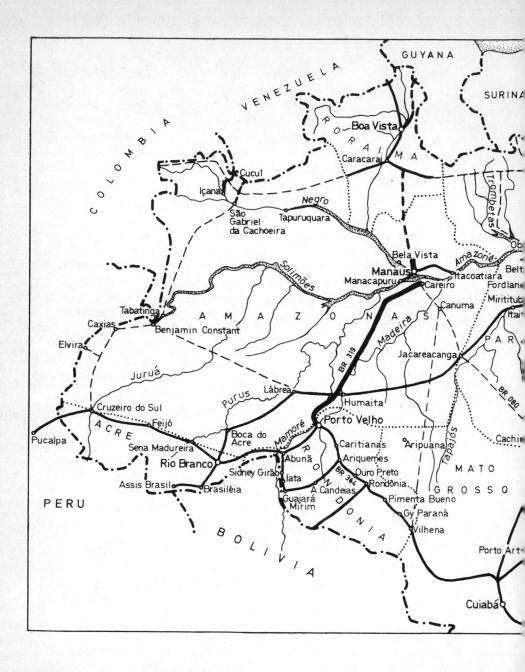

Fig. 1   Road and general reference map of Amazônia Legal (situation in late 1980)

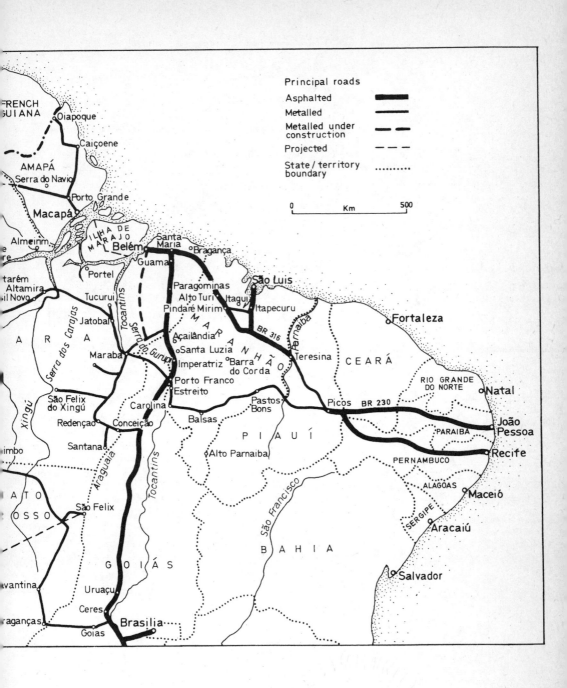

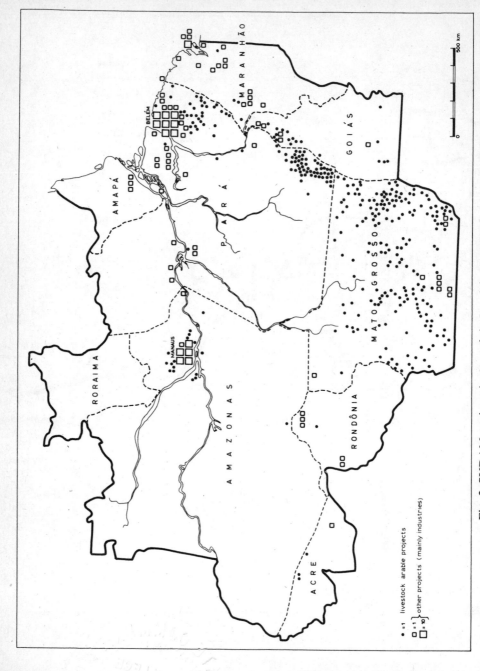

Fig. 2 SUDAM projects in Amazônia Legal (source: Kleinpenning 1977)

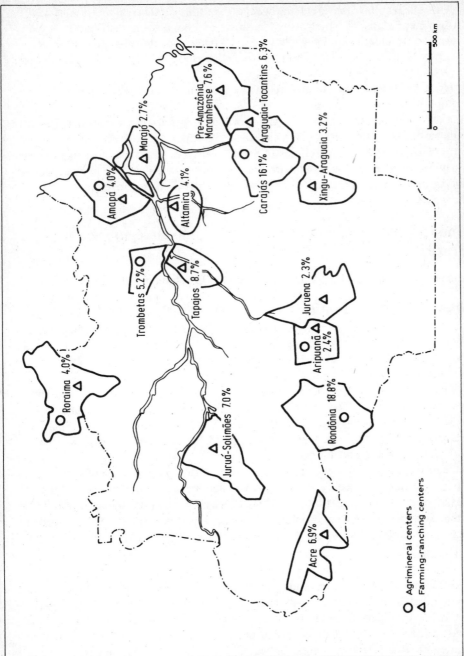

Fig. 3 Programme of agricultural and mineral poles in the Amazon Region – POLAMAZONIA (Figures indicate the part of the total budget allocated in 1975 to each pole)

Amapá 4.0%

Marajó 2.7%

Pre-Amazônia Maranhense 7.6%

Araguaia-Tocantins 6.3%

Carajás 16.1%

Altamira 4.1%

Xingu-Araguaia 3.2%

Trombetas 5.2%

Tapajós 8.7%

Juruena 2.3%

Aripuanã 2.4%

Roraima 4.0%

Juruá-Solimões 7.0%

Rondônia 18.8%

Acre 6.9%

○ Agrimineral centers

△ Farming-ranching centers

500 km

0

consequences have these had for the relative position of this region within Brazil?
2 Are there signs of noteworthy shifts in the population distribution within Amazônia under the influence of the development policy being pursued or of its related indirect effects, as a result of which there have been changes in the relative position of the subregions?
3 Have there been important shifts in the relationship between urban and rural population?

In answering these questions the analysis will concentrate on the period 1970–80, because this is the decade during which the most important development measures were taken, or in which the effects of earlier measures could manifest themselves most clearly. The most marked demographic changes are therefore to be expected during this period. Where necessary, however, attention is also paid to changes during the years 1960–70.

## Changes in the relative position of the Amazon region within Brazil

The population of the North[1] increased from 2.602 million in 1960 to 3.651 million in 1970 and 6.029 million in 1980. That of Amazônia Legal[2] was 5.160 million in 1960, 7.150 million in 1970, but had risen to 11.192 million in 1980 (Table 1). This means that the North accommodated only 3.7% of the Brazilian population in 1960, but that this percentage had risen to 3.9% in 1970 and to as much as 5% in 1980. The share of Amazônia Legal increased from 7.3% in 1960 to 7.6% in 1970 and 9.2% in 1980.

The population increase of the North was 40.3% during the period 1960–70 and as much as 65.1% for the years 1970–80. Amazônia Legal experienced an increase of 38.5% between 1960 and 1970, and one of 56.5% between 1970 and 1980. For Brazilians as a whole there was a growth of 33.1% during the 1960s and one of 28.2% during the following decade.

From these figures it is clear that the Amazon region is not an area of stagnation, but is even characterised by a rate of growth above the national average. This was already the case between 1950 and 1960. Since then, however, the trend has been intensified, giving rise to a population increase which is even comparable to that experienced during the rubber boom of the years 1890–1920.

It is useful to make a comparison not only with the country as a whole, but also with those regions which have long been known as the most important areas of immigration within Brazil. This will make it possible to show the relative position of Amazônia as a growth region. In the first place, a comparison is possible with the metropolitan regions of the nine largest cities (i.e. São Paulo, Rio de Janeiro, Belo Horizonte, Recife, Pôrto Alegre, Salvador, Fortaleza, Curitiba and Belém). The combined absolute population increase of these cities during the period 1960–70 was 8.5 million, accounting for no less than 36.8% of the total increase of Brazil. During the period 1970–80 the increase was 10.71 million, or 41.4% of the national growth.

The figures imply that the population of these metropolitan areas increased by 55.7% between 1960 and 1970 and by 45% during the following decade. The first percentage was still above the growth figure for the North and for Amazônia Legal, but in the following decade the relative growth of the North and of Amazônia Legal exceeded that of the metropolitan areas.

It will be clear, however, that very different absolute numbers are involved, so that it is understandable that during the 1960s the North accounted for only 4.5% of the national population growth and still for no more than 8.9% during the 1970s. Amazônia Legal accounted for 8.5% of national growth during the period 1960–70 and for 15.2% during the decade 1970–80.

The population growth of the Amazon region may also be compared with the population increase of the South and the Southeast combined, these regions forming the economic and demographic heartland of Brazil. During the 1960s the population of the seven states of the South and Southeast increased from 42.995 million to 57.016 million, and then to 71.961 million during the 1970s. This corresponds with a growth of 32.6% between 1960 and 1970, and of 26.2% between 1970 and 1980. The growth rate of the North and of Amazônia Legal was higher than these figures in both decades, but once again the difference in absolute numbers should be borne in mind. Thus the South and the Southeast accounted for 59.7% of national growth during the decade 1960–70, and of 56.1% between 1970 and 1980.

## Explanation of the relatively feeble attractiveness of Amazônia Legal

Although the countryside of northeast Brazil, because of its extreme droughts, unfavourable ownership and occupation relationships and continuing processes of enlargement of scale, can scarcely offer an acceptable existence to many country-dwellers, and although employment in agriculture is continuing to fall in the other parts of Brazil, the figures we have just given show that it is not the case that Amazônia exercises an exceptional attraction on the rest of the country. Despite the existence of large areas of unused land which are gradually being opened up by road construction, the 'surplus' agricultural population is not migrating *en masse* to the North. The share of Amazônia in the national population growth is too modest for that, certainly when it is remembered that a large part of the population growth there is accounted for by natural increase.[3]

The following circumstances, in particular, appear to exercise a negative effect on the volume of the migration flows to Amazônia Legal.

Table 1   Population changes in Amazônia Legal and its subregions, 1960–80

| Subregion | Area in km² | Population in 1960 | Share in 1960 (%) | Population in 1970 | Share in 1970 (%) | Population increase 1960–70 Absolute | As % of 1960 | Share in regional growth 1960–70 |
|---|---|---|---|---|---|---|---|---|
| Amazonas | 1 560 327 | 721 215 | 14.0 | 960 934 | 13.4 | 239 719 | 33.2 | 12.1 |
| Roraima | 230 104 | 29 489 | 0.6 | 41 638 | 0.6 | 12 149 | 41.2 | 0.6 |
| Acre | 152 589 | 160 208 | 3.1 | 218 006 | 3.0 | 57 798 | 36.1 | 2.9 |
| Amapá | 139 068 | 68 889 | 1.3 | 116 480 | 1.6 | 47 591 | 69.1 | 2.4 |
| NW Segment | 2 082 088 | 979 801 | 19.0 | 1 337 058 | 18.6 | 357 257 | 36.5 | 18.0 |
| W Maranhão (2) | 257 451 | 1 879 959 | 36.4 | 2 336 894 | 32.7 | 456 935 | 24.3 | 23.0 |
| Pará | 1 228 870 | 1 550 935 | 30.0 | 2 197 072 | 30.7 | 646 137 | 41.7 | 32.5 |
| N Goiás (2) | 285 793 | 348 278 | 6.8 | 549 050 | 7.7 | 200 772 | 57.6 | 10.1 |
| Mato Grosso | 881 001 | 330 610 | 6.4 | 612 887 | 8.6 | 282 277 | 85.4 | 14.2 |
| Rondônia | 243 044 | 70 783 | 1.4 | 116 620 | 1.6 | 45 837 | 64.7 | 2.3 |
| SE Segment | 2 896 159 | 4 180 565 | 81.0 | 5 812 523 | 81.3 | 1 631 958 | 39.0 | 82.1 |
| Amazônia Legal | 4 978 247 | 5 160 366 | 100.0 | 7 149 581 | 100.0 | 1 989 215 | 38.5 | 100.0 |
| Brazil | 8 511 965 | 70 992 343 | – | 94 508 583 | – | 23 516 240 | 33.1 | – |

| Subregion | Population in 1980 | Share in 1980 (%) | Population increase 1970–80 | | Share in regional growth 1970–80 | Population density per km² | | |
|---|---|---|---|---|---|---|---|---|
| | | | Absolute | As % of 1970 | | 1960 | 1970 | 1980 |
| Amazonas | 1 449 135 | 12.9 | 488 201 | 50.8 | 12.1 | 0.5 | 0.6 | 0.9 |
| Roraima | 82 018 | 0.7 | 40 380 | 97.0 | 1.0 | 0.1 | 0.2 | 0.4 |
| Acre | 306 893 | 2.7 | 88 887 | 40.8 | 2.2 | 1.1 | 1.4 | 2.0 |
| Amapá | 180 078 | 1.6 | 63 598 | 54.6 | 1.6 | 0.5 | 0.8 | 1.3 |
| NW Segment | 2 018 124 | 17.9 | 681 066 | 50.9 | 16.9 | 0.5 | 0.6 | 1.0 |
| W Maranhão (2) | 3 211 418 | 28.7 | 874 524 | 37.4 | 21.6 | 7.3 | 9.1 | 12.5 |
| Pará | 3 507 312 | 31.3 | 1 310 240 | 59.6 | 32.4 | 1.3 | 1.8 | 2.9 |
| N Goiás (2) | 782 306 | 7.0 | 233 256 | 42.5 | 5.8 | 1.2 | 1.9 | 2.7 |
| Mato Grosso | 1 169 812 | 10.5 | 556 925 | 90.9 | 13.8 | 0.4 | 0.7 | 1.3 |
| Rondônia | 503 125 | 4.5 | 386 505 | 331.5 | 9.6 | 0.3 | 0.5 | 2.1 |
| SE Segment | 9 173 973 | 82.0 | 3 361 450 | 57.8 | 83.2 | 1.4 | 2.0 | 3.2 |
| Amazônia Legal | 11 192 097 | 100.0 | 4 042 516 | 56.5 | 100.0 | 1.0 | 1.4 | 2.3 |
| Brazil | 121 150 573 | – | 26 641 990 | 28.2 | – | 8.3 | 11.1 | 14.2 |

Source: Anuário BASA 1971 and Sinopse Preliminar de Censo Demográfico 1970 and 1980
1 The figures of area have been taken from the Anuário BASA 1971. The figures for Maranhão and Goiás relate only to the area lying within the official boundaries of Amazônia Legal (see Notes 1, 2). If certain municipalities fell within those limits, therefore, only the relevant part of the municipal area is included. Until recently the area of Amazônia Legal was somewhat smaller (4.87 million km²), because only the part of Mato Grosso north of the 16th parallel was included. In 1977 Mato Grosso was split up into two new states: Mato Grosso do Sul and Mato Grosso. At this time the boundaries of Amazônia Legal were modified to include the whole of the new state of Mato Grosso.
2 The population figures relate to whole municipalities even though only part of their area may fall within the limits of Amazônia Legal. Municipalities with more than 25% of their area falling outside Amazônia Legal are not included in the population calculations.

1 The different, humid tropical environment, which requires considerable physical adaptation and brings with it dangers to health, as well as imposing very specific demands on the way in which colonists have to make a livelihood. Not for nothing is the Amazon region often described as a 'green hell'.
2 The great unfamiliarity of many people with the potentialities and limitations of the region is not compensated by adequate and intensive information and guidance on the part of the government, not even in the official colonisation projects.
3 The small-scale colonisation projects realised by the government (more specifically by the Instituto Nacional de Colonização e Reforma Agraria, INCRA) have so far had little success, either quantitively or qualitatively.
4 As a result, spontaneous colonisation forms the only alternative for many people. But because of their unfavourable location in relation to the economic and demographic core areas of the country and their inaccessibility, large areas offer little attraction for spontaneous colonisation either. There is scarcely any market for commercial production, so that in such areas colonists can only build up a precarious, more or less self-sufficient existence, especially since all kinds of basic provisions in such fields as education, health care and agricultural advice are lacking.
5 Those parts of Amazônia Legal which are favourably located in relation to the Southeast have become the field of operation of modern, large-scale, capital-intensive agricultural enterprises, which generally make use of taxation facilities offered by the government. Land speculators are also active in these areas. As far as land use is concerned, the emphasis is wholly on extensive cattle ranching, which scarcely provides permanent employment. Added to this is the fact that the majority of spontaneous occupiers are regarded by the large enterprises and the land speculators as undesirable elements, so that a fierce struggle for land has arisen in many places, ending in most instances to the disadvantage of the spontaneous colonists. These facts are obviously not unknown to many potential migrants and they have removed the desire to make the attempt to build up such a risky existence.

The effect of the above is to cause many country people who are struggling to survive to prefer to go elsewhere to find a living, particularly to the great cities, which are consequently growing at an explosive rate. The conseqence for the vast territory of Amazônia Legal is that the population is still modest, both absolutely and relatively (see Table 1).

## Population increase per state or territory

So far the changes in population size have been looked at for the North and Amazônia Legal as a whole without separate consideration of the growth figures for the individual territories or states or parts thereof. In this section, therefore, a closer examination is made of the population changes at the level of the states and territories, with attention being paid particularly to the period 1970–80, when the population growth was considerably greater than during the preceding date.

The principal data for this period are summarised in Table 1, which also includes figures for the years 1960–70, making possible comparisons between the two decades.

The table shows that the population increase of Amazônia Legal during the period 1970–80 was by no means evenly distributed over the region. Some areas grew considerably more strongly than others, but nowhere was there a decrease.

The population growth of Amazonas, Acre, northern Goiás and the western part of Maranhão between 1970 and 1980 was below the average for the whole of Amazônia Legal. Amapá grew at about the same rate as the regional average, while the growth figures for the other areas were considerably above the regional average of 56.5%. The most spectacular growth occurred in Rondônia, where the population quadrupled in only ten years.

As a result of the uneven growth there were some shifts in the relative positions of the subregions. The share of Amazonas, Acre, northern Goiás and western Maranhão in the total population of Amazônia Legal declined somewhat, while that of Amapá remained the same. The other subregions generally strengthened their position. The most remarkable changes were those for Rondônia and Mato Grosso.

Northern Goiás occupies a rather special position in that its share of the total population of Amazônia Legal increased during the 1960s and only decreased after 1970. As far as the three other areas which experienced a weakening of their position between 1970 and 1980 are concerned, this was a development which had already set in during the preceding decade.

Equally, if not more striking, are the figures from Table 1 relating to absolute population increase. Of this increase 83.2% is shown to have occurred in the southeastern segment, by which is understood Rondônia, Mato Grosso, northern Goiás, Pará and western Maranhão, which subregions together account for 58.2% of the surface area of Amazônia Legal. By contrast, the northwestern segment, which covers 41.8% of the surface area and comprises Acre, Amazonas, Roraima and Amapá, experienced only 16.9% of the absolute increase. The figures in Table 1 show that these striking differences also existed during the period 1960–70.

The fact that the population growth occurred predominantly in the southern and eastern part of the Amazon region is closely related to the circumstance that these subregions had a larger population, so that the natural increase could be much greater than in the states making up the thinly populated northwestern segment of Amazônia Legal.

A further factor, however, is the location relative to the economic and demographic heartland of Brazil, i.e. the South and Southeast. The distance to these core areas is much less for the southern and eastern subregions of Amazônia than it is for the northern and western subregions, especially since the southern and eastern subregions have recently been linked with the 'Centre' of Brazil by a number of important highways. Consequently, during the past decade migration from the Southeast to the Amazon region has been directed more to the southern and eastern subregions.

The highways just referred to have been completed successively since 1960. To be specific, the ones mainly concerned are the link between Belém and Brasília, completed in 1960, which opened up the north of Goiás and the south of Pará, and the link between Cuiabá and Pôrto Velho, completed in 1965, which provided not only Rondônia, but also western Mato Grosso, with a relatively good connection with the Southeast. In Mato Grosso, moreover, in addition to a section of the BR 080 road, a number of small access roads were constructed leading to the north, while the Cuiabá–Santarém link was opened to traffic in 1976. The effect of this latter road, however, should not be overestimated, since the period of four years between when it opened and the Census was relatively short, and the spontaneous settlement of colonists, land speculators and others along this link appears to be somewhat more controlled than along other roads, because the army – which constructed the road – has continued to exercise a certain measure of supervision.

Apart from being stimulated by its favourable location and the building of roads, the greater population increase on the southern and eastern margin of Amazônia Legal has also been encouraged by the fact that large investments have been, or will be, made here shortly. These investments have largely been made by investors from the Southeast and South of Brazil, who believe that the southern and eastern areas of Amazônia Legal afford the most favourable prospects for development because of their relative closeness to the economic 'Centre' of the country. The hundreds of large-scale cattle-ranching projects, which have been or are being realised in the Amazon region, with or without tax concessions, are therefore concentrated predominantly in Mato Grosso, northern Goiás and southern Pará (see Figure 2). In this connection, it is also significant that the southern and eastern margin of Amazônia Legal is much more favourable physically for cattle farming than the more northerly areas, where the tropical forest is denser.

Not only is temporary work created by the cattle-farming projects (within the framework of the clearances), after which the temporary workers often remain 'hanging about' in the area, but the cattle-farming projects, because of their extensive character and the large areas of land they consequently require, lead to the construction of numerous secondary and tertiary roads. These are sometimes no more than '*picadas*' (trails), but they improve accessibility and so encourage spontaneous colonisation. In the northern subregions of the Amazon region all this is much less in evidence, with the exception to some extent of northern Roraima.

The relationship between population growth and communications emerges somewhat more clearly when we consider the point of time at which various roads were completed and when the rapid population growth began. It then appears that the population growth of Rondônia was still relatively 'normal' by Brazilian standards during the 1960s (Table 1). The very spectacular increase dates mainly from the end of the 1960s and the 1970s (see Figures 4–8). The effect of the Cuiabá–Pôrto Velho road link, completed in 1965, of the propaganda carried on since then for the development and integration of Rondônia, and of the INCRA colonisation projects undertaken within that context is clearly demonstrable here. There was also an acceleration in the population growth of western Mato Grosso at that time. Northern Goiás experienced quite a strong population growth during the 1960s immediately after the completion of the Belém–Brasília link. During the 1970s the increase remained considerable, but was nevertheless at a reduced rate, because the areas along this road were then partly occupied and other subregions within the Amazon region had meanwhile been given better accessibility (see Figures 5–8).

The Transamazônica, completed during the 1970s, also resulted in a marked increase in the rate of population growth in the areas through which it passes, although in comparison with the north–south links between Belém and Brasília, and Cuiabá and Pôrto Velho, the influence of the Transamazônica is more modest, because a very small proportion of the population of the North lives in the municipalities which it opened up. This is not only because the highway was completed later, but also because it runs in an east–west direction. In so doing it links the 'demographic vacuum' with the Northeast, which although characterised by serious impoverishment and unfavourable subsistence prospects, so that it might provide many potential colonists, is much less able because of its economic weakness to function as a market and as a provider of capital for development projects. The greater part of the investments in Amazônia Legal therefore originates in the Southeast and not the Northeast. Moreover, because of its east–west course, the Transamazônica does not provide a favourable connection with the South and Southeast of Brazil and, particularly for the western areas along this highway, the distances are very great. A final point is that the official colonisation projects carried out along the Transamazônica have not been very successful. We shall return to the effects of the Transamazônica when we come to examine the population changes within the individual subregions. The road was mentioned here only to illustrate the importance of factors such as accessibility and distance from the economic and demographic heartland.

Western Maranhão occupies a somewhat special position. A quite large-scale spontaneous colonisation by simple peasants has already been occurring here for a

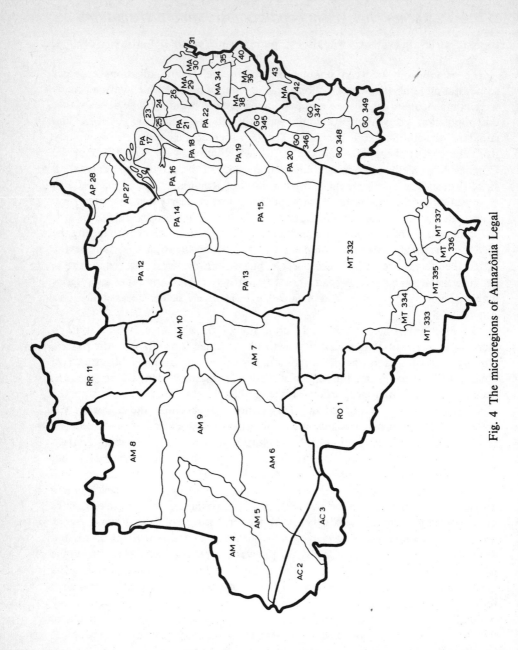

Fig. 4 The microregions of Amazônia Legal

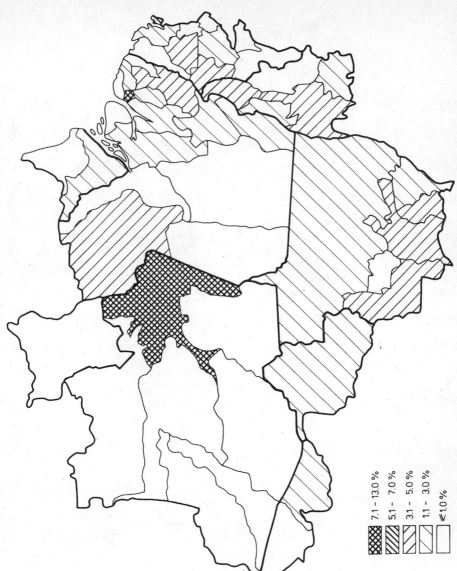

Fig. 5  Share of each microregion in the total population growth in Amazônia
Legal 1960–80

7.1 – 13.0 %
5.1 –  7.0 %
3.1 –  5.0 %
1.1 –  3.0 %
< 1.0 %

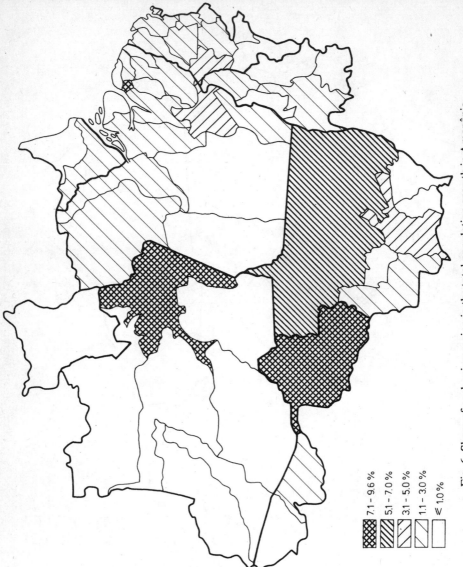

7.1 – 9.6 %
5.1 – 7.0 %
3.1 – 5.0 %
1.1 – 3.0 %
≤ 1.0 %

Fig. 6  Share of each microregion in the total population growth in Amazônia
Legal 1970–80

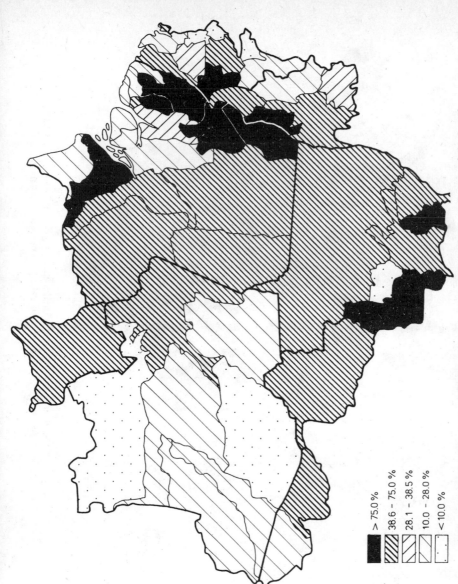

Fig. 7 Population growth in each of the microregions of Amazônia Legal 1960–70 (as % of 1960) (Brazil 33.1%; Amazônia Legal 38.5%; none of the microregions was characterised by a growth rate within the range 33.1–38.5%)

> 75.0 %

38.6 – 75.0 %

28.1 – 38.5 %

10.0 – 28.0 %

< 10.0 %

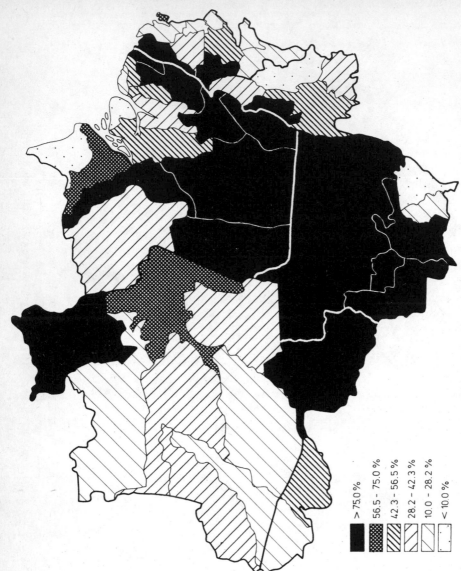

**Fig. 8** Population growth in each of the microregions of Amazônia Legal 1970–80 (as % of 1970) (Brazil 28.2%; Amazônia Legal 56.5%)

> 75.0 %

56.5 – 75.0 %

42.3 – 56.5 %

28.2 – 42.3 %

10.0 – 28.2 %

< 10.0 %

considerable time. A high proportion of the rural population which can no longer find a possibility of making a living in the Northeast has been migrating to this subregion. The explanation for this is to be found both in the proximity to the densely populated regions of the Northeast and the existence of large areas of state land. Another significant factor is that western Maranhão possesses a rather favourable natural environment by comparison with the drought polygon of the Northeast, while not yet presenting the more extreme characteristics of the humid tropical climate experienced in the more westerly parts of the Amazon region. Until recently, large-scale agricultural projects were absent or were so modest in number and extent as not to hinder the chances of the majority of the colonists of making a living. One could speak of an 'open' frontier. Only in recent years has this situation changed and, according to recent newspaper reports, there has been an escalation of conflicts over land-ownership.

Because western Maranhão already had a considerable population as a result of this spontaneous colonisation during the 1960s, a large part of the absolute natural population increase of Amazônia Legal occurred in this subregion. Nevertheless, there was a smaller relative and absolute increase during the period 1970–80 than in the more southerly marginal areas, so that the relative position of Maranhão has been somewhat weakened.

## Population changes at the meso- and microregional levels

In the preceding section the effect of location, road building, investment and other development activities was emphasised. The relationship between these variables and the population increase will emerge rather more clearly, however, if we now concentrate on the question of where within the subregions of Amazônia Legal the population increase has mainly occurred. For this purpose it is necessary to make an analysis at the level of the meso- and microregions. Such an analysis will also present an opportunity to identify more precisely the centres of gravity of settlement.

We shall not consider in detail the situation in the areas of the *northwestern segment*, since the occupation of this part of Amazônia is still very incomplete. Briefly summarising the results of Figures 5–10, the following may be stated.

In 1970 the population was very unevenly distributed. The microregions of Alto Purús, Macapá and Médio Amazonas and the municipality of Boa Vista,[4] which emerge as the main concentration areas, occupied only 21.6% of the total area of the four states or territories. Nevertheless, in 1970, they held 64.2% of the total population. In 1980, 69.2% of the population lived there, from which it may be concluded that no important changes have occurred in the population distribution and that the occupation of northwest Amazônia is still very fragmentary. There is even a tendency for the degree of concentration to increase.

The occupation pattern in the part of Pará lying north of the River Amazon also fits

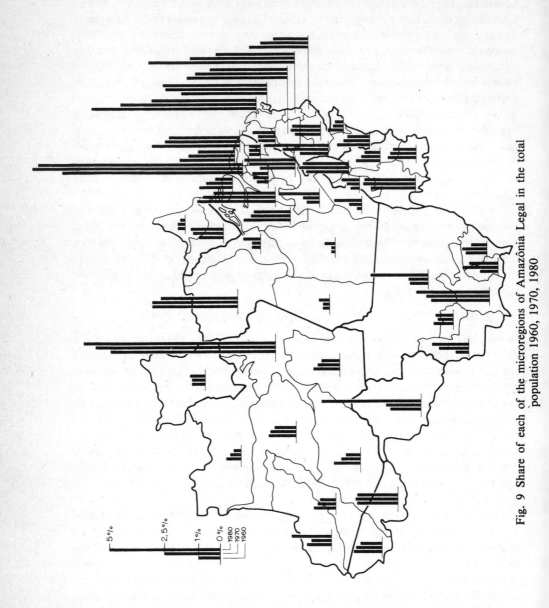

Fig. 9 Share of each of the microregions of Amazônia Legal in the total population 1960, 1970, 1980

within the picture outlined above. The six municipalities it comprises, which make up 22% of the area of the state, accommodate only 5.7% of the state population. The municipalities in question are Faro, Oriximiná, Óbidos, Alenquer, Monte

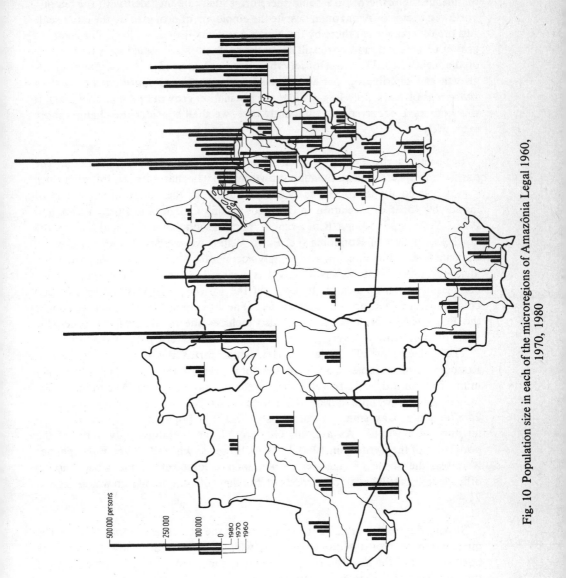

Fig. 10 Population size in each of the microregions of Amazônia Legal 1960, 1970, 1980

Alegre and Almeirim, which extend northwards from the Amazon to the frontier with Guyana and Surinam. Within these minicipalities the population is very much concentrated in the vicinity of the main river; their 'hinterland' is practically uninhabited. Northern Pará could therefore equally be included with the 'empty' northwest sector of Amazônia, despite the employment provided by the large-scale Jarí project established there by the North American firm of Ludwig. The centre of gravity of occupation in Pará still lies in the areas situated immediately on or south of the main river. With this observation, we have arrived at a discussion of the growth and distribution pattern of the population of the *southern and eastern subregions* of Amazônia Legal. Since the population growth of Amazônia Legal is shown to have occurred predominantly here, we shall consider the changes more extensively.

Beginning at the western corner, *Rondônia* first deserves our attention. The particularly spectacular population growth which has characterised this area since it was opened up in 1965 has occurred mainly in the zones which are most favourably located in relation to the roads linking Cuiabá and Pôrto Velho, and Pôrto Velho and Abunã/Rio Branco. The six municipalities making up the northeastern part of Rondônia (i.e. Pôrto Velho, Ariquemes, Ji-Paraná, Cacoal, Pimenta Bueno and Vilhena) accordingly account for almost the whole population increase of the territory.[5] Not only has nearly the whole of the spontaneous colonisation been concentrated here, but the various, relatively modest, official colonisation projects are also located here. The development pole designated under the POLAMAZONIA programme also includes the relatively more accessible parts of the territory covering as it does the northwestern part of Rondônia.

The municipality of Guajará Mirim, which forms the southwestern part of Rondônia and occupies 26.3% of the total area of the territory, is the only municipality not directly served by the roads mentioned above. Accordingly, this municipality grew little during the period 1970–80: the population rose from 24 879, which was small in comparison with the population explosion of the territory as a whole.[6] As a result Guajará Mirim contained only 7.1% of the population of the territory in 1980. In 1970, however, when the other municipalities were less the scene of large-scale spontaneous colonisation and when various official projects still had to be carried out, the share of Guajará Mirim was as high as 21.4%.

Striking differences are also to be observed in the new state of *Mato Grosso*. The microregion of Norte Mato Grossense, which (as its name shows) covers the northern part of the new Mato Grosso and, as such, occupies no less than 70% of the total area of the state, accommodated in 1970 only 10.6% of the population. Communications have been improved recently, however, with the building of simple access roads and the completion of part of the BR 080 road and of the road from Cuiabá to Santarém. It is therefore not surprising that this microregion experienced a remarkable increase during the 1970s, such that its share in the total population of the state rose to as much as 24.4%. In absolute terms there was growth from 64 878 to 285 168, i.e. more than a quadrupling. This growth is closely related to the further expansion of cattle farming (and sometimes also of arable farming and mining) and to the creation of two development poles (see Figures 7–10).

In 1970 nearly 90% of the total population was concentrated in the southern microregions of Alto Guaporé, Alto Paraguai, Baixada Cuiabana, Rondonópolis and Garças, which made possible a large absolute growth, amounting during the period 1970–80 to 60.5% of the total population increase of the state. Nevertheless, this demographic predominance began to weaken during the 1970s as a result of the spectacular increase just referred to in the more northerly zone.

The microregions situated in the southwest prove to have experienced the strongest absolute and relative growth; the increase in the southeastern microregions, by contrast, was less. This means that the western part, which is served by the road from Cuiabá to Pôrto Velho, belongs, as far as its growth pattern is concerned, with the area with a strong population increase defined in Rondônia (Figures 7 and 8).

The rather narrow and elongated shape of *northern Goiás* and the fact that this area is completely bisected by the Belém–Brasília highway lead one to suppose that no noteworthy differentiation is to be expected in the population increase within this region. Nevertheless, significant differences are observable when the figures for the microregions are compared. The microregions of Extremo Norte Goiano, Baixo Araguaia Goiana and Médio Tocantins Araguaia, and the municipality of Araguaçu, which are situated in the west, in the more immediate vicinity of the Belém–Brasília highway, prove to have accounted for 84.3% of the population growth during the decade 1970–80, and for as much as 84.8% during the preceding decade, even though they cover only 59.2% of the surface area of northern Goiás. The two microregions of Tocantins de Pedro Afonso and Serra Geral de Goiás, which are situated east of the Tocantins, and are, moreover, not directly bisected by the Belém–Brasília highway, although they are connected to it be a number of primitive roads, on the other hand accounted for only 15.7% of the population growth of northern Goiás between 1970 and 1980 (15.2% in 1960–70), although they cover 40% of this subregion. In 1960 the eastern microregions still held 35.6% of the population of northern Goiás, but the proportion had fallen to 24.4% in 1980. Because of the drawing power of the western areas, the population growth of the eastern microregions even remained below the national average.

*Pará* – the state with the largest population of Amazônia Legal – still shows a strong concentration in the northeastern corner, where the occupation process has been mainly concentrated over the past few centuries. The nine microregions located here, and which include the city of Belém, accommodated 79.6% of the population of the state in 1970 and still held 73.2% in 1980.[7] However, 62.4% of the population growth during the decade 1970–80 took place in this northeastern corner, so one cannot yet speak of striking shifts in the distribution pattern. At most there are incipient signs of this, because the area's demographic dominance has decreased somewhat. This incipient loss of position also affects the microregion of Belém, which contained 31.6% of the state's population in 1970 and 29.6% in 1980 (see Figures 7–10).

Various microregions in eastern Pará can attribute their growth partly to the fact that they are situated along or in the vincinity of the road from Belém to Brasília. This applies particularly to the microregions of Araguaia Paraense (020) and Guajarina (022), which had a combined population in 1970 of 188 102, and 403 785 in 1980, amounting to an increase of 114.6%. While the share of the two microregions in the total state population was 6.1% in 1960, by 1980 it had risen to 11.5%. To what extent accelerations in growth tempo are related only to the road building, however, and to the enhanced possibilities for agricultural exploitation arising therefrom, or are also the consequence of the greater influence of the city of Belém, or of other factors, cannot be determined without further research.

It is somewhat easier to measure the direct consequences of the construction of the Transamazônica. Although the eastern area opened up by this highway also falls generally within the sphere of influence of the Belém-Brasília highway, the more westerly section does not and, in any event, there is no large city (such as Belém) in the vicinity of the Transamazônica which can significantly influence the process of population growth. The effect of the Cuiabá–Santarém link on the population increase can also be discovered relatively easily.

The ten Pará municipalities which are today cut through by both the highways just mentioned still contained only 11.1% of the state population in 1970, but this proportion had risen to 13.9% in 1980 as a result of the fact that the population increased from 243 412 to 488 598 during the period concerned and thereby more than doubled.[8] The population growth in these municipalities during the period 1970–80 represented 18.7% of the growth in the whole of the State of Pará (14.2% if the municipality of Santarém is excluded). The most striking increase occurred in the municipalities of Marabá, Itupiranga, Jacunda, Altamira, and Itaituba, where the population tripled or more than tripled, mainly as a result of spontaneous and planned colonisation activities. If these, in themselves impressive, population changes are compared, however, with the effects of the Belém–Brasília link in northern Goiás and southern Pará, one is bound to conclude that the influence of the Transamazônica and the Cuiabá–Santarém link should certainly not be overestimated. The absolute population growth along both roads in 1970–80 was only about half that which occurred within the zone of influence of the Belém/Brasília link. The background to this has already been discussed in another connection.

Reference has also been made elsewhere to the fact that the part of Pará north of the Amazon still has only a small population. The conclusion in respect of Pará can in fact be that although there has been a somewhat wider dispersion of the population as a result of road construction and related activities, there have not yet been any fundamental changes in the distribution pattern. The designation of a number of '*polos*' has also as yet had only a small effect at the state level. Consequently, the long-occupied northeastern corner is still dominant demographically.

Lastly, reference should be made to *western Maranhão*. The northern part of this state has long had a denser population than the more southerly interior. This situation did not change fundamentally during the 1970s. The microregions of Gurupi (029), Baixada Occidental Maranhense (030) São Luís (031), Pindaré (034) and Mearim (035), plus nine municipalities, which together comprise the northern part of western Maranhão, in 1960 had 76%, in 1970 74.1% and in 1980 72% of the total population resident in the part of the state within Amazônia Legal. The percentages do show, however, that its position is beginning to weaken. The area which is gaining from it is the central zone, served by the BR 230 road and comprising the microregions of Imperatriz (038), Alto Mearim e Grajaú (039) and Medio Mearim (040) and a few additional municipalities. While only 15.7% of the population of western Maranhão lived in this central zone in 1960, by 1980 the proportion had risen to 21.9%. This shift is related not so much to the designation of the area as a development pole, as to the extensive spontaneous colonisation which has occurred in this area. The least populated area is the extreme south, the relative position of which was even weakened demographically (see Figures 9 and 10).

In view of the distribution pattern it is not surprising that population growth has occurred mainly in the northern part of west Maranhão. It is the area in which São Luis is situated and it has relatively the best communications. The main road from Fortaleza to Teresina and Belém passes through this northern part of the state.

If the distribution pattern of the population within west Maranhão is considered in a wider context, it appears that the more densely populated north links up with the northeastern part of the bordering state of Pará, where (as has been stated) the largest part of the population of Pará is resident.

In conclusion, the following may be stated with reference to the sub-areas of the *southeastern segment*. Because these sub-areas contained a larger population and migration was largely directly towards them, it was here that the population increase mainly occurred. The relatively large population increase, however, does not mean that growth was more or less uniform over the whole of the southern and eastern zone. It actually occurred in a limited number of subregions, often the areas which have already been settled for a long time or have the best communications or both. There in fact exists here a very marked fringe of denser population and high growth. This fringe includes the municipalities of northeast Rondônia, the microregions of southern Mato Grosso, those of north Goiás west of the Tocantins, the adjoining microregions of northeastern Pará and, lastly, the northern microregions of western Maranhão (Figure 10). The zone situated on the 'inward' side of this series of important growth regions had a very small population in 1960 and 1970, with the exception to some extent of the long-established population axis in the immediate vicinity of the Amazon. Essentially, there has been no radical change in this position despite the fact that certain subregions, such as the area lying within the sphere of influence of the Transamazônica, have seen quite a marked relative population increase.

What these facts essentially mean is that the population increase in southern and eastern Amazônia Legal may be primarily regarded as the result of a process which has been occurring in Brazil over a long period, i.e. the advance of the frontier of denser occupation from the Southeast and the Northeast. In other words, it is primarily a question of the increasing integration of new areas in southern and eastern Amazônia Legal into the Southeast, the economic and demographic heartland of Brazil, on the one hand, and into the Northeast, which may be regarded as a demographic core region, on the other.

This process has been accelerated by the construction of a number of north–south links; the most important east–west link (the Transamazônica) made a much smaller contribution. The agricultural and cattle-farming projects supported by the SUDAM also proved to have had an influence. The establishment of various industrial development projects in Belém primarily influenced the population growth of the city itself. The influence of the programme of planned colonisation carried out by the government and concentrated along a section of the Transamazônica, was relatively small. A similar programme was carried out in Rondônia, but here the possibilities for spontaneous colonisation played a greater part in the explosive population growth. The development poles designated within the framework of the Second Development Plan have undoubtedly had an influence on the population growth, but because of their recent creation they could have been of only limited significance, while the lack of adequate information makes it difficult to measure their effects. Moreover, it must be realised that there is generally an interaction at work in the sense that the government has capitalised on economic developments already in progress in the area concerned when deciding to designate one or more poles. It is exceptional for the development process to have been set in train by the designations (as in the case of Carajás).

In the light of the foregoing conclusions, the efforts to let Amazônia Legal have a greater share of the population growth will have the most success if the development measures are directed towards the areas which are most favourably located relative to the Southeast and Northeast and have good communications with them. In other words, the government would do well mainly to guide and support the process of the advancing frontier of more intensive occupation. Fewer results can be expected from the measures to develop the still extremely thinly populated regions west and north of the frontier. At best such measures create enclaves of development. Viewed in this light, a less hasty opening up of the extreme north of Amazônia Legal by means of the Perimetral Norte would be only sensible.

## Aspects of the urbanisation process

It would be beyond the scope of the present article to consider in detail the process of urbanisation. Instead we must limit ourselves to a few main features of the 1970s, during which period Amazônia Legal experienced its greatest demographic growth. In 1970, 56% of the Brazilian population was regarded as urban, but in Amazônia Legal no more than about 36% of the population lived in urban settlements (Table 2). This lower degree of urbanisation was closely related to the fact that, in the Amazon region, the emphasis was very much on agricultural activities. Considered in itself, however, the degree of urbanisation was not especially low, which is also understandable, since trading and transport activities (related to the gathering economy) were not unimportant there, mining had developed in a number of places, management and administrative functions had to be carried out, the agricultural population required urban services and the cities of Belém and Manaus, in particular, had grown because of a certain measure of industrialisation, based partly on the processing and working up of local raw materials and partly on the manufacture of various consumer goods. For Manaus there was the further factor that the city had experienced an explosive growth of its commercial activities as a free trade centre. Last, but not least, was the fact that many urban centres provided a temporary or more permanent home for workers who were trying to earn a

*Table 2  Size and growth of the urban population of Amazônia Legal 1970–80, by subregion*

| Subregion | Urban population 1970 | | Urban population 1980 | | Increase 1970–80 | |
|---|---|---|---|---|---|---|
| | Absolute | As % of total population | Absolute | As % of total population | Absolute | % |
| Amazonas | 409 278 | 42.6 | 869 020 | 60.0 | 459 742 | 112.3 |
| Roraima | 17 929 | 43.1 | 49 622 | 60.5 | 31 693 | 177.1 |
| Acre | 60 557 | 27.8 | 135 754 | 44.2 | 72 197 | 124.2 |
| Amapá | 63 785 | 54.8 | 106 424 | 59.1 | 42 639 | 66.8 |
| NW Amaz. Leg. | 551 549 | 41.3 | 1 160 820 | 57.5 | 609 271 | 110.5 |
| W Maranhão | 577 288 | 24.7 | 997 557 | 31.8 | 420 269 | 72.8 |
| Pará | 1 037 340 | 47.2 | 1 702 403 | 48.5 | 665 063 | 64.1 |
| N Goiás | 137 717 | 25.1 | 312 956 | 40.0 | 175 239 | 127.2 |
| Mato Grosso | 239 524 | 39.1 | 673 069 | 57.5 | 433 545 | 181.0 |
| Rondônia | 60 541 | 51.9 | 239 436 | 47.6 | 178 895 | 295.7 |
| SE Amaz. Leg. | 2 052 410 | 35.3 | 3 925 421 | 43.1 | 1 873 011 | 91.3 |
| Amaz. Legal | 2 603 959 | 36.4 | 5 086 241 | 45.8 | 2 482 282 | 95.3 |
| Brazil | 52 904 744 | 56.0 | 82 013 375 | 67.7 | 29 108 176 | 55.0 |

Source: Sinopse Preliminar do Censo Demográfico, 1970, 1980.

livelihood in forest clearance or other activities related to the process of further opening up and colonising the area.

By 1980 the degree of urbanisation for Brazil had risen to 67.7%; in Amazônia Legal it had reached 45.8%. In 1980 also therefore the degree of urbanisation still lay below the national average, which is not surprising in view of the still strongly agricultural character of this region. The as yet relatively modest level of urbanisation appears not only from the proportion of town-dwellers, but also from the fact that, of the 198 towns with more than 50 000 inhabitants identified in Brazil in 1980, only eleven were situated within the limits of Amazônia Legal. Four towns (i.e. Castanhal, Rondônopolis, Rio Branco and Macapá) had between 50 000 and 100 000 inhabitants, the remaining seven had more than that. They included Santarém Pôrto Velho, Imperatriz, Cuiabá, São Luís, Manaus and Belém. The latter two were by far the largest settlements.

Examination of the level of urbanisation by subregions shows that there were important differences both in 1970 and 1980. The degree of urbanisation was relatively high in the states of Amazonas and Pará, which contain within their boundaries the two largest cities of Amazônia and numerous smaller towns along the main river. This also applied to the relatively small territories of Roraima and Amapá, where (as we have seen) the small population is highly concentrated in or near the metropolitan core with little dispersion beyond that. The latter was incidentally still true of Rondônia around 1970. The degree of urbanisation was relatively low, on the other hand, in areas like Maranhão, Goiás and Acre, where there is a more dispersed rural occupation, partly by the larger agricultural enterprises, partly by simple small colonists.

A further striking fact is that the urban population almost doubled during the period 1970–80. This means that the high population growth which characterised Amazônia Legal during this period was not purely an increase of the rural population, but was accompanied by a considerable urbanisation. In fact, the rate of urbanisation in Amazônia Legal during that time lay well above the national growth rate. Examination of the urban increase at the state and territory level reveals that in some instances, there was an urban growth which was two to three times as great as the growth at the national level. The most spectacular changes occurred in Rondônia, the territory which (as we have seen) was characterised by a very explosive population increase.

The urban growth occurred partly in the larger centres of Amazônia Legal. The population of Manaus doubled during the 1970s, thanks to the free trade activities, increasing industrialisation, various agricultural development projects in the near environs and a greater service function for western Amazônia (related to greater accessibility). The population of the Belém metropolitan region rose from 656 351 in 1970 to 1 000 349 in 1980, a development to which, among other things, a number of industrialisation projects supported by the SUDAM will have contributed. The other metropolitan municipalities also experienced a marked population increase (Table 3). While the population of the eight metropolitan municipalities still accounted in 1960 for only 18.7% of the total population of Amazônia Legal, by 1970 the proportion was already 22.8% and, in 1980, 24.7%.[9]

Table 3 *Population changes in the metropolitan municipalities of Amazônia Legal, 1960–80*

| | Population | | |
|---|---|---|---|
| *Metropolitan municipality (1)* | *1960* | *1970* | *1980* |
| Belém (Pará) | 402 170 | 642 514 | 949 545 |
| Manaus (Amazonas) | 175 343 | 314 197 | 642 492 |
| Rio Branco (Acre) | 47 882 | 84 845 | 119 815 |
| Pôrto Velho (Rondônia) | 51 049 | 88 856 | 138 289(2) |
| Macapá (Amapá) | 46 905 | 87 755 | 140 624 |
| Boa Vista (Roraima) | 26 168 | 37 062 | 69 627 |
| São Luis (Maranhão) | 159 628 | 270 651 | 460 320 |
| Cuiabá (Mato Grosso) | 57 860 | 103 427 | 219 477 |
| Total | 967 005 | 1 629 307 | 2 740 189 |

Source: Sinopse Preliminar do Censo Demográfico 1980
1 The metropolitan municipality of the State of Goiás is situated outside Amazônia Legal.
2 The figure for 1980 is influenced by boundary changes.

The position of the metropolitan municipalities has therefore been strengthened rather than weakened.

What is striking, however, is not only the growth of the larger urban centres; numerous smaller places also 'profited' from the high population increase of Amazônia Legal. This is understandable, because the advancing colonisation process created a foundation for more and larger service centres (country towns). Moreover, many migrants settled precisely in these smaller towns – either temporarily or more permanently – as a base from which to carry out forest clearance and reclamation, or from which to consider the possibilities of establishing their own holdings. These were partly people who had never had farms of their own, but partly also peasants who had been driven out of the areas of spontaneous colonisation by large landowners, land thieves and speculators. It was particularly in the southern and eastern fringe that the urban settlements grew in number and extent, since that was where the population increase within Amazônia Legal mainly occurred.

## Notes

1 North Brazil is defined as the states and territories of Acre, Rondônia, Roraima, Amazonas, Pará and Amapá.

2 Apart from the 'North', Amazônia Legal also includes the part of Goiás lying north of the 13th Parallel, the whole of the recently created State of Mato Grosso, and the part of Maranhão situated west of the 44th Meridian.

3 Detailed and reliable migration data are scarce; in fact, no migration data at all are available for the period 1970–80, but it may be assumed that the level of natural increase in Amazônia Legal does not differ significantly from that in Brazil as a whole (1960–70): 33%; 1970–80: 28%). This means that, during the period 1970–80, about half of the population growth in Amazônia Legal can be attributed to natural increase. The average volume of the migration flow to Amazônia Legal was about 200 000 persons per year in that period, which is relatively modest when compared with the total population of Brazil (1980: 121 million).

4 Roraima has not yet been subdivided into microregions. There is only one microregion, which coincides with the territory and consists of two municipalities (Boa Vista in the north and Caracarai in the south).

5 Reference is made here to municipalities because Rondônia has not been subdivided into microregions.

6 To a small extent the limited growth is also related to boundary changes.

7 The microregions in question are Furos (016), Campos de Marajó (017), Baixo Tocantins (018), Tomé-Açu (021), Guajarina (022), Salgado (023), Bragantina (024), Belém (025) and Viseu (026). They cover 18% of the area of Pará.

8 The municipalities in question are São João do Araguaia, Marabá, Itupiranga, Jacunda, Portel, São José Porfirio, Altamira, Itaituba, Aveiro and Santarém.

9 Part of the population of metropolitan municipalities is classified as rural.

**Statistical Sources Employed**

Banco da Amazônia. 1970. Amazônia: Estatísticas Básicas. Belém. Anuário BASA 1971.

Instituto Brasileiro de Geografia e Estatística. 1971. Sinopse Estatística do Brasil 1971. Rio de Janeiro.

Instituto Brasileiro de Geografia e Estatística. 1971. VIII Recenseamento Geral do Brasil. Sinopse Preliminar do Censo Demográfico 1970. Rio de Janeiro.

Instituto Brasileiro de Geografia e Estatística. 1981. IX Recenseamento Geral do Brasil. Sinopse Preliminar do Censo Demográfico 1980. Rio de Janeiro.

# 2  Population changes in the Brazilian Amazon

SAMUEL BENCHIMOL

The complexity and continental size of the Amazon Basin (see Table 1) must arouse our imagination, when we consider its national and world scale:

1/20   of the Earth's surface
1/5    of available freshwater reserves in the world
1/3    of evergreen broad-leaved forest resources
1/10   of the world's living species
2/5    of South American land
3/5    of Brazilian territory

By contrast, the people who inhabit it represent only 3/1000 of the world's population. They number 14 million in the South American Amazon as a whole and about 11 million in the Brazilian Amazon, which consists of the States of Pará, Amazonas, Acre, Rondônia, Mato Grosso, the Federal Territories of Amapá and Roraima, plus Goiás north of the 13th parallel, and the State of Maranhão west of the 44th meridian.

Dramatic change, however, has been noted in the growth and distribution of the Brazilian Amazon population in the decade 1970–80, when it registered a demographic expansion of 54.5%, from 7 256 651 to 11 218 385 inhabitants.

The opening of the economic frontier, the finding and unlocking of mineral and forest resources, the construction of a network of highways, the availability of cheap land and colonisation programmes, all motivated the influx of migrants, tenants and farmers from the Centre–West and South Brazil. The peopling of Amazonia no longer derived exclusively from the poverty-stricken Northeast or depended on river transportation and floodplain settlements. It started to reflect the natural expansion of the southern and savanna frontiers of the Central Brazilian Plateau, along the southern Amazon tributaries of the Madeira, Tapajós, Xingu, Tocantins and Araguaia rivers, and through access provided by new roads in the uplands.

Although the actual population is still insignificant when we consider the 5 million km² of the Brazilian part of the Amazon Basin, encompassing 260 million hectares of equatorial rainforest and vast untapped natural and mineral resources, we should emphasise that this fact does not constitute a major obstacle for

Table 1 River basins of the Brazilian Amazon

| States and Territories | Total | Areas of basins (km$^2$) | | | | | |
|---|---|---|---|---|---|---|---|
| | | Amazonia | Tocantins Araguaia | Northeast | S. Francisco | Paraguai | Paraná |
| Pará | 1 248 042 | 1 049 002 | 166 893 | 32 147 | – | – | – |
| Amapá | 140 276 | 140 276 | – | – | – | – | – |
| Maranhão | 328 663 | – | 30 485 | 298 178 | – | – | – |
| Amazonas | 1 564 445 | 1 564 445 | – | – | – | – | – |
| Region to be demarcated | | | | | | | |
| Amazonas Pará | 2 680 | 2 680 | – | – | – | – | – |
| Roraima | 230 104 | 230 104 | – | – | – | – | – |
| Acre | 152 589 | 152 589 | – | – | – | – | – |
| Rondônia | 243 044 | 243 044 | – | – | – | – | – |
| Mato Grosso | 881 001 | 602 327 | 110 140 | – | – | 168 534 | – |
| Goiás | 642 092 | – | 494 675 | – | 2 779 | – | 144 638 |
| Totals | 5 432 936 | 3 984 467 | 802 193 | 330 325 | 2 779 | 168 534 | 144 638 |

Source: Departamento de Estudos Geográficos do IBGE.

development. The main difficulties are in insufficient knowledge of the humid tropics, rainforest management, soil conservation and agroforestry, and discoveries of new native or exogenous species of plants and animals that could well be adapted to these habitats and environments. These are the great challenges that the Amazonians now have to face, with the help of many dedicated scientists and scholars such as those attending this symposium.

This problem leads to the question of how much population the Amazon can absorb, now and in the future, without spoiling its natural resources and causing irreversible ecological damage. Since the optimal size of a population has a positive correlation with the carrying capacity of an ecosystem, and with the constraints of actual technology, infrastructure of services and environment management, we shall pursue a conservative demographic policy. We must, therefore, be aware that a Chinese or Indian style population explosion would not achieve a balanced social economic development. Simple statistics showing a population increase over the years, as presented in the tables, may not be evidence of progress or improvement in the quality of life and well-being of its people. On the contrary, overpopulation may not only impoverish the people but also cause so much damage and devastation that the natural resources would be irreparably lost in a few generations.

It is important to point out that human settlement and economic activities in the Amazon became viable because of the new technological revolution. Despite many calculated risks, this revolution enabled us to overcome the long distances and to solve many problems: though satellite telecommunication, infra-red radar photography, remote sensing, agroforestry research, rapid and cheaper means of transport, construction of a network of roads (making easier access to previously

Table 2 Vegetation types of the Brazilian Amazon km²

| States and territories | Land area in km² | Humid and super-humid rainforests of Amazonia | | | | | Sub-tropical rain-forest outside Amazonia | Sub-humid forest of the interior | Cerrado and cerradão | Pantanal complex | Cach-imbo complex | Campos | Campo liable to flooding | Littoral vegetation (manques, dunes, res-tingas and beaches) |
|---|---|---|---|---|---|---|---|---|---|---|---|---|---|---|
| | | Total | Super-humid forest of high Amazon | Terra firme | Igapó | Várzea | | | | | | | | |
| Pará | 1 227 530 | 1 156 648 | — | 1 081 868 | 38 456 | 36 324 | — | — | — | — | 12 132 | 33 333 | 14 559 | 10 853 |
| Amapá | 139 068 | 110 567 | — | 108 466 | 2 101 | — | — | — | — | — | — | 9 739 | — | 7 686 |
| Maranhão | 324 616 | 99 907 | — | 99 907 | — | — | 11 076 | — | 183 788 | — | — | — | 25 048 | 15 268 |
| Amazonas | 1 558 987 | 1 532 939 | 364 408 | 898 824 | 23 044 | 246 663 | — | — | — | — | — | 26 048 | — | — |
| Roraima | 230 104 | 172 924 | — | 166 340 | — | 6 584 | — | — | — | — | — | 57 180 | — | — |
| Acre | 152 589 | 152 006 | — | 134 650 | — | 17 356 | — | — | — | — | — | 583 | — | — |
| Rondônia | 243 044 | 207 986 | — | 191 514 | — | 16 472 | — | 1 321 | 20 701 | — | — | 14 357 | — | — |
| Mato Grosso | 881 001 | 504 667 | — | 504 667 | — | — | — | — | 294 189 | 72 987 | 1 219 | 6 618 | — | — |
| Goiás | 642 036 | 31 916 | — | 31 916 | — | — | — | 68 573 | 531 172 | — | — | — | — | — |
| Totals | 5 398 975 | 3 969 560 | 364 408 | 3 218 152 | 63 601 | 323 399 | 11 076 | 69 894 | 1 029 850 | 72 987 | 13 351 | 158 233 | 40 212 | 33 812 |

Source: Departamento de Estudos Geográficos do IBGE.

Table 3  Brazilian population growth (1872–1980)

Population and percentage increase

| Regions | Area (km²) | 1872 | 1890 | 1900 | 1920 | 1940 | 1950 | 1960 | 1970 | 1980 |
|---|---|---|---|---|---|---|---|---|---|---|
| *North* <br> Rondônia, Acre, Amazonas, Roraima, Pará, Amapá | 3 581 180 | 332 847 | 476 370 <br> 43.1% | 695 112 <br> 45.9% | 1 439 052 <br> 107.0% | 1 462 420 <br> 0.16% | 1 844 655 <br> 26.0% | 2 561 782 <br> 38.8% | 3 603 860 <br> 40.6% | 5 890 633 <br> 63.4% |
| *Centre-West* <br> Mato Grosso do Sul, Mato Grosso, Goiás, Federal District | 1 879 455 | 220 812 | 320 399 <br> 45.1% | 373 309 <br> 16.5% | 758 531 <br> 103.2% | 1 258 679 <br> 65.9% | 1 736 965 <br> 37.9% | 2 942 992 <br> 69.4% | 5 079 952 <br> 72.6% | 7 569 668 <br> 49.0% |
| *North-East* <br> From Maranhão to Bahia | 1 548 646 | 4 638 560 | 6 002 047 <br> 29.4% | 6 749 507 <br> 12.4% | 11 245 921 <br> 66.6% | 14 434 080 <br> 28.3% | 17 973 413 <br> 24.5% | 22 181 880 <br> 23.4% | 28 111 927 <br> 26.7% | 34 855 745 <br> 24.0% |
| *South-East* <br> Minas Gerais Espírito Santo, Rio, São Paulo | 924 924 | 4 016 922 | 6 104 384 <br> 52.0% | 7 824 011 <br> 28.2% | 13 654 934 <br> 74.5% | 18 345 831 <br> 34.4% | 22 548 494 <br> 22.9% | 30 630 728 <br> 35.8% | 39 853 498 <br> 30.1% | 51 727 924 <br> 29.8% |
| *South* <br> Paraná, Santa Catarina, Rio Grande do Sul | 577 723 | 721 337 | 1 430 715 <br> 98.3% | 1 796 495 <br> 25.6% | 3 537 167 <br> 96.9% | 5 735 305 <br> 62.1% | 7 840 870 <br> 36.7% | 11 753 075 <br> 49.9% | 16 496 493 <br> 40.4% | 19 035 500 <br> 15.4% |
| Brazil – totals | 8 511 928 | 9 930 478 | 14 333 915 | 17 438 434 | 30 635 605 | 41 236 315 | 51 944 397 | 70 070 457 | 93 145 730 | 119 079 470 |
| Percentage increase between censuses | | | 44.3% | 21.7% | 75.7% | 34.6% | 26.0% | 34.9% | 32.9% | 27.8% |
| Geometric media of annual growth | | | 2.01 | 1.98 | 2.88 | 1.49 | 2.39 | 2.99 | 2.89 | 2.48 |

inaccessible areas), and the building of an infrastructure of services, facilities and public utilities.

This advance of scientific knowledge led to recent discoveries of a great variety of minerals, such as manganese, iron, bauxite, kaolin, copper, tin and natural gas in Amapá, Carajás, Marabá, Jarí, Trombetas, Mapuera, Rondônia and Juruá. Mining activities, mostly capital-intensive and labour-saving, allow rational exploitation with a minimum of manpower, and less ecological damage. These findings reinforce our thesis that a region with such a bonanza of minerals and enormous hydroelectrical potential does not need to devastate and sacrifice our forest, which must be preserved and used adequately, since it is a biological endowment, not only to the Amazonians but to all mankind.

So the best guide to formulate an appropriate demographic and economic policy for the Amazon is to follow four rules of action. These guidelines are that all Amazon projects should be ecologically adequate, economically viable, politically acceptable and socially equitable. We have to admit that these guidelines have often been violated and many errors and omissions have been committed, as happens in most countries of the world, including the most developed and industrialised ones.

The population growth pattern of the Brazilian Amazon, which we now describe, shows how we reached the present figure of 11 million people in the Brazilian Amazon and 14 million in the whole Basin. To understand it, we must recall that the demography of the Amazon Basin is divided into five periods.

*The first, the pre-Orellana period*, in which about 2 million Amerindians lived sparsely dispersed, from the Incas of the Andes to the Tupinambás of the Atlantic coast; from the Caribs and Aruaks of the Guyanas to the Gês and Tapuias of the central plateau of Brazil. Some of them achieved a high degree of cultural accomplishment, for instance, the Incas in Cuzco and Machu Picchu who lived in the upper Amazon rivers of the Urubamba and Ucayali; and the Marajoaras in the Delta. These pre-Orellana Indians were able to develop their social and economic structure using primitive weapons and instruments which were well adapted to the environment and limitations of their diversified ecosystems.

*The second period, in the sixteenth century*, starts in 1542 with the expedition of Orellana, who first descended the Amazon river from Quito via the Napo. His expedition started the conquest of the Amazon, later disputed by Spaniards, Portuguese, Dutch, French and British. This phase was marked by violent disruption of tribal societies and the total or partial annihilation of Amerindian culture and society, through conquest, slavery and epidemics. In this period Spanish settlements were established in the upper rivers and the peripheries of the Basin, while the Portuguese and their Brazilian descendents established themselves along the main course of the Amazon and the main tributaries. This

*Table 4 Brazilian urban and rural population (1950–80)*

| Regions | Urban | | | | Rural | | | |
|---|---|---|---|---|---|---|---|---|
| | *1950* | *1960* | *1970* | *1980* | *1950* | *1960* | *1970* | *1980* |
| *North*<br>Rondônia, Acre, Amazonas, Roraima, Pará, Amapá | 580 867<br>31.49% | 957 718<br>37.80% | 1 626 600<br>45.13% | 3 046 129<br>51.69% | 1 263 788<br>68.51% | 1 604 064<br>62.20% | 1 977 260<br>54.87% | 2 847 007<br>48.31% |
| *Centre-West*<br>Mato Grosso do Sul<br>Mato Grosso, Goiás, Federal District | 423 497<br>24.38% | 1 007 228<br>35.02% | 2 437 379<br>48.04% | 5 118 092<br>67.75% | 1 313 468<br>75.62% | 1 935 764<br>64.98% | 2 635 880<br>51.96% | 2 436 777<br>32.25% |
| *North-East*<br>From Maranhão to Bahia | 4 744 808<br>26.40% | 7 516 500<br>34.24% | 11 752 977<br>41.81% | 17 585 618<br>50.44% | 13 228 605<br>73.60% | 14 665 380<br>65.76% | 16 358 950<br>58.19% | 17 276 289<br>49.56% |
| *South-East*<br>Minas Gerais, Espírito Santo, Rio, São Paulo | 10 720 734<br>47.55% | 17 460 897<br>57.36% | 28 964 601<br>72.68% | 42 848 230<br>82.79% | 11 827 760<br>52.45% | 13 169 831<br>42.64% | 10 888 897<br>27.32% | 8 904 421<br>17.21% |
| *South*<br>Paraná, Santa Catarina, Rio Grande do Sul | 2 312 985<br>29.50% | 4 360 691<br>37.58% | 7 303 427<br>44.27% | 11 880 533<br>62.41% | 5 527 885<br>70.50% | 7 392 384<br>62.64% | 9 193 066<br>55.73% | 7 155 896<br>37.59% |
| Brazil – totals<br>Percentages urban/rural | 18 782 891<br>36.16% | 31 303 034<br>45.08% | 52 084 984<br>55.92% | 80 478 602<br>67.57% | 33 161 506<br>63.84% | 38 767 423<br>54.92% | 41 054 053<br>44.08% | 38 620 390<br>32.43% |

Table 5  *Growth of population of Amazonia (Northern Region) (1872–1980)*

| | Area (km²) | 1872 | 1890 | 1900 | 1920 | 1940 | 1950 | 1960 | 1970 | 1980 |
|---|---|---|---|---|---|---|---|---|---|---|
| Para | 1 248 042 | 275 237 | 328 455 | 445 356 | 983 507 | 944 644 | 1 123 273 | 1 550 935 | 2 167 018 | 3 411 235 |
| Amapá | 140 276 | – | – | – | – | – | 37 477 | 68 889 | 114 359 | 175 634 |
| Amazonas | 1 564 445 | 57 610 | 147 915 | 249 756 | 363 166 | 438 008 | 514 099 | 721 215 | 955 235 | 1 406 354 |
| Roraima | 230 104 | – | – | – | – | – | 18 116 | 29 489 | 40 885 | 79 078 |
| Acre | 152 589 | – | – | – | 92 379 | 79 768 | 114 755 | 160 208 | 215 299 | 301 628 |
| Rondônia | 243 044 | – | – | – | – | – | 36 935 | 70 783 | 111 064 | 492 744 |
| Totals | 3 578 500 | 332 847 | 476 370 | 695 112 | 1 439 052 | 1 462 420 | 1 844 655 | 2 601 519 | 3 603 860 | 5 866 673 |

Source: Annual statistics, IBGE

Table 6  *Growth of population of Centre-West Region (1872–1980)*

| | Area | 1872 | 1890 | 1900 | 1920 | 1940 | 1950 | 1960 | 1970 | 1980 |
|---|---|---|---|---|---|---|---|---|---|---|
| Goiás | 642 092 | 160 395 | 227 572 | 255 284 | 511 919 | 826 414 | 1 214 921 | 1 913 289 | 2 941 107 | 3 864 881 |
| Mato Grosso (before division) | – | 60 417 | 92 827 | 118 025 | 246 612 | 432 265 | 522 044 | 889 539 | – | – |
| Mato Grosso | 881 001 | – | – | – | – | – | – | – | 601 042 | 1 141 236 |
| Mato Grosso do Sul | 350 548 | – | – | – | – | – | – | – | 999 452 | 1 386 803 |
| Federal District (Brasilia) | 5 814 | – | – | – | – | – | – | 140 164 | 538 351 | 1 176 748 |
| Totals | 1 879 455 | 220 812 | 320 399 | 373 309 | 758 531 | 1 258 679 | 1 736 965 | 2 942 992 | 5 079 952 | 7 569 668 |

Source: Annual statistics, IBGE.

division was finally recognised by the treaties of Madrid (1750) and S. Ildefonso (1777), which shaped the present political frontiers.

During this period there was a rapid depopulation of the area, aggravated by epidemic diseases such as smallpox, measles, malaria and influenza, to which the Amerindians had not developed immunity. There was acute scarcity of manpower for fishing, hunting, extraction of forest products and slash-and-burn subsistence agriculture.

The European conquerors and colonists mixed with the native Indians and the resulting inter-ethnic intercourse produced the present *caboclo* population which still lives and works on the floodplain riverbanks of the Amazon. Few survived in those very poor colonial days and in the decades following independence. The first Brazilian census of 1872 counted only 332 847 inhabitants in the two states of Pará and Amazonas.

*The third period* started with the massive migration of people from the northeastern states of Ceará, Pernambuco and Parahyba. This began in 1877 when a great drought ravaged and expelled its population and the rubber boom in Amazonia attracted about 300 000 afflicted migrants. Since the rubber tree occurs mostly in the southern part of the Amazon there was a shifting of population from northern and eastern Amazonia to the upland west and southwest frontier, pentrating deeply into the inter-fluvia of the Tapajós, Madeira, Purús and Juruá rivers. By the close of the nineteenth century, the population had grown to about 700 000. In the next two decades up to 1920 the population doubled, despite the recession years that followed the 1915 crash.

*The fourth period* comprised the depression years of the twenties and thirties, when Amazonia lost its monopoly of native rubber and was unable to meet Malayan plantation competition. In those twenty years, from 1920 to 1940, the State of Pará lost about 40 000 inhabitants, Acre around 13 000. The only exception was the State of Amazonas which registered a small gain in population. In fact, Amazonia, having lost its economic base of survival, was depopulated in this period. The regional gross product plummeted from £ 25 000 000 of the boom days of 1910 to about £ 200 000 in 1932. This depression caused a reflux of population from the upper rivers to the main course of the Amazon and the two principal cities of Belém and Manaus. A similar situation affected the Amazon-bound Peruvian, Colombian and Bolivian populations who attempted to survive in Iquitos, Leticia and Cobija.

*The fifth period* started during World War II when, as a result of the Japanese occupation of southeast Asia, the rubber estates were reactivated and the region received about 200 000 migrants from the Brazilian Northeast. In this phase, the Brazilian government started development efforts through the creation of several agencies to deal with finances and credit, agricultural research and health programmes; reorganisation of political space through the creation of new Federal Territories of Amapá, Roraima and Rondônia in 1943; planning and development – Superintendência de Valorização Econômica da Amazônia (SPVEA) founded in 1953 and later replaced by the present Superintendência de Desenvolvimento da Amazônia (SUDAM) in 1966. In the sixties, after transferring the new federal capital to Brasília in 1960, government action gained momentum with the construction of a network of roads to integrate the Amazon region to the rest of the country. In 1964, the Belém–Brasília highway was inaugurated. In the following decade construction began on the 3 300 km Transamazônica highway from east to west, the Cuiabá–Santarém road linking the Brazilian plateau to central Amazônia, the Cuiabá–Pôrto Velho–Rio Branco road integrating the Centre-West to the Northwest, the Pôrto Velho–Manaus–Bôa Vista road connecting the Southwest and central Amazônia to Venezuela.

These highways and pioneer roads opened new frontiers for colonisation and unlocked mineral resources in the forest hinterland. They broke the traditional pattern of settlement along the banks of rivers, especially those of the Amazon itself, with its silt-laden waters responsible for a generous floodplain of rich soil, abundant fish and cheap water transport. The interfluvial forests opened by these pioneer roads in most cases mask poor acid oxisols and ultisols, with high levels of toxic aluminium.

The ambitious programme of the Transamazônica colonisation and its partial failure provided some lessons, which range over environmental effects, ecological aggression, soil erosion after the removal of tree cover, spread of weeds and diseases. All this lowered the rate of human-carrying capacity of the soil and slowed down colonisation. However, we cannot assume that all human settlements failed in those hinterlands and interfluvia. In those areas where the forest soil base is dominated by red clays, probably derived from weathered basalt, or black soil perhaps generated from anthropogenic factors (as in many parts of the Transamazônica near Altamira, or in southwest Rondônia) colonisation is achieving success. In the former, spontaneous and government-inspired colonisation attracted a new wave of 300 000 migrants from the south and southeast, especially from Paraná, Rio Grande do Sul and Espírito Santo. In Rondônia, where smallholder farmers received grants of about 30 000 lots of 100-hectare homesteads, there is a boom in perennial agriculture of coffee, cocoa, rubber and guaraná. From this new experience, we can now assume that there are many habitats and ecosystems in Amazonia where nutrient-rich soils can support a substitution of forest canopy by ecologically oriented agroforestry. This ends the concept of the Amazon Basin as a single-faced and uniform region.

As a result of these recent trends and changes, the population has grown considerably. In the Northern Region (six states and two territories) the census data of 1950–70 show that the population doubled from 1 844 655 to 3 603 860 and increased by a further 63.46% in the decade 1970–80 to the present figure of

5 890 633 inhabitants. If we use the larger concept of the whole Brazilian Amazon Basin, the census data shows that the 5 363 308 inhabitants in 1960 increased to 7 256 651 (35.3%) in 1970 and to 11 218 385 in 1980, with a growth of 54.5% in the last decade. This population now represents 9.4% of the total Brazilian population of about 120 million people.

In this attempt to account for the observed population trends and changes and evaluate their significance, attention will focus first on Rondônia whose population increased by 333.0% in the decade 1970–80. Most of this growth is due to the opening of the frontier by the construction of the BR-364 road linking Cuiabá to Pôrto Velho. New population centres sprang up along this road and cities like Vilhena, Ariquemes, Cacoal, Pimenta Bueno and Ji-Paraná were born. This last, which in 1970 had 8 904 inhabitants, increased by 1 271.0% to 122 124 in 1980. Rondônia is now Amazonia's biggest agricultural centre of perennial and grain agriculture with a record of 300 000 ha of cultivated land, producing about 500 000 bags of coffee and 100 000 arrobas (15 kgs) of cocoa. Most of its farmers migrated from Paraná and Rio Grande do Sul, expelled by labour-saving mechanised soya agriculture which replaced the previous labour-intensive plantation system of coffee farms. This is the first agricultural revolution in Amazonia, generated by the nutrient-rich red-clay soil and by good farmers from the most developed agriculture of southern Brazil.

Table 7  *Geographical demography of Brazilian Amazonia*

| | | Population | | Percentage increase from 1970 to 1980 | Annual rate of increase per 100 inhabitants |
|---|---|---|---|---|---|
| | Area km² | 1970 | 1980 | | |
| Pará | 1 227 530 | 2 161 316 | 3 411 235 | 57.8 | 4.67 |
| Amapá | 139 068 | 114 687 | 175 634 | 53.1 | 4.35 |
| Amazonian Maranhão | 257 451 | 2 458 616 | 3 341 842 | 35.9 | 3.12 |
| Region to be demarcated Amazonas/Pará | 2 680 | – | – | — | – |
| Amazonas | 1 558 987 | 955 394 | 1 430 314 | 49.7 | 4.12 |
| Roraima | 230 104 | 40 915 | 79 078 | 93.2 | 6.31 |
| Acre | 152 589 | 216 200 | 301 628 | 39.5 | 3.39 |
| Rondônia | 243 044 | 113 659 | 492 744 | 333.5 | 15.30 |
| Mato Grosso | 881 001 | 601 042 | 1 141 236 | 89.8 | 6.62 |
| Amazonian Goiás | 285 793 | 594 822 | 844 674 | 42.0 | 3.57 |
| Totals | 4 978 247 | 7 256 651 | 11 218 385 | 54.5 | 4.45 |

Source: Annual statistics.

In the Amazon comprising the State of Mato Grosso and part of Goiás, we found a quite similar pattern. The opening of the above-mentioned BR-364 and of the BR-165 linking Cuiabá to Santarém gave an opportunity for private and government colonisation programmes. In Mato Grosso, the population increased

Table 8  Demographic Expansion in the Amazonia and Centre-West in the decade 1970–1980

|  | Resident population | | Urban population 1980 % | Relative increase | |
|---|---|---|---|---|---|
|  | 1970 | 1980 |  | 1980/70 % | 1970/60 % |
| 1 Eastern Amazonia |  |  |  |  |  |
| Pará | 1 161 316 | 3 411 235 | 48.9 | 57.8 | 41.7 |
| Amapá | 114 687 | 175 634 | 59.1 | 53.1 | 53.6 |
|  | 2 276 003 | 3 586 869 | 49.4 | 57.6 |  |
| 2 Maranhão (entire state) | 2 997 576 | 4 002 679 | 31.4 | 33.5 | 21.2 |
| 3 Western Amazonia |  |  |  |  |  |
| Amazonas | 955 394 | 1 406 354 | 59.9 | 47.2 | 34.8 |
| Roraima | 40 915 | 79 078 | 61.7 | 93.2 | 44.4 |
| Acre | 216 209 | 301 628 | 43.8 | 39.5 | 36.1 |
| Rondônia | 113 659 | 492 744 | 47.3 | 333.5 | 59.1 |
|  | 1 326 177 | 2 279 804 | 54.7 | 71.9 |  |
| 4 Mato Grosso (north) | 601 042 | 1 141 236 | 57.5 | 89.8 | 84.3 |
| 5 Mato Grosso do Sul | 999 452 | 1 368 803 | 67.0 | 36.9 | 74.5 |
| 6 Goiás (entire state) | 2 941 107 | 3 864 881 | 62.1 | 31.4 | 53.6 |
| 7 Federal District | 538 351 | 1 176 748 | 96.7 | 118.5 | 283.6 |
| Amazonia and Centre-West – total | 11 679 708 | 17 421 020 | 53.9 | 49.1 | – |
| Brazil – total | 93 215 311 | 119 024 600 | 67.5 | 27.6 | 32.9 |

by 89.8% from 601 042 in 1970 to 1 141 236 in 1980. The highest rate of increase was in the microregion of northern Mato Grosso with 345.0% and upper Guaporé-Jauru with 91.2% increase. In the State of Goiás, in the transitional zone from savanna to tropical rainforest, the lower Araguaia and middle Tocantins have the greatest population gains: settlement there has been facilitated by the opening of the Belém–Brasília paved highway.

In the State of Pará population changed from 2 161 326 in 1970 to 3 411 235 in 1980 (57.8%) as a result of many economic events such as the gold rush in Serra Pelada; the discovery of the Carajás mineral complex and the construction of the first Transamazônica railway from Carajás to Itaqui-Maranhão (890 km); the bauxite mining in Trombetas; the construction of the hydroelectric dam of Tucuruí on the Tocantins river (4 000 000 kW); the Jari project in Almeirim county; the gold rush and the BR-165 road from Santarém to Itaituba, on the Tapajós river; the colonisation settlements along the Transamazon Highway in Altamira and São Felix do Xingu; the black-pepper plantations and farms along the Belém–Brasília highway in the Bragantina, Guajarina and Tomé–Açu microregions.

In the metropolitan zone of Belém, the population in 1980 reached one million inhabitants, an increase of almost 50.0% over of the previous decade. This increase caused much stress and difficulty for the low-rent classes, as demonstrated by the enlargement of the shanty towns of the *baixadas* of Belém.

The State of Maranhão on the edge of Amazonia, which is a zone of transition from the dry and drought-ridden land of the Northeast to the tropical rainforest, has the greatest population density. In the 1980 census out of a total of 4 002 679, some 3 341 842 are included in the Amazon part of Maranhão, with an increase of 35.9% over the 1970 population of 2 458 616. Of this total, 68.0% are living in rural areas. Maranhão is the rice-basket of the Amazon having this year produced about 1 500 000 tons along the Tocantins river and in the humid valleys of the Gurupi, Mearim, Pindaré and Itapecurú rivers.

In the State of Amazonas, the population increased from 955 394 in 1970 to 1 430 314 in 1980 (49.7%), concentrated mainly in the city of Manaus, which grew 96.3% in the decade, from 312 160 to 634 759 inhabitants. This was mostly due to the institution of the Free Trade Zone of Manaus in 1967, which created about 50 000 jobs in the new industrial district, specialising in the assembly and manufacture of electronics, motorcycles, watches, jewellery, opticals, jute, textiles, veneer and plywood goods. In the hinterland, the historical trend of concentration in the middle Amazon continued, from the frontier of Pará up to Manacupurú (63.2%) and in the middle and upper Solimões (36.0%), all along the main course of the Amazon river. The northern part of the State of Amazonas registered the lowest density and continues to be remarkably uninhabited, after a population shift from the north to the south of the Basin, perhaps due to ultisol conditions, lean resources and impoverished black-water rivers.

In the territories of Amapá and Roraima there were small absolute gains in population in the decade 1970–80, of 61 947 and 29 163 respectively, although percentage-wise the increases were 53.1% and 93.2% in the last ten years. In the State of Acre, difficulties of river transportation during the summer and erosion and broken terrain along the BR-364 road during the rainy season when the state is isolated from the rest of the country, have hindered colonisation and prospects are dim until these problems are overcome. The population increased by 39.5% in the decade, from 216 200 to 301 628 in 1980.

## Conclusion

There has been a remarkable change in the size and distribution of the Amazonian population since World War II when the Brazilian government announced development plans.

Table 9 *Urban and rural population ratios (Amazon region, north) 1940–80*

| Years | Urban population | % | Rural population | % | Total population |
|-------|------------------|-----|------------------|------|------------------|
| 1940 | 405 792 | 27·7 | 1 056 628 | 72·3 | 1 462 400 |
| 1950 | 580 867 | 31·5 | 1 263 788 | 68·5 | 1 844 655 |
| 1960 | 957 718 | 37·4 | 1 604 064 | 62·6 | 2 561 782 |
| 1970 | 1 626 600 | 45·1 | 1 977 260 | 54·9 | 3 603 860 |
| 1980 | 3 046 129 | 51·7 | 2 847 007 | 49·3 | 5 893 136 |

Table 10  Urban population ratios 1970–80

| | 1970 | | | 1980 | | | Average annual growth 1970–80 |
|---|---|---|---|---|---|---|---|
| | Total | Urban | Urban percentage | Total | Urban | Urban percentage | |
| Pará | 2 167 018 | 1 021 966 | 47·16 | 3 411 868 | 1 669 662 | 48·94 | 4·67 |
| Amapá | 114 359 | 62 451 | 54·61 | 175 634 | 103 926 | 59·17 | 4·35 |
| Amazonas | 955 235 | 405 831 | 42·48 | 1 432 066 | 858 181 | 59·93 | 4·12 |
| Roraima | 40 885 | 17 481 | 42·76 | 79 153 | 48 885 | 61·76 | 6·81 |
| Acre | 215 299 | 59 307 | 27·55 | 301 605 | 132 174 | 43·82 | 3·39 |
| Rondônia | 111 064 | 59 564 | 53·63 | 492 810 | 233 301 | 47·34 | 15·80 |
| Northern Region | 3 603 860 | 1 626 600 | 45·13 | 5 893 136 | 3 046 129 | 51·69 | 5·04 |
| North-East | 28 111 927 | 11 752 977 | 41·81 | 34 861 907 | 17 585 618 | 50·44 | 2·16 |
| South-East | 39 853 498 | 28 964 601 | 72·68 | 51 752 651 | 42 848 230 | 82·79 | 2·64 |
| South | 16 496 493 | 7 303 427 | 44·27 | 19 036 429 | 11 880 533 | 62·41 | 1·43 |
| Centre-West | 5 073 259 | 2 437 379 | 48·04 | 7 554 869 | 5 118 092 | 67·75 | 4·04 |
| Brazil | 93 139 037 | 52 084 984 | 55·92 | 119 098 992 | 80 478 602 | 67·57 | 2·48 |

Table 11  Demographic growth of state capitals 1872–1980

| Municipalities of the capital cities | 1872 | 1809 | 1900 | 1920 | 1940 | 1950 | 1960 | 1970 | 1980 |
|---|---|---|---|---|---|---|---|---|---|
| Belém (Pará) | 61 997 | 50 064 | 96 560 | 236 402 | 206 331 | 254 949 | 399 222 | 633 379 | 934 330 |
| Macapá (Amapá) | – | – | – | – | – | 20 594 | 46 777 | 86 307 | 137 698 |
| São Luis (Maranhão) | 31 604 | 29 308 | 36 798 | 52 929 | 85 583 | 119 785 | 158 292 | 265 595 | 449 877 |
| Manaus (Amazonas) | 29 334 | 38 720 | 50 300 | 75 704 | 106 399 | 139 620 | 173 703 | 312 160 | 634 759 |
| Boa Vista (Roraima) | | | | | | 17 247 | 25 705 | 36 491 | 66 769 |
| Rio Branco (Acre) | | | | 19 930 | 16 038 | 28 246 | 47 437 | 70 959 | 117 113 |
| Pôrto Velho (Rondônia) | | | | | – | 27 244 | 50 695 | 64 522 | 134 621 |
| Cuiabá (Mato Grosso) | 35 987 | 17 815 | 34 339 | 33 678 | 54 394 | 56 204 | 56 828 | 100 865 | 212 929 |
| Totals | 158 922 | 135 907 | 217 997 | 418 643 | 398 313 | 663 889 | 958 659 | 1 570 648 | 2 688 096 |

Source: Annual statistics, IBGE

From 1940 to 1980, the population of the Northern Region increased from 1 844 665 to 5 890 633 inhabitants. If we consider the Brazilian Amazon Basin (Amazônia Legal), the present population is 11 218 385 — an increase of 54.5% over the 1970 Census, representing an average yearly growth of 4.45%. Most of this increase occurred rapidly in towns and cities where the ratio of urban to rural population increased from 27.7% in 1940 to 51.7% in 1980, creating problems of shanty towns, *palafitas* and *favelas* as happens in so many Latin American cities.

The forested uplands and interfluvia were crossed by a web of pioneer roads such as the Belém–Brasília, the Transamazon Highway, Cuiabá–Santarém, Cuiabá–Pôrto Velho–Rio Branco, Pôrto Velho–Manaus–Bôa Vista–Caracas serving as the backbone of the system. New migrants settled along these roads while the traditional population remained along the river banks or fled from their homes to the shanty outskirts of towns and cities, requiring a large social investment in housing, education and public utilities.

Despite the partial failure of some colonisation projects established on poor oxysols and ultisols along the Transamazon Highway, other projects located on the eutrophic soils along that road and in the southwest in Rondônia are achieving good results. These successes indicate that when experienced farmers work on a nutrient-rich soil and use cultivation methods adequate to the environment, combining perennial-tree cash crops with short-cycle grain for subsistence, the outcome has been positive.

Another observed trend is that the settlement of the Amazon no longer depends exclusively upon the poverty-stricken Northeast, acting as a safety valve to relieve its demographic pressures, economic distress and political strife. The area is now receiving migrants, tenants and farmers from the Brazilian Centre-West and South. It seems that the development of the region will be a natural expansion of the southern and the savanna frontier of the Central Brazilian plateau, fostered by improvements in scientific knowledge, discoveries of new resources and intelligent use of appropriate technology for the humid tropics.

Amazon development must be ecologically and scientifically sound and socially oriented. Well-intentioned government policies and incentives are not enough. They may be distorted and lead to an economic rush to cut, slash and burn, dig and drill, at the expense of human welfare and wilderness values. Unless such policies are accompanied by the creation of a new agroforestry ecosystem for the benefit of man, the results will be wasteful.

Balancing development and conservation to humanise and improve the natural ecosystems for the well-being of Brazil's people and of her South American neighbours with whom are shared the Amazon condominium; this is the great challenge of our generation.

# 3 Alternative migration targets and Brazilian Amazonia's closing frontier

## L. J. A. MOUGEOT

## Internal migrations, within Latin American countries: recent directional trends at the urban and regional levels

### The facts

Relatively more people in Latin America have recently been moving to middle-sized cities and frontier regions. Though major national cities and core regions scored the highest immigration rates in the past (Daland 1969 p. 30), flows to secondary settlements and sparsely inhabited areas have gained importance in many countries over recent decades. Metropolises exhibited falling total growth rates in the 1950s and 1960s in Mexico, Venezuela, Argentina, and Peru, with intermediate-sized cities growing more swiftly than the former during the more recent period (Table 1).

Table 1 *Average annual population growth rates for 6 Latin American countries, per city-size category (1960–70)*

| Country | City-size category | | | | |
|---------|---------|---------|---------|---------|---------|
| | | | | Major city | |
| | *50–100$^a$* | *100–250* | *250 over* | *1960–70* | *1950–60* |
| Brazil (50)$^b$ | (25) 6.99 | (15) 6.19 | (8) 7.37 | (2) 7.37 | 5.31 |
| Mexico (67) | (41) 4.88 | (18) 5.82 | (7) 4.42 | (1) 5.46 | 6.27 |
| Argentina (19) | (4) 2.42 | (9) 3.20 | (5) 2.98 | (1) 2.40 | 4.27 |
| Venezuela (14) | (6) 6.00 | (6) 7.25 | (1) 5.79 | (1) 5.26 | 7.52 |
| Peru (10) | (7) 9.17 | (2) 11.14 | (0) –$^c$ | (1) 8.60 | 7.32 |
| Colombia | –$^d$ | – | – | (1) 5.10 | 7.35 |

Source: Based on data in Fox (1975), pp. 53–58, 63–73, 78–80, 85–89, 93–96, 100–103.
Notes: a in thousands
    b numbers in parentheses refer to the number of cities involved
    c computation does not apply
    d data not available in source

Net immigration probably contributes less to total growth in metropolitan centres, due to migrants' higher fertility, than in smaller agglomerations with equivalent overall population increments. Trends amid the urban system are further differentiated regionally. Colombia witnessed a twofold directional shift; between 1964 and 1974 its thinly settled northwestern and eastern lowlands, as well as peripheral subregional centres – Pasto, Neiva and Cúcuta – exerted more attraction than their more occupied and central counterparts. In Brazil, frontierward migration increased over the 1950s and 1960s, and the Central West and North experienced higher net rates than the more densely settled northeastern and southern regions, both in total and cityward inward migration (Table 2; the 'Frontier' category includes Central West plus North).

## The meaning

Emerging alternative migration targets in Latin American countries suggest that people's search strategy for a better livelihood varies, as development proceeds over time and through space. In the past, benefits of densely occupied regions and disadvantages of their counterparts have been overrated, due to pervasive perceptual biases on the part of migrants. With improving communication networks and rising diseconomies of scale in the former regions however, smaller nuclei and the peripheries have lately come to receive growing numbers of outsiders. Some surveys even record significant portions of contingents now on the frontier, who have already spent some time in larger and more competitive environments, as revealed by immigration fields of towns and hamlets in central and southeastern parts of Amazonia (Jones 1981 p. 119; Unikel 1975; Faria 1976; Roberts 1978 p. 106). After 1940 however, a series of innovations were introduced in the agricultural and industrial sectors of national economies, such as: (a) capital-intensive technology, dictated by import-substitution policies; (b) petrochemical farming, dictated by agricultural export programmes; (c) ownership titling and production regulation, imposed by the private-property-based market economy; and (d) liberal legislation against abusive labour management. These changes have particularly hampered the absorption of labour by advanced regions, with spatial mobility becoming correspondingly less profitable. The following subsections further detail this argument (Chossudovsky 1981; Kowarick 1977 pp. 127–45).

*Mounting social pressures on resources in rural areas*

In the countryside, these post-1940 transformations have imposed mounting social pressures on available resources, thus leading to unemployment and displacement. Improved transport systems and communication networks have funnelled the advance of commercial agriculture into formerly subsistence areas, with a related rise in land values, land titling, rearrangement of production factors and modifications of work conditions. According to Ernest Feder rural unemployment is rising in Latin America.

The absorption rate of medium- and large-sized farms has been disproportionately small in the face of a rapidly growing agrarian labour force. Brazil's recent censuses illustrate this trend. Here, the number of agricultural workers increased from 12.6 millions in 1950 to 15.6 millions in 1960. Most of this additional manpower was found on small farms, whereas employment on large multifamily units sank by 35 per cent. Job slots on these large estates would have

Table 2 Urban population and its growth by region and city size, Brazil, 1950–70

| Region-category | | Total population (1000s) | | | Average annual growth rate | |
|---|---|---|---|---|---|---|
| | | 1950 | 1960 | 1970 | 1950–60 | 1960–70 |
| **Northeast** | | | | | | |
| Metropolitan | centre | 1 139 | 1 899 | 2 904 | 5.24 | 4.34 |
| (Fortaleza, Recife, Salvador) | periphery | 155 | 271 | 657 | 5.75 | 9.26 |
| Other 100 000+ | | 781 | 1 273 | 2 048 | 5.01 | 4.87 |
| 20–100 000 | | 501 | 850 | 1 393 | 5.42 | 5.03 |
| All 20 000+ | | 2 576 | 4 293 | 7 002 | 5.24 | 5.01 |
| Official urban | | 4 745 | 7 681 | 11 053 | 4.93 | 3.71 |
| **Southeast** | | | | | | |
| Large metropolitan | centre | 4 430 | 6 562 | 10 122 | 4.01 | 4.43 |
| (Rio and São Paulo) | periphery | 950 | 1 962 | 4 563 | 7.52 | 8.81 |
| Other metropolitan | centre | 862 | 1 655 | 2 682 | 6.74 | 4.95 |
| (Belo Horizonte, Curitiba, Pôrto Alegre) | periphery | 168 | 253 | 879 | 4.18 | 13.26 |
| Other 100 000+ | | 1 443 | 2 558 | 4 329 | 5.89 | 5.40 |
| 20–100 000 | | 2 008 | 3 573 | 5 673 | 5.93 | 4.73 |
| All 20 000+ | | 9 861 | 16 563 | 28 248 | 5.32 | 5.48 |
| Official urban | | 12 584 | 22 288 | 33 109 | 5.88 | 4.04 |
| **Frontier** | | | | | | |
| Metropolitan | centre | 241 | 375 | 603 | 4.52 | 4.87 |
| (Belém) | periphery | 1 | 2 | 3 | 7.18 | 4.14 |
| Other 100 000+ | | 168 | 496 | 1 331 | 11.14 | 11.04 |
| 20–100 000 | | 134 | 290 | 594 | 8.03 | 7.43 |
| All 20 000+ | | 544 | 1 163 | 2 531 | 7.89 | 8.09 |
| Official urban | | 1 004 | 2 036 | 4 064 | 7.33 | 7.16 |
| **Brazil** | | | | | | |
| Metropolitan | centre | 6 672 | 10 491 | 16 311 | 4.63 | 4.51 |
| | periphery | 1 274 | 2 488 | 6 102 | 6.92 | 9.39 |
| Other 100 000+ | | 2 643 | 4 327 | 7 708 | 6.11 | 5.94 |
| 20–100 000 | | 2 392 | 4 713 | 7 660 | 5.95 | 4.98 |
| All 20 000+ | | 12 981 | 22 019 | 37 781 | 5.43 | 5.55 |
| Official urban | | 18 783 | 32 005 | 52 085 | 5.47 | 4.99 |

Source: Reproduced from Merrick and Moran (1979 p. 15). The authors originally used data provided in Fox (1975).

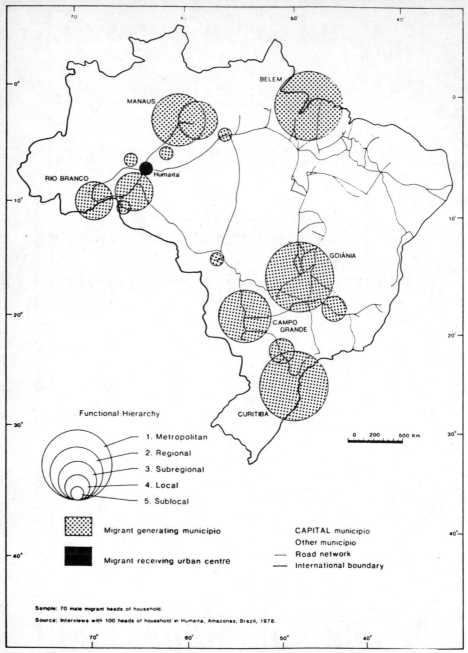

Fig. 1 Functional hierarchy generating direct migrants to the urban centre of Humaitá, Amazonas 1978

Note: Those who resided in metro and regional order *municípios* prior to moving to the urban centre constitute 18.57% of all immigrated informants. See Mougeot 1980a p. 88.

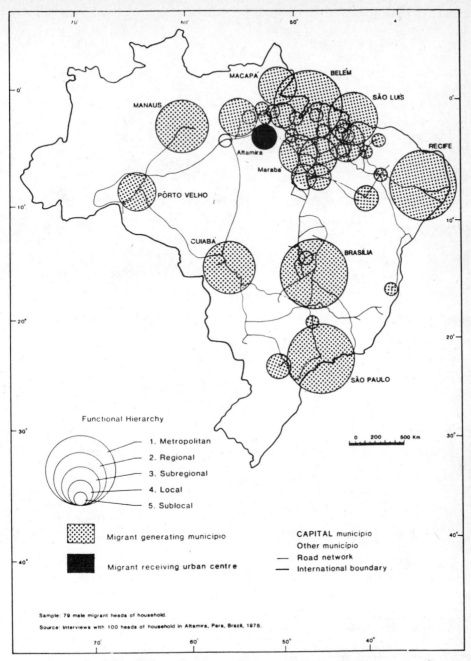

**Functional Hierarchy**

1. Metropolitan
2. Regional
3. Subregional
4. Local
5. Sublocal

Migrant generating município

Migrant receiving urban centre

CAPITAL município
Other município
— Road network
— International boundary

Sample: 79 male migrant heads of household.

Source: Interviews with 100 heads of household in Altamira, Pará, Brazil, 1978.

Fig. 2  Functional hierarchy generating direct migrants to the urban centre of
Altamira, Pará 1978
Note: Those who resided in metro and regional order *municípios* prior to
moving to the urban centre constituted 15.19% of all immigrated informants.
See Mougeot 1980a p. 88.

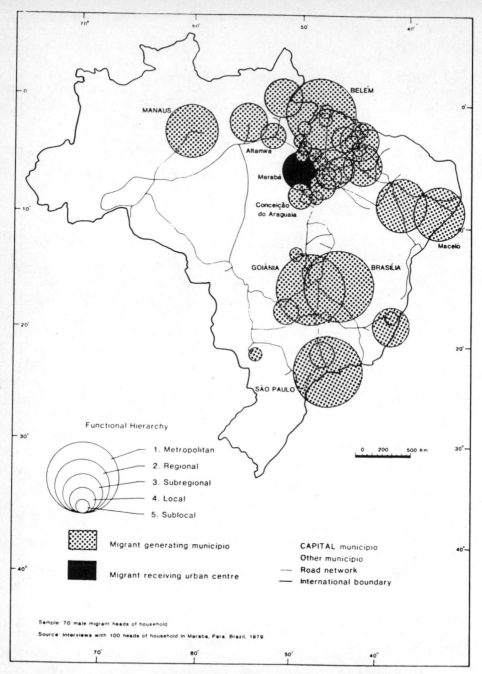

**Fig. 3** Functional hierarchy generating direct migrants to the urban centre of
Marabá, Pará 1979
Note: Those who resided in metro and regional order *municípios* prior to
moving to the urban centre constituted 25.71% of all immigrated informants.
See Mougeot 1980a p. 88.

vanished due to: (a) a massive shift toward labour-extensive livestock operations; and (b) large shares of permanent crops requiring less labour and more machinery. Also, more of the rural working population became engaged in non-agrarian occupations in the countryside during the 1960s. But such vacancies were predicted to become saturated and less well paid in the future (Feder 1971 pp. 33–5).

Growing social pressure on resources in rural areas has thus led to proletarianisation – creation of a propertyless agrarian population – throughout Latin American and Brazil in particular. Despite unabated cityward migration, Latin American families of smallholders and landless rural labourers have swollen in numbers, from 12.6 to 18 millions over the 1960–80 period, out of a total of 103.2 millions, nearly half of them in Brazil (Feder 1971 pp. 3–4; Martine n d p. 55). In the State of São Paulo, the proportion of permanent employees dropped from 34 to 24 per cent of sharecroppers and from 15 to 8 per cent between 1950 and 1960 (Gonzales and Bastos 1976 p. 260). The percentage of all rural workers in the country who did not own the land they cultivated rose from 19.2 to 38.1 per cent, over the 1950–75 period (Martins 1980 p. 46). In 1972 according to data from the Brazilian Institute for Colonisation and Agrarian Reform (INCRA), wage-earners in agricultural areas totalled 7.8 millions; of these, 6.8 millions were temporary jobbers and 1 million permanent workers (Martine n. d. p. 55).

These figures convey a reasonable pulse of the changes in rural work conditions that prompted both frontier and cityward migration in recent decades (Moran 1977). Between 1950 and 1970 for instance, net immigration to the central-western states of Paraná, Goiás, and Mato Grosso involved some 2.8 million people (Sanders and Bein 1976, p. 596). Furthermore, and largely due to their inability to retain access to land in the developed regions, growing numbers of agricultural workers are cast out towards marginal urban areas. In 1970 these accounted for 7, 13, and 15 per cent of the total agricultural manpower in Paraná, Pernambuco, and Goiás, respectively, and for 25 per cent in São Paulo (Gonzales and Bastos 1976, p. 241).

*Mounting social pressures on resources in urban areas*
In Latin American cities, industrial employment grew at faster rates than the urban population before 1950, but this tendency was reversed later on. Labour-absorption rates of manufacturing and craft sectors have remained constant at best in subsequent decades. Again, Brazilian performance mirrors the regional situation: the number of non-agricultural workers increased at a faster pace than urbanisation during the 1940s, with an opposite trend prevailing thereafter. (Kowarick 1977 pp. 128–9, 150).

Most crucial is the fact that cityward migration is associated with the expansion of an ill-defined tertiary sector. Latin America's sector-specific shares of total employment indicate that jobs provided by agriculture dwindled from 53.4 per cent to 42.2 per cent; those in goods and non-agricultural basic services fluctuated between 23.5 and 24.8 per cent; whereas recruitment by the mainly informal service sector rose from 23.1 to 33.0 per cent, between 1950 and 1969 (Kowarick 1977 p. 129). Large migrant flows from the fields are thus the main cause for high urbanisation rates. These are combined with low productivity, depressed salary levels for unskilled labour and shuddering inequality in both income and welfare distributions (Beier *et al.* 1976 pp. 381–2). This is certainly true of Brazil, where the real minimum monthly wage fell and the income profile worsened in all metropolitan areas during the 1960s. Most wage-earners with less than this minimum stipend in 1970 concentrated in civil construction and personal service occupations. Due to the growing insufficiency of bread-winners' income, more family members have been joining the labour force in recent years: the proportion of those aged 10–19 rose in the already saturated personal-service sector, which further contributed to low derisory salaries in those activities (Fraenkel and Souza 1976 pp. 51, 46, 38).

The soaring economic hardship of large numbers of urban residents engaged in agriculture, civil construction, crafts and repair services, petty vending, and other non-capitalised activities is useful in the drive toward modernisation. Labour surpluses within a given region are functional in that they provide the capital-intensive industrialisation process with an ever cheaper and servile labour force. This excess manpower also satisfies most of the demand for low-return services. All this saves capital that can be injected into those sectors where it becomes essential (Roberts 1978 pp. 167–8). In other words, the salary and occupational structure is subordinated to the needs of the production system. It thus ensures the maintenance of a reserve army within a given region (Martine and Peliano 1978 p. 182). This implies substandard living conditions and an appalling rating by the poor on most indices of well-being: widespread malnutrition, and mortality rates many times those of the middle classes or of the industrialised low-income groups. In the city of Santarém in the State of Pará, with approximately 200 000 inhabitants in 1980, three sample surveys (conducted by Brazil's Food and Nutrition Institute (INAN) in peripheral neighbourhoods in 1975 and 1977, and on the whole urban area in 1979, plus a citywide food-price study in 1980) reveal that: (a) the great majority of children aged 5 years or less are underfed, with nearly a fifth of these suffering from second- and third-degree malnutrition; (b) the proportion of undernourished youngsters increased during the 1975–9 period, particularly those stricken by second-degree malnutrition; and (c) a towering growth in urban prices of basic foodstuffs – well beyond that of the decreed minimum salary. These factors are largely responsible for this aggravated situation (Dutra 1981).

The labour reserve is that partly employed or unemployed component of the population that is relatively in excess in any given region. It is a most unstable segment both spatially and economically (Kowarick 1977 p. 105). In Brazil for instance, destitute groups predominate in cityward migration flows. Almost 60 per cent of urban migrants, with less than 5 years' residence in their census district in

1970, earned about one minimum wage; the percentage was larger for recent arrivals at those localities (Martine n d p. 52). An inability to gain or keep ownership and control of factors of production forces the poor to move repeatedly, within and between settlements. Case studies show that low-income household heads at all levels of the urban system often work far from their residence (Roberts 1978 p. 120. Mougeot 1976 p. 60). For instance, in a village well centred in its *município* in Maranhão, 14 per cent of 195 interviewees worked outside the *município*, with lengths of stay at remote workplaces ranging from 2 to 270 days, one month on average. Itinerants included rural jobbers and craftsmen who rapidly exhaust local demand for their products (Mougeot 1978 p. 13; Aragon 1978 pp. 88–94; Mougeot 1980 p. 123).

*Frontierward migration as an alternative search strategy*

The pervasive spatial mobility of the low-status labour force in well advanced regions not only sparks competition, but also depresses wages and curtails opportunities for individual progress. It also prompts traditional labour-intensive activities to be displaced from the more developed realm into other areas, where markets and accessibility are smaller and poorer.

Frontier settlement is part of this displacement process. This point is illustrated by a study of rates of urbanisation, unemployment and underemployment and their spatial variations throughout Brazil's Northeast during the decades 1950–70. Over this period, the densely peopled and industrialised coastal fringe was stricken by both rural and urban emigration. Changes in land use and working conditions reached the coastlands, and this acted as an impetus for migration in the absence of compensatory job expansion. For example, sugar-cane cutters were proletarianised and deruralised in the humid eastern zone when the Agreste, Pernambuco and Sergipe changed more decisively to land-intensive pastoral activities. On the other hand, the dismissed rural labour was not assimilated by formal urban sectors. On the contrary, industrial production has been further modernised, with ensuing reductions in the absorptive capacity of extractive and tranformation plants in most northeastern states between 1950 and 1970.

Such changes in agriculture and industry have had two outcomes. First, in the urban system unemployment grew in large cities and more urbanised *municípios*, whereas disguised underemployment become more frequent in smaller settlements and mostly rural *municípios*. Subregional centres were particularly stricken, as they stood at the crossing point of those two opposite positions in the urban hierarchy. Secondly, in contrast with what occurred on the more developed seaboard, the peripheral microregions of Meio-Norte, Sertão do Piauí, Médio and Sub-Médio São Francisco, and the Extremo Sul da Bahia, scored high rural and urban population growth rates, as well as increases in primitive agricultural and informal non-agrarian employment. Small towns sprang up in those frontier backwaters, where household-produced goods and services involve low technological costs and use family labour under self-employment or subcontractual arrangements. Products are then marketed through a network of local fairs to satisfy the basic needs of low-income populations in the more advanced coastal fringe (Guimarães Neto 1976 pp. 34–6, 42–3, 60–1).

In summary, the modern sector encroaches upon its traditional counterpart. It induces the latter to emigrate and entrench at a distance, where it can survive and remain functional. Modernisation thus involves a never-ending struggle for control of space by various socio-enconomic groups. In this struggle a class's chances of gaining control over the contended space varies during development. The very survival of low-status contingents is tied to further territorial discrimination, in the face of encroachment by higher-class counterparts. One may view frontierward migration as a displacement towards less disputed areas. It occurs at all levels, away from a surface artery, a central district, a metropolitan centre, a nation's core region, or a more industrialised country.

As a means of damping pressure on available resources in the more competitive regions, Latin American nations have been encouraging frontierward migration more strongly in recent decades. Frontier settlement is an explicit component of many development policies. It is preferred to the less viable labour-intensive industrialisation or equitable redistribution of land between the urban and rural sectors. In practice, however, it has meant little more than endorsing an already operative and largely self-sufficient process. In Brazil, prodigal efforts to utilise northern resources were heralded as providing land and progress opportunities for the surplus labour force (INCRA 1972 p. 1; Camargo 1973 pp. 5–8; Mahar 1978 pp. 22–3; Katzman 1977 p. 202).

Despite lessons taught by attempts at reform in the 1960s, the social utility of frontier settlement schemes in the 1970s was equally shortsighted; Policy statements emphasised the palliative virtues of uncontrolled environments, without clearly spelling out their role as a stage in the expansion of the national space-economy. Moreover, they neglected the spatial friction involved in this process, and thus underrated the rapidly fading benefits for most frontier settlers.

By and large, the transition from subsistence to commercial frontiers in Latin America has created few opportunities for the lower rural groups to settle and progress socio-economically. It was seen earlier that the bulk of frontierward migrants are negatively selected in generating areas, where modernising agriculture and manufacturing brings about under- and unemployment. It is also true that frontier land ownership by a few farsighted individuals has been preceding occupancy by the majority. The conversion from primitive to advanced frontier areas has required large landholdings and some migrant labour (Barraclough and Domike 1960 pp. 391–424; Hennessey 1978 pp. 126–37).

# The closing frontier in Brazilian Amazonia: recent inter- and intra-regional migration trends

### The facts

As of 1970 Brazil's North Region persistently absorbed little population from other regions of the country (Mendes 1971 p. 71; Batista 1976 pp. 32, 34; Keller 1977 p. 167; Santos 1980 pp. 59–63, 87–118, 315–7). Net immigration contributed trivially to the Region's total population growth during the 1950s and 1960s: merely 3 points of the 4 per cent 1950–60 decennial increase, and 2.3 points of the 1960–70 increment estimated at 40.3 per cent. Development programmes aimed at fostering inter-regional migration have brought little gain. Net immigration estimates for the 1960s vary from one author to the next, but all are deceptive in relation to the Region's public domain and the northeastern landless populace. Elza C. de Souza Keller calculates the net inflow to have been approximately 114 000; Fernando H. Cardoso and Geraldo Müller put forth 67 000.

José A. Magno de Carvalho and Morvan de Mello Moreira applied the census survival rate method and obtained estimates of 61 427 and 53 875. They claim that the net inflow rate for the *whole decade* was less than the Region's *average annual* population growth rate in the 1960s. More recent calculations suggest an average *negative* 0.2 per cent annual increment attributable to net immigration during the 1960s (Keller 1977 p. 174; Santos 1979 p. 138; Cardoso and Müller 1977 p. 40; Carvalho and Moreira 1976 p. 41; Carvalho *et al.* 1979a p. 229). The above figures give little credit to governmental programmes launched in the 1960s to attract labour surpluses from congested regions. One project, the construction of the Belém–Brasília highway, has had much overrated pulling and stabilising effects along the road's corridor (Hébette and Acevedo Marín 1979 pp. 158–62). State-level calculations by Martin T. Katzman indicate that, depending upon which assumption is selected, the highway would have induced a shift of the order of 160 000 to 320 000 people, into microregions in its neighbourhood. Another study estimates that net immigration at the microregional level was 174 000 – Belém, Goiânia, and Brasília excluded – of which 108 000 were absorbed by rural areas. Most of this local reshuffling took place outside the North Region (Katzman 1975 p. 104; Becker *et al.* 1978).

If programmes implemented within the North Region had any redistributional effects, these were more notable on an intra- rather than an inter-regional level. Between 1960 and 1970 net migration between *municípios* within the Region was three times greater than net immigration from other areas of Brazil. A comparison of 1950–60 with 1960–70 municipal rates of rural and urban population change, reveals that the North met with an ever-accentuated depopulation of its territory during those two decades. A growing share of the Region's 144 *municípios* suffered absolute rural and urban population losses. In terms of rural depopulation, the number of *municípios* with growth indices smaller than the regional natural growth rate (3.8 per cent) swelled from 94 in 1960 to 120 in 1970 (Carvalho 1973 p. 112; Keller 1977 p. 267; Carvalho *et al.* 1979a p. 229). *Municípios* with growth ranging from zero up to the regional figure grew from 93 to 102, whereas those with rates below zero went from 1 to 18. As for urban depopulation, the number of *municípios* with a growth smaller than the regional natural rate rose from 32 in 1960 to 46 in 1970. *Municípios* with figures ranging between zero and the regional rate went from 28 to 33, but those with below zero scores from 4 to 13.

The above differentiation concerning inter- and intra-regional migrant contingents conceals a more significant trend, which involves both contingents. Migration flows to developing frontiers in the North Region mostly comprise short-distance movers. These movers proceed from both depressed economic areas within the Region and high social-pressure cells on its periphery. At an inter-regional level, western Maranhão, northern Goiás and Mato Grosso were seen in the 1950s as major escape valves for the northeastern and southern landless. In recent decades, with increasing landholding concentration and land-intensive agricultural occupancy, those havens have begun to experience depopulation – and net emigration in many cases, with outmovers heading mainly towards southeastern Pará and Rondônia (Keller 1977 pp. 209, 221; Becker *et al.* 1978).

At the intra-regional level, a comparison of 1960–70 municipal rates of total population change with the Region's equivalent natural growth rate, shows that relative and absolute depopulation took place in the less dynamic and more occupied areas of the North (Figure 4). Areas that witnessed absolute depopulation may have been penalised by deteriorating conditions for extraction and marketing of plant products, such as the upper Rio Negro, or by being adjacent to capital or mining *municípios*. The latter are likely to have absorbed considerable emigration from the former. Three major regions underwent relative depopulation at the municipal level. The middle Amazonas and its southwestern tributaries, with an economy dominated by plant extraction, suffered less than the upper Rio Negro. This is possibly due to the former area's lower population densities, poorer accessibility to urban magnets, and a marketing system for agro-industrial staples in its lower central section. The second region is located in Pará; it includes Marajó Island and Bragantina–Salgado microregions. Traditional cattle-raising areas in Marajó are being outpaced by alternative livestock-fattening grounds that sprang up to satisfy rising urban demand. Improved road access to pastoral project areas and to major urban centres has contributed to suck people out of soil-depleted Bragantina and Salgado. On the northernmost edge of Amapá Territory, a third region has been plagued by declining fur trade and plant extraction: as a result it loses population to the territorial capital (Keller 1977 pp. 232–40).

Certainly, this 1960–70 pattern of population change by municipality does not convey a detailed image of spatial mobility. The size of northern *municípios* – disproportionate by Brazilian standards – and the frequent use of rivers as boundaries, are both responsible for an underestimation of long-distance moves.

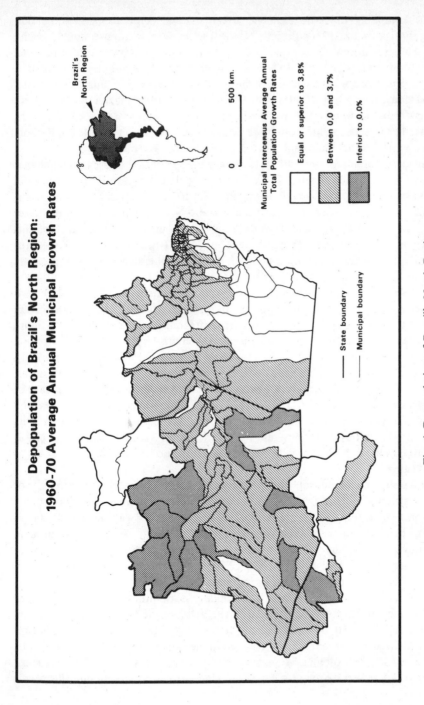

## Depopulation of Brazil's North Region:
## 1960-70 Average Annual Municipal Growth Rates

Brazil's
North Region

0       500 km.

**Municipal Intercensus Average Annual
Total Population Growth Rates**

Equal or superior to 3,8%

Between 0,0 and 3,7%

Inferior to 0,0%

State boundary

Municipal boundary

Fig. 4 Depopulation of Brazil's North Region
Sources of data: Carvalho and Moreira 1976 vol. I anexo 2; Keller 1977 p.
267; IBGE 1967.

Notwithstanding those deficiencies, several factual generalisations stand out. During the 1950s and 1960s Brazil's North Region demonstrated a limited ability to absorb populations from other areas of the country. Instead, intra-regional redistribution trends indicate greater spatial instability over those two decades, when more people concentrated in the major cities of Belém, Manaus, Pôrto Velho, and Macapá. Also, government-assisted developing frontiers, in southeastern Pará and Rondônia, have drawn their growth mainly from depressed areas within the Region. Migrants also came from more densely occupied areas outside the Region, such as western Maranhão, and northern Goiás and Mato Grosso.

A cursory examination of 1980 preliminary census data discloses evidence that reinforces some trends defined above. Assuming that the 1960s' annual natural growth rate remained unchanged throughout the 1970s, a conservative estimate is that one out of every four residents added to the North's population in the latter decade was an inter-regional migrant. It is highly probable that most of this inter-regional flow involved short-distance movers. It thus involved a low-status population proceeding from areas on the North's periphery, where social pressure on resources escalated further over the last decade.

The spatial distribution of growth among micrøregions within the North reveals patterns of depopulation already apparent in previous decades: (a) total and urban population growth is still greater in eastern Amazonia, where Pará's 1980 figure alone is equivalent to the 1970 population of the entire North – that state became predominantly urban in 1980 (64.2 per cent as opposed to 47.2 per cent in 1970); and (b) urbanisation continued at a faster pace in resource-utilisation project areas, such as the now mainly urban Araguaia Paraense (mean annual growth rate of 24.87 per cent in the 1970s), Tomé Açu (27.64), Baixo Amazonas (22.39), Marabá (16.63), and Xingu (16.54), as opposed to more settled and less dynamic areas, like the Baixo Marajó (7.84), Bragantina (7.77), and Médio Amazonas (7.38) (SEPLAN/FIBGE 1981 no. 1, 5, 18, 38; no. 6, 5; no. 23 5; no. 24 5).

**The meaning**

Limited empirical research has systematically addressed the process of frontierward migration in Brazilian Amazonia. One basic point of agreement in the fragmented literature is that unbridled changes under way in the Region's agrarian-production and land-tenure systems, along with infrastructural penetration, are rapidly closing openings for most settlers to advance socio-economically and stabilise themselves residentially. This crucial point receives detailed attention in the following paragraphs.

Concerning the North Region's changing agricultural production, plant extraction accounted for 41.1 per cent of the value of the regional gross primary product (GPP) in 1960, but only 22.6 per cent by 1969. During the 1960s, pastoral activities moved into areas formerly devoted to the extraction of rubber, Brazil nuts, and non-elastic gums such as *balata* and *chicles*. This is particularly true of eastern Amazonia – Pará and Amapá – where the share of plant extraction in this area's

GPP slumped from 31.1 per cent to 12.9 per cent. Changes were less pronounced in western Amazonia, where plant extraction still accounted for 34.1 per cent of this subregion's GPP in 1969 (Maia 1977 p. 366).

Along with agricultural transformation, Brazil's North Region underwent noticeable concentration of rural land-ownership between the late 1960s and early 1970s. According to a study by Amilcar A. Tupiassú and Simão R. Jatene, unit-specific Gini coefficients, based on INCRA's rural estate tenure data, climbed from 0.935 in 1967 to 0.972, in Acre; from 0.815 to 0.853 in Amazonas; from 0.854 to 0.879 in Pará; from 0.442 to 0.553 in Roraima; and from 0.799 to 0.869 in Amapá. In Rondônia, presumably due to INCRA's colonisation efforts, the index fell from 0.938 to 0.901. For the Region as a whole, establishments smaller than 100 hectares saw their average size shrink from 18.13 hectares in 1940 to 17.24 in 1975, while those covering more than 100 000 hectares nearly doubled their average size from 176 000 to 326 000 hectares (Tupiassú and Jatene 1978 pp. 119–23).

Improvements in infrastructure have aided the above structural changes. Accessibility to regional and extra-regional market centres dominated the spatial organisation of the North Region's agrarian economy by 1969. Outside Belém's belt of market-gardening and industrial crops, southeastern Pará in eastern Amazonia, and Rondônia in its western counterpart, are two areas increasingly specialising in pastoral land use. These subregions' links to northern and southern metropolitan markets were strengthened in the late 1950s and 1960s by the construction of the Belém–Brasília and Cuiabá–Pôrto Velho highways and the extension of state and municipal road networks. The pastoral corridor of the Amazonas river system has so far been less commercialised. In the State of Amazonas, upstream areas to the north and south of this central waterway are still closely tied to a subsistence economy with seasonal employment related to plant extraction (Maia 1977 p. 388–9; Santos 1980 pp. 62, 72).

In the more penetrated eastern and southwestern portions of the North Region, rural labourers and occupants are increasingly threatened by shifts in production types, rearrangement of work conditions, and conflicts over land tenure.

The reorientation of agrarian activities has caused much damage. Rubber estates have been abandoned, destroyed or converted, which resulted in some 24 130 tappers being laid off in the states of Amazonas and Pará alone. This labour force and its dependents are considered large enough to have influenced intra-regional migration patterns during the 1960s (Moreira and Carvalho 1976 p. 74).

Furthermore, although unpaid dependents still form the bulk of the Region's agrarian manpower, there has recently been a dramatic increase in the use of short-term employees during labour-intensive periods of the year, particularly in states with pioneer frontier areas. Whereas the number of permanent salaried workers grew from 20 353 in 1960 to 24 816 in 1975 (21.93 per cent increase), temporarily jobbers (used in the months when most required) soared from 298 268 to 528 233 (77.10 per cent) in just the period 1970–5. In any given census year, more occasional labourers were recorded than permanent ones. Between 1970 and 1975 high-season temporary out-hiring grew at a faster rate than the total working population (51.24 per cent). Peak-period temporary workers increase rapidly in states with active frontier areas: 1970–5 growth rates were 312.9 per cent in Rondônia, 94.33 per cent in Amazonas, and 77.7 per cent in Pará (IBGE 1960 II/I 12 pp. 36, 60; II/II pp. 12, 38, 72. Idem 1970 III/I pp. 30, 40, 202, 212, 364, 374; III/III pp. 30, 40; III/IV pp. 30, 40. Idem (1979 I/1 pp. 34, 40, 214, 220, 392, 398; 1/2 pp. 34, 40; I/4 pp. 34, 40). According to INCRA's rural-estate data, only 8.12 per cent of the Region's estates used permanent labour in 1972, and on those estates only 29 per cent of all wage-earners were permanent.

Cattle-raising operations had more estates (16.2 per cent) using permanent labour, as opposed to agriculture (9.66 per cent) and plant extraction (8.97 per cent) (INCRA 1976a vol. 1 p. 106; vol. 2 pp. 4, 38, 72). However, this probably reflects the former's capital-intensive character, rather than a genuine ability to absorb large numbers of permanent employees, whether on a per-hectare or per-estate basis. Though the census does not display the data needed to calculate labour/land ratios by type of activity, data on pastoral projects provides support for the argument. The federal agency for the development of Brazilian Amazonia (SUDAM) launched 368 projects, plus 65 extensions of existing ones, between 1967 and 1972 (Mahar 1978 p. 121; Katzman 1975 p. 77; Ferreira 1981 pp. 4–5). Most projects approved after 1967 were devoted to cattle-raising, and these are not labour-intensive. High technology levels are among the top criteria stressed by SUDAM when evaluating proposals, and those with high labour-absorption factors are accordingly not highly rated. As of 1975, areas of approved projects totalled 4 600 hectares in Amazonas and 2 556 000 in Pará; but jobs thus directly created in those states amounted to a mere 53 and 2 377, respectively! Dennis J. Mahar contends that such ventures are more attractive than industrial enterprises as anti-inflation investments (Carvalho et al. 1979b p. 97; Mahar 1978 pp. 152–4).

Concerning conflicts over possession of land, José de Souza Martins reports that of all land disputes and related deaths recorded throughout Brazil in 1975 and 1976, 60 and 90 per cent respectively occurred in Amazonia. In advanced frontier areas the number of conflicts grows rapidly: in southern Pará, they went from 43 in early 1976, to 55 in June, and then to 78 in December of that same year. In the adjacent state of Maranhão, 128 similar clashes were filed in 1980, with some affecting over a thousand people (Martins 1980 p. 87).

Beyond the above trends based on the census, case studies verify that the normal fate of displaced rural settlers is to swell a destitute and mobile labour reserve. They have become unemployed either due to the shift from subsistence to commercial agrarian activities, or have been cast out in the course of the move from small and untitled to large and registered landholdings. In general, evicted and laid-off farmers have been used temporarily in capital- or land-intensive projects, or have engaged precariously in informal service and craft occupations at nearby urban centres. Few had the information and skill needed to seize opportunities in less contended areas. The resulting socio-economic and residential insecurity of these populations has been observed in livestock areas of northern Mato Grosso, and along the Belém–Brasília highway in northern Goiás. These tranfsformations were seen to be happening at a faster pace in recent years in the state of Acre and in southeastern Pará. (Lisansky 1979, 1980; Rivière d'Arc 1977 p. 303; Rivière d'Arc and Apestéguy 1978; Dupon and Vant 1979 pp. 239–50; Hébette and Acevedo Marín 1979, pp. 158–69; Wesche 1981 pp. 136–40). Along the Pará segment of the Transamazonian Highway and the Rondônia portion of the Cuiabá–Pôrto Velho highway, government-sponsored colonisation schemes of family-scale commercial agriculture are isolated attempts to settle frontiersmen productively amid the adverse transformations that are under way. Despite all-out efforts unrivalled elsewhere in South America, Transamazonian schemes now appear to be justified by circumstances (Wesche 1981 p. 143; Bunker 1979 pp. 64–70). Though approaching capacity, they have to date proved less efficient than predicted, in terms of both target population absorption and socio-economic upgrading. First, farming experience prior to arrival has been more important than institutional assistance in helping the *colonos* to progress (Moran 1975 p. xviii; Wood and Schmink 1979 pp. 9–19). Also, not only have relatively few families been settled, but of those a significant proportion have left. Under ideal land-reform conditions, it was estimated that Brazil's surplus rural population would still amount to 2.8 million families or 14.5 million individuals in 1980. Meanwhile, official target figures for managed agricultural colonisation ventures in Amazonia were set at 100 000 families for 1974, and at one million for 1980. (D'Apole *et al.* 1972 p. 53 in Martine nd p. 57).

As of 1974, the schemes at Marabá, Altamira and Itaituba along the Transamazonian Highway, had taken only between six and seven thousand families (Cardoso and Müller 1977 p. 157). Indeed, annual rates of accumulated desertion on the part of Altamira *colonos* climbed from 12.69 per cent in 1971 to 32.97 per cent in 1977. These figures are based on 1971–77 data reported in INCRA's annual operational programmes of the Altamira Integrated Colonisation Project (PIC).

In the second half of the 1970s INCRA shifted most efforts to Rondônia, where it has since succeeded in altering tenure distribution. However, massive seasonal migration, overwhelmed settlements, burgeoning urban centres, and sharply intensified conflict over possession of land, have been hampering orderly settlement projects (Pimentel in Carvalho *et al.* 1977 III p. 370; Gall 1978). By mid-1977 some 28 000 families had been established by INCRA on its seven colonisation sites along the Cuiabá–Pôrto Velho highway. Forty-five per cent of these households were slotted in under insecure conditions, and there remained an additional 30 000 families to be attended to on the on-site waiting list. (Martine nd p. 78). A post-1974 turnabout in Amazonian development policy has further removed support from family-scale farming schemes towards large-scale natural-resource consortium projects (Brasil Minter 1975 pp. 19–20). Combined with the production and tenure changes noted earlier, this late revision of priorities is likely to erode the prospects of landless workers and middle-class agriculturists for access to land property and marketing channels. In the light of growing evidence, renowned Latin Americanist scholars have thus questioned the ability of current pioneer fronts to retain most of the labourers they attract:

> Despite the avowed goal of settling the Amazon, there is considerable evidence that the Brazilian government perceives people as an obstacle rather than an asset for development. (Katzman 1977 p. 81).

> The 'development' of Amazonia is already shaping up into what may become the most classic of all examples of resource exploitation, carried out by a tiny wealthy (minority) of individuals, through international companies, for the benefit of the populations of already wealthy countries in maintaining and augmenting their high living standards, and with minimal gain for the Brazilian poor. It will be convenient to blame only the developers. (Brookfield 1965, reprinted 1979, p. 204).

## Socio-economic advancement and residential stability during frontier development

Study areas were selected in Brazil's North Region to represent a cross-section of the frontier development process. Frontier regions characterised by different phases of economic occupancy were delimited and typified by the National Institute of Geography and Statistics (IBGE) (Maia 1977 pp. 380–90).

The urban hierarchy varies in complexity within each region, and in each an urban centre was chosen with a different hierarchical order. Ranks were in turn defined by IBGE, according to the function of cities within the urban system. All Brazilian municipalities were classified in five orders: (1) metropolitan; (2) regional; (3) subregional; (4) local; and (5) sublocal (IBGE 1972 pp. 1–112). In this study a sixth order is theoretically acknowledged, which corresponds to dispersed subsistence-economy hamlets (Frota in FUNARTE 1981 p. 26).

Four cities of the Brazilian North were selected: three possess increasingly higher hierarchical orders associated with advanced development phases. These represent three stages of urban evolution during frontier development. Stage One is indicated by a sublocal town, in a region of seasonal employment tied to export of non-perishable staples: Humaitá, in southwestern Amazonas. Stage Two is illustrated by a local town in a region with incipient pastoral activities: Altamira, in central Pará. Stage Three is exemplified by a subregional centre, in a region of diversified and intensive pastoral production: Marabá, in southeastern Pará. A fourth city, also located in an advanced frontier, is an example of a city that fails to lead the development of its region: Conceição do Araguaia, in southeastern Pará (see Figure 5 and Table 3) (Mougeot 198a pp. 49–85).

In a later section, rates of intergroup upward mobility are related to migrant

Table 3 Percentage distribution of municipal and microregion primary production values, by type of product and selected urban frontier centre, 1970

| Primary products | Humaitá* | | Altamira** | | Marabá*** | | Conceição do Araguaia** | |
|---|---|---|---|---|---|---|---|---|
| | Município | Microregion | Município | Microregion | Município | Microregion | Município | Microregion |
| Livestock slaughtering | 2 | 5.5 | 16.5 | 16 | 35 | 28 | 25 | 28 |
| Large animals | 2 | 1 | 9.5 | 8 | 33 | 25 | 18 | 19 |
| Middle-sized animals | 1 | 3 | 2 | 2 | 0 | 1 | 3 | 3 |
| Small animals | 3 | 4 | 5 | 6 | 1 | 1 | 4 | 6 |
| Permanent crops (jute, pepper, cacao, sugar cane, tobacco, mallow, etc.) | 3 | 4 | 6 | 9 | 1 | 4 | 6 | 5 |
| Temporary crops (cassava, maize, rice, etc.) | 29 | 36 | 58 | 53 | 9 | 25 | 55 | 54 |
| Plant extraction (nuts, rubber, non-elastic gums, etc.) | 63 | 54 | 20 | 21 | 55 | 44 | 14 | 13 |
| Total value (in thousands of cruzeiros) | 4 927 | 18 290 | 3 196 | 3 704 | 10 546 | 17 460 | 3 503 | 4 054 |

Sources: *IBGE, VIII Recenseamento geral. Censo agropecuário de 1970 (Rio de Janeiro: IBGE, 1974), série regional, III/IV, p. 153
**idem, VII Recenseamento geral. Censo agropecuário de 1970, série regional III/IV, p. 200
Note: Currency equivalent at the average exchange rate was US $ 217.723 per CR $ 1,000.00 in 1970, according to Latin America and the Caribbean Regional Office, The World Bank, Brazil – Human Resources Special Report.

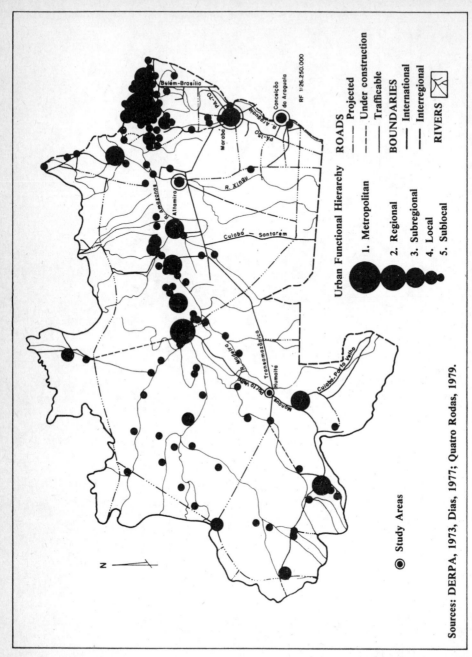

**Sources: DERPA, 1973, Dias, 1977; Quatro Rodas, 1979.**

Fig. 5 Brazil's North Region: urban functional hierarchy and transportation networks

retention rates. In this study, migration is an inter-locality move for residential purposes, whatever may be the duration of the stay at receiving points. The rate of migrant retention measures the relative ability of a place to retain its immigrants over a given period. The rate can be defined as the percentage of all those migrants who arrived at a place over the last decade (in this case 1968–78) still resident at that place at the end of this period.

Primary data required to calculate both socio-economic advancement and retention rates were obtained through structured interviews applied by the author to 400 individuals, at a rate of 100 per city.

It is contended that the ability of a city to retain its immigrants varies according to the socio-economic levels of migrants at the receiving centre, and the phase of economic development of the region. Individuals who come to the city with higher levels are more likely to remain at the centre than migrants with low status. Economic motives are dominant in the decision-making process in general, and of migrants to resource frontiers in particular. Therefore, migration can be viewed as a strategy for individuals to maximise their accessibility to opportunities. People tend to move to and remain where they perceive their chances to improve living standards as being better than elsewhere.

**Findings**

Findings are reported in three sections. The geographic and socio-economic selectivity of frontierward migrants is first examined in general terms, and trends are detected during frontier development. Then, socio-economic advancement at the receiving centres is looked at, both generally and in terms of variations in the process. Finally, results from those two sections further support the argument that migrant retention declines during frontier development, as a result of vanishing opportunities for the more destitute socio-economic groups.

**Geographic and socio-economic migrant selectivity**

The first series of results deals with geographic attributes of generating and receiving centres. They are associated with cityward migrants' occupational selectivity and mobility behaviour. General and stagewise differences are presented, concerning migrants' average length of moves from, and socio-economic levels at their previous residence, as well as differences in these people's ability to improve on previous achievement when moving to urban frontier centres. Also, changes are interpreted in the size, hierarchichal composition and pattern of the cities' immediate immigration fields. These changes relate to variations in the geographic and occupational selectivity of migrants, providing a basis for a stagewise model of cityward frontier migration.

*General statements*

Migrants at the selected cities come from both rural and urban areas at lower orders of the hierarchy. However, those from urban centres travel greater distances and come with higher socio-economic levels than those from the countryside or lower-order areas (Table 4). Furthermore, the former improve their previous

Table 4  Mean distances between previous places of residence of male migrant informants and receiving urban frontier centres, by receiving urban, frontier centre and by hierarchical order and environmental type of previous place of residence

| | | Intra-Municipal Migrants | Previous Places of Residence | | | | | | | | | | | | | | | | | | | | |
| Name and Hierarchical Order of Receiving Urban Frontier Centres | | | Metropolitan regional 1–2 | | | Intermunicipal Migrants | | | | | | | | | | | All Orders 1–5 | | | Intra and Intermunicipal Migrants All Orders 1–5 | | |
| | | | | | | Subregional 3 | | | Local 4 | | | Sublocal 5 | | | | | | | | | |
| | | Total n=83 | Rural n=1 | Urban n=44 | Total n=48 | Rural n=9 | Urban n=22 | Total n=31 | Rural n=8 | Urban n=26 | Total n=34 | Rural n=44 | Urban n=49 | Total n=93 | Rural n=62 | Urban n=144 | Total n=206 | Rural n=146 | Urban n=144 | Total n=290* |
|---|---|---|---|---|---|---|---|---|---|---|---|---|---|---|---|---|---|---|---|---|
| Humaitá 5 n=70 | b | 0 | 12 | 23 | 22 | 3 | 9 | 7 | – | 46 | 46 | 10 | 21 | 12 | 7.5 | 18 | 14 | 3 | 18 | 8 |
| | c | – | 1 | 14 | 14 | 0 | 3 | 5 | – | – | – | 13 | 13 | 12 | 10 | 13 | 13 | 7 | 16 | 12 |
| | d | 45% | – | 17 | 19 | 7 | 13 | 20 | 0 | 1 | 1 | 9 | 6 | 14 | 19 | 36 | 54 | 64 | 36 | 100 |
| Altamira 4 n=79 | b | 0 | – | 23 | 23 | 12 | 13 | 13 | 10 | 28 | 20 | 17 | 13 | 15 | 15 | 17 | 17 | 5 | 17 | 11 |
| | c | – | – | 15 | 15 | 6 | 8 | 7 | 6 | 17 | 16 | 11 | 9 | 10 | 10 | 12 | 12 | 9 | 12 | 12 |
| | d | –% | – | 15 | 15 | 2 | 8 | 10 | 3 | 4 | 6 | 13 | 22 | 34 | 18 | 48 | 66 | 52 | 48 | 100 |
| Marabá 3 n=70 | b | 34 | – | 20 | 20 | 10 | 13 | 12 | 5 | 10 | 10 | 6 | 1 | 7 | 7 | 13 | 11 | 6 | 13 | 11 |
| | c | – | 0 | 10 | 10 | 0 | 12 | 10 | 0 | 10 | 9 | 10 | 5 | 8 | 9 | 10 | 10 | 9 | 10 | 10 |
| | d | 5% | – | 26 | 26 | 3 | 9 | 11 | 3 | 16 | 19 | 19 | 20 | 39 | 24 | 70 | 94 | 30 | 70 | 100 |
| Conceição do Aragaia 4 n=71 | b | 0 | – | 16 | 16 | – | 6 | 6 | 3 | 6 | 5 | 8 | 7 | 7 | 6 | 9 | 8 | 3 | 9 | 6 |
| | c | – | – | 1 | 1 | – | – | – | 0 | 4 | 4 | 8 | 6 | 7 | 7 | 7 | 7 | 6 | 7 | 7 |
| | d | 30% | 0 | 7 | 7 | – | 1 | 1 | 6 | 15 | 21 | 20 | 21 | 41 | 25 | 45 | 70 | 55 | 45 | 100 |
| Total n=290 | b | 0 | 12 | 21 | 21 | 7 | 11 | 10 | 6 | 12 | 11 | 10 | 10 | 10 | 9 | 14 | 12 | 5 | 14 | 11 |
| | c | – | – | 12 | 12 | 5 | 8 | 8 | 4 | 13 | 12 | 11 | 7 | 9 | 9 | 11 | 11 | 14 | 11 | 24 |
| | d | 29% | 0 | 16 | 16 | 3 | 8 | 11 | 3 | 9 | 12 | 15 | 17 | 32 | 21 | 50 | 71 | 50 | 50 | 100 |

Source: Interviews with 400 heads of household in the North Region of Brazil, 1978–9
[a] Four cases excluded due to missing values
[b] Mean of individual distances expressed to nearest 50 km
[c] Standard deviation of mean value
[d] Row percentage of cases

occupational positions much more with frontier cityward migration than do the latter (Table 5).

*Stagewise differences*

In the process: (1) migration from within the *município* and towards the receiving centre decreases: this is probably due both to commuting and to service and employment deconcentration lessening the need for short-distance residential change; (2) the average length of moves increases between other generating areas and the receiving centre (however less so in the case of Marabá, where competing cities encroach upon its field); (3) people proceed from higher orders of the functional hierarchy and show better occupational levels originally; however, (4) they experience less advancement with migration, particularly those coming from urban areas; and (5) the geographic and socio-economic selectivity of intercity migration is further affected by the regional development situation of the receiving centre: for equal-order cities in regions with different phases of economic development, movers to more penetrated frontiers come from less distant nuclei at lower hierarchical orders. Worse, they also show lower previous achievement and less improvement with migration.

These city-based results agree with settlement theory that population transfer from more or less occupied areas becomes more frequent but ever less rewarding as the latter is further settled. Findings support the statement in classical and contemporary literature, that the dynamism of the frontierward migration lies in a never-ending search for equilibrium between economic efficiency and social equity. (Compare Frederick Jackson Turner's 1893 statement in Thompson (1975) with Paget (1960).) Individuals from both rural and urban scenes participate in this quest. Initially, a few enterprising and well-informed residents in remote and highly developed regions capture occupational vacancies arising on the primitive urban frontier. Local rural residents have their greatest chances to rise at this early stage, when they can readily perceive and reap opportunities in the nearby expanding job market. Those who succeed in doing so at this stage broaden their search space, thereby enabling themselves to sense alternatives whenever competition presses on. As the region is further occupied, the urban labour market grows but also becomes more specialised. Surface interconnection of the city and its information exchange with advanced regions are intensified.

At later stages, competition rises for job openings, as more intercity migrants head towards the now accessible frontier town. These people perceive themselves as less fit to remain in, or move to, demanding environments; instead they escape to less constraining markets where they can more easily practise previous or similar skills. It thus becomes increasingly difficult for countrymen to progress by moving directly to the urban centre. Under growing pressures on land, those unable to retain access to it and survive without resettling become, along with poorly skilled workmen, short-distance nomads between low-order places within the well developed frontier region.

Table 5　Mean social scores of male migrant informants according to occupations held at previous place of residence and upon arrival at the urban frontier centre, by receiving urban frontier centre and by hierarchical order and environmental type of previous place of residence

| Name and Hierarchical Order of Receiving Urban Frontier Centres | Previous Places of Residence | | | | | | | | | | | | | | | | | | | |
|---|---|---|---|---|---|---|---|---|---|---|---|---|---|---|---|---|---|---|---|---|
| | Intra-Municipal Migrants Total | Metropolitan regional 1–2 | | | Subregional 3 | | | Intermunicipal Migrants Local 4 | | | Sublocal 5 | | | All Orders 1–5 | | | Intra and Intermunicipal M All Orders 1–5 | | |
| | | Rural | Urban | Total | Rural | Urban | Total | Rural | Urban | Total | Rural | Urban | Total | Rural | Urban | Total | Rural | Urban | Total |
| | n–83 | n–1 | n–47 | n–48 | n–9 | n–22 | n–31 | n–8 | n–26 | n–34 | n–44 | n–49 | n–93 | n–62 | n–144 | n–206 | n–146 | n–144 | n–290* |
| **Humaitá 5** n=70 $X_1$[a] | 5.8 | 6.11 | 10.13 | 9.82 | 4.54 | 11.38 | 8.94 | — | 0.00 | 0.00 | 8.84 | 9.01 | 8.89 | 6.98 | 10.04 | 8.99 | 5.94 | 10.04 | 7.42 |
| $S_1$[b] | 3.47 | — | 5.89 | 5.75 | 0.45 | 9.23 | 8.00 | — | 0.00 | 0.00 | 6.98 | 3.44 | 5.92 | 5.38 | 7.09 | 6.65 | 4.11 | 7.09 | 5.67 |
| $X_2$[c] | 7.43 | 6.11 | 16.04 | 15.27 | 4.41 | 14.88 | 11.14 | — | 13.93 | 13.93 | 9.05 | 9.79 | 9.59 | 7.28 | 14.79 | 12.22 | 7.35 | 14.79 | 10.01 |
| $S_2$[d] | 4.84 | — | 8.13 | 8.25 | 0.36 | 11.29 | 10.27 | — | — | — | 8.91 | 2.08 | 7.26 | 6.73 | 8.78 | 8.81 | 5.37 | 8.78 | 7.62 |
| **Altamira 4** n=79 $X_1$ | 11.35 | — | 9.97 | 9.97 | 7.04 | 8.63 | 8.11 | 13.50 | 7.06 | 9.64 | 8.10 | 8.95 | 8.65 | 8.72 | 9.07 | 8.76 | 10.28 | 9.07 | 9.70 |
| $S_1$ | 6.93 | — | 7.59 | 7.59 | 0.80 | 4.87 | 4.18 | 3.78 | 3.63 | 4.75 | 5.29 | 5.61 | 5.40 | 4.97 | 5.94 | 5.86 | 6.28 | 5.94 | 6.11 |
| $X_2$ | 9.59 | — | 13.42 | 13.42 | 12.17 | 11.96 | 12.02 | 10.19 | 4.94 | 7.04 | 10.15 | 12.91 | 11.89 | 10.44 | 12.29 | 11.80 | 9.95 | 12.29 | 11.08 |
| $S_2$ | 6.04 | — | 8.40 | 8.40 | 6.76 | 5.08 | 5.00 | 8.46 | 2.10 | 5.32 | 5.25 | 16.70 | 13.53 | 5.35 | 12.26 | 10.82 | 5.76 | 12.26 | 9.47 |
| **Marabá 3** n=70 $X_1$ | 9.27 | — | 12.02 | 12.02 | 6.42 | 6.08 | 5.83 | 4.62 | 10.55 | 9.64 | 7.15 | 10.66 | 8.97 | 6.77 | 10.63 | 9.62 | 7.24 | 10.63 | 9.56 |
| $S_1$ | 12.22 | — | 4.12 | 4.12 | 1.37 | 1.25 | 2.49 | 0.58 | 6.30 | 6.17 | 6.27 | 8.59 | 7.63 | 5.50 | 6.11 | 6.16 | 6.90 | 6.11 | 6.55 |
| $X_2$ | 12.13 | — | 11.55 | 11.55 | 6.14 | 9.42 | 7.39 | 6.68 | 9.35 | 8.94 | 6.70 | 10.48 | 8.66 | 6.63 | 10.47 | 9.46 | 7.68 | 10.47 | 9.62 |
| $S_2$ | 13.56 | — | 7.04 | 7.04 | 1.76 | 3.93 | 4.40 | 1.00 | 7.99 | 7.36 | 6.75 | 8.70 | 7.91 | 5.87 | 7.34 | 7.15 | 7.75 | 7.34 | 7.52 |
| **Conceição do Araguaia 4** n=71 $X_1$ | 6.07 | — | 14.95 | 14.95 | — | 27.50 | 27.50 | 4.52 | 5.55 | 5.27 | 4.56 | 5.96 | 5.28 | 4.55 | 7.90 | 6.69 | 4.12 | 7.90 | 6.41 |
| $S_1$ | 4.92 | — | 8.32 | 8.32 | — | — | 0.00 | 0.73 | 2.37 | 2.09 | 1.38 | 5.44 | 4.02 | 1.24 | 6.95 | 5.81 | 5.03 | 6.95 | 5.58 |
| $X_2$ | 8.52 | — | 15.67 | 15.67 | — | 17.97 | 17.97 | 5.24 | 6.09 | 5.86 | 5.13 | 9.46 | 7.37 | 5.16 | 9.54 | 7.96 | 6.97 | 9.54 | 8.13 |
| $S_2$ | 6.95 | — | 8.21 | 8.21 | — | — | 0.00 | 1.61 | 4.22 | 3.67 | 1.97 | 5.87 | 4.88 | 1.85 | 6.53 | 5.71 | 5.64 | 6.53 | 6.06 |
| **Total** n=290 $X_1$ | 7.65 | 6.11 | 11.31 | 11.20 | 5.52 | 10.12 | 8.78 | 7.30 | 7.62 | 7.43 | 6.72 | 8.53 | 7.29 | 6.61 | 9.50 | 8.59 | 6.96 | 9.50 | 8.34 |
| $S_1$ | 6.04 | — | 6.10 | 6.08 | 1.34 | 7.57 | 6.71 | 4.23 | 5.21 | 4.99 | 5.14 | 6.56 | 4.66 | 4.65 | 6.46 | 6.10 | 5.69 | 6.46 | 6.09 |
| $X_2$ | 8.54 | 6.11 | 13.66 | 13.50 | 6.52 | 12.74 | 10.94 | 6.84 | 7.62 | 7.45 | 7.45 | 10.97 | 8.49 | 7.20 | 11.50 | 10.20 | 8.02 | 11.50 | 9.74 |
| $S_2$ | 6.28 | — | 7.79 | 7.78 | 4.12 | 8.06 | 7.63 | 4.02 | 6.15 | 5.67 | 5.82 | 11.22 | 6.12 | 5.36 | 9.09 | 8.37 | 5.96 | 9.09 | 7.85 |

Source: Interviews with 400 heads of household in the North Region of Brazil, 1978–9

Note: *Four cases excluded due to missing values

[a] $X_1$, mean of individual social scores corresponding to occupation held at previous place of residence

[b] $S_1$, standard deviation of $X_1$

[c] $X_2$, mean of individual social scores corresponding to first occupation held upon last arrival at urban frontier centre

[d] $S_2$ standard deviation of $X_2$

Only those who can learn about and break away to new vacancies in primitive outer regions strike greater socio-economic improvement. These people are a minority who possess wide search horizons; they originally have higher occupational status and proceed from higher-rank cities than most frontierward migrants. According to Lee (1966), these vanguard movers are the real frontiersmen. More numerous contingents with low standing, by virtue of constrained search spaces, 'fill up the territory' passed over by them.

*The case of non-leading frontier centres*

It is worth emphasising a more common situation where cities lack the strength needed to control the development of their hinterland. Two equal-order urban centres are compared, but they are located in regions in different phases of economic occupancy. Intermunicipal migrants who settled in the town of the more penetrated region come from less distant generating areas, show less socio-economic achievement at their former residence, and less improvement with migration (Tables 4 and 5).

Conceição do Araguaia attracts fewer individuals from high-order *municípios*, who moreover obtain less advancement at their new station. Whenever cities fail to lead the development of their region, they lose that functional centrality required to create occupational openings for well prepared individuals. In those circumstances, they may offer a refuge for migrants unable to cope in more contended markets. This seems to be the case with Conceição do Araguaia. This urban centre draws its migrants mainly (68 per cent) from local and sublocal *municípios* traversed by, or adjacent to, the Belém–Brasília highway between Marabá to the north and Goiânia to the south (Figure 6). Nearly 53 per cent of these migrants formerly worked in the primary sector: rural occupants (many of whom were forced to abandon or sell their plot of land) and cattle-ranch jobbers living in urban nuclei. Others were unemployed or skilled workmen who are ambulant to practise their craft.

Movers from low-rank *municípios* to Altamira, for instance, do proceed from more distant places and possess higher socio-economic positions originally, than those to Conceição do Araguaia (Tables 4 and 5, and Figure 2). The same is true with respect to Humaitá (same tables and Figure 2). Under this assumption then, people who ignore either of the above-mentioned courses and instead relocate at nearby low-order centres (such as Conceição do Araguaia) clearly do so because limited assets would render hazardous their survival in metropolitan environments, if it has not already done so. They may also envisage major obstacles to settlement in truly remote regions.

**Socio-economic advancement at urban frontier centres**

In this second series of results, an attempt is made to understand why some migrants, once arrived in the city, are more likely than others to repeat migration. Apparently, people moving to the frontier become part of a group unable to perform in larger urban centres. Also, their chances of staying in cities to which

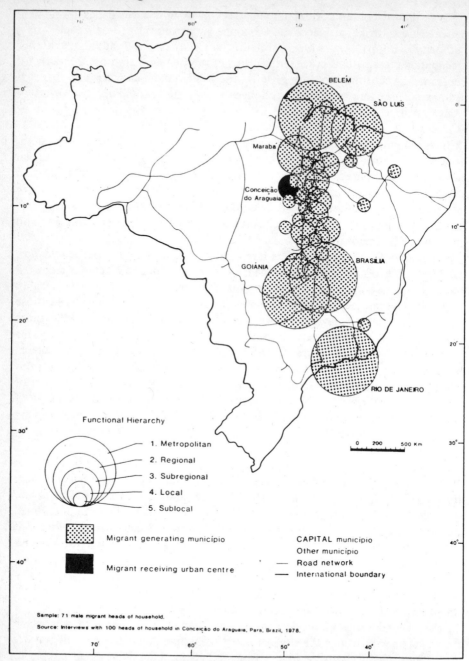

Functional Hierarchy

1. Metropolitan
2. Regional
3. Subregional
4. Local
5. Sublocal

Migrant generating município

Migrant receiving urban centre

CAPITAL município
Other município
— Road network
— International boundary

Sample: 71 male migrant heads of household.

Source: Interviews with 100 heads of household in Conceição do Araguaia, Pará, Brazil, 1978.

Fig. 6  Functional hierarchy generating direct migrants to the urban centre of Conceição do Araguaia, Pará 1978

they migrate vary sharply from one socio-economic class to another, at distinct stages of urban evolution.

### General statements

The urban frontier acts as a refuge for unsuccessful cityward migrants. Movers who reside or have resided in frontier towns were found to possess lower achievement levels than other cityward migrants. This difference persists when holding constant the hierarchical order of their present residence as well as their educational level or period of residence (Tables 6–9). Therefore, individuals who move to the frontier probably do so because they have been, or at least think of themselves as less capable of achieving high socio-economic levels.

Conversely, results imply that relatives who have moved to centres other than frontier cities are more successful. Given equal education or equal period of adjustment, they score on better occupations than their frontier counterparts. This could be due to their having received a better education, greater exposure to competitive environments in their previous migration history, or to differences in life-cycle stages. Today, most live in metro-regional and subregional centres, where

Table 6  *Mean social scores of cityward male migrants who never resided at the surveyed frontier centres, by educational level and hierarchical order of present place of residence*

| Educational level (years completed) | Metro-politan-regional 1–2 n=102 | Hierarchical order of urban centres | | | |
|---|---|---|---|---|---|
| | | Sub-regional 3 n=54 | Local 4 n=35 | Sublocal 5 n=57 | All 1–5 n=248 |
| none (0) n=51 | 21.6[a]<br>8.76[b]<br>5.39[c]<br>10.8[d] | 31.4<br>10.30<br>7.88<br>29.6 | 21.5<br>9.29<br>8.45<br>31.4 22.8 | 25.5<br>7.83<br>7.93<br>20.6 | 100.0<br>9.11<br>7.40 |
| primary (1–7) n=107 | 38.3<br>9.03<br>3.67<br>40.2 | 23.4<br>8.76<br>5.39<br>46.3 | 12.1<br>9.01<br>3.85<br>37.1 | 26.2<br>9.58<br>7.23<br>49.1 | 100.0<br>9.11<br>5.17<br>43.1 |
| secondary (8–11) n=32 | 59.4<br>12.44<br>9.53<br>18.6 | 12.5<br>10.94<br>5.08<br>7.4 | 9.4<br>10.58<br>3.27<br>8.6 | 18.7<br>16.94<br>5.96<br>10.5 | 100.0<br>12.92<br>8.12<br>12.9 |
| college (12 or more) n=58 | 53.4<br>45.08<br>30.51<br>30.4 | 15.5<br>16.60<br>26.44<br>16.7 | 13.8<br>13.42<br>16.38<br>22.9 | 17.3<br>29.10<br>23.90<br>17.6 | 100.0<br>33.54<br>29.82<br>23.4 |
| All (0 or more) n=248 | 41.1<br>20.58<br>23.81<br>100.0 | 21.8<br>10.68<br>12.06<br>100.0 | 14.1<br>10.24<br>9.24<br>100.0 | 23.0<br>13.38<br>13.91<br>100.0 | 100.0<br>15.31<br>18.42<br>100.0 |

Source: Interviews with 400 heads of household in the North Region of Brazil, 1978–9
[a] Row percentage
[b] Mean of individual social scores
[c] Standard deviation of mean value
[d] Column percentage
n=number of respondents

they show higher socio-economic status with longer periods of residence (Table 8). Although they may not represent large-city migrant populations in general, their high occupational positions may conceal the fact that formerly disadvantaged workers among them have left. Most of those who remain are unlikely ever to consider relocating in frontier towns. Similarly, migrants at the latter stations probably view these settings as less demanding, thereby enabling them to hold to or improve their livelihood more easily.

### Stagewise differences

Although frontier towns may appear as havens of opportunity, considerable differences exist through time and space within the urban frontier. Shifts can be observed in the range of occupational openings and the kind of people who are benefitted, as the frontier city evolves. As the urban centre ascends to higher hierarchical orders with further frontier development, migrants' attainment tends to remain constant (Table 7). In agglomerations of equivalent order but in regions with different phases of economic development, migrants in more penetrated regions show lower average socio-economic levels (Tables 5 and 7).

Table 7    Mean social scores of male migrants who reside or have resided at the surveyed frontier centres, by educational level and urban frontier centre of residence

| Educational level (years completed) | | Name and hierarchical order of frontier centres | | | | |
|---|---|---|---|---|---|---|
| | | Humaitá 5 n=249 | Altamira 4 n=198 | Marabá 3 n=191 | Conceição do Araguaia n=193 | All n=831 |
| none (0) n=236 | a | 6.8 | 7.5 | 6.0 | 6.5 | 6.69 |
| | b | 5.0 | 6.9 | 5.9 | 5.0 | 5.62 |
| | c | 32% | 22% | 29% | 29% | 236 (28%) |
| primary (1–7) n=462 | a | 8.4 | 8.5 | 8.5 | 7.9 | 8.33 |
| | b | 6.8 | 6.3 | 8.3 | 6.6 | 7.27 |
| | c | 54% | 59% | 55% | 55% | 462 (56%) |
| secondary (8–11) n=76 | a | 13.5 | 14.1 | 16.9 | 8.7 | 13.30 |
| | b | 11.7 | 7.2 | 9.2 | 7.9 | 9.36 |
| | c | 7% | 10% | 11% | 9% | 76 (9%) |
| college (12 or more) n=57 | a | 15.1 | 13.0 | 11.3 | 17.9 | 14.39 |
| | b | 10.6 | 17.5 | 13.2 | 27.9 | 17.69 |
| | c | 7% | 10% | 5% | 6% | 57 (7%) |
| All (0 or more) n=831 | a | 8.7 | 9.2 | 8.8 | 8.2 | 8.73 |
| | b | 7.4 | 8.4 | 9.1 | 9.4 | 8.53 |
| | c | 100% | 100% | 100% | 100% | 831 (100%) |

Source: Interviews with 400 heads of household in the North Region of Brazil, 1978–9
[a] Mean of individual social scores
[b] Standard deviation of mean value
[c] Column percentage
n=number of respondents

Table 8    *Mean social scores of cityward male migrants who never resided at the surveyed frontier centres, by period of residence and hierarchical order of present place of residence*

| Period of residence in years | | Hierarchical order of urban centres | | | | |
|---|---|---|---|---|---|---|
| | | Metro-politan regional 1–2 n=102 | Sub-regional 3 n=54 | Local 4 n=35 | Sublocal 5 n=57 | All 1–5 n=248 |
| 0–2 n=35 | a | 9.6 | 8.6 | 15.0 | 25.8 | 14.4 |
| | b | 6.3 | 5.4 | 19.3 | 25.8 | 16.7 |
| | c | 10% | 18% | 17% | 16% | 14% |
| 3–5 n=57 | a | 19.5 | 14.9 | 7.0 | 8.9 | 14.3 |
| | b | 23.9 | 21.0 | 2.2 | 5.8 | 18.7 |
| | c | 22% | 26% | 17% | 44% | 23% |
| 6–10 n=36 | a | 21.2 | 8.6 | 8.3 | 12.1 | 13.7 |
| | b | 25.8 | 2.7 | 8.1 | 12.1 | 17.0 |
| | c | 12% | 13% | 20% | 29% | 14% |
| 11 or more n=120 | a | 22.7 | 9.7 | 10.5 | 12.0 | 16.5 |
| | b | 25.2 | 7.7 | 5.2 | 9.7 | 19.3 |
| | c | 57% | 43% | 46% | 40% | 48% |
| 0 or more n=248 | a | 20.6 | 10.7 | 10.2 | 13.4 | 15.3 |
| | b | 23.8 | 12.1 | 9.2 | 13.9 | 18.4 |
| | c | 100% | 100% | 100% | 100% | 100% |

Source: Interviews with 400 heads of household in the North Region of Brazil, 1978–9
[a] Mean of individual social scores
[b] Standard deviation of mean value
[c] Column percentage
n=number of respondents

It was noted earlier that with equal education, frontier cityward migrants attain lower socio-economic levels than their counterparts in other urban centres. However, with more education, the former improve their status to a greater extent than do the latter. The social score distance between more and less educated individuals is greater at the frontier centres; people unable to take higher-scored occupations with equal education may enhance their status by moving to frontier towns (Tables 6 and 7). This appealing trait of the urban frontier fades away however, as the frontier evolves. As the frontier city evolves the social scores of the uneducated decrease, those of the primary-taught remain constant, those of the secondary-educated increase, and those of the college-learned decrease (Table 7). Thus, openings for migrants at both ends of the educational scale seem to collapse in the process. The trend is even more pronounced when comparing centres of equal order in different regions. Migrants to Conceição do Araguaia, in the more advanced frontier, show limited additional achievement with further education, as opposed to those in Altamira. During frontier urban evolution, shrinking opportunities should be particularly detrimental to less educated individuals. As a result of observed trends, it is contended that the socio-economic quality of repeated

Table 9    Mean social scores of male migrants who reside or have resided at the surveyed frontier centres, by period of residence and urban frontier centre of residence

| Period of residence in years | | Name and hierarchical order of frontier centres | | | | |
|---|---|---|---|---|---|---|
| | | Humaitá 5 n=249 | Altamira 4 n=198 | Marabá 3 n=191 | Conceição do Araguaia n=193 | All n=831 |
| 0–2 | a | 7.2 | 7.3 | 9.4 | 9.4 | 8.2 |
| n=301 | b | 7.0 | 7.0 | 13.3 | 12.8 | 9.9 |
| | c | 4.7% | 29% | 27% | 38% | 38% |
| 3–5 | a | 9.6 | 10.1 | 6.4 | 7.8 | 8.5 |
| n=205 | b | 7.8 | 10.7 | 3.9 | 6.8 | 7.7 |
| | c | 23% | 25% | 29% | 22% | 25% |
| 6–10 | a | 10.7 | 10.7 | 11.3 | 6.7 | 9.5 |
| n=182 | b | 7.5 | 7.5 | 8.2 | 5.7 | 7.2 |
| | c | 15% | 21% | 21% | 32% | 17% |
| 11 or more | a | 10.2 | 9.4 | 8.7 | 9.1 | 9.3 |
| n=143 | b | 7.4 | 8.2 | 7.9 | 8.0 | 7.8 |
| | c | 14% | 25% | 23% | 8% | 17% |
| Total | a | 8.7 | 9.2 | 8.8 | 8.2 | 8.7 |
| n=831 | b | 7.4 | 8.4 | 9.1 | 9.4 | 8.5 |
| | c | 100% | 100% | 100% | 100% | 100% |

Source: Interviews with 400 heads of household in the North Region of Brazil, 1978–9
[a] Mean of individual social scores
[b] Standard deviation of mean value
[c] Column percentage
n=number of respondents

migrants worsens during frontier development. Migrants who have left the frontier towns had lower occupational ranks than those who presently reside at the same centres. This difference is found to hold during frontier development, and when the migrants' educational level or period of residence is kept constant (Tables 10–13). Whereas migrants residing at the centres exhibit higher socio-economic positions with more education or longer periods of stay, this is not necessarily the case for leavers (Tables 10–13). Repeated-migrants are thus unlikely to improve their standing at the frontier cities.

The occupational status of leavers generally falls during frontier urban evolution. Not only do they have higher achievement levels in Humaitá (Stage One) than their counterparts in Marabá (Stage Three), but the gap between emigrants' own performance and that of present residents in narrower in Humaitá than in Marabá (Tables 10 and 12). The tendency for leavers to come from lower-rank working groups than residents, during frontier development, is also verified by comparing two nuclei of equal order in two different regions. At early stages, repeated-migrants exhibit high socio-economic levels and move to high-order places, while at later stages they demonstrate lesser achievement and relocate in lower-order areas. For instance, in Humaitá (Stage One) some 55 per cent of leavers worked in group 4 and

Table 10   Mean social scores of male migrants now living in frontier towns, by educational level and urban frontier centre of residence

| Educational level (years completed) | | Humaitá 5 n=202 | Altamira 4 n=164 | Marabá 3 n=52 | Conceição do Araguaia n=154 | All n=672 |
|---|---|---|---|---|---|---|
| none<br>(0)<br>n=194 | a<br>b<br>c | 7.3<br>5.3<br>31% | 8.0<br>7.2<br>24% | 6.6<br>6.6<br>27% | 6.6<br>5.2<br>32% | 7.1<br>6.0<br>29% |
| primary<br>(1–7)<br>n=379 | a<br>b<br>c | 8.8<br>7.1<br>55% | 8.5<br>6.5<br>60% | 9.0<br>10.1<br>55% | 7.9<br>6.9<br>55% | 8.6<br>7.7<br>56% |
| secondary<br>(8–11)<br>n=60 | a<br>b<br>c | 12.2<br>9.9<br>7% | 16.2<br>7.7<br>8% | 16.1<br>9.4<br>14% | 10.3<br>8.5<br>8% | 14.0<br>9.1<br>9% |
| college<br>(12 or more)<br>n=39 | a<br>b<br>c | 16.7<br>11.5<br>6% | 16.6<br>20.0<br>8% | 14.0<br>15.4<br>4% | 25.8<br>35.0<br>5% | 17.9<br>20.2<br>6% |
| 0 or more<br>n=672 | a<br>b<br>c | 9.1<br>7.5<br>100% | 9.7<br>9.0<br>100% | 9.5<br>9.8<br>100% | 8.5<br>10.2<br>100% | 9.2<br>9.0<br>100% |

Source: Interviews with 400 heads of household in the North Region of Brazil, 1978–9
[a] Mean of individual social scores
[b] Standard deviation of mean value
[c] Column percentage
n=number of respondents

5 activities in that city and 48 per cent were living in regional and subregional centres, at the moment of the survey. On the other hand, in Marabá (Stage Three) 65 per cent were in group 5 and 6 while in that centre 58 per cent went to places of sublocal order. At a large stage, people moving to the frontier settlement are those who do not see themselves fit for coping in higher-order agglomerations. Whenever they fail to improve, they are likely to further migrate downward in the functional hierarchy. None the less, it should be noted that migrants who have left the surveyed frontier towns have higher socio-economic levels at their present homeplace than those who used to live at former centres of equivalent order. This statement is still valid when the hierarchical order and the level of education, or period of residence are held constant (Tables 11 and 14). When leaving, migrants move essentially (77.63 per cent) to places at local and sublocal orders of the functional pyramid, mainly rural areas (59.6 per cent). They find it necessary to escape to less disputed environments, namely the countryside, in order to hold on to previous attainment or undergo some progress (Tables 13 and 15).

**Socio-economic advancement and migrant retention during frontier development**
People remain where they perceive living conditions to be better than elsewhere. Previous results show that migrants who reside in frontier cities augment their

Table 11   Mean social scores of male migrants who have resided at the surveyed frontier centres, by educational level and urban frontier centre of residence

| Educational level (years completed) | | Name and hierarchical order of frontier centres | | | | |
|---|---|---|---|---|---|---|
| | | Humaitá 5 n=44 | Altamira 4 n=34 | Marabá 3 n=37 | Conceição do Araguaia n=36 | All n=151 |
| none | a | 4.9 | 4.5 | 4.5 | 5.6 | 4.86 |
| (0) | b | 2.6 | 1.5 | 3.5 | 3.6 | 2.92 |
| n=42 | c | 34% | 15% | 40.5% | 19% | 42(28%) |
| primary | a | 6.7 | 9.0 | 6.0 | 8.2 | 7.37 |
| (1–7) | b | 5.6 | 4.2 | 4.7 | 5.8 | 5.21 |
| n=76 | c | 48% | 50% | 46.5% | 62% | 76(50%) |
| secondary | a | 18.6 | 8.7 | 11.0 | 4.1 | 10.28 |
| (8–11) | b | 21.5 | 2.3 | 4.1 | 3.8 | 10.53 |
| n=16 | c | 9% | 18% | 5% | 12% | 16(11%) |
| college | a | 7.4 | 13.9 | 6.9 | 25.9 | 16.20 |
| 12 or more | b | 3.3 | 14.7 | 9.8 | 33.7 | 19.42 |
| n=17 | c | 9% | 18% | 8% | 12% | 17(11%) |
| 0 or more | a | 7.0 | 9.1 | 5.9 | 8.6 | 7.62 |
| n=151 | b | 7.4 | 6.4 | 4.6 | 11.1 | 7.78 |
| | c | 100% | 100% | 100% | 100% | 151(100%) |

Source: Interviews with 400 heads of household in the North Region of Brazil, 1978–9
[a] Mean of individual social scores
[b] Standard deviation of mean value
[c] Column percentage
n=number of respondents

socio-economic levels with longer time of residence. Those who have not bettered their situation after a given period of adjustment are more prone to resume space-searching. The probability of migrating increases with each additional move. The economic improvement they found with repeated migration may be only shortlived; studies have shown that frequent movers experience more occupational wandering than durable socio-economic advancement (Martine and Peliano 1978 p. 177; Aragón 1978 p. 114; Nelson 1976 p. 743; Fraenkel and Souza 1976 p. 33).

According to Alistair Hennessy, the market for individuals with expertise in higher-order occupations expands during frontier development. Therefore, in the more penetrated frontier regions of Latin America, upward mobility is 'virtually' impossible for rural dwellers, but there exists a high spatial mobility. Numerous case studies refer to reduced opportunities in the countryside which act as an incentive to migrate.

When migrant retention is measured by means of a rate, the general hypothesis above is confirmed. Humaitá, Altamira, and Marabá have rates of 77, 77, and 80 respectively. Altamira's index is higher than the one scored by an equal-order city in a more penetrated region, for Conceição do Araguaia is rated at only 68 (Table 16) (Silva 1981 p. 62–7, 132, 143, 154–63). Intercity variations in migrant retention,

Table 12   Mean social scores of male migrants residing at the surveyed frontier centres, by period of residence and urban frontier centres of residence

| Period of residence in years | | Name and hierarchical order of frontier centres | | | | |
|---|---|---|---|---|---|---|
| | | Humaitá 5 n=202 | Altamira 4 n=164 | Marabá 3 n=152 | Conceição do Araguaia n=154 | All n=672 |
| 0–2 n=229 | a | 7.6 | 7.2 | 11.1 | 10.1 | 8.7 |
| | b | 7.5 | 7.4 | 15.5 | 14.3 | 11.1 |
| | c | 45% | 27% | 24% | 38% | 34% |
| 3–5 n=163 | a | 9.1 | 10.5 | 7.0 | 8.4 | 8.7 |
| | b | 6.5 | 11.8 | 4.0 | 7.3 | 7.9 |
| | c | 29% | 24% | 28% | 19% | 24% |
| 6–10 n=162 | a | 12.0 | 11.1 | 11.6 | 6.7 | 9.8 |
| | b | 7.7 | 7.4 | 8.3 | 5.9 | 7.5 |
| | c | 15% | 23% | 24% | 38.4% | 24% |
| 11 or more n=118 | a | 10.6 | 10.3 | 8.7 | 9.2 | 9.7 |
| | b | 7.9 | 8.4 | 8.4 | 8.9 | 8.3 |
| | c | 14% | 25% | 24% | 8.4% | 18% |
| 0–10 n=554 | a | 8.8 | 9.5 | 9.8 | 8.4 | 9.1 |
| | b | 7.4 | 9.2 | 10.2 | 10.3 | 9.2 |
| | c | 86% | 75% | 76% | 91.6% | 82% |
| 0 or more n=672 | a | 9.1 | 9.7 | 9.5 | 8.5 | 9.2 |
| | b | 7.5 | 9.0 | 9.8 | 10.2 | 9.0 |
| | c | 100% | 100% | 100% | 100% | 100% |

Source: Interviews with 400 heads of household in the North Region of Brazil, 1978–9
[a] Mean of individual social scores
[b] Standard deviation of mean value
[c] Column percentage
n=number of respondents

and socio-economic mobility rates of occupational groups, indicate that this is due to two facts: (1) the extent to which individuals with agrarian background move upward directly influences their residential stability; and (2) the extent to which migrants with occupational skills advance socially affects their residential stability. However, once in the city they become upwardly mobile. The ease with which they get better jobs reflects lack of competition from individuals better fit for any vacancy that might arise. Most workers moving into group 5 are former subsistence farmers and/or rubber tappers who frequently retain access to land, but who also work in urban construction projects or as road maintenance workers. Group 5 activities are a means for people to survive initially, while waiting for better openings; some 31 per cent of primary-sector workers entered group 5 on arrival, but only 11 per cent were still in it at the time of the survey. Agrarian labourers moving to group 4 take up skilled manual occupations as masons, carpenters, or mechanics. The lack of competition at this stage is shown by public-works departments that recruit and train on site in Humaitá (Stage One), but subsequently transfer personnel from other cities to Marabá (Stage Three). Opportunities for

Table 13   Mean social scores of male migrants who have resided at the surveyed frontier centres, by period of residence and urban frontier centre of residence

| Period of residence in years | | Name and hierarchical order of frontier centres | | | | |
|---|---|---|---|---|---|---|
| | | Humaitá 5 n=44 | Altamira 4 n=34 | Marabá 3 n=37 | Conceição do Araguaia n=36 | All n=151 |
| 0–2 | a | 5.5 | 78 | 5.4 | 7.2 | 6.4 |
| n=66 | b | 4.4 | 5.3 | 4.2 | 6.1 | 5.0 |
| | c | 57% | 38% | 35% | 42% | 44% |
| 3–5 | a | 13.5 | 8.3 | 3.7 | 6.6 | 7.2 |
| n=41 | b | 15.1 | 3.2 | 2.0 | 5.5 | 7.2 |
| | c | 14% | 25% | 32% | 37% | 27% |
| 6–10 | a | 7.5 | 7.5 | 4.9 | 6.9 | 6.8 |
| n=21 | b | 6.9 | 2.4 | 5.2 | 2.7 | 4.9 |
| | c | 18% | 12% | 13% | 11% | 14% |
| 11 or more | a | 6.8 | 9.2 | 9.0 | 7.6 | 8.4 |
| n=22 | b | 2.8 | 2.4 | 5.8 | 3.2 | 3.7 |
| | c | 11% | 23% | 19% | 8% | 15% |
| Total | a | 7.00 | 9.1 | 5.9 | 8.6 | 7.6 |
| n=151 | b | 7.4 | 6.4 | 4.6 | 11.1 | 7.8 |
| | c | 100% | 100% | 100% | 100% | 100% |

Source: Interviews with 400 heads of household in the North Region of Brazil, 1978–9
[a] Mean of individual social scores
[b] Standard deviation of mean value
[c] Column percentage
n=number of respondents

unskilled workers may also explain why cattle ranchers expressed difficulties in finding cheap jobbers in the town.

Those who ascend to group 3 are rural occupants favoured by the Madeira Agrarian Project, where they become proprietors of 100-hectare land tracts. It will be seen at a later stage that group 4 workmen compete with agrarian workers to become middle-sized rural proprietors. Most agriculturists living in Humaitá have their tract nearby, and rent it to others while they themselves manage a city-based business. Thus, at this stage, migrants find positions in the occupational scale hardly obtainable elsewhere. Given the extensive job mobility of rural labour, many now in higher job groups were formerly in the primary sector. They thus give these strata high rates of past advancement. The high rates of past and expected mobility in all groups at this stage mirror the dynamism of the migrants' socio-economic structure, and account for generally high retention rates.

At Stage Two most migrants with rural occupations at their previous residence are upwardly mobile. However, their access to higher groups is more restricted than it was before. Also, at this stage, group 5 occupations are less transitional, since an equal percentage of agrarian workers were in that group both upon arrival and at the time of the survey. It would be difficult for primary labourers to enter group 3, if

Table 14  Mean social scores of male migrants who have resided at the surveyed frontier centres, by educational level and hierarchical order of present place of residence

| Educational level (years completed) | | regional 1–2 n=23 | Metro-politan regional 3 n=21 | Sub-Local 4 n=46 | Sublocal 5 n=61 | All 1–5 n=151 |
|---|---|---|---|---|---|---|
| | | | Name and hierarchical order of frontier centres | | | |
| none | a | 10.3 | 8.0 | 4.5 | 6.8 | 6.3 |
| (0) | b | – | 5.2 | 4.2 | 5.2 | 4.9 |
| n=42 | c | 4% | 38% | 26% | 28% | |
| primary | a | 7.5 | 9.6 | 10.8 | 9.6 | 9.8 |
| (1–7) | b | 4.0 | 4.7 | 6.7 | 5.7 | 5.8 |
| n=76 | c | 35% | 43% | 52% | 57% | 50% |
| secondary | a | 6.3 | 19.8 | 23.8 | 16.3 | 12.3 |
| (8–11) | b | 6.3 | 17.6 | 26.0 | 11.8 | 12.5 |
| n=16 | c | 39% | 10% | 4% | 7% | 10% |
| college | a | 10.7 | 17.5 | 10.7 | 17.2 | 13.6 |
| (12 or more) | b | 13.4 | 0.7 | 10.3 | 9.4 | 10.2 |
| n=17 | c | 22% | 10% | 10% | 10% | 11% |
| (0 or more) | a | 7.9 | 10.7 | 9.3 | 10.1 | 9.6 |
| n=151 | b | 7.5 | 7.1 | 8.5 | 7.1 | 7.6 |
| | c | 100% | 100% | 100% | 100% | 100% |

Source: Interviews with 400 heads of household in the North Region of Brazil, 1978–9
[a] Mean of individual social scores
[b] Standard deviation of mean value
[c] Column percentage
n=number of respondents

they were not favoured by government-sponsored agricultural projects; in the absence of such projects their retention rate would probably fall, as in the case of Conceição do Araguaia. People in groups 4 and 5 at the time of the survey show lower mobility rates than earlier; percentages of individuals in either group who were in those strata prior to immigration are greater in Altamira than in Humaitá.

At Stage Three, most migrants who formerly had low-skilled rural occupations but remain in the city are upwardly mobile. But their access to higher groups is even more limited than at Stage Two. When living in the urban area is more expensive, and access to subsistence farming less likely, incomers who continue working the land have a very low retention rate. Those in Marabá who 'plough the fields' also need an employment in the city. For instance, many men in the Cidade Nova sector are both assistant masons and rural jobbers in order to meet urban living expenses. Families in the neighbourhood were reported to have returned to the interior because the bread-winner could not find a city-based job. Marabá's high retention rate is largely caused by its high rate of group 4 workers. By entering group 5, rural

Table 15   Mean social scores of male migrants who have resided at the surveyed frontier centres, by period of residence and hierarchical order of present place of residence

| Period of residence in years | | regional 1–2 n=23 | Metro-politan regional 3 n=21 | Sub-Local 4 n=46 | Sublocal 5 n=61 | All 1–5 n=151 |
|---|---|---|---|---|---|---|
| 0–2 n=79 | a | 4.8 | 9.1 | 8.5 | 9.5 | 8.7 |
| | b | 6.2 | 5.5 | 8.7 | 6.6 | 7.2 |
| | c | 26% | 67% | 60% | 51% | 52% |
| 3–5 n=30 | a | 7.7 | 32.2 | 9.2 | 12.4 | 11.2 |
| | b | 5.7 | – | 6.4 | 7.8 | 8.0 |
| | c | 30% | 6% | 17% | 23% | 20% |
| 6–10 n=20 | a | 8.7 | 8.4 | 9.2 | 7.0 | 8.2 |
| | b | 1.5 | 2.1 | 6.4 | 5.0 | 4.7 |
| | c | 17% | 14% | 13% | 12% | |
| 11 or more n=22 | a | 10.8 | 13.7 | 15.0 | 10.8 | 12.0 |
| | b | 12.0 | 5.6 | 13.0 | 8.5 | 9.6 |
| | c | 26% | 14% | 9% | 15% | 15% |
| 0–10 n=129 | a | 6.9 | 10.2 | 8.8 | 10.0 | 9.2 |
| | b | 5.2 | 7.3 | 7.9 | 7.0 | 7.1 |
| | c | 74% | 86% | 91% | 85% | 85% |
| 0 or more n=151 | a | 6.9 | 10.2 | 8.8 | 10.0 | 9.2 |
| | b | 5.2 | 7.3 | 7.9 | 6.9 | 7.1 |
| | c | 100% | 100% | 100% | 100% | 100% |

Source: Interviews with 400 heads of household in the North Region of Brazil, 1978–9
[a] Mean of individual social scores
[b] Standard deviation of mean value
[c] Column percentage
n=number of respondents

jobbers improve their chances of remaining in the city where there is a greater market for crafts, street vending and low-skilled personal services. Group 4 members have a very high rate of retention. Their residential stability could be explained by their access to an unusual number of employment sites. Rural migrants find jobs in construction and transportation, for instance in the federally-subsidised urban relocation area of Nova Marabá, bridge construction over the Itacaiúnas river, the Tucuruí hydroelectric project, and civil engineering sites along the PA–150 and PA–70 highways. The city is also the labour-recruiting base for the Serra dos Carajás iron-ore mining project.

*The case of non-leading frontier centres*

In the more developed frontier regions, settlements that fail to develop into more advanced towns are less able to retain their immigrants than cities of equal order in less penetrated regions. This is because such towns have fewer unskilled and semi-skilled job opportunities. For example, similar percentages of migrants who originally had primary jobs are upwardly mobile in Altamira and Conceição do

Table 16 Migrant retention rates and intergroup upward mobility rates, by occupational group and urban frontier centre

**Name and Hierarchical Order of Urban Frontier Centres**

| Occupational Group at the Time of the Survey or When Last Left the Frontier Centre | Humaitá 5 n=146 MRR[a] % | Humaitá 5 IUMR[b] Expected % | Humaitá 5 IUMR[b] Past % | Altamira 4 n=75 MRR % | Altamira 4 IUMR Expected % | Altamira 4 IUMR Past % | Marabá n=76 MRR % | Marabá IUMR Expected % | Marabá IUMR Past % | Conceição do Araguaia 4 n=105 MRR % | Conceição do Araguaia 4 IUMR Expected % | Conceição do Araguaia 4 IUMR Past % | All n=402 MRR % | All IUMR Expected % | All IUMR Past % |
|---|---|---|---|---|---|---|---|---|---|---|---|---|---|---|---|
| 1–2 n=9 | 50 | 0 | 73 | 100 | 0 | 75 | 100 | 0 | 64 | 83 | 0 | 25 | 80 | 0 | 64.5 |
| 3 n=33 | 90 | 9 | 61 | 60 | 4.5 | 48 | 100 | 46 | 46 | 75 | 0 | 64 | 81 | 16 | 57 |
| 4 n=101 | 79 | 67 | 88 | 60 | 25 | 35 | 95 | 19 | 54 | 50 | 9 | 55 | 70 | 24.5 | 56 |
| 5 n=105 | 81 | 83 | 71 | 65 | 55 | 62 | 67 | 56 | 47 | 71 | 50 | 80 | 73 | 58.5 | 64 |
| 6 n=65 | 82 | 61 | 0 | 75 | 59 | 0 | 46 | 81 | 0 | 50 | 54 | 6 | 61.5 | 61 | 2 |
| 7 n=89 | 78 | 90 | 0 | 100 | 100 | 0 | 73 | 50 | 0 | 79 | 100 | 0 | 81 | 88.5 | 0 |
| 1–7 uw[c] | 77 | s=13.7 | | 77 | s=18.9 | | 80 | s=21.8 | | 68 | s=14.6 | | 75 | s=7.8 | |
| 3–7 uw | 82 | s=4.8 | | 72 | s=16.8 | | 76 | s=21.9 | | 65 | s=14.1 | | 73.5 | s=8.2 | |

Source: Interviews with 400 heads of household in the North Region of Brazil, 1978–9
Notes: a MRR Migrant retention rate: the percentage of all migrant relatives who arrived at the town during the decade up to the year of the survey, and who were still residing at the town at the time of the survey. The decade is 1968–78 for Humaitá, Altamira, and Conceição do Araguaia, and 1969–79 for Marabá.
b IUMR Intergroup upward mobility rate: the percentage of male migrant informants working in that group at the time of the survey, who worked in lower jobs at their previous place of residence. Expected IUM is the percentage of male migrant informants working in that group at their previous place of residence, who worked in better jobs at the time of the survey.
c Unweighted means of group-specific migrant retention rates, with their corresponding standard deviation(s). Equivalent means weighted according to case frequency of each occupational group are: 80.1 (1–7) and 80.6 (3–7) in Humaitá, 69.3 (1–7) and 68.9 (3–7) in Altamira, 73.7 (1–7) and 73.3 (3–7) in Marabá, 64.8 (1–7) and 63.6 (3–7) in Conceição do Araguaia, and 73.1 (1–7) and 72.8 (3–7) for all four urban centres.
n=number of respondents

Araguaia, but those in the latter achieve less improvement. Agrarian workers moving to a local town have their residential stability sapped by the advanced phase of frontier development. They cannot depend on urban employment and commuting access to land for their own subsistence as readily as they still do in Humaitá (Stage One), nor on prospects of becoming middle-sized rural proprietors as in Altamira (Stage Two). In the 1960s, work openings on nearby cattle ranches permitted rural jobbers and construction labourers to work in the countryside while dwelling in the nearby town. With the termination of those activities and the westward movement of the labour front, migrants with land-based jobs who live in the city must commute over ever-greater distances, and remain for long periods on ranches or at placer-mining sites. They thereby undermine their residential stability. In fact, most leavers (77.7 per cent) who had agrarian employment during their stay in Conceição do Araguaia have moved to the interior of the *município* (mainly to the rapidly growing nuclei along the PA-150 highway) where they keep similar jobs. There is a vigorous market for crafts and personal services in the transportation hub of Marabá. But in Conceiçaõ do Araguaia seasonal unemployment affects those who enter such group 5 activities as potters or assistant masons. In order to survive, many members of this group accept any job available during wintertime, sell their possessions, or even move to unclaimed areas. Some took short-term employment on ranches, who would have preferred to leave the city, if they could only own a tract of land in the countryside. While group 6 workers have been penalised by landholding concentration and labour-extensive livestock operations, group 4 workmen in the city have been hurt by the lack of construction projects and expansion in local transportation functions (Carvalho *et al.* 1979b II p. 97; Hébette and Acevedo Marin 1979 pp. 158–69). Most leavers (69.2 per cent) with group 4 occupations in Conceição do Araguaia live in the interior of the *município*, where they persist in the same group or have fallen to an even lower level.

Based on the situation at centres in developed regions in southeastern Pará, one can speculate on scenarios that could unfold in the less-advanced frontiers. In Humaitá, for instance, unless ongoing rural settlement programmes are strengthened (as they were in Altamira in the early 1970s), a growing number of local subsistence farmers may be forced to relocate in less accessible areas. More probably, they will take shelter in the nearest urban settlement and engage in low-paying jobs on surrounding estates. This is the situation typically encountered in Conceição do Araguaia. In the process, migrants' spatial mobility should increase while their socio-economic progress lessens.

At Altamira, settlement on the Integrated Colonisation Project was approaching full capacity of the usable area in late 1979. Many *colonos* indicated that abandoned *colonias* in the scheme had been acquired and consolidated by individuals who transformed them into pastures. This land-use practice was noticed during field recognition along the Altamira–Marabá segment of the Transamazonian Highway.[1] Officials in Belém confirmed that INCRA was requesting further discriminatory actions to expand the usable area under its jurisdiction, involving 500-hectare units of land for livestock operations. These changes should ultimately depress the retention rate of group 6 migrants. On the other hand, Altamira expects some growth of its transport and construction activities. Although group 4 members may earn less advancement through PIC openings in the future, they should raise the residential stability when tapping alternative employment sources. They might work on the projected dam site on the Xingu river, new road linkages with São Felix do Xingu and Santarém, and the SUDAM-sponsored urban housing project.

## Summary

This study has put forth three interrelated arguments. Firstly, the post-1940 modernisation of agricultural and industrial sectors in Latin American heartlands, has led to a gradual opening of outer regions to settlement. Secondly, frontierward migration is part of the displacement process, whereby labour-intensive, traditional, low-return activities escape to less contended areas; as such, this is a mechanism for the release of social pressure that has been endorsed and stimulated by official frontier development policies in many countries.

Thirdly, and contrary to policy assumptions, recent case studies – particularly those focusing on Latin America's major settlement frontier, Amazonia – agree that the transformation of subsistence into commercial economies has harmed the settlers' socio-economic betterment and residential stability. These two aspects of land occupancy tend to deteriorate at a growing rate during frontier development. The integration of outer regions to core space-economies has relied on increasing interference by governmental policies. Despite these, today's more primitive frontiers suffer to an even larger extent those socially adverse structural changes that took place in the now well advanced national cores. This is particularly true of Brazilian Amazonia.

## Acknowledgements

Financial support to undertake fieldwork is gratefully acknowledged. It was provided by The Canada Council and the United States Social Science Research Council, for research in Cali, Colombia (1972–3); and by the Humanities and Social Sciences Division of The Canada Council, the Universidade Federal do Pará (UFPa), and the Núcleo de Altos Estudos Amazônicos (NAEA), in Belém, Brazil, for surveys in Brazilian Amazonia (1978–9). The author is indebted to advanced undergraduate students of the Facultad de Arquitectura, Universidad del Valle, in Cali, and to students of the Curso Internacional de Mestrado em Planejamento do Desenvolvimento of NAEA, for their logistical and critical assistance during data collection in Cali and Açailândia, respectively. Many early ideas have been either expanding or reformulated in this paper, through reflection on a communication about labour mobility, by Jean Hébette and Rosa Acevedo Marin and discussed in a NAEA seminar on 5/7/81, and in response to comments contributed by Luis Eduardo Aragón, Jane Felipe Beltrão, and Maria Tereza Couceiro Simões, in a subsequent NAEA debate of a subsidiary text by the author. Views and errors still present in this paper however, are his sole responsibility.

Delivery of this paper was made possible thanks to financial support granted to the author, by the Conselho Nacional de Desenvolvimento Científico e Tecnológico (CNPq), the Universidade Federal do Pará (UFPa), and the organisers of the 44th International Congress of Americanists, as well as The British Council.

## Note

1 This trend was also observed by Sawyer *et al.* (1979 p. 154); Wesche (1981 p. 139); and Moran (1981 pp. 143–6). Sawyer *et al.* further report that, out of the total 2.5 million hectares already expropriated for colonisation purposes within Altamira's PIC polygon, 86% remains either unsettled or untitled. In 1976, 500-hectare-plus lots absorbed more than 58% of the area already settled and /or titled. Also, squatters had invaded significant proportions of the polygon, including the entire area of the Projeto Anapú, Jarauçú, and the Reserva Florestal of the Transamazonian Highway.

# 4  An assessment of a decade of colonisation in the Amazon Basin

EMILIO F. MORAN

## Introduction

The past decade has brought major transformations to the Amazon Basin. From weak and unpredictable attempts at penetrating the Basin, the eight nations with Amazonian territories have initiated projects that indicate a significant degree of national economic commitment to the effort at integrating the lowlands. This effort has been led by Brazil, the country with the largest portion of the Basin and the one with the strongest national economy.

Since 1964, Brazil has had the most coherent Amazonian development strategy. Their strategy is inspired by the geopolitical writings of Golberry do Couto e Silva (1957) − a figure of consistent influence since 1964 in shaping Brazilian national and international policies. Since 1964 the Brazilian authorities have announced a series of interventions that, when taken as a whole, provide an interesting picture of the thrust of Brazilian policy for the Amazon. Operação Amazônia was followed by the creation of SUDAM, the Amazonian Development Agency. In 1971 the Programme of National Integration allocated considerable funds to highway construction and colonisation. By 1972 SUDAM had prepared documents that would serve as a basis for the First Plan for Amazonian Development (1972–4). Development schemes followed on each other with a rapidity which is hard to comprehend. In 1975 the Geisel administration announced the POLAMAZONIA programme simultaneously with the Second Plan for Amazonian Development. In 1980 the Figuereido administration called for national reflection on how best to develop the region. The Third National Development Plan (1980–4) for the first time since 1964 fails to give a distinct and separate Amazon Development Plan but states that the region's development is the primary responsibility of the private sector.

This paper will begin by analysing these policy shifts and particularly the performance of colonisation institutions in the Brazilian Amazon. The paper will then try to show that the same implementation problems which stood in the way of Brazilian efforts during the 1970s had earlier taken place in the other countries with Amazonian territories − and continue to take place for the same underlying reasons: an unwillingness by policy-makers to extend equal status to the frontier within national priorities, and to treat the Amazon as the *terra incognita* which it is when it comes to specifying forms of resource use.

## Highways and colonisation

In 1970 the Medici administration in Brazil announced a Programme of National Integration that would seek to integrate the Amazon into the national economic development priorities. This was to be done, first, by building roads across the Basin and along the frontier with the other countries with Amazonian territories. Alongside this road-building scheme, land would be made available to landless peoples from throughout Brazil – with special preference given to Northeasterners. The Amazon was given the status of a National Security region and land was appropriated to achieve stated goals with the minimum of legal dispute. A new *autarquia* was created to promote and implement the colonisation scheme, the National Institute of Colonisation and Agrarian Reform (INCRA).

The government mobilised an impressive array of resources in this highway and colonisation scheme: colonists were offered 100 hectares of land, a ready-built house either along the highway or in nucleated settlements (agrovilas), agricultural credit at 7 per cent annual rate (inflation was running at 15 per cent then), access to other farm inputs such as fertilisers, roads to markets, schools, and medical services. At least 51 government agencies were mobilised to serve the incoming population (Moran 1975). Perhaps because the scheme seemed to have such positive social goals, such as giving land to the landless, the scheme attracted many young Brazilians who poured themselves into their work and wore nationalistic T-shirts to promote the new spirit.

There can be little doubt that the social and demographic goals of the Transamazon Highway Colonisation scheme dominate the earlier discussions. The scheme was hailed by many as a solution to the underemployment and overpopulation of northeast Brazil, as a solution to the inequities in access to land elsewhere in Brazil, and as a reasonable way to use the legendary wealth of the Amazon. This optimistic media and government point of view was not shared by some scholars. Tambs (1974) noted that the geopolitical goals of the Escola Superior de Guerra were consistent with this Amazon highways initiative. Panagides and Magalhães (1974) noted that the integration of the Amazon fitted into the plants to generate enough foreign exchange to help solve the severe negative balance of payments problems facing Brazil.

In the tradition of *proyectismo* (Poleman 1964), Brazilian authorities set their sights very high in projecting the achievements to be expected from the highways and colonisation scheme. INCRA and the Ministry of Agriculture projected that at least 100 000 families would settle along the margins of the Transamazon Highway within the first three years. No less than 66 *agrovilas* were scheduled for construction, together with three larger settlements that would function as service centres for the *agrovilas*. Production goals for the small farmers coming from northeast and south Brazil were no less ambitious: 1500 kg of rice per hectare;

800 kg of beans/ha; 20 000 kg of manioc/ha; 1500 kg of corn/ha; 1200 kg of cotton/ha; and 600 kg of cacao/ha (Ministério da Agricultura 1972 p. 197).

The Transamazon scheme appeared to be endowed with a degree of planning rarely known in Latin American development planning. The Ministry of Agriculture produced a detailed plan of rural urbanism that detailed the spatial distribution of the new settlements and detailed their functions in accordance with their structural positions (Camargo 1971). The scheme proposed for the Transamazon Highway did not constitute a project-specific design but was, rather, a 'rational' plan for land use and settlement applied to the Amazon under the constraints of time imposed by presidential fiat.

Not only was the highway and colonisation plan very specific about the form and function of settlements and the production goals of the sector, but it even specified the amount of seed that would be used, the brands of insecticide and herbicide to be used, and the man-days of labour for each stage of the agricultural cycle. Table 1 summarises the crop-specific projections made by the Ministry. Although it might be argued that these projections could do no harm and might even help field technicians apply a fair standard to the colonists, such an argument assumes that

Table 1    Transamazon Colonisation Project projections

| Crop | seeds | yields | man-days labour |
|------|-------|--------|-----------------|
| Rice | 21 kg/ha | 1500 kg/ha | 56.5 md/ha |
| Beans | 35 kg/ha | 800 kg/ha | 48.5 md/ha |
| Corn | 14 kg/ha | 1500 kg/ha | 32.5 md/ha |
| Manioc | none | 20000 kg/ha | 20.4 md/ha |

Source: Altamira 1. Brasilia: INCRA (1973) pp. 165, 185

Table 2    Colonist Agency mutual obligations

*Obligations of the colonist towards INCRA:*
1   Reside with family on the lot
2   Cultivate the lot with the family
3   Observe the rules of the Project
4   To reforest areas damaged
5   To maintain life insurance on one's self
6   To pay INCRA for services and improvements provided by agency
7   Not to turn over, rent or mortgage the lot for at least 5 years
8   To pay punctually the loans provided
9   Not to divide the property, even for inheritances
10   Not to change the purpose of the property
11   Not to become a disturbing influence on the Project

*Obligations of INCRA towards the colonists:*
1   To provide sale/resale contract in 20 years
2   To provide a definitive title to the property on payment of amount owed
3   To provide assistance to start agricultural work
4   To guarantee free exercise of agrarian activities
5   INCRA may cancel all terms of the agreements if the colonist does not live up to the agreement

Source: INCRA office in Altamira, 1973. Moran, fieldnotes.

the field technicians had access to the central planning criteria. The colonists were held to lengthy obligations towards INCRA, while INCRA held itself to many fewer obligations towards the colonists (see Table 2). For example, the most important planning document, Altamira I (Ministério da Agricultura 1972), emphasises that those areas that have low soil fertility *will be left as forest reserves* [emphasis mine]. In the area near *agrovila* Vila Roxa, wherein I carried out a year-long study (Moran 1981), nearly one-third of the colonists either chose, or were assigned to, infertile plots. Yet, when the land's infertility became clear, INCRA and the Bank of Brazil would not cancel the debts colonists had incurred in their efforts to bring land that could not support crops into production (Moran, field notes 1974). I have noted elsewhere that the earliest INCRA administrator in Altamira sought to identify fertile land areas with the help of local *caboclos*, but that the rate at which colonists arrived made it impossible for him to stick to his original intention of selective land assignments – choosing, instead, to divest himself of all responsibility for the quality of the land on which farmers were settled. Implementation policy became that farmers were taken to the entrance to a forest opening and told to find a piece of land to their liking. I have demonstrated elsewhere that the newcomers from northeast and south Brazil applied incorrect criteria to soil selection (Moran 1977, 1981). INCRA personnel did not suffer from the consequences of not following the directives of Altamira I about setting aside soils of low fertility for forest reserves; however, the colonists who chose those areas were saddled with debts and in many cases lost control of land on the scheme.

Despite the presence of more than 51 government agencies, and elaborately detailed plans, by 1972 the colonisation scheme was already having trouble coping with the arrival of less than ten per cent of the colonists projected to arrive. Not only were the technicians having trouble coping, but so were the colonists themselves. Despite the spotty record of directed colonisation when it came to colonist selection (Nelson 1973), the government sought to apply criteria that would favour landless Northeasterners with large families. I have explored elsewhere the inappropriateness of the government criteria. Size of family and years of experience in agriculture were poor predictors of farmer performance. More accurate were items such as previous land-ownership and stability of residence, together with past experience with banking institutions and evidence of investment in durable goods (Moran 1975, 1979, 1981). The accuracy of these indicators was confirmed by Fearnside (1980) in another colonisation area of Altamira.

Despite the involvement of government agencies in the development of the Transamazon colonisation scheme, the lack of all-weather roads re-emerged as a constraint (see Crist and Nissly 1973). Without adequate roads for year-round transportation, the rural sector cannot develop. Lack of all-weather roads leads to isolation, loss of production due to moulding of produce, decreased health status, and reduced access to credit and other input facilities (Nelson 1973; Lewis 1954). Costs of building the Transamazon Highway proved to be at least three times the amount budgeted for – and led to the decision to reduce the construction of the all-important feeder roads connecting farms to the main trunk. This decision virtually guaranteed that a small-farm sector would not develop and that investments made into this sector would be re-evaluated, as indeed they were in 1974 just three years after the project was initiated. So clear was this process that many farmers asserted that the government intended them to fail and that was why there were so many administrative malfunctions in the colonisation process.

Colonists prepared their land in most cases on the assumption of completed feeder roads, and as a result overplanted given the condition of most feeders. As much as 50 per cent of production rotted on the farms due to moulding and the difficulty of getting to the areas. A few farmers were able to market small amounts to maverick entrepreneurs who invested in trucks and braved the poorly built roads in order to buy the rice below market price in the hope of making a hefty profit. Without them even more farmers than did default would have had to abandon the colonisation project due to defaults on bank loans.

Despite the apparent extensive preparation and planning engaged in by INCRA and other entities of the Ministry of Agriculture, the availability of seeds to the farmers was inadequate. In the first year, when there were less than one thousand families to serve, seeds were distributed close to the appropriate time and the yields of farmers were not far off the mark of projections, considering that they were often asked to contribute to infrastructural projects near the highway. In agricultural year 1971–2, farmers in the *agrovila* Vila Roxa averaged 1053 kg/ha of rice and a few of them exceeded the projection of 1500 kg/ha given by INCRA (Ministério da Agricultura 1972). The disappointing results discussed for post-1974 refer to the agricultural years 1972–3 and 1973–4. The reasons for the poor yields of rice in those two years were largely out of the hands of the farmers. The rice failure of 1972–3 (i.e. yields averaged 534 kg/ha) was largely the result of the promotion by INCRA of a rice seed inappropriate to the area. The seed came from the State of Pernambuco and was a fast-growing variety of about 90 days to maturity. In the rainfall pattern of the Altamira region, this meant that the rice was at its peak of fullness at the peak of the rainy season in March and that the rice lodged. Farmers who did not plant that particular variety of seed did relatively well and were within range of the desired projections, but the frequency of rice failure was such that the aggregated averages showed a disastrous result. The failure was blamed on the farmer, rather than on the providers of the seed. The production problems of 1973–4 (i.e. 597 kg/ha) were due to the early arrival of the rainy season and the difficulty of getting a good burn from fields cleared. This is a disaster comparable to a drought in a dry region and it seems incorrect to blame the farmer for a climatic event. The farmers postponed burning as long as possible, as is normal throughout the humid tropics in order to obtain the driest possible slash and the best burn results.

Access to other agricultural inputs was not easily available to most farmers. By and large, only limited amounts of fertilisers and insecticides were available in Altamira. The colonists faced the many pests and diseases of crops with little assistance (see annual reports of IPEAN and the summaries in Moran 1981 and Smith 1982). The process of modernisation of the agricultural sector did not proceed as scheduled by INCRA. The original plan indicated that by the second year the farmers should be starting on industrial crops such as rubber, cacao and pepper. Farmers who sought to transform their farm operation generally could not get the seeds for these perennials and continued planting manioc, rice, beans, and corn instead. The continuation of this pattern was viewed by government as indicative of the traditionalism of the farmers, not as a product of the failure of the agencies to deliver promised seeds and other inputs.

I will not belabour the many other malfunctions of colonisation that took place (for details see Moran 1981 and Smith 1982). The promised land titles were not easy to obtain and this delay in getting registered titles made it difficult for farmers to obtain sufficient credit to start major production projects. In addition, the insecurity of title affected many farmers by leading to distrust of government and lack of effort in their farms. Most houses were not yet built when farmers arrived and were shoddily constructed. There was no allowance made for the large size of families that had been encouraged in the selection process. Medical and education services were provided but they were limited mostly to the inhabitants near the main trunk of the Transamazon Highway. *Agrovilas* and houses on the side roads were rarely served by health and educational services and were being abandoned by the third year of the colonisation process. Thus, the inefficient issuing of titles, the lack of delivery on roads, agricultural inputs, houses, services, and credit facilities suggests that there is both a structural and a behavioural resistance to responding to the needs of the small farmer in the process of agricultural and national development.

What the Transamazon Highway Colonisation Scheme proved was that there is a serious, and recurrent, problem in the linkage between functional performance and the planning process of Brazilian development. As we shall see in the pages that follow, this problem recurs throughout the other countries with Amazonian territories and suggests a deepseated problem in the structural organisation of development institutions.

## Other colonisation areas

The performance of colonisation agencies throughout the Latin American countries with Amazonian territories is no better than that of INCRA. In a recent review of colonisation projects east of the Andes, Schuurman (1981) suggests that the Amazon continues to be treated as a backward frontier — one that can provide goods of economic interest to the growth poles of the nation, but not one to receive significant investments for internal development.

During the past decade, the Colombian Oriente did not have any Colombian growth poles located there. The emphasis continued to be on the coast and the central areas of the country with an emphasis on the urban areas. The same can be said about Ecuador's policies for the past decade: priority in national expenditures continued to be given to the coast and only a very tiny fraction of the investment was given to the Oriente or the rural sector away from the major cities. Bolivia continues the same pattern. Less than 4 per cent were spent on the agricultural sector during the decade when 60 per cent of the population were making a living from agriculture. Peru, after Brazil, has the most coherent Amazonian development strategy, in the light of its vast Amazonian territory. Yet, even here, the development plan of 1971–5 gave priority to the coastal cities and the 1975–8 plan gave priority to industrial and urban development of the coast. Clearly, then, the Amazon remains a backwater of the national budget, despite the apparent importance given to it with regard to the achievement of greatness in national ideologies.

In a recent study of the colony of Satipo in Peru, Shoemaker (1981) points out that the frontier settlement had an unfavourable market relationship with Lima and the rest of Peru, and the major problems in adjusting the settlement had to do with the dependency of Satipo on the rest of Peru. He suggests that the only, and most efficient, way to overcome the problems of colonisation in the Amazon, is by making the region more of an equal partner in the process of development, rather than the colonial entity which it tends to be treated as.

Throughout the Spanish-speaking countries, the rates of attrition from colonisation projects are even more discouraging than in Brazil. Rates as high as 95 per cent have been reported in the first three years of the Alto Beni of Bolivia, 60 per cent in Santa Cruz de Bolivia, as compared with 30 per cent in the Transamazon Highway. Among the reasons commonly given for the attrition rates are lack of all-weather roads, lack of basic health and educational services, and insecurity of title. These are the same factors that recur throughout the region and which continue to be inadequately addressed by government planning.

Among the reasons often given for the development of the Amazon one can note the need to give people without land access to it, and the need to integrate the vast Amazonian territories into production. Yet, the planning agencies in government consistently treat the Amazon as if it were one of the familiar regions near the capital – and make no allowances for the differences in processes and constraints that exist on frontiers. Frontiers are by very definition not well known and unintegrated into national goals. In order to bring a frontier into the nation several constraints must be dealt with: the price of land, the lack of skilled managers, the lack of knowledge of specific resource-use strategies, and the difficulty of finding markets for inadequately understood demand for exotic products and production constraints.

The cheap price of land in the Amazonian frontier, encouraged by subsidisation of capital and other forms of fiscal incentives, has encouraged patterns of resource abuse that would not have taken place if a tax policy had made such misuse costly.

In addition, by cheapening the price of land, the cost of qualified management of Amazonian development has also been increased (Norgaard 1979). The result of a cheap land policy has been to push native peoples off their lands, and serious land conflicts between colonists and Indians (Davis 1977). An indirect consequence of this process has been the loss of aboriginal know-how and its replacement by naive resource-use strategies.

The most serious constraint to the development of the Amazon is not the absence of adequate soils, nor is it the lack of labour, or even an insufficient amount of capital. Rather, the lack of management capacity at all levels of institutional functioning makes the process of Amazonian development extremely hazardous from both an environmental and a social point of view. Amazonian development planning has been characterised by the same classic biases which analysts have shown contribute to the maintenance of underdevelopment: a bias toward macro-models in plan formulation to the neglect of micro-planning; a bias towards the quantitative aspects of planning to the neglect of crucial but unquantifiable aspects such as human resource development; and a bias towards detailed planning to the neglect of implementation (Meier 1976 p. 851). Most of the problems we have discussed in the earlier portions of this paper deal with just such implementational problems: the non-delivery of promised houses and services, the delivery of the wrong seeds, the delivery of credit too late to use effectively, etc.

The result of a cheap land policy and an expensive management policy are intimately related to the lack of adequate knowledge of management of the rainforest. By not integrating the native peoples of the Amazon into the generation of a knowledge base for management, the result is that maladaptive knowledge all too frequently makes its way into the region, sometimes with disastrous results. For example, it has long been advocated that the floodplain (várzea) ought to be given preference in cultivation since it is a far superior land base to the acid soils of the uplands. However, recent research by Goulding (1980, 1981, 1982) gives strong evidence that clearing the igapós may very well destroy Amazonian fisheries since many fish species seem to rely heavily upon rainy-season feeding in the flooded forest for reproduction and weight gains. Findings such as this could have been generated by careful discussions with local fishermen who could have attested to the behaviour of fishes in the floodplain. The same can be said for forms of agroforestry that are being shown to be an excellent balance between production and conservation (Denevan, this symposium Volume 1).

While it is understandable why governments prefer to overdetail their planning schemes, given the lack of depth in adminstrative capacity, until it is recognised that overspecified plans actually contribute to the institutional inflexibility that has been noted to be in part responsible for the problems of implementation, the Amazon will continue to be mismanaged, even when the necessarily skilled people are in place. To begin to deal with the recurrent problems of Amazonian development and colonisation, two types of change are necessary: first, to address the immediate need of allocating more funds to managerial training and create needed incentives to make it attractive to go to, or remain in, the Amazon; secondly, the structure of decision-making needs to change in order to allow the then available managers to seek to adjust the broad brushstrokes of macro-plans to take micro-reality. In short, managers need to be delegated authority at the local level and to be held responsible for their actions in adjusting plans to local constraints. The result might then be more responsible management and clear levels of responsibility. Both farmers and government would then know who failed to deliver according to expectations.

While all countries have learned many lessons from the past decade of colonisation efforts, there is very little evidence that any of the central constraints that keep the region in its underdeveloped condition have been addressed. In a recent paper (Moran 1982) I have tried to show that the current Rondônia frontier shows few signs of being free of the major constraints noted before. Farmers continue to be settled with a pre-existing land capability map at a scale inappropriate to farm management, roads are still seasonally impassable, titles are issued years after the farmers have been in the area, credit is provided late, and there has been no provision to obtain a knowledge base from the native population. Instead, the efforts continue to be made piecemeal and with little recognition of the importance of timing to the efficient use of inputs. Among the few success stories that have been recorded are those from Bolivia in which Mennonite and Japanese colonists, left alone by institutions but located near markets and with good quality roads have been able in a space of but a few years to mechanise and achieve levels of income rare in the Amazon.

## The Amazon: A knowledge frontier

Any careful reading of the development planning literature from any of the Latin American countries with Amazonian territories will reveal an astounding fact: if we look at the books commemorating the latest development plan, it would appear that we already have the knowledge we need to tackle the area. On the other hand, reading the scientific literature on the Amazon reveals quite the opposite. Scientists continually emphasise that we have not even scratched the surface of Amazonia and that most of the basic processes are scarcely understood. Ecologists point out that we have not yet identified even a tiny fraction of the species present in the Amazon — much less understand the complex nutrient cycles present. What we do know is that they are very complex and that in some cases, such as the blackwater river basins, it is easy to devastate the region by destroying the nutrient cycling mechanisms (Herrera *et al.* 1978). Agronomists are just beginning to establish the extent of different soil types in the Amazon and the response of some of them to management (Sánchez *et al.* 1982; Nicholaides *et al.* 1982). Anthropologists have only in recent years begun to study the cultural ecology and ethnoecology of native Amazonians, thereby helping us to understand the forms of management that have been developed from long experience in the region (Hames and Vickers, in press; Moran and Hill, in press; Moran 1977; Posey 1982).

Why do we have such different views presented about the region? Governments are under considerable pressure to provide for the needs of their peoples, while at the same time having considerable resistance to change in the *status quo*, especially the rights to land in already occupied areas. The frontier offers a desirable free land that appears to give access to the disenfranchised. However, it has been noted time and again that colonists going to the frontier end up in most cases losing rights to land because after the initial period of occupation (Foweraker 1981), the large landowners enter the region and through force or their knowledge of the law, are able to push the poor off the lands they have cultivated at great personal cost (Schmink 1982; Wood and Wilson 1982). It is highly unlikely that colonists will be able to gain access to land unless governments are capable of specifically keeping the larger operators out – something which is questionable both on economic and political grounds. There is room in most economies for a small-farm sector capable of producing items of daily consumption and great local demand with greater efficiency than the larger operator. Economic policy can give the small operator considerable advantage in the struggle between sectors by providing small landholdings within access to market areas and providing inputs and ownership rights in a timely manner. At the same time, the government can still provide access to larger areas to private largeholders, especially in areas at greater distance from urban areas, thereby not pre-empting those areas for the small-farm sector. The advantage, or preference, of the larger holders has traditionally been for export and plantation crops. Those can be exploited as long as there are either processing plants or ports nearby. They do not require the proximity of urban centres to absorb their produce.

There is no logical political reason why nations with Amazonian territories must open the territory all at once. As long as there is a systematic effort to integrate the Amazon, political goals can be seen as progressing. Moreover, there is a great likelihood of support from a larger proportion of the population if the effort is clearly in the direction of human resource development and the creation of employment in the gradually opening frontier. This, of course, requires considerable reallocation nationally, given the preference for traditional careers in most Latin American countries. The number of persons choosing medicine and law over engineering, agronomy, and applied anthropology is still small. However, Brazil has shown in recent years that if salaries are raised sufficiently it is possible to transform this system of career preferences to some degree.

Recent volumes on colonisation and development in the Amazon make it clear that there has been progress in knowledge about the processes of settlement and resource use in the Amazon (cf. Barbira-Scazzocchio 1980; Moran 1983; Schmink and Wood in press) since the state of our knowledge at the beginning of the 1970s (cf. Wagley 1974). The rapidity with which knowledge is accumulating gives one hope that in the near future we may know enough to have greater impact upon public policy. It has been noted in recent papers that the Amazon has not proved to be a demographic frontier capable of absorbing surplus populations from overpopulated regions in the Andean highlands or the Brazilian coast (Wood and Wilson 1982). It has also been noted that the Amazon is not a resource frontier, given the poverty of many soils, the lack of infrastructure, and the low level of skills available regionally. I would argue that the true frontier role of Amazonia, in the short term, is a knowledge frontier. The Amazon holds the world's richest fauna and flora, its very vastness provides the great hope for the future of dealing with many diseases and projected agricultural needs. However, it can do none of those things at present.

The Amazon can serve a positive purpose for each of the countries who have portions of it, and for the world at large, if the thrust of efforts is to understand it. It would be naive to think that the forces that have been initiated will stop overnight – but neither do they need to be further accelerated. There are enough areas of the Amazon cut by roads, populated by a great variety of peoples with varied levels of income, education, and goals to provide any nation or group of nations with the ideal experimental setting for studying the forms of resource use appropriate to the region. Such a process would deal with a number of current problems simultaneously. By slowing the incentives to cheap land, the pressure on native peoples will decline and this would give more time to scientists to study the ethnoecology of native peoples and come up with ways to help them adjust to the future occupation of many areas. Ecologists and agronomists will have time to test the variety of crops and biological relations which help maintain stability and productivity in specific sites. The development of human resources will allow educators and others involved in training to experiment with forms of education that can best address regional needs.

Finally, this slowdown would begin to acknowledge that development is a time-bound process and that like time it is made of segments representing incremental complexity and adaptation. Thus far, colonisation efforts have not acknowledged that development must take place within the complex environment of international, national, regional, and site-specific constraints. Development planning has been nationalistic in goals – thereby ignoring the impact of fluctuations in international markets on the demand for products aimed at in development planning. Likewise, regional constraints are viewed as inconvenient artifacts that can be overcome by spending sufficient funds to bring in skilled personnel from other regions – thereby not recognising the lack of knowledge that external agents often bring to resource management, especially in large countries like Brazil where ignorance of other regions can be nearly total. For development in a region to take place, there must be internal changes in the structure of the relations of the region with the rest of the country and with other nations. This can only be effectively done when there is conscious awareness of the tendency of all regions to treat other regions as resource frontiers, rather than as equal partners. This means that priority must be given to developing the human resources of the frontier region and providing a labour market that encourages them to remain there, rather than be drained away by already developed regions. Also forgotten by most macro-development planners is that resource management is largely a site-specific process that requires considerable flexibility in institutional capacity. The planning designs that have so far guided colonisation have been marked by overly detailed planning and implementational schedules that are totally inappropriate to the state of knowledge of the Amazon region. The Amazon must be known a great deal better before anyone is in a position to take fixed positions on how to develop it. Above all, the Amazon requires intellectual and political flexibility.

# 5 Misdirected expertise in an unknown environment: standard bureaucratic procedures as inappropriate technology on the Brazilian 'planned frontier'

STEPHEN G. BUNKER

The economic incorporation of non-capitalist societies into a modern capitalist world system and its problematic consequences have been extensively analysed (Oxaal *et al*, 1975). Numerous studies have focused on the economic and political roles of national states in this incorporation (Leys 1975; O'Donnell 1978; Evans 1979). Far less attention, however, has been paid to the effects generated by the organisation of the national state itself, especially in large countries, where development has been regionally unequal.

The imposition of bureaucratic organisations and procedures which have evolved with specific forms of industry and commercial agriculture in the more developed regions of a single country may function less well in the social and physical environments of less developed regions (Bunker 1982). State planners in such a situation are likely to carry over operating assumptions appropriate to the dominant system with which they are familiar into environments which present them with considerable ambiguity and uncertainty. Recent Brazilian state programmes in the Amazon Basin reflect these problems highlighted by the extreme economic and ecological differences between the Brazilian centre and its tropical frontier (Bunker 1980).

The authoritarian regime established in 1964 inherited a bureaucratic system which had evolved during the dependent capitalist formation of the centre-south regions. While this regime did alter both the structure and the procedures of parts of this bureaucracy, a great deal of it remained essentially unchanged. The state assigned different parts of its Amazon development programmes to agencies whose functions in the centre-south most closely corresponded to its perception of necessary tasks in the north. This extension of established agencies into new areas occurred because the state planners knew too little about this unfamiliar environment to devise new bureaucratic forms for the Amazon; because the logic of administration in Brazil was increasingly centralist, and because bureaucratic agencies were not anxious to see rival agencies performing tasks which could be defined as part of their own jurisdiction. Thus, in addition to becoming an economic periphery of the Brazilian centre (or semi-periphery, *pace* Wallerstein), the Amazon became an institutional, administrative, and political periphery, subject to the imposition of modern bureaucratic organisations and procedures which had evolved in a very different physical, social, and economic environment.

The energy-intensive, expansive, and competitive nature of bureaucratic organisation enhanced the disruption and irrational effects of this imposition (Bunker 1984). The struggles of the various agencies to secure and expand their own budgets and jurisdiction took priority over the achievement of policy goals. The extreme political and economic weakness of Amazonian human communities relative to the resources these agencies controlled left these communities highly vulnerable to the ideological and procedural biases built into these bureaucratic agencies. It also left them little recourse against the policy distortions which inter-agency struggles for power produced.

The transfer of established agencies to work in the Amazon was particularly significant in the rural development and colonisation projects. A series of functionally specific agencies had emerged in the centre-south to encourage the integration of agriculture with the expanding urban market there. Separate small agencies were formed to provide particular services such as rural extension, crop price supports, technical assistance, and sufficient warehouses to assure markets. Others fomented and supervised cooperatives, others titled and registered land, and others carried out official colonisation and land reform.

The rural extension agencies, following the US model on which they were organised, were loosely tied to agronomic research institutions based in agricultural colleges. Special emphasis was placed on credit, which was in almost all cases provided individually. Banks required guarantees for these loans, so the documentation of land-ownership was also a major goal of the agencies.

These agencies essentially facilitated processes which capitalist development in the centre-south was already bringing about. Government plans for rural development in the Amazon, however, called for the rapid transformation of entire regions, little affected by the development of capitalist industry and agriculture, which were to be populated by peasant migrants from other regions. The relative independence of the functionally specific rural development agencies, which was appropriate to facilitate the development of capitalist and market-integrated agriculture in the centre-south, was not appropriate to the tasks of the deep state-directed transformations implied by development plans for the Amazon. The prior structure of the agricultural and rural development agencies did not permit the effective central coordination required for such an undertaking. Different agencies responded to different administrative levels, had different fiscal and statutory bases, and operated under very diverse patterns of authority. The centralising tendencies of the authoritarian regime reinforced the subordination of regional and local offices of each agency to its national headquarters, where there was little knowledge of conditions in the Amazon and little contact with other agencies operating there. There was even less contact with the local state government agencies with which many of these national agencies also had overlapping functions.

Each agency tended to transfer its own structure and its own procedures to the Amazon and to impose them on its new clients. The imposition by each agency of its own, imported procedures brought about a haphazard form of modernisation. Different agencies, and agents, of government had been assigned control of resources on which local populations increasingly depended. As access to these resources could only be achieved by compliance with bureaucratic regulations, individual success required rapid adaptation to exogenous modern institutions. Bureaucrats in the field typically interpreted compliance with new bureaucratic procedure as a criterion of worthiness to participate in government development programmes. Modernity thus became an ideology and a mission of individual bureaucrats, serving to justify both their unequal distribution of public resources and failure of their less successful clients (see also Wood and Schmink 1979). Because this bureaucratic perception was fragmented, however, by the specific functions and attributions of each agency, the individual bureaucrats were able to ignore the fact that the accumulated costs of compliance for most of their clients were greater than the benefits which enforced or imposed modernisation offered them. Competition and bargaining between the different agencies enhanced this bureaucratic insularity (Bunker 1979, 1982).

These agencies also transferred the goals, the procedures, and the technologies appropriate to the economy and ecology of the centre-south to their operations in the Amazon. Because of their emphasis on agricultural credit, and their orientation to commercialisation, there was little interest in the improvement of subsistence crops and strategies, although health instruction – primarily focused on sanitation – was stressed. In many areas, farmers' cooperatives were promoted as a means to encourage commercialisation and to return more productive capital to commercial farmers.

Rice, beans and corn – staples in the centre-south – were all aggressively promoted, despite evidence that there was little local market for some varieties of beans and for some of the rice. Manioc, the high-yielding staple of the Amazon which is admirably suited to most of the poorer soils there, was ignored, as were other tropical plants, like bananas, for which there is a steady local market. Except for a limited programme to improve the production of jute, an eminently commercial crop, little attention was paid to *várzea* cultivation, as there was little understanding of or sympathy with the technology required. Many agents found the changing, watery *várzea* environment uncomfortable and threatening.

Agents also tended to have little understanding of the vegetable extraction, hunting, and fishing which formed an important complement to agricultural subsistence and income. The special problems of swidden agriculture based on shifting slash-and-burn techniques were also ignored. The emphasis on titling land conflicted with the requirements of extensive periods of fallow. The geometric patterns of land distribution designed for the colonisation projects were superimposed on the varied and often broken Amazonian topography with no allowance for the peculiarities of soil types, drainage, or access to water on the individual lots. In one colonisation project, agents distributed seed that had been tested only in a temperate zone. The seed germinated poorly, and most of the colonists who planted it suffered crop failure, had to default on their bank loans, and went further into debt trying to feed their families until the next season. Because of their orientation to commercial agriculture, many agents tended to promote a limited number of crops and to discourage the diversified cultivation of numerous species which balanced subsistence diets and which limited susceptibility to pests, plagues, and crop failure (see Janzen 1973).

Some of the individual agents did learn a great deal about local techniques and requirements, but their effective use of this information was limited by agency goals and procedures as well as by the job criteria on which they were judged and which determined their chances of promotion. Frequent transfer of personnel, and the fact that the most effective were rewarded by being posted to urban headquarters, also limited the extent to which individual agents could adapt. Transfers between the colonisation projects on *terra firme* and the ecologically, economically, and socially very different *várzea* were especially problematic.

Thus, agencies organised to operate in an increasingly homogeneous modern capitalist economy were redirected to perform several different, incongruent, tasks in an extremely heterogeneous set of rural economies. Furthermore, all of these economies required adaptation to podological and climatological circumstances quite different than those of the ecological zones further from the Equator.

## Discontinuities in rural development programmes

The impediments this haphazard, imposed modernisation and ecologically inappropriate technology created for effective rural development programmes were further aggravated by ambiguities and discontinuities in government policy. The colonisation programmes were primarily aimed at gaining legitimacy for a national state facing various forms of rural unrest and violence. The remote location of the Transamazon Highway assured that these programmes would constitute a drain on national budgets out of proportion to any economic return. At the same time, however, rural development programmes in other parts of the Amazon had primarily economic goals. The rapid urbanisation of the Amazon required cheap, reliable food sources. Thus, part of the rural development programmes were aimed at the economic goals of stimulating commercial agriculture in areas accessible to urban markets, while other parts pursued the political goals of easing the social tensions and conflicts over land in other regions of Brazil.

The rural development agencies were therefore faced with a peculiarly diverse set of circumstances. The bulk of their budgets were assigned to the publicly visible colonisation projects. These areas, subject to fairly dense government activity, were relatively immune to the violent conflict over land which occurred in other parts of the Amazon. A smaller portion of their budgets involved their work along the other new roads, where the rapid influx of large enterprises and rapidly rising land values subjected their small-farmer clients to expulsion. Finally, in some of the traditional areas of settlement along rivers, their main task was to supplant the *aviamento* system, where the extremely low rates of exchange discouraged significant increases in production (Bunker 1979).

The proliferation of different nationally-based agencies after 1970, the fragmentation of responsibilities for rural development, the resulting difficulties of coordination between them, and the diversity of rural development goals did little to improve the effectiveness of rural development programmes in the Amazon. The multiple agencies involved in rural development were organised and funded in ways which compromised their orientation toward effective rural development plans or toward a profitable integration of the small farmer into a market economy. Most of them were in some way or another patrimonial bureaucracies in the sense of controlling resources and sustaining themselves from the sale of resources or services. Almost all of them served other clients besides small farmers and, because of the patrimonial nature of their funding, tended to be responsive to more powerful economic and political interests than those of the small farmers (Bunker 1979, 1983).

## Government agencies: Hierarchical power, dependency, and exchange

These problems were further complicated by the wide-ranging jurisdictional powers assigned to INCRA and to the SUDAM. INCRA's wide range of derived power gave it great control over various resources crucial to rural development. It was therefore able to subordinate other agencies more directly involved in rural development, creating dependency and achieving submission through exchange. Its dominant position within the rural development programmes led to serious distortions, however, precisely because of INCRA's vulnerability to pressures and demands from other sectors. The *Banco do Brasil* and SUDAM, whose mandates were even more subject to other interests than were those of INCRA, also had sufficient resources to dominate the agencies directly involved in rural development. Conflict between INCRA and SUDAM aggravated this problem. The subordinate position of the rural development programmes reflects both their divergence from the central thrust of Brazilian development planning, with its emphasis on the concentration of income and of the means of production, and the position, marginal and subordinate, of their clientele, the small farmers.

Rural development agencies derived insufficient power to achieve their stated goals and could only function through contracts and concessions from more powerful agencies. These contracts were worked out in negotiations and bargaining. These raised costs for the programmes. The concessions entailed impeded or deflected the rural development agencies from their assigned purposes. Division of responsibility between multiple specialised agencies aggravated the problems caused by dependency and the need to bargain.

The need to bargain varied between agencies according to the type and scope of the power they derived. The position of each agency in the bargaining process reflected its own interests in terms of the mandate imposed by the source or sources of its derived power. Comparison of these agencies' organisation and activities shows some of the ways that power derivation and consequent exchange regulations between the agencies involved in colonisation, rural extension, and technical assistance created, in part, the structure of the environment within which the small farmer in the Amazon had to operate, and the ways that the structure thus created impeded the formation of politically and commercially effective small farming communities.

In addition to INCRA, the agencies directly involved in colonisation and rural extension in the Amazon included:

EMATER (Empresa de Assistência Técnica e Extensão Rural), the local state agencies of a national public company, EMBRATER (Empresa Brasileira de Assistência Técnica e Extensão Rural); its projects included a programme of technical assistance to low-income farmers, orientation and managerial assistance, guidance for agricultural cooperatives, and the preparation of projects for loan proposals.

The local state governments' Secretariats of Agriculture, often involved in extension work and in colonisation of state lands.

CIBRAZEM (Companhia Brasileira de Armazenagem) a public company subordinate to the Ministry of Agriculture (MA), which maintained a network of warehouses in areas where those provided by private enterprise are insufficient.

CFP (Comissão de Financiamento de Produção), an '*autarquia*' under the MA, which determined the minimum prices to be paid for particular crops and controlled the funding for this programme.

CEPLAC (Commission for Cacao Cultivation), which derived its revenue from a national tax on cacao exports, and was promoting cacao cultivation in the Amazon, in some states independently, in others through contracts with and subsidies to EMATER.

The following agencies were indirectly involved in rural development, but exercised considerable control over other agencies' programmes through their control of financial resources:

The *Banco do Brasil*, in addition to administering the minimum price payments for the CFP, provided loans to small farmers in the official colonisation areas and near some of the larger urban centres through special agreements with EMATER. Rural development programmes absorbed a very small proportion of its resources.

The BNCC (Banco Nacional de Crédito Cooperativo) made loans to cooperative societies both for their own use and for secondary loans to members.

BASA (Banco da Amazônia S.A.) continued its regular credit operations after the failure of its agricultural cooperative programme. Its subsequent involvement with rural development programmes was minimal, though it did make extensive loans for large-scale agriculture and ranching.

SUDAM, the major planning, coordinating, and executing agency for the Amazon, provided limited resources for various of these programmes. It was funded in turn by a variety of other federal programmes. Its major concerns, however, were with large industrial, mining, and agricultural enterprises.

PIN (Programa de Integração Nacional), and later POLAMAZONIA (Programa de Polos Agropecuarios e Agrominerais da Amazônia), were programmes rather than agencies, but their directorates controlled funds for which all of these agencies competed. The various state governments, and their own planning agencies, as well as the various national ministries, also provided funds and political leverage.

All of these agencies functioned through power derived both as authority and as funding from different sources and at different administrative levels of articulation. In no way were they accountable to any one central planning authority. In fact, the proliferation of *convénios* or inter-agency contracts in many cases led to an agency's being accountable to several different other agencies. INCRA, an *autarquia* under the Ministry of Agriculture, enjoyed semi-autonomy, had its own resources, and the power to make decisions, but EMATER, as a 'public company in private law' received practically all of its funding already tied to particular projects, either in grants from the Ministry of Agriculture or through *convénios* with the SUDAM and other public organs. It also received revenues from planning work done on commission for banks and private enterprises. The local state Secretariats of Agriculture received funding from the state governments but were also dependent on *convénios* with INCRA and with the SUDAM.

The differences between INCRA and EMATER provide a number of examples of the ways that the different sources and derivations of power between agencies structured the organisation of rural development.

INCRA derived power directly from the federal level, both as budget and in its legally established patrimonial power over federal lands. Though subordinate to the Ministry of Agriculture (MA), its direct control over these lands, and its receipt of the monies deriving from both the land tax and its own land sales, gave it considerable autonomy from the MA. It was able to use its derived power in exchange relations with powerful economic groups interested in acquiring land. Its benefits from these exchange relations far outweighed whatever it might have gained from well executed rural development programmes, whose clients had few resources with which to bargain.

EMATER, in contrast, derived very little power directly from either the federal or the state level, either in terms of funds or in terms of authority or jurisdiction. It had no autonomous control of resources. While a much greater share of its efforts than of INCRA's were dedicated to rural extension for small farmers, its derived power was insufficient for its own assigned tasks.

In order to function at all, EMATER was forced to operate through a series of exchange relations, defined through constant bargaining with other agencies not primarily concerned with rural development, such as the *Banco do Brasil*, the BNCC, the local state Secretariat of Agriculture, the SUDAM, and INCRA, as well as with large-scale agricultural enterprises. Its dependence on these agencies and enterprises forced it to shape its programmes to their special requirements, and to use a portion of its own resources to attract them to further exchange relations. Even in the rural extension programme oriented to the small farmer, EMATER's exchange relations led it to comply with the interests of other sectors. As the small farmers did not have sufficient resources to bargain with EMATER, they had the least influence on its behaviour.

The structure in which EMATER had to operate, by providing certain restrictions and certain opportunites, led it to negotiate services which its derived power enabled it to offer in exchange for resources it did not control. Thus, its orientation to the needs of the small farmer, although not compromised as INCRA's was by the tensions of multiple mandates (Bunker 1983) was still subject to distortions from its dependence on agencies whose primary clientele was based in economically and politically more powerful sectors. Its dependent position left it with insufficient control over resources to programme effectively its own activities.

EMATER's mandate was simpler than INCRA's but was restricted by its almost total dependence on other agencies. Its work was frequently interrupted by delays in the funding arrangements established through *convénios*.

EMATER could maintain the financed programmes only through collaboration with and submission to other agencies. EMATER was thus relegated to serving as intermediary between the farmer and more autonomous, stronger agencies. Its major efforts in extension were devoted to preparing and accompanying loan requests for the *Banco do Brasil*, basically acting as the Bank's technical assessor. It was constrained to concentrate on rural credit, as an important part of its extension budget came from a 2% commission which it received from the Bank on each approved loan project. This commission created a tendency to favour large loans and thus concentrate on larger and more prosperous enterprises.

EMATER's programme to establish cooperatives depended not only on collaboration with banks, but also on the good graces and support of INCRA, which had statutory jurisdiction to supervise all cooperatives. It had to submit requests to INCRA for loans, concession of land to build facilities, and technical assistance. In other areas, it had to renegotiate the old debts of cooperatives which were originally funded by BASA. The need to utilise existing structures, which created EMATER's dependence on INCRA and BASA for its work with cooperatives, was itself a necessary consequence of the limited budget which EMATER received for this programme. Once the cooperatives were functioning EMATER served as intermediary between them and the BNCC in order to obtain credit.

EMATER's extension work was limited by CIBRAZEM's location and operation of its warehouses, because its compliance with the *Banco do Brasil's* requirements depended on the farmer's receiving the guaranteed minimum price for his produce, and because the CFP only paid minimum prices where there was an authorised warehouse. Although a public company under the Ministry of Agriculture, CIBRAZEM supported itself by storage charges and was loath to install facilities without assurance of sufficient return. EMATER's dependence on other agencies meant that it had no resource base of its own with which to obtain compliance with CIBRAZEM. As there was no effective pressure on CIBRAZEM, it was usually slow in rectifying the problems it caused for the small farmer.

Similar types of negotiation and bargaining had to be carried out by other agencies as well. Because INCRA formally controlled all land in colonisation areas, other agencies had to secure authorisations from INCRA to establish their operations. In most cases, this involved relatively simple loan arrangements, but in cases where the agency needed to erect permanent structures the decision had to pass through both the regional and the national offices of INCRA. Rivalries between the representatives at both the local and the regional levels frequently complicated and delayed these procedures. EMATER agents assigned to a cooperative established by INCRA in one of the colonisation projects spent years bargaining with INCRA for land to build a warehouse, in large part because a cooperative established by another INCRA programme opposed the concession to the first cooperative. A cacao nursery which CEPLAC wanted to establish in one of the colonisation areas was delayed for over two years while agencies of the state government, EMATER, and INCRA negotiated over location and control. Similar complications beset the plans for experimental stations to be run by a federal agricultural research agency. In the state of Pará, where CEPLAC had been obliged by the state government to operate through special contracts with EMATER, EMATER agents maintained that CEPLAC representatives deliberately delayed fiscal transfers necessary for EMATER's cacao programme in order to discredit the agency and regain control of the programme.

The *convénios* and fiscal transfers between agencies frequently meant that the agencies most directly in contact with farmers had least influence in the establishment of policy and the allocation of resources. This led to particularly severe problems in more remote areas, where communication facilities were limited. Decisions taken by INCRA or SUDAM to fund particular crops or support particular activities were incorporated into contracts with less powerful agencies, generally in negotiations at the regional level. Project goals were then communicated to the field offices of the less powerful agencies. These local offices had little recourse against inappropriate or impractical goals, as their regional superiors were generally unwilling to renegotiate entire *convénios* with INCRA and the SUDAM. In one instance, this kind of decision making resulted in a local supervisor being instructed to devote over a third of his budget to doubling corn production in an area where no corn was grown. In another case, a branch bank was directed to manage emergency loans for buying cattle in a distant flooded area at precisely the time that local farmers needed to process their crop loans. In order to deal with the emergency loans, this bank had to close its regular credit operations until after the proper planting time had passed.

The interference, discontinuity, conflicting mandates, uncertainty, and the drain on personnel time and travel expenses which the need for inter-agency bargaining and agreements created were exacerbated by the fluctuations, vacillations, and direct reverses of general state policy for the Amazon. One of the executive directors of EMBRATER, in Brasília, who had earlier supervised ACAR-Pará's (EMATER's predecessor) Transamazonian programmes, told me that he was in a meeting with the planning sector of the Ministry of Agriculture in 1976 when he was informed that the PIN, from which ACAR received most of its funding for the Transamazon, had been ended and replaced by POLAMAZONIA. Even though, as he said, one programme had simply taken all the money from the other, the entire ACAR Transamazon project was left without any funding. He had not previously been informed of the change in budgetary control. After extensive negotiations, he was able to get renewed, but considerably reduced, funding from POLAMAZONIA. The negotiations themselves, together with the new accounting procedures and transfer channels which had to be established, took so much time that there was a long lapse in budget and salaries for ACAR's agents and programmes. He described the entire process as the same money going through a thousand circles ('*O mesmo dinheiro dando mil voltas*').

He also told me that the decision to transform ABCAR, an 'association' directly dependent on the Ministry of Agriculture, into EMBRATER, a public company, had been an attempt to escape ABCAR's dependence on the goodwill of the Minister of Agriculture after a disastrous fight between the Minister and the head of ABCAR. He said the result of the transformation, however, had been to subordinate EMBRATER to the local state governments, to CEPLAC, to INCRA, to the *Banco do Brasil*, and to other specialised agencies to the point that EMBRATER 'was going crazy with *convénios*'. The advantages of drawing resources from multiple agencies were clearly offset by the extra work, the delays, and the complexities of multiple bargaining relations. These in turn had been imposed on the new company by demands from these agencies, and from the private sector, that EMBRATER serve other interests than those of small farmers. ACAR was transformed into EMATER at the time the state was abandoning its social welfare programmes in the Amazon, so EMATER suffered the consequences of the change in policies which had favoured the interests of its primary clients, colonists and small farmers, at the same time it suffered the delays and interruptions in the funding arrangements on which it depended.

## The effects of inter-agency bargaining on agent morale

The power differentials and bargaining between agencies at the regional and state levels subjected the field agents of the less powerful agencies to excessive and to conflicting or incompatible assignments and to the lack of necessary equipment. The complex funding arrangements which resulted from EMATER's multiple *convénios* frequently left vehicles and boats without necessary gasoline or spare parts because of delays in transferring funds. EMATER agents whose primary tasks, and salaries, were established by CEPLAC would be requested by their local superiors to perform essential services or to loan their equipment and vehicles to agents paid and financed by INCRA or SUDAM when CEPLAC funds had arrived and the others' hadn't, or vice versa. The considerable solidarity between agents confronting the isolation and hardships of extension work in remote areas was severely strained by the conflict between the performance of the tasks on which the individual agent was assessed and the needs of the local office as a whole.

The frequent delays in salary payments also undermined agent morale. In 1976, delays of budgetary transfers from INCRA, SUDAM, and POLAMAZONIA left some EMATER agents without slaries and without the gasoline necessary to do their work for over six months. Many of the agents were also acutely aware of the discrepancies between the tasks imposed on them by *convénios* and the more general goals of their own agencies. This was especially true of the multiple reports which had to be filed for the various agencies which funded specific projects and for the banks which provided agricultural credit. The forms which agents were required to fill out, and on which most of them believed their career chances were decided, frequently had little to do with their own definition of the tasks they felt they should be performing.

Centrally established policies and goals aggravated these problems. In order to prevent land tenure concentration in the colonisation areas, INCRA rules specified that no settler could get more land if he had already received a lot. This rule was designed for the newly opened colonisation areas, where families received 100-hectare lots. It was also applied, however, to older colonisation areas assigned to INCRA supervision. In Monte Alegre, a colonisation area located in the lower middle Amazon region in the State of Pará, colonists had been assigned much smaller lots several decades before. INCRA and EMATER policies required them to title these lots during the 1970s in order to participate in the rural development programmes. The small lots had by this time had been overused and the soils seriously depleted. The farmers were not allowed to move to land which new roads were opening up, so they were obliged to assume the costs of surveying and titling their small, increasingly poor lots. Agents were aware of the problems this policy was causing, but felt obligated to continue the pressure on the peasants to title their land, as the agents' and the agencies' performance was assessed according to number of titles assigned and the amount of credit applied for and used. Similar problems emerged in the soil-depleted areas around Belém and Manaus.

A particularly dramatic instance of the irrationality of centralised policy and procedural controls occurred in the extensive and densely settled *várzea* areas around Santarém. The massive importation of labour to the bauxite mines of Pôrto Trombetas greatly expanded the local demand for beef. Local merchants sought special PROTERRA (Programa de Redistribuição de Terras e de Estímulo à Agroindústria do Norte e Nordeste) loans for pasture formation from the Bank of Brazil. The bank required titled land as a guarantee. The only titled land in the area was in the Brazil-nut groves, which provided a substantial part of local peasant income and of local export revenues. There were ample other lands available more cheaply, but as these were untitled, the aspiring ranchers bought and burned Brazil-nut groves. This led to the explusion of relatively dense peasant settlements. There were direct confrontations and some violence. The actual revenues produced on the pastures were less than they would have been from the Brazil nuts, but, because the labour absorbed in cattle management was much less, the income from cattle was much more concentrated (see Bunker 1981). In this case, the unintended results of bank lending policy directly countered rural development goals for the area.

Job-accounting procedures also distorted other agency goals. In 1977, EMATER and several other agencies were directed to initiate a 'low-income programme' whose aim was to increase the income of a third of the farmers in various areas from what was defined as low income to what was defined as medium income. The agents who examined the forms on which their performance was to be recorded soon realised that the only way to assure that they would reach their goals on paper was to select farmers who were already prosperous. Many of the agents I talked to were aware of and disturbed by this distortion of a programme whose goals they believed in, but they defended their actions by saying that this was the only way that they could satisfy their regional superiors. Other agents complained that, although they were encouraged to work with the poorest farmers, and were repeatedly told that they should not overemphasise agricultural credit, the performance records they were required to submit stressed amount of credit provided. They claimed that agents who did not push a lot of credit were passed over for promotions and for the coveted transfers to urban centres.

In addition to imposing high costs on smallholders, the stress on credit encouraged extension agents to work with larger, more prosperous, farmers. Bank managers and agents frankly admitted a preference for making larger loans in order to restrict their own operating costs. Largeholders were also perceived as more creditworthy and were likelier to be able to afford the considerable costs of titling and registering their land. For all of these reasons, the larger loans tended to be approved more quickly and easily. Because agents perceived that their job performance would be judged in part by the amount of credit provided to farmers, they felt constrained to work with the more prosperous farmers. In some cases, agents urged farmers to apply for credit to buy machinery so costly that there was little chance of their repaying the loan.

The establishment of INCRA as supreme authority over land title impeded access to credit for medium-size operations which had previously dealt with banks on the basis of personal trust or on the basis of various land-use deeds, authorisations, and titles formerly conceded by either municipal or local state governments. In law, INCRA was to accept all valid previous titles, but INCRA procedures were slow and the areas to be discriminated were vast in relation to the agency's personnel, budget, and other priorities. In many areas, there was still considerable doubt and controversy over which areas were under INCRA jurisdiction and which areas were under local state jurisdiction. Banks were usually unwilling to accept earlier titles under these conditions, and so favoured those who could acquire INCRA titles.

Agents complained frequently of the difficulties that erratic funding, inadequate communication, and delays caused in their relations with the peasants and farmers they worked with. Most defined their primary work as convincing their clients to accept new technologies and increase commercial production. They believed that in order to be successful, they had to establish trust and authority with their clients, and that agency problems made it more difficult for the farmers to believe in them. Younger than most of their clients, usually from the ecologically very different regions of the centre-south, most expressed a strong assurance in the superiority of the economic and social values they believed they represented over what they defined as the backward methods and goals of the local farmers. At the same time, they felt a strong desire for approval and acceptance by the farmers in whose communities they were temporary, outnumbered newcomers. Administrative breakdowns, errors, and delays made them uncomfortable and resentful of the bureaucracies they worked for, because these undermined the basis of their local authority and acceptance.

Though immensely critical of the organisations they served, very few agents expressed any reservations about the value to the farmers of the general goals which they believed these organisations represented. Although they resented the undermining of their authority by agency error, they tended to attribute resistance to their programmes to ignorance, laziness, or Amazonian rural culture rather than to the extreme uncertainties which participation in government programmes imposed on the farmers as well as on the government agents.

## Programme distortions and limitations

Because the rural development and colonisation programmes depended on power derived from a diversity of sources, in some cases sources whose major concerns were evidently directed to other sectors of the economy, there were serious contradictions between them. The limitations on the power derived by the most active agencies reduced their programmes to efforts at mediation between other agencies, such as banks or storage companies, which directly controlled crucial resources. By providing services for these agencies, they augmented their own derived power through exchange relationships, at the cost of submission to the more powerful agencies' requirements. The organisation which resulted from this type of exchange at the regional and state levels reflected differentials of power between various political and economic sectors at the national level. The agencies which served the interests of nationally and regionally dominant classes by promoting highly capitalised agricultural and industrial activities derived much more power than agencies oriented to small-scale, labour-intensive production. The submission of the latter agencies to the former led to the fragmentation of programmes and to the inefficiency with which they were implemented.

In addition to being inefficient and cumbersome, the rural development programme imposed a series of modern institutions to which peasants had to adapt in order to participate. The bureaucratic procedures imposed on the peasants obliged them to adapt to a series of land-tenure, commercial, and credit institutions based on private property and individual contract and geared to the socially complex forms of industrial production and exchange in the Brazilian centre. Access to credit for fertilisers, seeds, tools and labour might allow some peasants to increase production, but the high costs of transport and storage and the forced sale to non-competitive buyers often so reduced their profits that they were unable to pay back their loans or recuperate the costs of bureaucratic procedures to obtain legal title to land. The costs of these procedures often constituted a large percentage of yearly marketing revenues for smaller farmers. This shifted a large proportion of the costs of rural development onto the individual farmers who were least able to afford it.

The over-riding emphasis on individual credit in rural extension programmes was especially costly. It forced the peasants to deal with modern institutions for measuring and registering land which actually endangered their continued occupancy. Land laws dating back to 1850 theoretically protect the occupant who has worked and improved land for 10 years if his right to occupancy is not challenged during that time. Legal procedures are costly and complicated, however, and the peasant farmer on formally untitled land can rarely compete with large-scale agricultural enterprises who can pay for these procedures in areas they penetrate.

Because rural development programmes generally involve the establishment of modern capitalist institutions, the peasant who does not deal successfully with them is more likely to be injured than helped by programmes of rural development. The centralising state-capitalist system imposed new institutions which reflect its model of the whole economy, and conflicts between the different levels of government result in vacillations and changes in the institutions legitimating and guaranteeing occupation and ownership of land. Adaptation to these rapid institutional changes requires capital, access to information and technical or judicial assistance, and frequently, political influence. As peasants do not have these resources, they are increasingly vulnerable to exploitation by those who do. Thus, despite their expressed aims, rural development programmes in the Amazon become instruments for Brazil's strategy of capitalist expansion through the concentration of means of production. The excessively complex modern institutions which underlie the bureaucracy's standard operating procedures systematically prejudice the peasants. Both the fixed costs and special knowledge required for compliance favour large and highly capitalised enterprises, contribute to the expulsion of peasants from their land, and increase discrepancies between rural classes.

In summary, the marginal economic and political position of the Amazon, and within the Amazon of peasant communities, has meant that:

1 Rural development programmes are discontinuous and inadequately funded.
2 They are subordinate within and to agencies which also serve development functions for nationally dominant classes. Rural development figures as a minor part of the most powerful agencies' total mandates. This has also led to the fragmentation of rural development responsibilities among multiple agencies. Competition between these agencies impedes their effective coordination.
3 Peasants are forced to adapt to procedures best suited to the economies of other classes and other regions. Rural development programmes in the Amazon oblige peasant-farmers to acquire numerous personal documents, most importantly a title to land – and to confront individually the bankers, transporters, and warehouse managers and buyers who control the infrastructure which is necessary to integrate the peasants into a market economy. All of these individual adaptations are expensive, and increase the possibility of loss on any year's crop.
4 Finally, the transfer of agency goals and procedures from other parts of Brazil disrupts ecologically adaptive subsistence and commercial strategies while imposing new costs on household economies.

## Conclusion

Rural development programmes for the Amazon were distorted by private-sector penetration of the state apparatus and competition for its resources; bureaucratic inefficiency associated with excessive complexity; lack of effective governmental control and coordination; the accumulated residues of past political and administrative arrangements; and discontinuities of government commitment caused by shifts in the relative power of different segments of the government itself. The authoritarian Brazilian regime was unable to overcome either the legacy of extreme power differentials which the Amazon's extractive history had formed or the problems of major regional differences within its own borders.

The state was forced to operate through agencies inherited from what Roett

(1978) has described as a patrimonial state, a governmental apparatus in which various agencies controlled certain economic and political sectors and derived part of their own political and economic base from that control. The state was able to mount highly ambitious new programmes aimed at transforming the Amazon, but it had to operate through an administrative structure established by earlier regimes and geared to the socio-economic organisation of other areas. Power differentials and bargaining between agencies, rather than centrally established policy, were the primary determinants of actual programme decisions.

The south-central regions of Brazil are extensively industrialised, but the State affects and is affected by vast areas within its national boundaries where modern economic and organisational systems are only tenuously established. Analysis of colonisation and rural development programmes in the Amazon suggests that a comprehensive model of the Brazilian State must take the political and administrative effects of unequal regional development within a single nation into account. The extensive literature on internal colonialism and regional inequality indicates that this problem is shared by many developing countries.

## Acknowledgements

This research was done while Dr Bunker was Visiting Professor at the Nucleus of Higher Amazon Studies, Federal University of Pará, Belém.

# 6     Land development in the Brazilian Amazon with particular reference to Rondônia and the Ouro Prêto colonisation project

LAERCIO L. LEITE and PETER A. FURLEY

## Introduction

Land colonisation in the Federal State of Rondônia has proceeded at a faster rate than in any other area of the Brazilian Amazon with the exception of the eastern Transamazon Highway. (Figure 1). The penetration of roads into the western Amazon spurred on by political and social rather than economic motives, has brought in its wake government, private and both official and squatter settlements. Fortunately Rondônia has a larger proportion of favourable natural resources for agricultural development than most other areas in the rainforest. The earliest IBRA colonisation schemes were not in a position to appreciate the differences in land quality and were sited largely in *várzea* areas along the Madeira river and its tributaries. Subsequent INCRA schemes have been situated along the BR 364 which, by coincidence in following the old telegraph line of Col. Rondon, traverses some of the potentially most useful soils in the state.

This paper analyses the progress of colonisation especially during the first decade of the Ouro Prêto Integrated Colonisation Project (PIC Ouro Prêto) which lies in the centre of Rondônia. (Figure 2). It seeks to set out measurable criteria of success and to examine whether success is related to land quality. Constraints to development have been identified by means of field interviews. Finally there is an assessment of the degree to which the Project's objectives have been realised.

## Background to settlement and development in the area

The Ouro Prêto area was not settled in any permanent sense prior to the establishment of the project, except possibly by Indian groups for whom there is little information available. Until the mid-1940s nearly all the migrants to Rondônia came from the north and northeast of Brazil, travelling by water and settling along the main navigable rivers — the Madeira and Mamoré. The main activities were restricted to gathering forest products such as rubber, or cultivating traditional subsistence crops like rice, beans, maize and cassava. After the decline of rubber

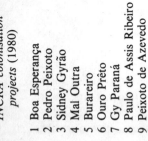

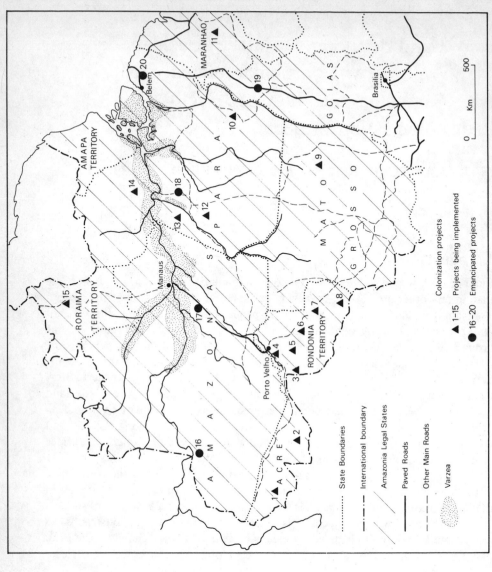

Fig.1  Amazônia Legal and INCRA Pic (Projeto Integrado de Colonização)
schemes. Source: INCRA ANOS (INCRA 1980)

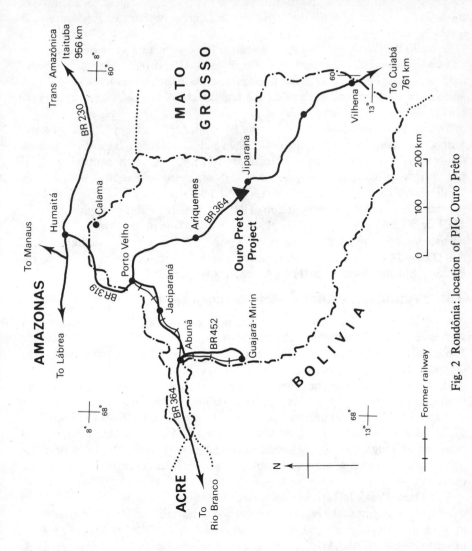

Fig. 2 Rondônia: location of PIC Ouro Prêto

profitability in the 1940s, the government of the Territory (as it was at that time) became concerned over a lack of food supplies and the slow pace of development; this led to proposals for colonisation and settlement. Seven small projects were set up over the next 20 years along the course of the abandoned Madeira–Mamoré railroad (the 350 km from Pôrto Velho to Guajará Mirim) (IBGE 1979a). However these settlements made little progress owing to the infertile soils, a lack of government financial and technical support, inadequate management, the remoteness from markets and incentives and the non-agricultural background of most settlers. Consequently the schemes never grew beyond a subsistence crop level.

By 1970 the Territory[1] was still one of the least populated parts of Brazil, with 111 064 inhabitants in 243 044 km² (IBGE 1977b). This represented a density of 0.45 person per km² but half of this population lived in the two towns of Pôrto Velho and Guajará Mirim, and the bulk of the remainder lived along rivercourses in the northwest of the Territory.

The road network developed after the BR 364, running from Cuiabá to Pôrto Velho, was opened to vehicles in 1967. The road passes through some of the most fertile soils of the *terra firme* in the Brazilian Amazon. Migration from the south via Mato Grosso followed rapidly and mostly comprised agricultural labourers or smallholders from the southern states who had been driven out by increased mechanisation and by the substitution of labour-intensive coffee by soya and wheat. The lure of land-ownership and the availability of 100–ha plots at low cost attracted an astonishing number of migrants (Pacheco 1979) and the population rose to 520 000 by 1978 representing a 21% growth rate. This took place mostly along the BR 364 and the developing INCRA projects (Figure 2).

## The selection and establishment of the project

The establishment of official colonisation projects in Brazil is governed by land statutes enacted in Law 4504 (Brazil 1964), and Decrees number 56795 (Brazil 1965) and 54428 (Brazil 1966). The projects which were then set up (see Figure 1), embody four main socio-economic objectives: (1) to attach people firmly to the land, (2) to increase the standards of living, with particular emphasis upon the health and eduction of colonists, (3) to contribute to regional economic growth through taxes, increased consumer power and by contributing to the food supply of urban centres, and (4) to promote the rational exploitation of land resources. In addition, although this is not specifically stated, it is clear that the Brazilian government has been seeking to establish a finer political control over its border areas.

The Ouro Prêto Integrated Colonisation Project is the largest official land development scheme in the region. The decision to start the project came after a visit in 1968 by officials from IBRA, the predecessor of INCRA, to study a private project set up by CALAMA near Jiparaná (Vila Rondônia). They were impressed by the fertility of the area and by the numbers of immigrants wishing to become colonists (Wesche 1978). The project was created on 15 August 1969 by Decree 63104.

In addition to the general socio-economic objectives of colonisation, there was also the intention to clarify the land titles in this part of the Territory and to eliminate illegal land appropriation which was rife in the western Amazon and particularly evident in Mato Grosso and Rondônia at that time. Furthermore there was a desire to extend small farm units to cater for the demand for land from landless farm labourers throughout the country. Large commercial enterprises were being encouraged separately by generous tax incentives.

Unlike some other INCRA schemes, development at the Ouro Prêto site was not preceded by detailed assessments of the land resources, as for example in the PIC Sagarana Project in Minas Gerais (Leite and Furley 1982). The precise choice of site was governed by the availability of large tracts of unoccupied public land (notwithstanding the complicated arguments over tenure), the accessibility provided by the BR 364, the proximity to areas already settled, and the observations of good crop performance at the CALAMA site. Speed and pragmatism were necessary to avoid excess uncontrolled land occupation by *posseiros* (squatters), and the first migrants were settled in 1970.

The evolution of the Ouro Prêto scheme followed the guidelines established by INCRA (INCRA 1971). However, this methodology only deals with development after a project has been set up. The choice of site and the selection of appropriate sizes of farming plots precedes the Programação Operacional, and in the case of Ouro Prêto, this stage was completed somewhat arbitrarily without detailed survey. Of the 12 basic components involved in a Programação Operacional, 6 are directly controlled by INCRA and the remainder are the responsibility of other government organisations or by the settlers themselves with INCRA having a coordinating role.

For each component, three phases were distinguished representing (1) implantation, (2) consolidation and (3) emancipation. Thus each component could be at a different state of completion, and in a large project such as Ouro Prêto, new colonists are being added continuously whilst some of the land titles were 'emancipated' by 1975.

## The environment and the settlers

Evaluation of the success of the project requires a close scrutiny of the environmental resources and of the potential of the settlers as well as the formal structure of the colonisation scheme. One of the first moves by INCRA after the project was established, was to commission a detailed survey of the land resources. An agreement was reached in 1971 with CEPLAC (Commissão Executiva do Plano da Lavoura Cacaueira), an organisation with interests in the development of cocoa which had been operating successfully in cocoa development since 1957. Their first report for the Ouro Prêto area (Silva 1973) indicated that the soils and climate were more suited to tree crops than short-cycle crops. Around 65% of the initial 60 000 ha were considered to be Class II land with a 'good suitability' and 15% was Class II/III land with 'moderate suitability'. The remainder was classed as unsuitable for cocoa (and by implication most other forms of agricultural development). The amount of good quality land in the project area was therefore high in proportion to Rondônia (Furley 1979) or to the Brazilian Amazon as a whole (van Wambeke 1978).

Subsequent surveys have confirmed this environmental potential. By 1977 230 000 ha had been surveyed (Dias and Melo 1976; Carvalho and Peixoto 1976; Silva 1973) with soil maps produced at a scale of 1: 125 000. Within about a year the results of the large-scale Projeto Radambrasil surveys were also available providing further evidence of the agricultural potential of the better soils: see Figure 3 (DNPM 1976, 1978, 1979; Furley 1980). The soil units with the highest potential are capable of supporting arable and pastoral farming as well as silviculture. They are eutrophic, having medium to high levels of fertility indicated by the base saturation (over 50%), and are potentially useful reserves of exchangeable cations with low contents of exchangeable aluminium. Mesotrophic soils, with between 30 and 50% base saturation, also provide opportunties for short-cycle as well as perennial crops. Even some of the dystrophic soils (with less than 30% base saturation) can be used with care although on the whole their nature precludes arable development.[2]

The 100-ha plot-size typical of the initial land allocation, was not based on any experimental evidence. The plots were approximately rectangular, 500 by 2000 m, and 50% was supposed to be maintained as forest reserve. There were, in addition, 46 plots of 200 ha where livestock was to be the main activity. Since 1980 however, migrants have been settled in 50-ha plots – a political decision based partly on the demand and partly on the fact that the larger plots were not being fully or effectively utilised. The plots were laid out in a geometric grid pattern to either side of the BR 364 with secondary roads every 9 km perpendicular to the main road giving access to '*glebas*'. The secondary roads give access in turn to tracks at 4-km intervals linking individual farms (Figure 4).

The number of settlers far exceeded the original expectations. The target of 500 families was surpassed in 1972 after only two years and the steepest rise occurred in the period from 1972 to 1976. By the latter date there were 4670 families officially settled and this figure had risen to 5050 by early 1980 when the field survey for this paper was undertaken. However in the six months between January and June, 1980, a further 2165 families applied for plots and 1655 were selected, making a grand total of around 6700 families by mid-1980 and excluding the many unofficial squatters in and around the project area. Of these official colonist families 4060 had received land titles by mid-1980, whilst the remainder were given provisional land titles (Autorização de ocupação) which allowed them to receive short-term credit for seasonal crops. The squatter familes can acquire ownership rights if the land, in plots of less than 100 ha, has been occupied for at least one year, developed with family labour and if the farmer has no other agricultural land to his name. In the early years, squatters marked out plots in the same manner as those laid out by INCRA and many have eventually been incorporated in the expansion areas of the original sector (POP1 or Projeto Ouro Prêto, sector 1) shown in Figure 4. In addition a number of families have worked as sharecroppers within the official project area or as salaried workers until plots became available. Thus the total number of families has greatly exceeded the official number of settler families. For instance during a field sample of 105 plots, in POP1 it was found that there were 212 families living in the area. Most of the migrants have come from the south and east; of the families interviewed 35% came from Paraná, 24% from Mato Grosso (North plus South) and 24% from Espírito Santo but they had been born in the eastern states, particularly Minas Gerais and Espírito Santo.

By 1980 therefore, the Project extended over the very considerable area of 512 585 ha in four sectors; there were 5050 families officially settled, 80% with land titles, and many other families were either accepted and waiting for their applications to be processed or were squatting at the fringes and/or working as sharecroppers.

## Land quality and farming success

The present investigation concentrated upon POP1 because the families in this area had been settled for the longest period (at least seven years) and similar opportunities had been available in terms of credit, technical and mangement advice and selling opportunities during this period. Settlers from the fringes in POP2 and POP3 were later included in order to afford a comparison. It was assumed that a colonist who had been in the area for over seven years should have had more opportunities to develop his farm than one who had settled in the area for shorter periods of time.

The object of the field survey was to devise criteria of farming success and then to test whether they were related to land quality as defined in the soil units established by Silva (1973). Altogether 105 farms were surveyed; 61 of these farms were in POP1 (from a total of 580 in that sector) and 44 in POP2; (a further 3 represented farms on the margin of the first developed sector).

Farms were stratified according to the variations in soil fertility (Silva 1973) and grouped as follows:

1 40 plots in POP1 having 50% or more of their area containing soils with medium to high nutrient status. There were 401 farming plots in this group with an average of 92% of their area having medium to high nutrient soils.
2 21 plots in POP1 with less than 50% of their soils in the medium to high nutrient status category. There were 179 plots in this group with an average of 80% low nutrient soils.
3 In addition 44 plots on the fringes of POP2 and POP3 were studied. They were not officially recognised in the initial land allocation. This group of plots was not related to soil type but the families were interviewed to see whether the period of settling had affected success.

The most obvious criteria for assessing relative success would have been yields from farm produce or profits. However the measurement of these factors is notoriously difficult and unreliable. Yields are not measured accurately at present

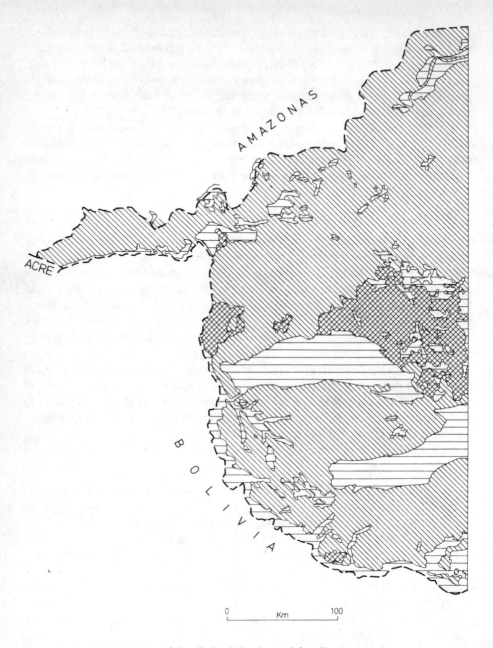

Fig. 3 Soils of the Federal Territory (after Furley 1979)

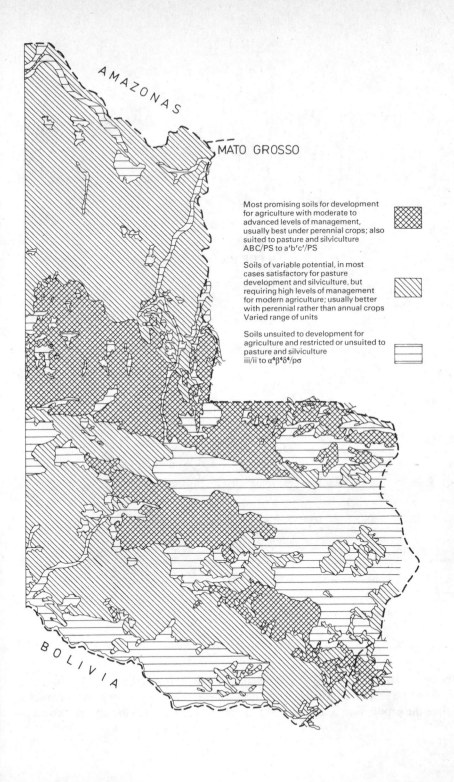

A M A Z O N A S

MATO GROSSO

Most promising soils for development
for agriculture with moderate to
advanced levels of management,
usually best under perennial crops; also
suited to pasture and silviculture
ABC/PS to a'b'c'/PS

Soils of variable potential, in most
cases satisfactory for pasture
development and silviculture, but
requiring high levels of management
for modern agriculture; usually better
with perennial rather than annual crops
Varied range of units

Soils unsuited to development for
agriculture and restricted or unsuited to
pasture and silviculture
iii/ii to $\alpha^4\beta^4\delta^4$/p$\sigma$

B O L I V I A

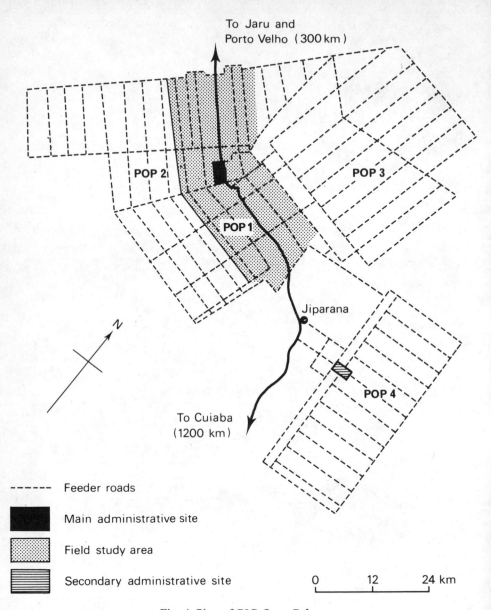

To Jaru and
Porto Velho (300 km)

POP 2

POP 3

POP 1

Jiparana

POP 4

N

To Cuiaba
(1200 km)

------ Feeder roads

Main administrative site

Field study area

Secondary administrative site

0          12         24 km

Fig. 4 Plan of PIC Ouro Prêto

either by the INCRA agricultural advisers or by the farmers themselves, although there are some estimates possible from the products sold in shops or sent to market. Much of the production is consumed on the farm or is bartered locally and is never properly enumerated. The estimation of profit is equally hazardous because so much of the produce fails to reach a money market and because farmers are naturally reluctant to reveal the full extent of any success.

The basic criteria utilised in the assessment of a settler's success in this survey were therefore measurements of possessions and farm improvements. The four main criteria adopted were domestic animals, agricultural machinery, household possessions, and farm buildings:

**Domestic animals**

This category included all animals except poultry. Domestic animals factor scores were accumulated:

$$da = \quad (cattle + pigs + horses + other\ animals).$$

Scores ranged from 0 to 164 with a predominance of low scores (Table 1). Over 50% of the domestic animals were owned by less than 20% of the settlers and over half of the animals were cattle with 30% belonging to 7% of the settlers. There was evidently a considerable variation amongst the colonists although there was no clear relationship with land quality. The difference between the means of the A and B groups was not significant at the 5% level. Furthermore the mean figure for the C group of colonists was only slightly lower and not significantly different. It would appear therefore, that the earlier start afforded to the pioneer settlers was not sufficient for them to have made a very much greater success than later arrivals and this may be partly due to the initial difficulties in getting the project going. The numbers of animals are small in comparison with the areas under established pasture and this indicates that there is understocking. The low level of development is further illustrated by the absence of processing facilities; milk is either consumed fresh or is used in the production of home-made cheese, and there are no meat-processing facilities.

It may well be therefore, that the project has not progressed sufficiently far for a clear understanding of the livestock variations.

Table 1    Data for the factor domestic animals: sample survey (frequency distribution)

| Size group of domestic animals | % of total no. (3372) | % of total no. of farms | |
|---|---|---|---|
| 0–20 | 15.6 | 49.5 | overall |
| 21–40 | 19.6 | 20.9 | mean 32.1 |
| 41–60 | 17.5 | 11.4 | |
| 61–80 | 22.1 | 10.5 | range 164 |
| 80 | 25.2 | 7.7 | |

Mean scores: Group A 34.0; Group B 34.8; Group C 29.1

**Agricultural machinery**

The degree of agricultural development in a commercial enterprise should be mirrored by an increasing number and diversity of machines and farming aids. In the present survey (the agricultural machinery factor) was compiled from

am =    [tractors (2) + plough (1) + harrow (1) + cultivator (1)
        + ploughing machine (1) + threshing machine (1) + spraying machine (1)
                    + diesel engine (1) + chain saw (1)]

Scores ranged from 0 to 8 with 25% of the settlers interviewed scoring zero. Only 12% scored over 4. See Table 2. The most common aid was, perhaps not surprisingly, a chain saw (56%) followed by spraying machines (31%). However there is no significant difference at the 5% level between the means of the A and B groups, nor between the pioneer and the more recent colonists (C). Thus neither the quality of the land nor the length of residence time between POP1 and the expansion areas alongside have had any influence upon this aspect of farming success. Indeed the small number of farming aids must indicate that farming operations are labour-intensive and consequently the amount of land farmed will be determined by the availability of labour. Nevertheless the range of implements in use could suggest that a relatively advanced approach to agriculture is in the process of being adopted.

Table 2    *Data for the factor 'agricultural machinery': sample survey (frequency distribution)*

| Size group of agricultural machines | % of total no. of machines (183) | % of total of settlers (105) |
|---|---|---|
| 0 | 0 | 24.7 |
| 1–3 | 63.9 | 62.9 |
| 4–6 | 27.9 | 10.5 |
| 7–8 | 8.2 | 1.9 |

Overall mean: 1.7; Range 0 to 8
Mean scores: Group A 12.0; Group B 1.6; Group C 1.5

**Household possessions**
This factor should also indicate relative success and in the present survey the score for possessions (p) was derived from

p = [cars and/or vans (2) + refrigerator (1) + television (1) + radio (1)
        + gas cooker (1) + electricity (1) + piped water (1) + water filter (1)]

Scores ranged from 0 to 6 with a predominance of low scores (70% less than 3). See Table 3. Radios were the most frequent possession (83% of sample) along with water filters (66%); piped water was available to 18% of the settlers interviewed and 17% had neither a van nor a car. Electrical power was not available to all sites and this will have affected some items such as refrigerators and televisions.

Once again the means for the A and B groups were not significantly different, indicating that land quality does not have appeared as yet to have influenced prosperity. The means for the A and B groups were significantly greater than those

Table 3   *Data for the factor 'household possessions': sample survey (frequency distribution)*

| Size groups of possessions | % of total no. of possessions (215) | % of total no. of settlers (105) |
|---|---|---|
| 0 | 0 | 10.5 |
| 1–2 | 49.3 | 60.9 |
| 3–4 | 40.9 | 24.7 |
| 5–6 | 9.8 | 3.9 |

Overall mean: 2.0; Range: 6.0
Mean scores: Group A 2.2; Group B 2.4; Group C 1

for C but it should be emphasised that the overall levels were very low. It appears that the later arrivals have not managed to acquire the same level of personal possession and the findings tend to suggest that this criterion may prove more useful as the project develops although the reasons for prosperity do not yet appear to be related to soil fertility.

**Farm buildings**

The nature and range of buildings may also be used as an indicator of the investment a family has placed in the farm and would only be constructed where there is a measure of success. This factor (fb) was compiled from:

[storehouse (1) + maize store (1) + grain store (1) + corral (1) + pigsty (1)]

A maize store (*paiol*) is distinguishable from either a storehouse or a grain store by its architecture or function which is exclusively to store maize on the cob. Grain stores (*tulhas*) are usually employed to store unsacked grains such as rice or maize and also unsacked coffee berries. Storehouses contain all the remaining items such as farming tools, pesticides and fertilisers. Grain would normally be bagged before being placed in a storehouse. Scores ranged from 0 to 6 with 66% of the sample scoring between 1 and 3. Pigsties are the most common farm building (73%), followed by corrals (64%) and maize stores (58%). See Table 4.

As with the previous factors the means for groups A and B were not found to be significantly different at the 5% level, nor were there significant differences between the older farms and the non-pioneer farms. Since storehouses are relatively easy and inexpensive to construct, the findings tend to suggest that storable surpluses are not as yet being generated. The only additional observation from these figures is that the number and variety of farm buildings is sufficient to justify the contention that permanent agricultural settlement has been successfully established in the area.

## The areas farmed and farming practice

The areas farmed and the nature of the crops grown were also examined. Cleared pasture land has not been included in the sample survey and the factor area farmed (am was drived from:

am =

(area in perennial crops + area in biennial crops + area in annual crops)

The perennial crops include cocoa, coffee and rubber; the biennial crops are mostly sugar cane and cassava whilst the dominant annual (short-cycle) crops are rice, maize and beans. Intercropping was found to be a common farming practice and a convention was devised to calculate the areas for each crop (discussed in Leite 1982).

Table 4  Data for the factor 'farm buildings': sample survey (frequency distribution)

| Size group of farm buildings | % of total no. of farm buildings (286) | % of total no. of settlers (105) |
|---|---|---|
| 0 | 0 | 5.7 |
| 1–3 | 53.8 | 65.7 |
| 4–6 | 46.2 | 28.6 |

Overall mean: 2.7; Range: 6.0
Mean scores: Group A 2.8; Group B 3.0; Group C 2.5

Table 5  Areas farmed: sample survey (frequency distribution)

| Size groups of areas farmed (ha) | % of total area farmed (11003.5 ha) | % of total no. of settlers (105) |
|---|---|---|
| 0– 9.9 | 24.9 | 53.3 |
| 10–19.9 | 41.2 | 32.4 |
| 20 | 33.9 | 14.3 |

Overall mean: 10.5; Range: 66.0
Mean scores: Group A 18.6; Group B 17.1; Group C 16.4

The areas farmed per family plot varied widely from 1 to 86 ha. However the means for groups A, B and C are not very different (Table 5) and no significant differences on the basis of either land quality or pioneer versus non-pioneer colonisation can be detected.

However there is a linear relationship with time because on the whole, a 100 ha plot can only be cultivated at a rate of between around 6 and 10 ha per year using family labour without mechanisation. The pattern of agricultural development appears to follow similar trends whatever the area farmed (Figure 5).

In the sample area none of the 105 farming families had cultivated the same tract for short-cylce crops for more than three years. This was mainly as a result of weed invasion and only a few of the colonists remarked on lower yields after the second year.

There was a high rate of deforestation: within 10 years colonists had been able to clear all the areas to which they were entitled under existing legislation (i.e. 50% of their plot). By 1980 5514.5 ha of the total 11003.5 ha had already been cleared. Most was used for pasture whilst the most common perennial crop was coffee (82%

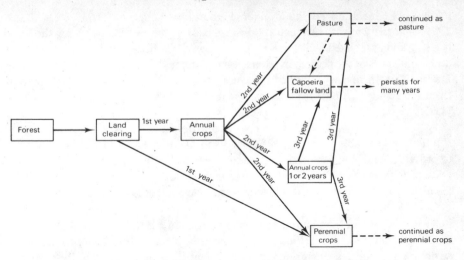

Fig. 5 Diagram of the farming activities following deforestation

of the colonists), usually worked in smallholdings of less than 10 ha. Interestingly the 50% forest conservation rule seems to have been observed overall, but nearly a fifth of the area was already *capoeira* in 1980 (land cultivated for one or two years and then abandoned): see Table 6a. This does not suggest an advanced form of agriculture and such an impression is re-inforced by the findings in the sample survey that no liming nor terracing was used, that only 4% of the farmers used fertilisers and 19% sprayed their crops (Table 6b).

## Evaluation of the project

The objectives of the project were never defined quantitively and therefore only qualitative observations can be made.

The objective of improving living standards is difficult to measure. To do so would require data on living standards prior to migration, and precise information on incomes, capital and general social conditions was not available and could not be collected satisfactorily in the field. In answer to general enquiries, settlers tended to compare their conditions at the time of the survey with those at the time of their arrival rather than before migration. The majority of settlers found it easier to provide food for their families than in their earlier situations and felt that educational facilities were better or at least as good as before. However there was a consistent view that health service facilities were worse than earlier (in 1980 there was only one doctor and a hospital with 40 beds in Ouro Prêto for an estimated population of 50 000). Housing conditions were often poor; nearly one fifth lived in *tapiris* with earthen floors, palm-frond roofs and wattled walls. However we feel that the housing does not reflect the economic performance of the settlers but rather the level of education. The adult illiteracy is estimated at over 50% (World Bank 1979) and the project administration must bear some responsibility for the poor housing and associated health hazards. The cost of industrial building, of materials and remoteness of the project must also contribute to the low quality of the housing. Despite these problems, most of the colonists seemed to gain a great satisfaction from the acquisition of legal titles for the farms and from the relatively good crop yields.

A further objective of the project was control of the occupation of the region. INCRA was not able, with the staff at its disposal and the high rate of immigration, to prevent illegal land occupation, particularly in the early years. However, disputes and conflicts were nowhere near as great as those found elsewhere in the Territory (as in the Gleba Prosperidade, Cacoal, or Imóvel Aliança, Pôrto Velho: Gall 1977; Bourne 1978; CETR 1980). On the whole the land-tenure situation was satisfactory in 1980 with 80% of the colonists having acquired land titles (95% of the sample study). Furthermore the objectives of creating a small or medium-sized farm structure and permanent agricultural settlement have been successfully achieved. This is supported by the numbers of families settled, the insignificant turnover of colonists, the proportion of land occupied by perennial crops and the numbers of farm buildings and permanent facilities.

Despite the unreliable or non-existent data on the area farmed, crop yields, livestock and timber production, tax revenues, growth of commercial and industrial enterprises, there is ample evidence that the project has contributed to regional growth. By 1976 Ouro Prêto was estimated to be producing 60% of Rondônia's requirements in rice and was self-sufficient or in surplus in many food crops such as beans, maize and cassava (INCRA 1976b). Since then a number of the perennial cash crops have come into production increasing the amount and diversity of the agricultural products sent to market.

The data for the sample survey conducted during the 1979/80 agricultural year supported this view. The average colonist farmed 10.5 ha with perennial crops, 6.2 ha with short-cycle crops and kept on average 18 head of cattle and 13 pigs. This is clearly in excess of family or local requirements. The fact that there are numerous small shops and businesses in Jiparaná and Ouro Prêto, that the project now contains well over 50 000 inhabitants farming large areas and sending out increasing quantities of primary products, and equally presenting a growing demand for goods and services, are all indicators of the positive contribution of the project to regional growth.

It is more arguable whether there has been a rational utilisation of land resources. The best use of land resources compatible with the broad socio-economic and political aims of the project would probably imply a limited cultivated area except for perennial crops, a diversification of crops and animal production, the adoption of modern farming practices and management techniques, with the aim of developing sustainable levels of productivity.

Table 6 (a)    *Land use in the 1979/80 agricultural year: sample survey*

| Land use | Area (ha) | % of total area | % of total land cleared |
|---|---|---|---|
| Forest | 5489.0 | 49.8 | – |
| Pasture | 2180.5 | 19.8 | 39.5 |
| Perennial crops | 1105.5 | 10.0 | 20.0 |
| *Capoeira* | 973.5 | 8.8 | 17.6 |
| Annual crops | 653.5 | 5.9 | 11.8 |
| Other uses | 601.5 | 5.7 | 11.3 |
| Total | 11003.5 | 100.0 | 100.0 |

(b)    *Farming practices adopted by colonists in sample survey*

| (%) | | (%) | |
|---|---|---|---|
| Irrigation | 0 | Intercropping | 58 |
| Contour planting | 22 | Spraying | 19 |
| Terracing | 0 | Ploughing | 2 |
| Fertilising | 4 | Harrowing | 2 |
| Liming | 0 | Improved seed | 15 |

These aspirations cannot be said to have been fulfilled at present. The land-use data given in Table 6 camouflages some dangerous trends. Although the 50% forest conservation legislation has been generally observed, a number of plots have been completely cut over and the project has only been in operation for a short period. There is little likelihood that the forest can be conserved in patches or individual farming plots as pressures increase with time. In any case the legislation has been criticised by a number of ecologists (eg. Goodland and Irwin 1974, Sioli 1973, Gifford 1981) on the grounds that it is unworkable and impossible to monitor effectively and that the fragments left are in any case too disturbed for conservation purposes and could not minimise the irruptions of pests and diseases. Only a small portion of the forest is used effectively during clearance. The volume of standing timber has been assessed at 100 to 170 $m^3$ ha$^{-1}$ but since loggers only extract the most valuable species, the effective yield is often below 5 $m^3$ ha$^{-1}$ (SEAC 1980), and the bulk of the standing crop is burnt. In addition to such wasteful clearance practices the land is underutilised. Nearly one-fifth of the area is in the form of *capoeira* and the 40% in pasture is understocked (averaging less than 1 head of cattle per hectare). There has also been considerable criticism (e.g. Hecht 1982) of early optimistic research work on pasture extension in forest areas (e.g. Falesi 1976); many ecologists put grazing at the bottom of their list of acceptable developments in forest areas (e.g. Goodland 1980) and there is serious doubt as to whether pastoralism is a sustainable and useful way of exploiting forest areas of Brazil (Fearnside 1979).

The farm practices themselves leave much to be desired. Very few modern techniques are utilised, including liming and fertilisation as well as land management such as terracing and contouring. There is a high risk of erosion in the cultivation of the steep slopes within and surrounding the colonisation area. On the other hand, perennial crops appear to give a good return and are both ecologically and in the long term economically better suited to the area. Tree crops avoid the frequent ground disturbance associated with short-cycle crops, they protect the ground surface from excess radiation and raindrop impact, they maintain higher levels of organic matter and moisture both above and below the ground surface, and they are also labour-intensive making a better use of family labour and guaranteeing a more stable long-term future than arable cultivation. Although it was not a direct object of the field survey, the sample of farmers interviewed who concentrated on perennial crops were found to be better off in terms of material possessions and housing than the remaining colonists. The greater use of tree crops native to the area would also make use of the natural nutrient-cycling mechanisms, well adapted to dystrophic soil conditions, and so conserve the limited nutrient supply.

Finally, evaluation of the project requires a consideration of the factors which have limited development over and above the environment and geographical isolation. Four factors have had a notable influence – the road network, the level of credit and technical assistance, the administration of the project, and the settlers themselves.

The difficulties of maintaining the all-weather roads and the inadequate feeder roads, have restricted access to the main service centres and markets at critical times of the year. Feeder roads are inadequate because of their impassibility in the wet season and because there is decreasing accessibility away from the main roads. Some colonists are 50 km or more from services. Agricultural extension officers have also found it difficult to reach the less accessible parts of the project. The ratio of road length to the number of settlers has worsened since 1971, but on the other hand the overall road conditions have improved since the beginning of the project. With limited access to markets there is a greater necessity for adequate storage and, as indicated earlier, the on-farm storage facilities were inadequate in 1980, and no cooperative facilities existed except those for cocoa. Furthermore, the condition of the BR 364, the only road link with the major markets of the south and east, frequently halted movement and hindered traffic flow throughout the worst of the 4–5 month wet season. Paving of the BR 364 was approved by federal authorities in 1980 and is well under way so this constraint is likely to be eased in the future.

The necessity for providing credit and technical assistance has always been recognised (INCRA 1971, 1976b). Although INCRA was not the direct provider of credit, it administered the land titles which allowed access to banks. However, the nearest bank in the early days of the project was in Pôrto Velho (350 km) and the road conditions together with delays in issuing land titles were significant in restricting development particularly over the first five years. This may partly account for the lack of measurable difference in farming between the A or B and C groups surveyed. Credit for cocoa began in 1973 but by 1974/75 only 5% of the colonists had received financial aid. Financing of rubber began in 1975 with 37 colonists. Coffee was not financed until 1976. Thus from 1974 to 1977/78 only

14% of the official colonists received credit for the planting of the three perennial crops (INCRA 1979). This lack of credit meant that progress was inevitably slow; farming failed to develop to a commercial scale as rapidly as anticipated and the most suited crops (perennial trees and bushes) got going late in the project. The farming families in the sample survey at POP1 were better off in this respect than the remainder because of their proximity to the main road and the fact that they obtained land titles earlier and were amongst the first to receive loans. Many of the plantations are still immature and the long-term prospects are thought to be very good.

A further problem has been the fact that credit was made available for holdings too large for the average family. Finance was available for 10 ha of rubber or cocoa and between 5 and 10 ha for coffee. Estimates for the average family labour force work out at around 600 man-days per year (INCRA 1974) but the estimates for the labour requirements of 10 ha of rubber or cocoa are 1300 and 1000 man-days per year respectively (SEAC 1980). This implies a reliance on hired labour or sharecroppers and labour is expensive (new arrivals have the acquisition of land as their priority, Mueller 1980). As labour costs are high and market prices vary (especially international prices for primary products), so some growers have abandoned part of the original area for which they were financed. At the same time other potential growers cannot obtain finance for the more realistic lower acreages. The financing of short-cycle crops faces similar sorts of difficulties with the additional problem that the loans are of short duration and have to be repaid soon after harvesting. Methods of financing have therefore contributed to the slow development of the project.

INCRA's administration of the project has to bear some of the responsibility for the limited growth but there were a number of factors outside INCRA's control. Experimental field evidence was lacking on the best methods for developing farms in the region, help which was supposed to come from other government departments often failed to materialise, and finally the administration had to cope with an unexpectedly high influx of migrants, many of whom became squatters. On the other hand there were some mistakes for which they have to take the blame. The grid pattern of plots failed to take account of the environmental differences. Thus some plots are situated completely within areas containing the best soils whilst others are totally within the poorest soil groups or have severe management problems owing to slope or drainage. As yet these factors do not seem to have made much difference, but they are likely to prove more significant as the project develops. Forest clearance was thought by the colonists to commensurate with land improvement and cutting proceeded faster than necessary because squatter families believed that such improvements would help in securing possession. One of the outcomes of this lack of control is the large area today classified as *capoeira* or as underutilised pasture. Furthermore the sizes of plots related neither to environmental resources nor to the labour capabilities of a family. In addition, the implementation of the project in the early stages was supervised on the whole by young and relatively inexperienced advisors.

It can be argued that the settlers themselves represent one of the major resources of the region and have not been helped to fulfil their potential. Mueller (1980) makes the point that the colonists have had to struggle against all kinds of difficulties, some of which were avoidable or the effects of which could have been mitigated. With greater backing, he argues, and with technical and financial support, the settlers can still contribute handsomely to the development of the State. Many of the incentives for the settler were later seen to be misdirected — for example the availability of credit for the cultivation of excessive areas of land and the unchecked forest clearance. The removal of forest from watercourses and steep slopes is particularly serious and the process cannot be blamed upon the settlers who have not had experience in managing such an environment. Equally the failure to adopt liming, fertiliser and other appropriate farming techniques is partly due to education, lack of technical direction and the absence of subsidies for expensive farm inputs. The costs of such inputs are calculated at over three times those for a smallholder in the south of the country. Many of the problems hindering a commercial level of production require solutions beyond the capabilities of the individual colonist.

## Conclusions

A number of specific conclusions may be derived from this discussion:

1 The four criteria adopted for the measurement of a colonist's success do not indicate that differences in land quality have, as yet, influenced prosperity. However this does not mean that the better soil resources should not be husbanded carefully as their influence will probably be felt more strongly as the project develops.

2 The pioneer settlers in POP1 have not managed to develop their agricultural holdings to a significantly greater degree than later settlers but they do have higher levels of household and personal possessions. Once again this may be a reflection of the early stage of development and greater differences should be observable over the next decade.

3 Some of the objectives of the project have been achieved but a number of deficiences are also apparent:

(i) standards of living: standards of housing and health are still low but education and subsistence levels appear to have improved and the majority of the colonists interviewed appear to be satisfied with their progress (1980).

(ii) occupation of the region: this objective has been fulfilled and there are many signs of a permanent and increasingly successful project development although there is a serious lack of control and monitoring of some aspects, notably in the promotion of a sound agricultural plan.

(iii) contribution to regional development: this contribution has been less than anticipated because of the failure to develop commercial levels of agriculture and greater farming prosperity; at the same time there are several positive features and the rate of contribution appears to be accelerating.

(iv) rational utilisation of land; this cannot be said to have been a complete success; there has been excessive forest clearance and the agricultural plan at least in its initial form, lacks sustainability. The natural resources of the area are not being exploited or conserved in a manner which would satisfy either agriculturalists or ecologists. A redesigned plan, with modification to the 50% forest conservation legislation to allow for a single unified forest block instead of fragmented patches, greater emphasis on perennial rather than ground crops or grass and greater technical assistance on the management of land, would help in achieving sustained production. The 100 ha plots seem to be too large for the average family as witnessed by the extent of *capoeira*.

It would be helpful to have a clearer silvicultural policy allowing forestry to be developed alongside agriculture. It would also be of value to establish alternative management techniques to test the physical and economic viability of different farming practices. Such measures should include multiple cropping and agroforestry techniques.

4 The major constraints to farming development, apart from the environmental difficulties and geographical isolation, are the financing and credit arrangements and the condition of the BR 364 and feeder roads.

5 The project has had a low economic performance over the first decade of its existence. This can be ascribed in part to deficiencies in planning and administration but cannot fairly be blamed upon the settlers.

6 The future prospects for some aspects of the project seem particularly good, notably for perennial tree and bush crops, but future development will require further assistance with storage, processing and marketing.

## Notes

1 The Federal Territory of Rondania became a full state in December 1981 (Lei Complementar No. 41, 23.12.81).

2 Once a clear forest policy has been established for the evergreen forest it should be possible to extend silviculture, particularly on the mesotrophic soils which are marginal for farming (Gifford 1981). All these estimates of agricultural potential are based on medium to high levels of management skill.

# 7   Seasonality and capitalist penetration in the Amazon Basin

## JANET TOWNSEND

## Why seasonal analysis?

> To everything there is a season and a time for every purpose under heaven, a time to be
> born and a time to die; a time to plant and a time to pluck up that which is planted
>
> Ecclesiastes 3: 1–2.

*Seasonal analysis* has recently been promoted by rural development specialists at
the Institute of Development Studies, Sussex, England (Chambers *et al.* 1979,
1981). Although the approach is pragmatic and reformist, it also offers scope to
more critical theorists. For two reasons the seasonal dimensions of rural poverty
tend to be much underrated. First is the 'dry season bias', under which researchers,
experts, professionals and officials tend to undertake rural visits and research in the
dry season. Surveys, even of nutrition or health, may be made at a time of atypical
wellbeing; seasonal adversities may be greatly underestimated. Secondly,
disciplinary and professional specialisation hinders the understanding of seasonal
linkages between different factors. A doctor may observe seasonal patterns of
morbidity but not of indebtedness, but it may be sickness at a time of heavy debt
which leads to permanent impoverishment rather than the sickness alone.

Chambers distinguishes between 'screw' and 'ratchet' effects in rural poverty.
The 'good' seasons of the year might be expected to offset the 'bad', with difficult
times screwing poor people down into their poverty with the process being reversed
in seasons of abundance or good health. But seasons can also act irreversibly, as
ratchets rather than screws. Illness at harvest may cost an indebted farmer his title
to his land. Or inadequate rain in one season may force a farmer below subsistence
production, so that he must buy food and even seed at seasonally high prices;
indebtedness building up from a series of inadequate wet seasons may again cost
him his land, his control over the means of production. These ratchet effects are
mathematically not cycles, down and up again, but catastrophes. To locate all these
phenomena correctly, we need interdisciplinary, year-round research. Whenever we
fall short of this, we should remember that rural people often see more of the whole
than outside specialists, and may be able to broaden our tunnel vision.

Human life is characterised by cycles or pulses of differing periodicity or
wavelength, from the heartbeat through circadian rhythms and circannual rhythms
to the life cycle, the product cycle and economic cycles such as the Kondratieff long

wave (Kondratieff 1926). In examining food systems and rural poverty, we need to increase our awareness of circannual (year-long) rhythms and cadences through field research and the incorporation of concepts and analytic techniques from time geography and chronobiology.

The geographer has traditionally defined seasons as 'periods of the year which are characterized by special climatic conditions' (Moore 1968): these are above all seasons of temperature in temperate latitudes, seasons of rainfall in the tropics, with a great range of periodicities in temperature, rainfall, daylight and other variables. To the biologist, seasonality 'is the occurrence of certain obvious biotic and abiotic events or groups of events within a definite limited period or periods of the astronomic (solar, calendar) year' (Lieth 1974): events not in the atmosphere but the biosphere. Phenology is defined as 'the art of observing life cycle phases or activities of plants and animals in their temporal occurrence through the year' (Lieth 1970). Human seasonality, however, is generated not by habitat but by the forms and relations of production. Hardesty (1975) measures the human seasonality of an area not by climate but by the length of the annual harvest periods, but even that is no measure of seasonal stress. Many aspects of human activity affect the occurrence of seasonal stress, the degree of hardship undergone and the differential effect of seasonal stress within society.

Although '*Seasonal Dimensions to Rural Poverty*' (Chambers *et al.* 1981) draws almost exclusively on south Asia and sub-Saharan Africa, the questions raised are of equal interest in Latin America.

## Habitat seasonality

Some components of climate, such as polar radiation, are true circannual cycles and recur with absolute regularity around the solar year. Others fluctuate from year to year in amplitude, phase and even frequency; some of these fluctuations may show a secular trend over a period of years (Stoddart and Walsh 1982). Two aspects of climatic seasonality are therefore significant in habitat seasonality: the circannual regularities and the year-to-year fluctuations. A single short rainy season will dominate rural life; the problems will be greatly compounded if the timing and amount of precipitation fluctuate from year to year.

Climatic seasonality acts as a '*zeitgeber*' to force other rhythms (Halberg and Katinas 1973) in the biosphere. Cycles and variability in rainfall and temperature create the conditions of growth for plants and livestock, pests and diseases.

Quantitative indices of climatic seasonality tend however to be of limited utility. Walsh (1980, 1981) has developed indices of rainfall seasonality which permit mapping at a very general scale (Figure 1). As Walsh (1981) points out, they only include the likelihood of variability in so far as the dry, highly seasonal climates do tend to be more variable, and they can only ignore secular change over the years. Yet in northeast Brazil, a fortnight's delay in rainfall may render cropping impracticable, while in humid areas of the Amazon with a short dry season, rain in

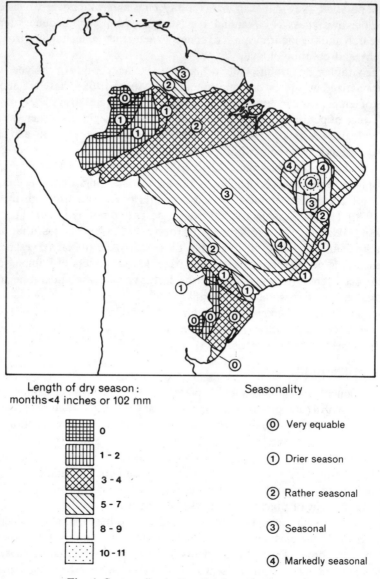

Length of dry season:
months <4 inches or 102 mm

Seasonality

| | | |
|---|---|---|
| ▦ | 0 | ⓪ Very equable |
| ▤ | 1 - 2 | ① Drier season |
| ▨ | 3 - 4 | ② Rather seasonal |
| ▨ | 5 - 7 | ③ Seasonal |
| ▥ | 8 - 9 | ④ Markedly seasonal |
| ▒ | 10 - 11 | |

Fig. 1 Seasonality in Brazil (after Walsh 1981)

the dry season may prevent the burning locally essential to cropping (Townsend, field data; Smith 1976a). 'Slight' oscillations in phase and amplitude, let alone the frequency of the rainy season, are far more likely to bring human catastrophe than is absolute rainfall seasonality.

In seasonal analysis, a clear understanding of habitat seasonality is of great importance, but deterministic hypotheses should not be overemphasised. Maps from Walsh's seasonality indices will inform us better about one component in rural poverty; they will not explain it. Chambers *et al.* (1979) saw a wet/dry seasonality as an explanation of tropical poverty, and posited a common scenario in agricultural communities:

> the worst times of the year are the wet seasons when, at the same time, there are food shortages, high food prices, hig demands for agricultural work, and high exposure to infection . . . These factors combine to make the wet season a time of stress and crisis for all, but especially for women, children and the poorer families. The wet season is marked by loss of body weight, low birth weights, high neonatal mortality, poor diet and malnutrition, poor child care, sickness, indebtedness and loss of production through sickness and weakness. It is a time when many poor people become poorer.

This scenario is indeed widespread, but it is not universal. Also, it might be expected that the stress might be most acute in the most seasonal habitats (as does appear to be the case in nutrition (Schofield, 1979)), but even for cultivators the response is varied. Chambers (in Chambers *et al.* 1981) emphasises that each environment should be examined independently. As his contributors demonstrate, stresses in northern India occur in the hot, dry season; rainfall seasonality in Bangladesh is not high; circannual climatic events are similar in the Gambia and northern Nigeria, but circannual human events are not. Similarly, in Latin America land is more abundant and weed control may be by forest fallow. Labour demands for weeding in the wet season are then much less, and it is the dry season which sees not only harvest abundance, but harvest labour demands and heavy labour requirements for clearing new land. Again, the Brazilian *sertão* is humanly much more susceptible to drought than regions of similar habitat seasonality in the African Sahel (Hall 1978). The plan to relieve poverty in the Northeast by moving people to a region of lower seasonality and higher rainfall along the Transamazônica has been an admitted failure.

## Seasonal analysis

Seasonal stress is to be found in Amazonia in many forms: seasonal hunger, malnutrition, disease, natality, labour demand, child neglect, demand for social spending, indebtedness, price swings, migration and transport problems. The pulses of life and society are phased to the '*zeitgeber*' of climate; the final relationship of all the cycles, with their different periods, all operating simultaneously, is, in the biological sense, a 'rhythm'. Each area has its characteristic rhythm, as individual and distinctive to it as its landscapes, and perhaps as compounded of success and catastrophe. In the rhythms, in the landscapes, we are ultimately observing not environmental determinism but the reproduction of the mode of production – the working out of social, not astronomical forces (Figure 2).

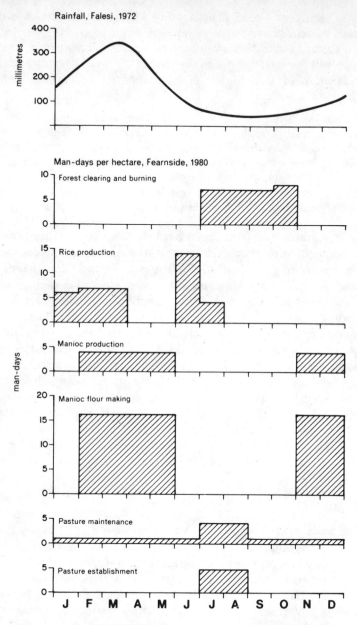

Fig. 2 Transamazonica seasons, Altamira

Of the infectious *diseases*, it is malaria and the diarrhoeal and respiratory diseases which are notably seasonal in the Americas. Their ecologies, however, are very complex and the phase relations with climate may vary greatly with local environments, as illustrated by Smith (1976a) and Moran (1976, 1981) for malaria on the Transamazônica. Linkages with debt and crop failure are likely, and gastroenteritis is itself a major precipitating cause for protein-energy malnutrition (Teruel *et al.* 1973). Conversely, of course, malnutrition facilitates infection, and malnutrition itself varies seasonally. Other seasonal variations in human behaviour affect disease transmission, resistance to infection and likelihood of recovery. Indoor crowding against wet or cold promotes respiratory infection; seasonal visits to particular sites for cultivation, hunting, fishing or bathing may give opportunities to vectors; seasonal labour migration may carry disease; agriculture itself is the main cause of trauma (accident); at times of peak labour demand, caring for the sick may be less practicable.

At an apparently less serious level, seasonal peaks in the activities of biting insects are a widespread problem which can have very real effects on agricultural activity although little mentioned in the literature, save by Smith (1976a) and Moran (1976). On the Transamazônica, *similium* bites increase in the planting and harvesting periods of rice. They cause intense irritation and loss of sleep; children and some adults also develop a haemorrhaging syndrome from them. Farms where the biting is particularly severe find seasonal labour hard to obtain for the harvest, and families may actually abandon their lots at these times and seek respite in the villages and towns, thereby reducing labour inputs at critical periods.

Probably the feature of habitat seasonality in Amazonia most familiar to field researchers is the effect on transport.

*Seasonal transport problems* are common to most areas and may act as pacemakers in the economies of whole regions. Circannual changes in the friction of distance can operate at all scales, from a farmer's access to his fields to a region's access to markets. Riviere (1972) has detailed the rhythm of Roraima (northern Brazil) and its overall gearing to friction of distance. Only since early 1978 has there been a road link to the rest of Brazil: until then, movement out was by the Rio Branco or by air. The Rio Branco is a usable waterway for only five months of the year, and only for a much shorter time at the highest flood can large riverboats reach Roraima. This has restricted capitalist penetration and created a high cost of living with frequent seasonal shortages – even, in bad years, of basic foods. Other aspects of friction of distance are out of phase: in the wet season, when river transport becomes practicable, movement across the savanna by jeep and truck becomes impossible save on the very restricted tarmac; the best and surest means of travel is the horse. The intensity of social life therefore varies enormously between wet and dry seasons; the sheer difficulty of overland movement in the wet season also governs the annual routine of the cattle economy. The yearly roundup for the branding of calves, vaccination, drenching and castration takes place in the dry, but before the opening of the road, it was also necessary to have a lesser, wet-season roundup to select cattle to go downriver for sale, despite appalling working conditions in the corrals.

Although the reasons are little understood, in Latin America road transport tends to be cheaper and more effective than river transport: a town such as San José de Guaviare in eastern Colombia, accessible by air all year, by river after a fashion all year, and by road (opened 1971) only in the month of January, conducts a surprising proportion of its trade with the outside world in that month. Such cycles are widespread in areas of high rainfall from Mexico to Paraguay.

Seasonality of access can be as serious in economic terms as can harvest loss through flood or drought: access too has its periodicities and its catastrophes. There are also direct effects on health when health care may be not only, as always, expensive and inappropriate, but totally inaccessible. Periodicity of access will be a serious obstacle to the achievement of primary health care.

All human societies have their counterseasonality strategies, whether conscious or otherwise. Hunters, gatherers and fishers may migrate with their food or change their food with the seasons; cultivators may store or diversify; in the examples just considered, of seasonality of access, the tarmac road and the all-weather airstrip defy the seasons and make an important stage in capitalist penetration. Any successful food system must incorporate counterseasonality. In rural poverty, counterseasonality is as critical to survival as is production itself and should be as carefully considered in any planned interventions. Seasonal analysis of a problem, a system, an area must examine not only the cadences of stress and compounding of stress by linkages/temporal coincidences within the rhythm, but the 'mechanisms' by which stress is lessened or avoided. In food systems there are essentially three possible forms of counterseasonality: food production throughout the year, food storage, and reduction of seasonal labour peak by the use of tools or machinery to reduce labour inputs. Systems of reciprocity, redistribution and the market are all effectively forms of storage. All are bounded by the total time available to the population – the 'packing of time-consuming activities in population time-budgets' (Carlstein 1978).

## Counterseasonality in the Amazon Basin

Prior to conquest by the Iberians, a range of non-capitalist modes of production incorporated very different degrees of organisation of production and social division of labour. For pre-agricultural societies, the choice of counterseasonal strategies would be between
1 moving from one activity to another through the year (Figure 3)
2 using different spaces through the year (Figure 3)
3 any combination of these two.
Survival depends on both a system for finding food at all seasons and on resisting a seasonal 'failure' in any one year when some regular periodicity fails, of fish, fruit or game. It appears that both highly specialised and highly diversified groups existed. Agriculture allows an increasingly intensive occupation of space–time: Carlstein (Figure 4) has shown how an increased frequency of cropping effectively colonises

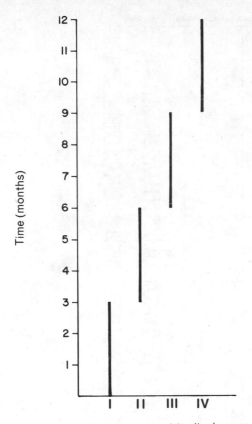

Fig. 3 Counterseasonal strategies changing activity and/or place

| **eg:** | ACTIVITIES | SPACE | ALTITUDINAL ZONES |
|---|---|---|---|
| I | hunting | riverside | pasture |
| II | fishing | swamp | potatoes |
| III | gathering fruits | high forest | maize |
| IV | gathering tubers | seasonally flooded floodplains | coca |

time at the same place and (Figure 5) how irrigation again extends use of time at the same place.

By the Conquest, water management was developed in a wide range of environments, from irrigation in the dry lands, through terracing for water retention on slopes to raised fields in the lowlands, probably for both irrigation and drainage: all would promote permanent cultivation and multicropping through the year. Today the Llanos de Mojos are seasonally flooded and little populated, but the

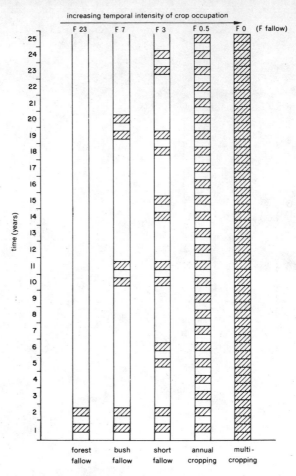

Fig. 4 Increasing occupation of space–time: Carlstein 1973, 1978

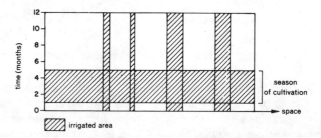

Fig. 5 Temporal expansion in resource occupation: Carlstein 1978

square, artificial lakes with inlet and outlet channels were apparently constructed and used for retreat cultivation. Raised platforms there reach 25 by 300 m (Denevan 1966). Similar relic agricultural ridges and platforms may lie under the Amazon forests, particularly in more seasonal areas (Denevan 1980). Modern ridged-field cultivation in eastern Venezuela certainly operates on moisture control in an area of pronounced dry season (Denevan and Bergman 1975): labour investment in the initial ditching is heavy, but sustained cultivation is then possible with light labour inputs.

The main lowland cultigen, manioc, was available from at least 3 000 BC (Pickersgill and Heisen 1977) and is exceptionally seasonal as it stores well in the ground.

Possibly all dense pre-Columbian populations depended on water management, but other strategies were certainly employed. In the wet lowlands, retreat cultivation was practised by seasonal rivers; domestic refuse fertilised permanent house gardens and created anthrosols (Smith 1980). Forest-edge species of animals may have been allowed to feed on cultivated gardens while themselves being cropped for food (Linares 1976): this reduced protein seasonality, acting as a pseudo-domestication. Diversity of domesticates and wild foods, polyculture and intercropping may have been basic and widespread.

The best known counterseasonal use of altitudinal range must be Murra's verticality model (1960, 1972, 1975), under which activities are timed by altitudinal space (Figure 3). A community would fill the agricultural calendar by exploiting different ecological niches at different seasons, thus maximising both labour use and production throughout the year. The scheduling problems could be extraordinarily complex (Guillet 1981) but such strategies were essential for survival; Winterhalder and Thomas (1978) estimate crop failures today as equivalent to one year in seven.

A few examples of pre-Conquest societies under non-capitalist modes of production serve, therefore, to demonstrate the fundamental importance of counterseasonality strategies, and the wide range adopted in a variety of environments. Recent studies of Amerindian groups yield much fuller pictures of the sheer diversity per group. None can be taken as packaged survivals of a pre-Conquest world; there has been far too much migration, disease and destruction by slaving and warfare. With that caveat, however, they may be considered as non-capitalist fractions.

Anthropologists fortunately retain an interest in the agricultural calendar, although few work on time use, time allocation or energy budgets. A few exceptional Amerindian groups can be identified whose agriculture is almost aseasonal, such as the Yanoama of western Amazonia (Smole 1976). That is, among the Yanoama, someone might be clearing land for a new garden at almost any time of year; there is no clearly defined horticultural seasonality other than the life cycles of the different varieties of cultivated plants – but the actual crops and techniques are still controlled by habitat seasonality. Even the Yanoama rely above all on dependable, planned food production. This continues even in times of war, and hunting is subordinated to both horticulture and collecting. Cutting and burning occasion the prolonged periods of intensive labour, not planting, weeding or harvesting. Seeds are of minor importance: most propagation is by stem and root cuttings, so there is no planting season.

Far more typical than the Yanoama would be the Yukpa of the northwest (Ruddle 1974), whose 45 cultivated crops are grown in a clear annual cycle, closely related to the marked dry season and the double rainfall maxima of the wet season. Fishing is incorporated in the cycle at the time of low labour demand; in the hungry season, hunting and gathering are practised. Polyculture, interplanting and the consumption of a wide range of foods including invertebrates do much to reduce seasonal stress. Male labour demand peaks when land is cleared, female labour at harvest and processing. When labour is lost from disease, injury or death, kin obligations replace it. Cultivation alone would not ensure a balanced diet, but hunting, fishing and insect gathering provide animal proteins and fats, while wild fruits and leaves yield essential vitamins. Ruddle argues that it was the complexity of the cycle which assured Yukpa subsistence, now threatened by cash-cropping and even livestock — but that is another story.

A common problem in these cultures is a 'hungry season' when a basic food supply such as manioc is assured but the gardens do not yield a balanced diet. Among the Tapirapé, the phrase 'I am hungry' means 'I am hungry for meat or fish'; there may be manioc in abundance (Wagley 1977). There, however, at the hungry time of the heavy rains, hunting is hampered by difficulty of movement, although game is at its most abundant; fish, too, is caught mainly in the dry season, for fish traps are used as the water recedes. Overall, tropical rainforest Amerindian cultures vary greatly and include many combinations of cultivating, gathering, hunting and fishing, many variations of age and sex distribution of labour and many responses to habitat seasonality. Diversity of productive activities in time and space is perhaps the common characteristic of their circannual rhythms, with manioc as the common basic theme. Covering the hungry season is critical; often tropical subsistence agricultures yield energy output–input ratios of 10–20: 1 but still may not achieve food security because of seasonality (Norman 1978; Haswell 1981).

Far more widespread in the American tropics today is the *pre-capitalist mode* of production, where wide variety of forms of peasant production are subordinated to the capitalist mode. Petty commodity producers and 'semi-proletarians' are to be found in varying relations with different forms of capital in varying concrete conditions as diversity at the household level yields to increasing social divisions of labour. The investigation of these relations is of the first importance, but it is convenient for this paper to adopt the generalisation of an articulation of pre-capitalist modes of production to the capitalist mode (Wolpe 1978).

In hot, wet Amazonia many forms of production have noteworthy seasonal dimensions. Fishing is a major seasonal subsistence and cash activity, recently studied in depth by Smith (1981) at Itacoatiara for a diverse mosaic of biotopes on the floodplains of the Amazon and its tributaries. Here habitat seasonality is powerful: the composition of fish communities changes radically during the year with fluctuations in water levels; fishing methods are adapted to water depth, fish movements and fish abundance. Only by deploying many different fishing methods at different times of the year on different sites is it possible to catch fish all year – about 100 species in all, caught by at least 12 different methods. Wealth derives from specialisation, while poverty must put diversity to use. The seine nets, which call for the most outlay, prove to yield much the largest catch per effort and indeed catch the most fish, but can only be used in daylight on debris-free sites. Poor and part-time fishermen are able to exploit more difficult sites with differing techniques. Although most fish is locally consumed, bottom trotlines are now set in the main channel of the Amazon at low water for the giant catfish, which are sold to freezing plants and end in supermarkets in Manaus, Brasília and the south. (Similar fish from other areas are exported to the United States.) Despite this multi-level sales structure, production appears to be essentially petty commodity; vertical integration still begins at the freezing plant, not on the river. Conservation is very much a matter of ad hoc tradition. Legal controls prohibit the use of dynamite (ineffectively) and impose minimum lengths by species for consumption – again ineffectively and possibly not on sound biological grounds. Experience with much more seasonal fisheries in Colombia (Townsend 1976) suggests that once the market develops or friction of distance is overcome, legal constraints are impossible to enforce as differentiation of producers proceeds.

One 'resource' against seasonal stress which is widely utilised from the Andes to the Amazon is borrowing and consequent indebtedness: important both in proletarianisation and in the reproduction of pre-capitalist modes of production. Rubber collectors, for instance, can only operate in the dry season (Wagley 1953), while Brazil nuts are collected when they fall after fruiting in the wet season (Velho 1972). In both cases, the same cycle of indebtedness is to be encountered: the collector is in debt to the trader, the trader to the import–export firm, in Belém or Manaus. In a simple operation of usury capital, large companies send out merchandise on credit to traders, traders advance the necessities of life to collectors, and collectors are often trapped into a lifetime's debt (Ianni 1978).

Smith (1976a, 1978) and Moran (1976, 1981) both concluded that inappropriate choice of a seasonal grain crop prejudiced the chances of colonists on the Transamazônica. Along the Highway, forest vegetation is well adapted to withstand the dry season. Manioc and plantains can survive the dry season, but planting of maize and rice must be timed to take advantage of the wet season (the length of which increases westward). The agricultural cycle is highly seasonal (Moran 1981) and the actual area a settler can cultivate is a function of (1) the length of the dry season, for clearing and burning and (2) the availability to him of labour or credit to hire labour (Smith 1976) or buy a powersaw (Moran 1981). At

29 man-days per hectare to clear and burn (Fearnside 1980), space very clearly becomes a function of time.

Upland rice was the officially promoted crop, but is much less productive in yield, calories and profitability along the Highway than manioc (Smith 1976). Rice competes poorly with weeds, so that a long dry spell after felling is essential to give a very thorough burn. Birds and pests also render harvest imperative immediately after ripening: again a heavy labour demand in a tight time constraint. Storage is then a problem, with moulds, rats and pests, while marketing is beset with difficulties (Moran 1981). For manioc, on the other hand, planting and harvesting are much more flexible to family possibilities (Figure 2). Manioc can also be processed into flour, year-round, by the family. It is then not subject to predation and can be stored when access to market is impeded by the roads (Smith 1976a, 1978). Smith and Moran have also developed some analysis of the linkages in seasonal stress. The major peak in simulid biting (above) coincides with the rice harvest; peak malaria transmission coincides with the critical time of planting in the early part of the rainy season; accidental injury is second only to malaria in causing lost labour time, and is a direct function of agricultural activities, particularly felling and clearing. These linkages differ in type. All directly cause lost labour time, but the greatest exposure to simulid bites can be avoided just by not growing rice, while the peak malaria time is the optimum time for planting not only rice but maize, manioc or plantains (the only advantage of manioc is that it can still be planted later in an emergency), and accidental injury could only be eliminated by stopping forest clearing and agriculture altogether. Seasonal bites are easy to avoid, malaria difficult, accident impossible.

Transamazon colonists who began on the Highway with resources of their own have been notably the more successful (Wood and Schmink 1978, Schmink 1977). Within this group, those of local origin have been more successful still (Moran 1981). Locals obtain higher yields, presumably from greater local knowledge; they also intercrop and multicrop, keeping the ground under constant cover, and employ wild game and wild fruits to supplement their diets and to lower expenses; manioc flour is an important cash resource. Seventy-odd crops are cultivated, many of them in multistoreyed house gardens. Although (Smith 1976b) there are still wild food resources which are refused but would be acceptable to Indians, year-round nutrition for 'local' colonists is better than for those relying on seasonal grains (Moran 1976). Yet official credit was restricted to rice, corn, beans, one perennial crop and, of course, cattle by banks and development agencies (Moran 1981), exposing colonists to seasonal stress.

Foweraker (1981) has traced the operation of violence, law, lawlessness and the State in the separation of peasants from the land. He has perhaps understated the role of merchant/usury capital and indebtedness in capitalist penetration – in which, of course, the State and finance capital have an important place. Seasonality may be shown to have great significance in those indebtedness cycles in which colonists lose their land on the forest 'frontier'. This may be demonstrated by reference to Colombia where, unlike Brazil, a man who works unoccupied land has the legal right to obtain full title to it, and has had since 1936. There are many abuses, but from the creation of the agrarian reform institute INCORA in 1961, until the late seventies, titles were indeed extensively granted. This titling of land in colonisation areas accounted for most 'agrarian reform' activity in Colombia and although only a minority of colonists have been affected, titles add great value to land in facilitating credit and sale and are held in high regard.

In most Colombian colonisation areas (Townsend 1976, 1977) the leading edge or frontier of colonisation is composed of crop farmers producing maize, upland rice and manioc; diversification is usually poor. Both costs and risks are high; credit is expensive and short-term (normally six months), whether obtained from store-keepers, traders or the state development bank. Often there are great similarities with the debt cycle of rubber and Brazil-nut collectors in Amazonia: very commonly, a store-keeper will supply the necessities of life until the first harvest, when the colonist hopes to pay off the debt and farm independently. Far more commonly, he is caught in a cycle of indebtedness: home-made alcoholic brews are illegal in Colombia, unlike the Central Andes; the store-keeper is also the source of beer and rum, and at harvest time will often import a supply of prostitutes. Seasonal harvest spending then calls for more borrowing to finance the next harvest. Some evidence for the critical effect of this harvest spending may be found among the evangelical converts in these areas. They often escape the debt cycle and make successful use of credit, apparently because they eschew drink and prostitution.

Save in the most isolated areas, only the poorest, least creditworthy, rely on family labour – and they are often part-time farmers, selling their labour. Most colonists, particularly after they have established themselves with the first harvest, seek credit to hire seasonal labour for forest-felling and for harvest. At first sight, it is strange to encounter large migratory work-forces in regions where every family is bitterly poor. The labour is in fact financed from outside: entrepreneurial ability and access to credit are critical. Colonists rank the quality of management of a frontier farm above all other considerations in determining whether a farm pays – above fertility, accessibility, even farm size (Townsend 1977). The colonist needs to be a skilled manager of both the complex agricultural cycle and the credit system.

But this is only a stage. As on the Transamazônica (Moran 1981), the almost universal ambition is to move into cattle. Attempts to establish stable petty commodity production of cash crops are rare, although it may be found where plantains are produced on fertile, seasonally flooded land with good access to urban markets. Otherwise:

1 Yields fall very rapidly and the colonist is unlikely to be able to secure a sufficient reserve for forest fallow; the crops are staple foods for the cities and their prices are held too low to warrant fertiliser and herbicide, particularly as transport costs are by definition high.

2 Cattle are an escape from compound seasonal stress: seasonal transport risks (cattle can be stored on the hoof and can even provide some of their own transport), seasonal hazards to crops, problems of managing seasonal labour – many of the problems of social and habitat seasonality.

3 Cattle carry higher status.

The pioneer, then, will attempt to become a cattle farmer – to achieve control over the means of production by relying on family labour and a small, permanent, wage-labour force. He will try to clear as much land as possible, employing seasonal labour and always at a risk that a fluctuation in habitat seasonality or a miscalculation will cost him the land which he has been using as collateral with the trader or the bank. In some areas, the commonest way for land to change hands is for the bank to foreclose (Townsend 1976). Powerful differentiation processes are at work. After cropping, land will be laid down to grass; if crops have been unusually profitable, cattle will be bought, but more commonly cattle will be obtained on credit or a grazier's cattle will be cared for. Exceptionally, the French or farmer road to capitalist production (Kay 1980; de Janvry and Ground 1978) will be won and a stable cattle farm achieved; far more commonly the land or the 'improvements' will be sold to those with more capital or better access to credit. Even if INCORA have not granted freehold titles to the land, title to the improvements is relatively secure and well recognised by Brazilian standards; it may well have been cadastrally registered. Peacefully and legally, the colonist then functions as a cheap way of clearing forest for pasture, which is then cheaply appropriated for ranching. In Caquetá, a World Bank project has shown that credit facilities do enable the colonists to take the farmer road, achieving about fifty head of cattle on fifty hectares: given exceptional access to credit at critical stages, debts are met and farms as well as ranches prove practicable. Normally, the credit is much cheaper and more accessible for the already prosperous.

Cattle breeding and even fattening then become counterseasonal strategies, whose success is an element in what Parsons (1976) has called the 'grass revolution of the American tropics' and Feder (1979) 'hamburger and frankfurter imperialism' or 'a vast, continent-wide strategy to turn Latin America into one big cattle ranch'. Although Falesi (1974, 1976) and Alvim (1980) see ranching as viable for the Amazonian habitat, the agroecosystem is unproductive, wages are low, employment is extremely low (Feder 1979; Souza Martins 1980). Ranching in Amazonia is extractive: it collects and removes in the cattle the few nutrients of an oligotrophic ecosystem while absentee landlords do the same for the profits.

The primitive accumulation in which Amerindian groups with their highly diverse subsistence strategies and frontier farmers with their assortment of cropping patterns are dispossessed of their land by large landowners or capitalist entrepreneurs for cattle ranches is very differently mediated in different social formations. Foweraker (1981) has uncovered the role of violence in Brazil and the mediation of the State; elsewhere, violence still occurs but may receive less tacit support from the State where other devices are available. The same cycle of land use may be found in Mexico with massive support from the World Bank (Feder 1979) and in Costa Rica (Spielmann 1974) where violence is relatively uncommon and a myth of rural concensus is widely held (Seligson 1979). Probably the interaction of expensive credit and seasonal stress operates widely on the pioneer frontier to displace colonists, often without the violence and legal complexities of Brazil. But situations change: reports suggest that recently in Colombia, INCORA has almost ceased titling land, and farmers have been forcibly dispossessed by gunmen of land to which they hold full freehold title; they appear to be without redress. Violence is, of course, widespread in Colombia and seems now to be incorporated into class conflict on the frontier for purposes which were served for twenty years by habitat and socio-economic structure.

The capitalist modes of production in the Amazon basin (restricting ourselves to non-mineral primary production) naturally manage the possibility of seasonality rather differently. Cattle ranching is a suitable counterseasonal strategy where both land and cattle are cheap as it simply evades certain heavy seasonal costs. Lumbering is able to deploy seasonal labour for a necessarily seasonal activity. In a few areas, production and transport costs render cropping economic on a permanent, high-energy, high-technology basis. The economics of hydroponic rice and timber plantations at Jarí remain obscure. Of the great variety of other forms of production, none appear likely to expand greatly in the short term. Fully capitalist relations of production are rare in rural areas and a strong dependence on pre-capitalist modes is common.

What are the possibilities? Research by North Carolina State University at Yurimaguas, Peru, suggests that 'continuous production can be achieved in the Amazon with adequate fertilisation': that appropriate fertiliser will enable continuous cultivation of basic food crops or good pasture on most level sites in Amazonia (Sánchez *et al.* 1982). Most colonists — and indeed most Andean peasants — would reply that appropriate fertiliser is rarely available in the lowlands and almost never economic for basic foods, while advice as to which is the appropriate fertiliser is totally unavailable. Large landowners can get soil tests and suitable fertiliser, and on occasion do — in Colombia, usually for pasture. Any sustained breakthrough in the economic application of fertiliser in the lowlands will lead to rapid capitalist penetration.

Interest among researchers at present is more among more diverse, low-energy strategies. In 1964, Tosi and Voertman argued that the importation of grain-and-pasture agroecosystems to the humid tropics has been inappropriate, and that imitation forest agroecosystems should be developed. This is now a widely held view; Uhl and Murphy (1981), for instance, submit from work with diverse *conuco* systems on the Río Negro (southern Venezuela) that natural succession provides a model for the construction of sustained-yield agroecosystems. Field trials are under way in lowland Peru (Rios 1979), lowland Ecuador (Bishop 1979), near Manaus and possibly (Brisco 1979) on the Jarí project. Such strategies would by definition be counterseasonal and imply a shift from specialisation to diversity; the prospective systems are often described as the base for a prosperous peasant economy, notionally on the southeast Asian model (Kunstadter *et al.* 1978). At present, 'forest garden' production is far more a feature of Middle America (Wilken 1977; CATIE 1979) than of Amazonia. Polycultural swidden does occur in Amazonia, but Amazon Indians more often plant their fields 80 to 95% with manioc and solve their production problems with long fallow (Moran 1981). Substantial investment in research and extension would be required to promote diverse sustained-yield agroforestry; this is impossible for the peasants and appears not to interest any fraction of capital. Research and development is far more in ranching and in monocultural plantations – *Gmelina arborea* and *Pinus caribea* at Jarí, *Guilielma gasipaes* (peach palm) for Del Monte cattle feed in Costa Rica.

Technically, agroforestry has great attractions as a diverse, counterseasonal agroecosystem providing excellent nutrition and high employment. But it will not in itself provide satisfactory food systems in lowland Amazonia save in a context of major structural change.

## Conclusion

In Latin America today, most agricultural change in tropical areas is either towards increased seasonal stress or towards the one counterseasonal strategy which is ecologically undesirable and does nothing to solve the problems of poverty: cattle ranching.

Seasonal analysis, preferably on an interdisciplinary basis, offers an important tool both to critical theorists and to reformists. Where there is acute seasonal stress, it is unlikely that simple intervention which identifies the 'enemy' as habitat seasonality will be effective, or so the case of northeast Brazil suggests: nor can capitalist accumulation be stopped in its tracks. Nevertheless, seasonal analysis can do much to identify events certain to lead to permanent impoverishment at the household level: downward ratchets may easily be created by compound effects of seasonality. Seasonality *per se* remains a function of both habitat seasonality and culture, but a clearer apprehension of the nature of habitat seasonality at a particular site may be critical to understanding the role of local practices and external influences in actual seasonal stress.

Seasonality problems and counterseasonal strategies in Latin America demonstrate the importance of seasonality itself. We can identify complex and successful traditional counterseasonal strategies, but we find that many were reduced or destroyed in the colonial period and that (more important for present purposes) many are under threat today. Seasonality proves important not only in case and regional studies but in work on thematic topics as diverse as nutrition, transport and labour. Finally, local, national and international mechanisms are involving seasonality as just one more ratchet which works upwards for the haves and downward for the have-nots. If a significant fraction of the funds being poured into research and development of beef-cattle production in the tropics could be diverted into counterseasonal strategies leading at least to a high level of permanent employment, food systems in the Amazon Basin might be somewhat more secure.

# 8 Replacement of traditional elites: an Amazon case study

DARREL MILLER

## Introduction

The economic and social development of the Brazilian Amazon since the construction of the Transamazon and other Amazon Basin highways has been the focus of research in a variety of disciplines. Much of this research has been concerned with the small-farm sector (Moran 1975, 1981; Kleinpenning 1975; Smith 1976a; Fearnside 1978; Wood and Schmink 1979). The results of this research chronicles the structural, economic, and ecological constraints which have worked against unqualified success for the colonists and migrants who continue to flock to the region.

In spite of overwhelming evidence to the contrary, we must keep in mind that there have been some *limited* successes. Moran (1981) estimates that 40% of the colonists in the *agrovila* where he did his initial study are surviving as small farmers in spite of the constraints. Elsewhere, I have noted that a new urban middle class has been created in a number of small cities which lay in the path of the Transamazon Highway (Miller 1979, 1982). The creation of this new middle class is a direct result of the federally-funded Transamazon project, but I should hasten to point out that this was not a component of the original Transamazon plan nor does it in any way compensate for the many failures among the colonists in the small-farm sector. It does, however, point up a common pattern. In rural Brazil, commercialisation and industrialisation have opened up new opportunities, but these new opportunities 'have most often often been taken by commercial elites and few real benefits have accrued to the rural peasantry' (Forman 1975 p. 84).

In this paper, I should like to focus on another aspect of 'success' in the Transamazon region – namely the replacement of traditional elites by members of the urban middle class from other areas of Brazil. This latter group, by competing and, in many cases, by totally replacing the former, have become the new local elite. As such, they represent a new pattern for the Amazon – one which sees the further intrusion of the national social and economic model into Brazil's last frontier (Velho 1976; Cardoso and Müller 1977; Fleming–Moran and Moran 1978). By elites, I am simply referring to a small minority within a community who wield power. In no sense am I referring to elites in Lipset's (1967) terms as being prerequisites for development. I use this term because of the problems associated with using categories such as lower, middle, and upper class in such disparate communities as São Paulo and the small riverine cities in the Amazon Basin.

Much of the impetus for these changes has come from the tax incentives and investment opportunities available to large-scale investors under the First and Second National Development Plans (PND I and PND II) in addition to the extensive highway construction and colonisation provisions of the former. In fact, with the de-emphasis of colonisation under the PND II, major investors have become dominant in many frontier areas encouraged by the POLAMAZONIA programme (cf. Mahar 1979). Schmink (1981 p. 26) notes that about two-thirds of the land in the *município* of São Felix do Xingu (located in the southeastern corner of the State of Pará) has been reserved for large-scale investors even before the highway (PA279) to the community has been completed.

Despite such conditions, the traditional elite do not simply disappear when large-scale investors begin to move in. One of the principal foci of this paper will be the discussion of areas of conflict between the two groups and the outcome of these conflicts. The data will show that: (1) traditional elites did not disappear but lost some of their power (both political and economic); (2) some traditional elites survived by carving out new niches or reserving old ones for themselves; (3) new elites had most success in the economic sphere; (4) resentment and antagonism existed between traditional and new elites; and (5) elites migrate in and out of Amazon communities in accordance with economic cycles and, as a result, most have no roots in the community. The data on which these conclusions are based were collected in the *municípios* of Gurupá and Itaituba in the State of Pará in 1974 and 1976–77.[1] The first section of the paper will present the traditional economy and elites of the Amazon. The second section will examine a specific community on Brazil's Transamazon Highway. The third and fourth sections will discuss the areas of conflict within that community, and the last section will review the processes involved and place them in the context of regional economic fluctuations.

## Traditional elites of the Amazon

The term 'elite' as it is used in this paper – a small minority who exercise power within a community – is particularly appropriate to describe the elites in traditional, riverine Amazon communities. These traditional elites, often no more than one or two families in a community, can be traced back to the original traders who set up trading posts in and around Indian villages. The trader functioned as the local power broker between the outside world and those living within the parameters of his trading area. His position, although all-powerful within his trading area, was still rather low in the hierarchy of 'multiple dependencies' which characterise the economic history of the Amazon Basin (Cardoso and Müller 1977 p. 13) – one based on extractivism and a dependency on the international or national market.

One of the best known and most important products extracted from the Amazon tropical forest is rubber. Although rubber was not the first – a long list of jungle products precedes it during the first three centuries of European contact – it was certainly the most widely extracted and has left a legacy in almost every Amazon community, including those which will be used as case studies in this paper. For this reason, I should like to present a brief description of some salient features of the rubber boom years which have a direct link to the analysis of present-day elites.

By 1870, the demand for raw rubber began the largest economic boom the Amazon had yet experienced. The distribution of rubber trees over the Amazon rainforest was, of course, not equal nor were all areas equal in terms of quality of the rubber extracted. The quality and quantity of the latex as well as location on a major trade route were all factors which affected the economic success of communities or trading posts located throughout the Amazon. The labour force working the rubber trails during the boom period – approximately 1870–1914 – came mainly from the northeast of Brazil. Except for a few towns and cities, the rubber areas were remote outposts with few modern amenities available to the vast majority of those involved in the collection of rubber. Immigrants, lured to the Amazon by tales of vast riches, for the most part found the life exacting and the rewards few.[2]

The elites during the boom period lived primarily in the cities of Belém and Manaus. Opulence and extravagance became the norm as wealthy rubber barons imported the best Europe had to offer, built palatial houses, and attended social and cultural events patterned after those in European capitals. Both cities boasted opera houses and other modern conveniences. But not all elites were residents of the two major cities of the Amazon. Charles Wagley (1976) gives a detailed description of local rubber barons in the town of Itá. The lifestyle of the elite was similar to that of the two state capitals – only lacking the scale. Even lesser-known towns, such as Itaituba, located on the Tapajós river, evidenced some of the elite excesses of the rubber years. Although it could not match the amenities of Itá as described by Wagley, Itaituba could boast a post office, a grand town hall, eight or nine stores, a bakery, and a row of large houses parallel to the river where the important traders and functionaries lived. An article in a local newspaper of the time describes the town hall as decorated with carpets, crystal chandeliers, vases of French porcelain and mirrors bordered with marble from Carrara, Italy. Houses were built in the colonial style with balconies. Foodstuffs and merchandise were imported exclusively from Europe.[3]

By 1914 Asian rubber began to reach European markets and as the price of rubber fell it was accompanied by a concomitant drop in commerce and population in the Amazon Basin. Although the rubber trade has never fully died out – fluctuations occurred during the late 1930s and World War II (Murphy 1960 p. 46) – the rubber barons and most of the traders and merchants left the Amazon leaving behind a labour force (though many of them also emigrated) and a hierarchical social system for organising the labour force. Population in Itá and Itaituba had dropped by two-thirds and one-half, respectively, by 1920.

The rubber barons, itinerant river traders, trading-post operators, merchants, functionaries, and rubber collectors who occupied positions within the social hierarchy came principally from outside Amazonia. They came to earn their fortunes and then to return to their native states. Natives of the region came out into the hinterlands and, if and when their fortunes were made, returned to the urban centres of Belém and Manaus. In the case of Itaituba, it is interesting to note that informants referred to three or four leading merchants who dealt in rubber during World War II when the region experienced a mini rubber boom. None of these merchants or their families operated in Itaituba during the first rubber boom. Almost all of the original rubber elite left Itaituba after the boom turned into a bust. Those few families or individuals who remained returned to the ways of the old itinerant river traders and traded up and down the river. The merchants who arrived in Itaituba during World War II were newcomers to the region. Three of the four major merchants during that period came from the Northeast. The fourth was a native of a city near Belém. In brief, the merchants (and I believe to some extent all immigrants to Amazonia) came to exploit an extractive economic boom, to make their fortunes, and then to return to more urban areas in other regions.

## A Transamazon community

The *município* of Itaituba in the southwest corner of the State of Pará provides an excellent example of the fate of traditional local elites in the face of rapid change. A *município* rich in natural resources and land (the largest in area in Brazil) historically it has followed the traditional Amazon cyclical economic pattern. It is traversed from south to north by the Tapajós river, which served as a major transportation route for the extraction of tropical forest products and served as a trade route between Mato Grosso and the cities of Pará (Tocantins 1877). Its location in the path of the Transamazon Highway and the concomitant massive immigration has made it one of the major growth areas in the Amazon. The rubber era was probably the zenith of the community's history, but the current 'highway' boom has far surpassed that period in terms of growth and change.

The town of Itaituba today, with a population of 20 000 according to the 1980 census, is strikingly different from the Itaituba of the pre-highway period. Pictures of Itaituba during the early and late 1960s show a bucolic, rural, isolated Amazon village – largely unchanged since the years following the rubber boom. First Street, parallel to the river, is covered with grass in many places. Colonial-style houses with tile roofs line one side and a number of large mango trees line the other. Cattle and horses graze along the riverfront. Few people are walking in the street except for a small group in front of the post office and one of the two trading posts. The only vehicles are the trucks owned by the *município* or one of the local merchants.

Today, First Street is alive with activity. Although it is still a dirt street, there is very little grass. A taxi stand is situated near one of the mango trees at the dock. Businesses and agencies occupy almost all the empty lots. Street lights and electric wires run along the new sidewalk. The lack of heavy automobile traffic is due primarily to the poor condition of the street rather than a lack of vehicles. A cloud of dust hangs over the busiest areas during the dry season and during the wet season small rivulets turn the street into an exaggerated washboard.

The business district has spread to Second Street which during the early 1960s was primarily a residential street with mango trees down the centre and little more than a patch to serve pedestrian traffic. Today, Second Street carries more vehicle traffic than any other street. The mango trees are all gone, as are most of the residences. Stores and other businesses line both sides of the street from one end of town to the other. Traffic makes crossing the street difficult at times. Litter, mud, and dust attest to the street designation as Federal Route BR230 (the Transamazon Highway) through Itaituba.

On Third and Fourth Streets in the 1960s residents had to continually keep cutting back the encroaching forest. Now there are no more lots for building. Residential areas stretch an additional twenty blocks into the forest. Neighbourhood stores, churches and housing for wealthier residents dot this area where ten years ago only the socio-economically marginal townspeople lived. Many of the latter have been selling their ramshackle houses built on now-expensive lots and building much better houses in new neighbourhoods. Automobiles, electricity and running water are now facts of life in every neighbourhood.

Growth in Itaituba over the last twelve years is attributable to two main factors – the Transamazon Highway and the exploitation of numerous deposits of fluvial gold in the interior of the *município*. In 1970, construction on the Altamira to Itaituba section of the Transamazon Highway began in the west at Itaituba. In 1972 the highway was opened from Estreito on the Belém–Brasília highway to Itaituba and in 1974 a second section was opened to Humaitá in the west. By that time the segment of the Santarém–Cuiabá highway north of the Transamazon had been completed and the southern section to Cuiabá was completed in early 1976. Major sections of each highway passed through the *município* intersecting at a point near the town of Itaituba. The construction of these two highways and the planned colonisation carried out by the federal colonisation agency (INCRA) provided impetus for a tremendous growth spurt. By 1974 there were 8000 residents in the town in addition to the colonists living along the Transamazon Highway. At about this same time policy at the federal level began to shift away from small farming and colonisation. Planners felt that agricultural goals could not be met given the natural and institutional constraints. Indeed, with the poor quality of soils around Itaituba and problems of credit, transportation, storage and the like, life for small farmers along the Transamazon both east and west of Itaituba was at no better than the subsistence level.[4]

The road, however, remained a key factor in the growth of Itaituba even though the Second National Development Plan (PND II) envisioned the Amazon as a 'resource frontier' (Mahar 1979 p. 26). In 1975 the POLAMAZONIA programme appeared defining Itaituba's development role as a '*polo de mineração*' (mining pole). The national Mineral Resources Research Company (CPRM) began surveying the *município* in 1976 and found large deposits of limestone in a colonisation area and a newly designated national park. Neither seemed suitable (cost-wise) for extraction anytime in the near future. Concurrent with colonisation and highway construction, the extraction of gold continued. The gold deposits were hardly a recent discovery. Tocantins (1877 p. 90) reports that the explorer Jõao de Sousa Azevedo extracted gold at two places during an eighteenth-century expedition up the Tapajós. By 1981, aided by the facilities of overland transport and the increased urban amenities, the number of miners (*garimpeiros*) had increased to 40 000 and the number of mines (*garimpos*) to several hundred. Itaituba had become the supply, transportation, and personnel headquarters for a major gold rush.

Policy planners had originally hoped to resettle countless Northeasterners on their own lands in the Amazon and, at the same time, make the area at least self-sufficient in food production if not a net exporter of food. With the policy shift toward mining, it was hoped that the country would be able to export vast mineral riches. Instead, although still roughly in the category of mining, we have a traditional Amazon boom based on the extraction of a relatively limited resource which, when it is exhausted, will leave the community without an economic mainstay. In the interim, however, Itaituba is flourishing economically and supporting a significant elite group. The following two sections will present the major arenas – economic and political – of the elites in Itaituba.

## The economic area

Emphasis on economic matters in the Amazon merely reflects the importance of the extractive model in understanding the attitudes of those who have settled there either temporarily or permanently over the past three centuries. The Amazon has long had the image of a vast treasure trove ripe for plundering. The attitudes of the current economic elite – landowners, merchants, and the like – are no different. The outsiders who have recently arrived because of the Transamazon boom, who are economically successful and have thus been recognised as 'elite', came for many of the same reasons as the traditional local elite who arrived during earlier boom periods. None the less, attitudes of the traditional elite towards the newly arrived entrepreneurs reflect their very real misgivings about losing control of the commercial sphere. The traditional elite see the newcomers as opportunists who are crowding an already very crowded economic sector. The more urban lifestyle of many of the newcomers is seen as inappropriate for life in a rural community. Observation of actual behaviour revealed that the traditional elite were involved in exploiting almost every new economic sector and were, thereby, just as opportunistic as the newcomers. The younger members of traditional elite families often socialised with the newcomers and to an even greater extent, adapted aspects of their lifestyle.

Identifying members of the current elite according to specific criteria was extremely difficult. Using income as a criterion was next to impossible, since informants were less than candid about total earnings. As a result, I used ownership of a major business, ownership of large tracts of land or of central city real estate, and participation in elite community events. Of a total of 326 merchants, landowners and professionals in the city of Itaituba, using very liberal interpretations of the parameters, 69 individuals or families could be identified as 'elites'. These included 36 bureaucrats, politicians or professionals and 33 merchants and landowners. Some individuals overlapped categories. When this occurred, the individual was classified according to his full-time or most important activity. Of the former group, 10 had lived in Itaituba in the pre-highway period. They will be discussed in greater detail in the next section. Of the merchants and landowners, only seven dated from the pre-highway period. Of these seven, three date from World War II or before, three arrived in the early 1960s and one is a native of the region but born in 1949. An effort was made to trace former elite families who had fallen on hard times. Two families who had been considered elite in the past were located. Their life histories revealed a gradual fall from elite status beginning before the highway boom. Three other families had moved from Itaituba after the highway came, but little is known of their current residence or status.

According to the above data, approximately one-quarter (26 per cent) of the individuals classified as elites are members of the traditional elite. Less than one-half of those (10 per cent of the total) are active in the commercial or business sphere and less than one-half of that group (4 per cent of the total) can be traced back to the original rubber-trading elite. Judging from the historical records and interviews with older informants, this does not represent a wholesale replacement of the traditional elite by newcomers. Considering that the traditional elite had almost total control over the economic sector in pre-highway times, these individuals saw their monopoly broken in a significantly expanded local economy. Interviews with several of the traditional elite revealed a strong resentment that their fortunes did not rise geometrically with the expanded economy. It would be revealing to establish the extact proportion of the economy which they control, but the data are incomplete and I suspect reliable data is unattainable. However, in all seven cases the merchants agreed that they were financially much better off with the coming of the highway than they were before.

Five of the traditional elites are merchants. Each was able to capitalise on the rapid population expansion during the early 1970s. A composite picture of their methods and approaches will provide an example of their ability to find new niches. Data are based primarily on the life histories of three specific individuals, but may be generalised to all five. Each of the merchants dealt in the trading of rubber, Brazil nuts and Amazon hardwoods until the mid-to-late 1960s when gold mining began in earnest in a variety of *garimpos* scattered through the *município*. At this point in time, those men involved in the collection of rubber abandoned their rubber trails and began panning for gold. This change required a concomitant adjustment on the part of the merchants. One abandoned his itinerant trading up- and downriver to establish a store for provisioning *garimpos*, another set up a bakery, and the third, Itaituba's most successful merchant who held the rubber concession for the entire *município*, also focused his attention on buying gold and provisioning the *garimpos*.

By the early 1970s, each merchant had adjusted to a change in the primary extractive product in the *município*. The community had also undergone a slight increase in population (from 1300 to 2000). With the beginning of construction of the highway from Itaituba eastward towards Altamira, population, services, and lifestyles have not stopped changing.

With the arrival of construction crews in 1970, and the first colonists two years later, all merchants began to expand their operations. This meant stocking a greater variety and quantity of goods along with improving marketing techniques to correspond more closely with those in urban centres in other parts of Brazil. Two merchants presently operate large (for the Amazon) general merchandise stores with many of the trappings of supermarkets and department stores. A third has opened a combined appliance, office supply and furniture store including a xerographic service.

The remaining traditional elite members became more directly involved in the buying of gold and provisioning of mines. Both arrived in Itaituba in the early 1960s, working in various *garimpos* as merchant or miner or both. One has become Itaituba's wealthiest citizen, employing several thousand miners, operating several planes and warehouses as well as owning 20 000 hectares of land and 3000 head of cattle. He, and his colleague, were the first to realise the importance of Itaituba as a central warehousing point for provisions and a base for the small planes which are the only transportation link to the mines. The opening of the highway only strengthened Itaituba's role, as goods could be brought in by truck from southern Brazil in greater quantities and at lower prices. With the current gold boom in the *município* (estimates centre around US\$ 3000 000 000 per year), those involved in buying gold are only becoming wealthier.[5]

The increasing wealth of the gold buyers is in marked contrast to the stagnant or decreasing fortunes of the five merchants mentioned above. Increasing competition and fluctuations in the economy have taken their toll. Newcomers bring with them new ideas, new methods, a greater access to capital and credit and more experience in dealing with the bureaucracies which tax or oversee many aspects of local business. In short, the greater intrusion of the nation economy and the state and federal bureaucracies have created new conditions which are beginning to outweigh the initial advantages of the traditional local elite. One merchant is currently in serious economic difficulty. Others could soon follow.

From the discussion of specific cases, one can see a trend toward the replacement of some of the traditional elite in the commercial sector. Cattle and landholdings by each have remained largely unaffected to date. The gold buyers are riding the crest of yet another Amazon boom, and if their gains are invested wisely, they should retain their elite status. Certainly, however, the total control the traditional elite had over the economy is lost. Similar trends and consequences are also present in the political arena discussed in the next section.

## The political arena

Three separate groups are most visible in the political arena. They include the municipal government, the bureaucrats employed by the various state and federal agencies, and the military officers stationed at the army base ($53^a$BIS). There are certainly other individuals and groups involved in political events within the community (cf. L. Miller 1981), but the three above-mentioned groups are the most powerful and best organised. The concerns and arenas of all three groups overlap somewhat, but each has a specific power base. For those involved in municipal government, there is control over the municipal budget and allocation of municipal lands. The various bureaucracies have their individual budgets and control over resources in almost all sectors of the community as well as linkages with powerful individuals and/or bureaucracies at the state and national levels. The local military officers, in a nation ruled by the military, have considerable prestige and power owing to their membership in the national ruling group.

The Transamazon region is a national security area (*área de segurança nacional*). As such, the mayors of the communities in the path of the highway must be appointed by the president. In addition to the mayor, there are eight municipal councillors and a small administration encompassing the mayor's office, a vice-mayor (chosen from among the eight councillors), a treasurer (chosen from among the councillors), a purchasing agent, and a secretariat headed by an elected Secretário do Município, who handles some administrative details and assists the mayor in some of his tasks. The eight councillors and the secretary of the *município* are elected, ideally, every four years. The last scheduled elections were in the fall of 1981.

The mayor of Itaituba has served, at the pleasure of the federal government, since 1969. He was elected to that office in 1954 and served as mayor from 1955 to 1958. He and two other men have served as mayor of Itaituba, alternating terms, since 1951. All three men are still active in local politics. All are members of the local elite dating from World War II and before. Traditionally, the office of mayor has been extremely important in the Amazon. Given the boom-bust nature of the economy of that region, the municipal budget represents the one continuous and assured source of income although, granted, it is relatively small when compared to more 'developed' communities. In times of economic hardship, having a position or job with the municipal government means that one has an assured cash income to buy foodstuffs and manufactured goods not locally produced, whereas others must turn (or return) to subsistence farming and hunting to feed their families. For example, in the Amazon River *município* of Gurupá in 1974, the export-prohibition on unprocessed logs led to the collapse of the local lumbering industry. Temporary municipal jobs such as cutting the grass in the plaza or paving a street became important sources of income and political favours for the mayor. It is not surprising, then, that residents in almost all Amazon *municípios* look upon the mayor as an intercessor between themselves and the state government – the ultimate dispenser of goods, services, and benefits.

Taking into account the historic role of municipal governments in the Amazon, it is not surprising that in an era of intense development activities, economic expansion, and population growth, the local elite in Itaituba have reserved the arena of local government for themselves. All eight members of the municipal council are long-term residents dating from before the coming of the Transamazon Highway. They include two former mayors, three merchants, a notary, a lawyer, and a pharmacist. Although each has a full-time occupation, all are also involved in cattle raising and/or land speculation. As in the case of São Felix do Xingu noted by Schmink (1981), the distribution of land in the municipal agricultural colony adjacent to the city and distribution of lots in new residential areas have netted substantial financial gains for all councillors. One, who owns a small bar, devotes much of his time to convincing the poorer residents to trade their dilapidated housing on valuable central city property for new houses on lots in newer neighbourhoods. The councillor then sells the lots for a considerable profit to merchants in the expanding commercial district. Land is a perennial investment for local elites; however, confusion over land titles has reduced total local investments in land to those areas in which INCRA, the colonisation and agrarian reform agency, can give 'clear' titles. It is interesting to note that purchases of large tracts of land as reported by Schmink (1981) for São Felix do Xingu and in the Marabá sector have not occurred in Itaituba. Purchases of large tracts of land are principally for the purpose of raising cattle. Transportation to market and the suitability of the terrain for cattle raising have proven to be negative constraints for that type of development in Itaituba. Cattle raising for local consumption is practised by several local landowners. At present gold is a much more lucrative investment.

Control of the local purse-strings and other financial advantages linked to control of the local government have kept a small group of the local elite in a position to compete with a tide of outsiders who have surpassed them in other sectors. Indeed, in both the neighbouring Transamazon Highway *municípios* of Altamira and Marabá, technocrats from outside the community have been appointed mayors, thus eliminating many or all of the advantages local elites might have accrued from total control of the municipal government.

A second political arena involves the bureaucrats working for the 28 state and federal agencies (as compared to seven in the pre-highway period). All top administrators, except for the post office and the state school system, come from large urban areas outside of the Tapajós region. The practice of sending state tax collectors and other bureaucrats from the state capital to rural and isolated *municípios* is a common one for the Amazon. This was true for the *município* of Gurupá in 1974 and in 1948 (Wagley 1976 p. 106). Wagley noted that these bureaucrats from outside the community were considered 'First Class' largely due to their high and steady salaries. In Itaituba today the relatively high salaries (some receive a hardship supplement for having to work in such a backwater) set the bureaucrats apart from most of the local population and also from the local elite. They also have proportionately more education (at least into the secondary level) and considerably more urban experience which allows them to take advantage of available credit at banks and benefits offered by any of the other agencies.

The administrators who work in Itaituba can carry out their jobs in any way they see fit. Few supervisors in the state capital view a trip to Itaituba with much relish. Thus, there is considerable latitude for local administrators with a concomitant lack of communication with the next administrative level. This, along with the aforementioned advantages, has allowed a high proportion of upper-level administrators to dabble in entrepreneurial activities in almost every sector of the economy. Several have made considerable financial gains in agricultural commodities (primarily upland rice) and gold mining.

None of the bureaucrats has attempted to become involved in local politics. Most are hoping for an eventual posting to an office in a larger city or a financial killing in one of their extra-agency dealings. None expressed a long-term commitment to Itaituba. They have families and roots elsewhere and represent a transient component of the local elite. Their lifestyles and attitudes make them stand out in sharp contrast to the traditional elites while at the same time providing the local residents with a look at urban Brazilian lifestyles. This difference in lifestyles has caused a revolution in the commercial sector, bringing the significant changes discussed in the previous section.

A final group in the political arena are the military officers from the army base ($53^a$BIS). In many respects, the officers are similar to the administrators and bureaucrats in terms of educational level, high salary, and urban experience but they are distinctly different in that they are representatives of the ultimate national authority and as such are the ultimate arbiters of law and order in Itaituba. Indeed, before the establishment of the army base, law and order was a haphazard affair handled by a local sheriff (*delegado*) and three assistants. The sheriff was more or less diligent and generally handled things in a personalistic style. The circuit judge appeared every six months to try serious cases. With the immediate presence of the military, the current sheriff is diligent in enforcing laws in the urban areas of the *município* and attempts to control crime in the more isolated *garimpos* in the interior.

In discussions with military officers, it was clear that they perceived their role as bringing civilisation to the interior, or as one officer put it, 'educating the poor *caboclos*'. Indeed, military personnel provided a number of much-needed services in both formal and informal programmes. One of the military doctors manned a mobile medical unit which provided medical care to rural areas on a regular monthly basis. The other opened up an office in town to serve the urban residents. The base dentist saw local residents in his office three mornings a week and provided free dental care to children in the town's four elementary schools. Nineteen-year-olds from Itaituba and the surrounding area received their basic training at the base including instruction (and assistance) in maintaining proper hygiene, securing necessary documentation (such as drivers' licences, identification cards, social security cards and worker identification cards), and other similar learning experiences which would, to a greater or lesser degree, make them more productive members of Brazilian society.

On a more informal level, officers' wives formed the nucleus of the middle-school (grades 5–8) faculty due to their high levels of education attained in other regions of Brazil. The base frequently contributed funds and manpower to a wide variety of community events: athletic, social and civic. Because of their position as local representatives of a national elite, army officers were much sought after as patrons for such events, a very clear indication of their elite status.

In short, even in the absence of direct election of top local officials, a considerable expansion of the political sector has occurred concomitant with population growth spurred by extensive immigration. It is not surprising, therefore, to see outsiders – agency administrators and military officers – assuming positions among the political elite. The traditional local elite have been partially replaced as sole power brokers in the political arena.

## Conclusions

The case of Itaituba demonstrates what occurs when traditional elites face a new set of conditions and are placed in direct competition with representative individuals of urban middle-cass backgrounds. For the traditional local elite in Itaituba, there were many initial advantages to being in the community at the beginning of the highway boom. Individuals with a small amount of capital were able to capitalise on economic growth in the commercial and land sectors. But along with the construction workers and colonists, came other entrepreneurs, bureaucrats, etc., who also wanted to cash in on the boom. Although many of these were at a distinct disadvantage in terms of knowledge of the local community and ownership of land, they brought with them a number of advantages including, most importantly, experience with the national Brazilian society and economy.

What I expected to find when I first asked myself about traditional elites during my fieldwork, was a gradual and almost total replacement. Of course, this did not occur. The local traditional elites showed a surprising degree of flexibility and adaptability to the changing conditions and increased competition. In fact, almost all of the local elite in Itaituba at the beginning of construction of the highway are still active and viable members of the current elite group. Some, particularly three councillors, owe their current status more to their social position in pre-highway times than to any business or entrepreneurial acumen. For the most part, they are successful. They do not have, however, the degree of control over the community they once had. They are simply a few among many, although most admit that they are financially better off. Sharing membership in the elite group and the 'spoils' from 'their' community has created some resentment on the part of the traditional elite. By the same token, some of the new elite remember the obstacles thrown in their path during the early days of the boom.

The economic sphere has proven to be the most lucrative for the newcomers, although positions in the bureaucracy have attracted many others. In 1977 there were over 300 entrepreneurs at all levels and almost 200 bureaucrats (including families, 6.7% of the population). Many more have probably arrived during the current gold boom. The traditional elite has managed to keep a foothold in both the economic and political arenas. Control over the municipal government has been their most successful area of influence.

Taking a broader perspective, the importance of regional economic cycles cannot be overestimated. With each economic boom, elites and peasantry alike have migrated to the Amazon. When the boom ends, depopulation occurs especially in the more isolated areas. In this region there are not vast numbers of landowners who are tied to the land. We so often hear of rural Brazilian peasantry migrating from the Northeast to southern Brazil and from the South to the new frontier areas, but throughout the history of the Amazon, elites have also migrated to make their fortune and then most often to return to their native region.

There are some indications that the current boom may be somewhat different. The intrusion of national social and economic institutions into the region has been unprecedented. Certainly, if gold becomes harder to find, there will be some degree of retrenchment, but the bureaucrats, the successful small farmers, the large landowners, and the merchants who serve them will most probably remain. The community's role as a transportation hub and the vast quantities of land still available will ensure its viability for some elites and non-elites alike.

## Acknowledgements

Professor Miller was formerly with the University of William and Mary, Williamsburg, Virginia.

1 Research for the 1974 field trip was sponsored by the Tropical South America Program at the University of Florida. The 1976–7 trip was sponsored by a grant from the Organisation of American States (PRA–54903).
2 See Castro (nd) for an account of an immigrant's experience in the Amazon.
3 Belém, Pará, 12 October, 1969.
4 Moran (1981) feels that this decision was made on the basis of incorrect analytical procedures by policy makers. He notes: 'The result is a structure of decision-making

insensitive to micro-level variability and with a tendency to homogenization of both environment and social variables.' (Moran 1981 p. 23).

5 I should note that the wealthy gold buyer mentioned here is classified as elite due to his economic status, but his lack of education, lowly family origins, and gruff demeanour make him an unsuitable guest in some elite homes.

# 9 Innovations in colonising Bolivian Amazonia

J. COLIN CROSSLEY

## Introduction

The history of directed colonisation in Bolivia over the last thirty years has been a catalogue of difficulties. Lessons from earlier experience have been applied with considerable success at San Julián where over 1600 families were settled in 1972–80. An important role has been played by a group of American missionaries inspired by the United States frontier experience. But are Bolivian circumstances comparable? More generally, can colonisation satisfy the aspirations of Bolivian small farmers for a higher standard of living?

## Recent history of colonisation

Official or directed schemes of colonisation in the Alto Beni, the Chapare and in parts of Santa Cruz (see Figure 1) have followed a common pattern in certain respects which has led to serious difficulties:

1 Inadequate care has been taken in the selection of land for settlement: much land in the Chapare later proved liable to flooding; some soils at Yapacani in Santa Cruz proved to be exceptionally infertile. The Alto Beni scheme was rescued from laying out holdings on the floodplain only by the timely advice of members of the British Tropical Agricultural Mission in 1963 (Crossley and Johnson 1977 pp. 20, 30, 32).

2 Holdings have been laid out in 'piano-key' fashion, as parallel rectangular strips fronting onto an access track. The construction of houses on such strips created physical and social isolation for the settlers and contributed to land abandonment. It also led to spontaneous migration to small towns and lesser nucleated settlements, from which the colonists now commute daily or weekly to work on their holdings (Crossley 1977 p. 8).

3 A tolerable road network has been constructed only several years after the foundation of the colony, the new settler normally finding only bulldozed trails. Thus the main highway to the Alto Beni thirteen years after its foundation was still only an unsurfaced if graded road, frequently impassable in wet weather. The Chapare and Cuatro Ojitos colonies in contrast enjoy asphalt highways to the outside world; yet in the latter, the author found in 1975, the majority of holdings remained accessible only by earth roads which had been recently graded through

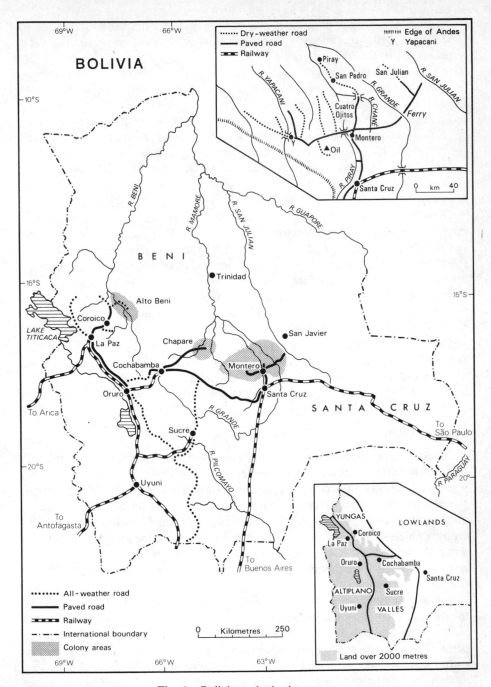

Fig. 1  Bolivia: colonisation areas

the collective effort of the settlers, over fifteen years after the colony's foundation. Under the worst conditions vehicular access is possible for only a few days at a time, even in the 'dry' season.

4 In plains areas lacking permanent streams, wells are necessary for water supply. Given the piano-key layout, it has been impossible to construct wells conveniently accessible to all.

5 Programmes of official assistance to the colonists have not been constructed carefully enough. Thus early settlers in the Alto Beni received credit requiring repayment long before their enterprises were commercially viable. More generally, aid has been given in a paternalistic way, creating dependence rather than self-reliance, and leaving the settler unable to cope when the programme has ended.

Given such problems it is not surprising that high annual rates of abandonment have been reported in directed colonies, for example 52 per cent in the Alto Beni, 46 per cent in the Chapare and 32 per cent at Yapacani during the period 1964–9 (INC/BID 1969 pp. 43–8). It should not be overlooked that spontaneous colonisation, accounting for large numbers of settlers but less well documented, has also suffered from all but the last of the difficulties discussed above.

Nevertheless to emphasise the failure and abandonment rates is to a degree misleading. Except where holdings have been left on account of their physical unsuitability, the land vacated has usually been taken over by new settlers or by neighbours. In a survey carried out in 1975 in the directed and spontaneous colonies of the Cuatro Ojitos/San Pedro/Piray district the author found no evidence of holdings being totally abandoned (except through flooding) or of their being acquired by large landowners (Crossley 1977 pp. 6–7).

## Piray Colony

In the Santa Cruz area the lands around and between the towns of Santa Cruz and Montero have for centuries been held in large estates. Colonisation by small farmers began only a third of a century ago, along three axes radiating from Montero: westwards through Yapacani (ultimately intended to link up with the Chapare), northwards through Cuatro Ojitos and San Pedro, and eastwards to the Rio Grande which served as a barrier during the 1960s. Along the northern axis, where directed colonisation (Cuatro Ojitos) had given place beyond the R. Chané to spontaneous ventures, the process ended in 1969 with the establishment of Piray Colony.

Still lacking adequate advice on land selection – some land has since proved liable to serious flooding – the colony also suffered from access problems: only a bulldozed trail provided a 5 km link to the seasonally open main road. From a social point of view, however, Piray marked a turning point in several respects. From the start it was intended that farmhouses should be built together in a nucleated village, though the farmlands of the 140 settlers continued to be laid out along traditional lines in the surrounding area. Secondly the settlers, who arrived together, were provided with a coordinated orientation programme designed to impart techniques of forest clearance, cultivation and house construction and to advise on hygiene and nutrition. The need for such a programme arose because most of the settlers came from the temperate highlands of western Bolivia, few having previously farmed on their own account in the tropical lowlands. Additionally a small revolving loan fund provided the resources for limited ventures into the productive use of credit. Finally the underlying spirit of the colony was a combination of self-reliance and mutual support underpinned by the establishment of community institutions of self-government based on participatory democracy.

The whole concept was slowly formulated by the organisers of Piray, a group of American and Bolivian members of the Methodist, Catholic and Mennonite churches who came together to form the United Churches Committee (Comité de Iglesias Unidas – CIU). Having worked individually for several years in the colonies in such fields as agriculture, education, nutrition, social work and pastoral care they had first formed a joint venture the previous year to assist in the rehabilitation of evacuees from a flood disaster. The resources for both projects came in the main from Oxfam, as well as the respective churches.

Visiting Piray in 1975 the author found an established community enjoying a lively self-government and now only periodically visited by the CIU. Credit facilities were about to be expanded, thanks to the interest taken by a large regional savings and loan cooperative. The colonists depended upon the arrival of merchants with trucks for the sale of their sole cash crop, rice. But collectively they decided upon the minimum price they would accept.

## The San Julian Colony

When CIU's preoccupation with Piray ended in 1971 it looked for new opportunities to repeat and refine its orientation programme. The National Colonisation Institute (Instituto Nacional de Colonización – INC) had in 1968 begun to settle the San Julián area, identified in 1966 by the British Mission as the largest area of moderately good soils in the lowlands still awaiting colonisation (Crossley and Johnson 1977 pp. 30, 32, 36). At first INC adopted the traditional layout of parallel strips beside a road, in this case that between the Rio Grande ferry and San Javier. This was shortly to become an all-weather highway designed as a section of a new national route linking La Paz and Santa Cruz via Trinidad.

However as CIU arrived on the scene INC was already planning to experiment with a new layout of holdings radiating from a central 2-ha communal plot. In this fashion houses could combine location on individual holdings with clustering to form a nucleated village (Figure 2, Inset). Each *núcleo* was to comprise 40 holdings of approximately 50 ha, together occupying a square block. The area allocated for each block, however, was to be 5 km square, the excess being devoted to roads, the central plot, and to a surrounding reserve of forest. In addition the *núcleos* were to be disposed about the main access road in the manner depicted in Figure 2, the intention being that the central *núcleo* of each group of nine would also assume certain central-place urban functions.

INC and CIU agreed to cooperate in settling colonists in *núcleos*, whose layout lent itself excellently to the operation of an orientation programme. Under the initial contract CIU was solely responsible for orientation. CIU was, however, unable to offer adequate human resources for a major settlement initiative. In the four years 1972–5 only seven *núcleos* were settled, the colonists totalling 233 and the CIU personnel never exceeding eight (Figure 2).

Meanwhile USAID, disillusioned by the results of earlier Bolivian-directed colonisation schemes, was impressed by the new programme at San Julián and offered financial support for its expansion. Under new agreements reached in 1975, INC, CIU and USAID combined in a five-year plan (1976–80) to settle 4440 families in *núcleos* disposed along a new all-weather highway. US loans to INC were to finance this road, the Brecha Casarabe, and lateral feeder roads as well as the installation of wells and pumps in the centre of each *núcleo*. CIU was to operate the orientation programme but INC was to assume progressively the financing of an expanded orientation team and ultimately its control. The president of CIU, an American, was also taken onto the INC payroll as trouble-shooter. Oxfam and the churches again funded CIU's part of the operation, with the British Ministry of Overseas Development co-funding the Oxfam share. In this manner therefore CIU hoped to be able to assist in the settling of far more people than it could otherwise have done and INC hoped to acquire new expertise in the hitherto deficient social component of its work.

In the event what has happened is judged by most observers, both outside and participating, to have been a success though one that must be qualified in certain directions. As a result additional international support has been forthcoming for the further development of San Julián. The CIU personnel are again participating, though they have now constituted themselves as a non-church organisation, the Integral Development Foundation (Fundación Integral de Desarrollo – FIDES).

During the second phase 1372 families have been settled in 34 *núcleos*. Although this constitutes only 31 per cent of the number planned, the rate of settlement has been almost five times that of the first phase of INC/CIU cooperation. In all, between 1968 and 1980, 1861 new farms have been created, including 256 of the earlier piano-key type, and an estimated total population of 5440 has been established on the land (for these and succeeding details, see INC/CIU 1981 and Figure 2). In the peak year 1977, orientation personnel rose to 32 (19 INC, 13 CIU) and declined at the end to 21 (17 INC, 4 CIU).

The costs of the 1976–80 phase are estimated at US$ 1 million, including salaries, infrastructure, supplies and transport, or $ 711 per settler. Excluded are the costs of constructing the main Brecha Casarabe highway and of INC posts already on the establishment. Roughly one-half was contributed by INC, one-third by CIU,

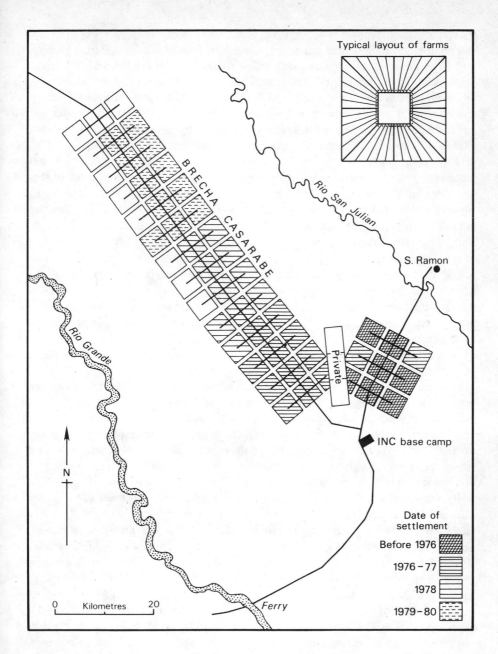

Typical layout of farms

BRECHA CASARABE

Río San Julian

S. Ramon

Private

Rio Grande

INC base camp

N

0    Kilometres    20

Ferry

Date of
settlement

Before 1976

1976 – 77

1978

1979 – 80

Fig. 2 San Julián colony

the rest being attributable to World Food Programme supplies.

The total area allotted to settlers at San Julián amounts to 96 000 ha, of which 30 500 lie along the national route (including piano-key holdings) and 65 500 along the Brecha Casarabe. In addition some 18 per cent of the land along the Brecha originally assigned for colonisation proved to be liable to flooding or to be subject to rival claims by private individuals or cooperatives. Future conflicts for the settlers were avoided either by early resolution of claims or by not proceeding to establish *núcleos* in disputed localities (Figure 2). Such action, while prudent, served to destroy the geometrical basis for designating a town for every nine *núcleos*. Legal security for the colonists comes only from the granting of titles and most of this work remains to be done. Because inadequate resources had been devoted to surveying the individual holdings, only 33 000 ha were ready in 1981 for the bureaucratically lengthy process of titling, and not a single title had been granted.

By Bolivian standards progress with road construction has been good: 88 per cent of *núcleos* received a graded and ditched road either before the arrival of settlers or during the orientation programme; all are now so provided. Surfacing the Brecha road has however stopped long before its end and lack of maintenance is causing the steady deterioration of all unsurfaced roads. Equally importantly, though outside the remit of the colonisation programme, no steps have been taken to replace the ferry across the Río Grande by a bridge. Worse still, surfacing of the Montero–ferry–San Javier highway was undertaken without any feasibility study of bridging the gap at that site. Recent studies reveal the cost of a bridge would be prohibitive. The alternatives under consideration are a site many kilometres downstream requiring new roads on either side of the river or utilising the existing railway bridge 60 km upstream and constructing even longer new roads. Until the problem is solved settlers at San Julián and indeed all inhabitants of the lands to the north and east will continue to suffer from the expensive and unreliable ferry service which effectively prohibits the commercial development of any highly perishable commodity that requires processing or marketing west of the river.

By the same standards provision of water supplies has also been good. Every *núcleo* had one well bored before or during the orientation programme. In a few cases however the water quality was so dangerous that several deaths were caused, and it was undesirably low in other cases. Following analyses in 1977 the Public Works Department recommended that settlement should be prohibited if analysis proved a supply to be unsafe. This recommendation was circumvented by seeking no further analyses prior to settlement.

The process of installation and orientation of settlers in each *núcleo* followed a standard pattern: INC was responsible for erecting in advance two communal dormitories and an eating hall and for recruiting and delivering the colonists in groups of 40 families. The arrival of new groups was phased over the early months (May to July) of the dry season. Any delay meant that the four-month programme and the preparation of the land for cultivation would not be completed before the onset of the summer rains and the colonists' future would be imperilled. On occasions CIU refused to start the programme when urged to accept groups too late in the season.

The orientation team comprised an agricultural extensionist, a home-improvement advisor, a promoter of cooperativism and a health auxiliary, all of whom cycled to each *núcleo* in turn to conduct courses and give advice, as well as social promoters one of whom was resident in each *núcleo* for the duration of the programme. In addition an administrator coordinated the work and drivers, and store-keepers and surveyors provided support. The American trouble-shooter regularly travelled between the central (La Paz), regional (Santa Cruz) and zonal (San Julián) offices of INC and the field in order to overcome problems and if necessary to circumvent bureaucratic delays by calling on the flexible resources of CIU. Radio transceivers provided essential communications for both normal purposes and emergencies. During the years 1977 to 1979 the team produced manuals for the guidance of new and future staff on such topics as agriculture, cooperativism, health promotion, nutrition, home improvement and social promotion.

The aims and tasks of the programme remained much as those outlined for Piray except that course contents were pared down to exclude theory and practical details not of immediate value and hence interest to the settler. Food was provided free by the programme using WFP supplies, local purchases and the *núcleo's* own vegetable garden. Other prime necessities were sold through a newly established system of consumer cooperatives. Although this was imposed from above, representatives in each *núcleo* were trained progressively to assume management responsibility.

According to the evaluation the communitarian aims would appear to have been reasonably successful. All *núcleos* continue to elect councils and to hold regular village meetings. Internal conflicts are resolved by the community. In all *núcleos* work on road maintenance is still done communally. At a higher level most groups of *núcleos* have elected councils, with largely recreational functions. These in turn have created a Federation of San Julián Settlers which, at the time of the author's visit in 1979, was venturing by its own initiative into the collective marketing of maize. The majority of *núcleos* retain a consumer cooperative with a combined membership of 800 and annual turnover of $ 100 000.

The extent to which these organisations are characterised by genuine participatory democracy remains unclear. Solidarity has certainly been undermined where ethnic differences exist within or between *núcleos* – highlanders from both Quechua and Aymara regions constitute, with the lowlanders, three groups of different language and culture. Conversely, *núcleos* composed of members of the same highland community have not exhibited the stability and leadership that might have been expected: the authoritarianism and conservatism of traditional leaders are ill-suited to the innovatory needs of the new environment.

Nor has the major role played by women in the orientation teams served at all to dent the traditional male domination of village society. This is however hardly surprising since the evaluators recognise that the (male-dominated) membership of CIU itself paid inadequate attention to the promotion of equality.

As at Piray a limited credit scheme started by CIU was expanded with the arrival of a large savings and loan cooperative. A branch office was opened in mid-1976 and by the start of 1981 the local membership, to whom responsibility had been delegated, totalled 600.

In the agricultural sphere colonists have naturally acquired the techniques of forest clearance, burning, and cultivation. The role of instructor played by small farmers of local origin has also helped to bridge the cultural gap. In contrast the programme appears largely to have failed in its endeavour, for sound economic and nutritional reasons, to promote self-sufficiency and the cultivation of a wide variety of legumes and other vegetables. The majority now grow only rice or maize.

The health status of the settlers remains basically unknown for lack of records. Whereas weights of both adults and children were regularly recorded during the months of the orientation programme – and the majority were found to have gained weight, contrary to the normal tendency – no subsequent measurements were made. Records of the INC medical service at its San Julián base camp reveal that gastroenteritis, pneumonia and skin diseases account for 71 per cent of outpatient treatments. The failure of INC to run a mobile doctor service, for lack of transport and commitment, was widely criticised. On the other hand there appears to have been a universal adoption of such preventive health measures as the use of latrines, which every settler was required to construct. Regular yellow fever, DTT (diphtheria, totasus and tetanus), measles and polio vaccinations, begun during the programme, have also continued.

From the colonists' point of view the best single criterion of success of the orientation programme ought to be the rates of abandonment of holdings. Data have however been collected only since 1975 and their presentation in the evaluation allows of more than one interpretation. Comparisons with national figures quoted previously cannot be made with confidence. The low rate of abandonment within a year of settlement (under 5 per cent) suggests considerable success in the programme's primary aim of easing the colonist's adjustment to his new environment. Yet, as the author was informed in 1979, participants who failed to complete the programme were not officially registered as settlers. Conversely the cumulative percentage for abandonments within four years (28) may exaggerate the real rate. Most holdings abandoned have been transferred to new settlers, in whose selection the original colonists have played a key role, preference being accorded to friends and relatives. Nevertheless, if abandonment rates by late arrivals is above average, the percentage of original settlers still in occupation after four years must exceed the implicit figure of 72.

In concentrating upon the needs of newly arrived settlers the orientation programme by design excluded consideration of problems that would emerge subsequently, such as the maintenance of soil fertility and the development of markets. Given its limited resources and its desire to see installed as many small farmers as possible, CIU cannot fairly be criticised for its preferred emphasis. Nevertheless the very success of the San Julián programme, in accelerating colonists' adjustment and in providing access roads to markets from the start, advanced by years the second or consolidation stage of colonisation when advice is required on better techniques and on commercialisation. Since many colonists early express their aspiration to commercial success, it is probable that continuing abandonments are attributable to the frustration of those desires. It will be argued below, however, that such frustrations may be caused by more than the mere absence of a consolidation programme.

A major aim of CIU in cooperating with INC was to train an orientation team and devise structures for permanent incorporation into INC, in order that orientation should become a standard part of its work. In this task CIU failed. Although Bolivián staff were trained by CIU and shared its commitment to the service of the colonists, although INC took these people onto its established payroll, and although most of the successive directors of INC shared CIU's aims, bureaucracy combined with political events to prevent the desired incorporation. Decision-taking in INC was highly centralised, with a rigid chain of command from central office down through regional and zonal offices to field staff. Services were also highly compartmentalised. The orientation programme needed flexibility, delegation of authority to the field, and the close coordination of many different services. To graft such a programme onto the existing structure, especially in the face of an often suspicious middle management, proved impossible. At the end too a *coup d'état*, which brought to power a repressive military regime, gave the *coup de grâce* to CIU's hopes when most of the orientation staff were dismissed.

Nevertheless for the duration of the contract the partnership between INC and CIU had notable achievements. With no change in the directorate of CIU and only one change of administrator the partnership brought a stability and continuity to the programme when on average the Director of INC was changed every fourteen months and local heads were replaced every nine months. The short chain of command within CIU (directorate–field administrator–field staff) coupled with the delegation of considerable authority to the lowest level, the flexibility of budgetary allocations, and the mutual trust which existed within the organisation provided much scope for a rapid response to needs and for circumventing bottlenecks inherent in INC's structure. The independence, both collective and individual, of CIU's directorate also allowed CIU to exert an unstated threat to withdraw if INC failed to comply with its side of the contract. Given that CIU was dominated by Americans and that the third partner was USAID, some community of interest might be expected and cannot be denied. Yet CIU at times confronted bottlenecks that could be attributed more to USAID than to INC.

In the end it seems likely if unprovable that thanks to this unique partnership considerably more people were satisfactorily installed on their new holdings than would otherwise have been the case.

## Structural problems of colonisation

For many Americans the idea that homesteading on the frontier of settlement is the cornerstone of the nation's democracy is part of their mythology. More immediately some of the Americans of the CIU are themselves the children and grandchildren of small farmers of the Midwest. Not surprisingly the author found a desire, either conscious or subconscious, to replicate in Bolivia a way of life that for them was satisfying in their homeland. But there exist salient differences in the character of the American and Bolivián frontiers (for the author's view of the historical differences see Crossley 1961). In particular, differences in production conditions and in opportunities for commercialisation need stressing.

**Production conditions**

Although the sizes of the American homestead (160 acres or 64 ha) and the San Julián holding (50 ha) are similar, their physical potential differs greatly. Most of the American farm was cultivable on a permanent basis. In the absence of cheap hired labour animal traction was essential if the farmer was fully to utilise the land. As a result a high *per capita* production was possible.

In the Bolivián colonies in contrast no way has yet been discovered of utilising all the land permanently. Shifting cultivation is still the only proven way of achieving adequate yields and if the rotation of the land is too rapid yields decline, as early colonists with 20-ha holdings have discovered. Furthermore, leaving tree-stumps in the ground − because their removal is costly, whereas allowing them to rot provides much-needed nutrients − restricts the colonist to manual cultivation techniques. In consequence, in the absence of hired labour, he can utilise no more than 5 ha at a time. Hence *per capita* production is low and incomes earned are no greater than a farm labourer can command (Maxwell 1980 p. 165). According to Maxwell, mechanised destumping and land preparation can free the farmer from this straitjacket (p. 167). Maxwell's later observations however reveal that soaring costs of mechanisation, coupled with the soil compaction resulting from the use of heavy equipment, may have closed this avenue of escape (Maxwell 1983 personal communication). Neverthless both these difficulties could be obviated through the use of animal traction, as advocated by CIU's president, following American practice (Graber 1976). The long-term effects of its use, however, also remain unknown.

Putting most of the land under permanent pasture and practising dairying affords another option. But this is open only to farmers who enjoy rapid and reliable transport to a processing factory and is therefore unlikely to be available to San Julián colonists in the foreseeable future. Sadly the only enterprise which has proved able consistently to yield a high income from a limited area is the tree crop, coca; but its production is most actively discouraged for moral and medical reasons.

**Commercialisation**

In the United States the colonisation process was accompanied by the general expansion of roads and railways, of towns and cities, of industries and commerce, and of exports (in the late nineteenth century) to an industrialising Europe which had a growing demand for cheap agricultural produce. Thus as aggregate production by settlers increased the growing markets both near and far were able to absorb that increase.

In Bolivia today little of this applies. Its national population of 5 million is small and the purchasing power of the majority is low. Admittedly the city of Santa Cruz is the boom town of the republic, having grown from 43 000 in 1950 to over 300 000 today. Admittedly too some of San Julián's earlier colonists have developed a profitable line in growing tomatoes for Santa Cruz. But at the macro-level of total national demand the real problem is revealed. In the early 1960s economic policies of encouraging import-substitution agriculture appeared to combine happily with social policies of siphoning off excess population in the rural highlands to new areas of colonisation in the lowlands. But long before the tide of migrants could be satisfied the supply of sugar cane exceeded demand and quotas had to be imposed. Similarly in the late 1970s the National Rice Board which offered guaranteed prices collapsed under the burden of unsaleable stocks. Or again, two milk-processing plants, near Cochabamba and Montero, drawing their supplies from a few hundred farmers appear to satisfy total national demand for milk products.

Doubtless untapped markets exist for specific products at particular times and locations. Market information services are, after all, underdeveloped and transport and storage facilities merit improvement. Rising urban populations also create new market opportunities.

Yet it may be argued, and demonstrated, that the main problem for Bolivian farmers lies not simply in the fact of a low aggregate demand but rather in the ratio of producers to consumers. A generation ago, for sound political and social reasons, large farms were expropriated under the Agrarián Reform Act and their land was distributed among small farmers. Expectations that this process would create family farms of adequate size for all could not be fulfilled for the simple reason that there was insufficient cultivable land in farms to give all beneficiaries such a holding.

In the same way it may be calculated that in any country such as Bolivia where half or more of the population directly depend on agricultural production for a living and supply most of their own needs, and where the other half or less of the population are non-agricultural, then there exists on average only one customer at best for every producer. Under the circumstances where such a demographic balance exists it is concluded that, regardless of the political system obtaining, there is no way in which all farmers can achieve a satisfactory livelihood from the exchange or commercialisation of their production. The problem can be alleviated only by the long-term shift in the demographic balance or by expanding exports.

In this last respect the Amazonián lowlands of Bolivia are especially badly located, as only high-value products can withstand the transport costs to distant markets. Thus in 1977 transport costs to Atlantic ports accounted for 21 per cent of the f.o.b. price for sugar, but only for 8 per cent of the price for cotton (Maxwell 1980 p. 170).

For a country like Bolivia, it may be concluded, the process of colonisation which creates thousands of new farms and brings into cultivation tens of thousands of new hectares has serious social implications. The major one is that, if the colonists break out of their straitjacket and achieve high levels of production and productivity or if the larger farms nearer to Santa Cruz increase output, then on balanace it will be at the expense of other producers who are smaller and less efficient. Only careful planning could avoid the resultant distress.

# 10  Social change in the *garimpo*

MARIANNE SCHMINK

The small-scale placer-miner, working with his rudimentary tools to extract gems and minerals, is a figure surrounded by legend. In Brazil, where their presence is probably the most significant, such miners are known as *garimpeiros*, a term originating in the eighteenth century to refer to those who worked in the extraction of diamonds in defiance of prohibitions by the Crown.[1] Despite subsequent changes in legal status, the marginal image of the *garimpeiro* has persisted, along with widespread legends of his adventurous, colourful lifestyle. Detailed studies of the *garimpeiro* are, however, extremely rare.

Brazilian placer-miners were present from the seventeenth and eighteenth centuries in the diamond- and goldfields of the states of Minas Gerais and Mato Grosso, and later in Bahia (Baxter 1975 p. 2). In the present century, *garimpagem* has been primarily concentrated in Mato Grosso, Goiás and the Amazon states. While no reliable population figures exist for *garimpeiros*, a 1973 survey counted a total of 284 000, of whom ninety per cent were concentrated in these states, nearly half (114 000) in the State of Pará (Fundação de Assistência aos Garimpeiros 1973, cited in Baxter 1975 p. 15). A study of the most active placer-mining regions carried out in 1981 similarly found seventy per cent of the 148 000 *garimpeiros* to be located in these states, nearly half (70 000) in Pará (Guimarães *et al.* 1981, cited in Salomão 1982 p. 15). These figures contrast with the slightly more than 47 000 workers employed in Brazilian mines in 1980, highlighting the importance of *garimpagem* within the mining sector (Brasil 1981, cited in Salomão 1982 p. 15).

Placer-mining has some features in common with other extractive activities typical of the Amazon region, as well as some distinctive elements that make *garimpeiro* society unique. Among the latter is a well developed set of norms and beliefs often referred to as the '*lei do garimpeiro*'. A complex system of labour relations, and its accompanying ideology emphasising both independence and solidarity, have evolved in the *garimpo*. Their particular features have varied in different regions and periods, especially in response to changing relations with landowners, mining companies, and the Brazilian State.

This study will focus on the impact of contemporary social change on the *garimpo* tradition in the Amazon region. Case study material will be presented to illustrate two forms of interventions that transform the socio-economic and ideological systems of the *garimpo*.[2] First, the imposition of control of commerce by mining companies is shown to disrupt the labour relations system of the *garimpo* as capitalistic norms are introduced. Second, direct federal intervention in selected areas reinforces the breakdown of traditional social relations, and represents an attempt to impose an ideology more appropriate to the goals of the Brazilian State. These changes are interpreted within the specific context of the frontier setting in southern Pará. Before turning to the analysis of social change, however, the paper begins by outlining the principal features of the *garimpo* tradition.

## The *garimpo* tradition

*Garimpagem* is defined by its small scale and rudimentary technology, the main features of which have changed little over the centuries. Different types of deposits require distinct forms of technical production, varying both with the characteristics of the location and with the type of mineral (Baxter 1975 pp. 133–75; Sales 1955 p. 17). The minimal tool kit of the *garimpeiro*, however, has remained relatively simple, including shovels or other digging instruments, carrying vessels, and sieves or pans for cleaning the gravel (*cascalho*). The principal technological innovation has been the use of small motorised pumps to move water, introduced in the 1940s (Baxter 1975 p. 302).

The system of labour, supply and production is complex and variable, but the central axis is the *meia-praça* relationship between the *fornecedor* (supplier), and the direct producers, or *garimpeiros*. These two figures provide, respectively, the capital and labour that goes into the extraction of minerals. The supplier furnishes to his workers at least their basic food rations during the time they are working, and sometimes also equipment or other supplies. These provisions are referred to as the *rancho* or the *saco*. The *garimpeiro* contributes not only his own labour, but often basic tools and sometimes other elements (such as a share in the cost of gasoline to operate water pumps).

The term *meia-praça* refers to the work relations that exist between the supplier and *garimpeiro*, but is also used to refer to the *garimpeiro* himself who works under this system (Sales 1955 p. 34). In this way his particular social definition is distinguished from the more global term *garimpeiro*, which refers to independent miners or indeed to all those who make their living in the *garimpo*. (For example, prostitutes in the *garimpo* are commonly referred to as '*garimpeiras*'.) In return for their respective contributions to the *meia-praça* relationship, supplier and *garimpeiro* divide equally between them whatever returns accrue during their association. Concretely, the supplier has right to half the production, and the other half is equally divided among all the *garimpeiros* in his *turma* or work crew.

The *meia-praça* system has some elements in common with the traditional system of *aviamento* in Amazonia, used mainly for extraction of such forest products as rubber and Brazil nuts. This system involved a supplier and producer contributing capital and labour in a similar way. Suppliers were themselves supplied by larger-scale merchants, who were in turn tied to a monopoly of exporters. Products moved 'up' the system as supplies moved 'down' to the producer. In a similar way, the *fornecedor* in the *garimpo* generally receives credit and supplies from a merchant who is, in turn, tied to one or more mineral buyers.

The *garimpo* system nevertheless differs from the traditional *aviamento* in some important ways. The *aviamento* system relied on creating and maintaining debt ties between producers and suppliers (and between lower- and higher-level suppliers) to tie labour to often isolated and difficult work conditions. The *garimpeiro* also works under adverse conditions, has no guarantee of medical assistance or other benefits, and is subject to summary dismissal by his supplier at any moment. However, he does not incur any debt to his supplier. Once the claim has been worked, if there are no returns the *garimpeiro* owes nothing. This constitutes a critical difference between the two systems that provides the basis for the independence of the *garimpeiro*. Furthermore, the element of luck inherent in the mining activity holds out a possibility of sudden wealth that was not present for the traditional collector in the *aviamento* system (Salomão 1981 p. 43).

The 'gamble' of the *garimpo* is always cited by *garimpeiros* as being its principal attraction. Its 'wheel of fortune' holds out the possibility that each person might 'strike it rich' or *bamburrar*. There are a wealth of folk beliefs and taboos in the *garimpo* surrounding such good fortune. Chief among these is the notion that wealth must be spent lavishly, rapidly, and ostentatiously – traditionally on drink, women, and fine clothing. The so-called 'fever' of the *garimpo* which keeps miners moving from one *garimpo* to another is the desire for these moments of wealth. According to the law of the *garimpeiro*, those who begin work with the idea of rationally investing their returns are doomed to *blefar* or *dar blefe* (Come up with nothing). Similarly, tradition has it that if *garimpeiros* don't throw away the earnings from their first good strike, they will never have another. This ethic leads to such stories as that of the *garimpeiro* who paid for taxis to carry his hat around town, or another who plastered the body of a prostitute with Cr$ 1000 bills while she slept.

The *garimpeiro* takes pride in his independence, and in his role as a courageous pioneer working in new areas to find hidden riches. Alongside this apparently individualistic orientation, however, is an elaborate system of ethics that promote solidarity. Given the uncertainty, isolation, and harshness of *garimpo* life, it is this strong mutual support which sustains *garimpeiro* society. Thus one of the strongest tenets of the law of the *garimpeiro* is that, no matter how scarce, food is shared freely among *garimpeiros*. Similarly, tradition has it that theft between *garimpeiros* is virtually unknown, and claims are scrupulously respected even when their owner is absent for months. The legendary violence of the *garimpo* is generally confined to the brothel where the combination of women, drink and gambling can be explosive (Salomão 1981 p. 43). When crimes are committed, they are handled by a committee of the whole which expels the criminal and takes up a collection for the victim. From this standpoint, the ostentatious spending encouraged by the *garimpeiro* ethic functions as a sort of levelling mechanism that reinforces the strong sense of kinship and solidarity which characterises the *garimpo*.

The *meia-praça* relationship and its accompanying ideology of independence, risk-taking, and solidarity form the heart of *garimpo* culture, and society. But the strength of the various elements, and variations in the system, depend on the particular characteristics of each *garimpo*. Some placer miners work independently, or as day labourers, although work as a *meia-praça* is preferred by the majority who have few resources of their own (Baxter 1975 p. 284; Equipes Pastorais 1982 p. 54). The existence of a strong *meia-praça* system with large work crews depends primarily on the wealth of the *garimpo*, which attracts potential suppliers. In the *garimpos* at Poxoréo, Mato Grosso, for example, during the boom period in the 1930s and 1940s, 90 per cent of the *garimpeiros* worked as *meia-praças*, commonly in teams of 18–20 men. By the mid-1970s when mining was in decline, it was difficult to find a patron: while 63 per cent of the *garimpeiros* worked as *meia-praças*, only 8 per cent worked in groups larger than two people, and most worked alone (Baxter 1975 pp. 311–12, 212).

Internal differentiation in the *garimpo* is also more complex than described here. Some tasks are specialised, especially those requiring more skill during the washing phase. Some *garimpeiros* hire out on a daily basis to other crews for this task, in turn hiring their own temporary replacement. Whole crews may also exchange labour for some tasks, a practice known as *troca de dias*. More formalised partnerships known as *sociedades* may also exist between *garimpeiros* or suppliers. On the other hand, the divisions between supplier and *meia-praça* may often be indistinct. In some cases a supplier may work as part of his own crew, receiving the two shares corresponding to his two roles. Furthermore, in the traditional *garimpo* there is some degree of mobility between supplier and *meia-praça*, which strengthens feelings of identity and solidarity (Equipes Pastorais 1982 pp. 67–9; Salomão 1981 pp. 41–2).

The hierarchical structure of patron–client relationships may also be complex. In *garimpos* located on private land, the landowner has a legal right to collect a 10 per cent share of all minerals extracted. The owner himself, or his agent, establishes a presence in the *garimpo* to collect this tax and carry out other administrative tasks. By tradition, similar shares may also be demanded for access to water, or for use of a pump (Baxter 1975 pp. 240–1). In some cases, the *garimpo* itself has an 'owner' who was responsible for opening the area, and usually has financing from merchants or mineral buyers. In remote areas such as those of the Tapajós region, *garimpos* with access only by small planes are known as 'closed' due to the monopoly control exercised by their owner. He controls commerce, transportation, and purchase of ore and may also have his own private security force. Ownership of the brothel allows him to recapture the profits of the *garimpeiro*. While the owner's monopoly permits him to manipulate prices and hence exploit the supply system to his advantage, he is also responsible for maintaining supplies through seasonal shifts in production, assuring the subsistence of the *garimpeiros* (Salomão 1981 pp. 43–4). In an 'open' or 'tame' *garimpo*, by contrast, the owner's monopoly is broken and competition between merchants and mineral buyers is present. The owner of the *garimpo* may charge a landing fee for use of the airstrip.

## The *garimpeiro* and the companies

Since 1817, when legislation first permitted the formation of mining companies in Brazil, sporadic government actions on their behalf have presented a potential threat to the *garimpo* (Baxter 1975 p. 10; Salomão 1982 p. 18). Under normal circumstances, research permits granted to mining companies do not interfere with the extractive activities of *garimpeiros* in these areas, but when production rights are given, the *garimpeiros* are expected to leave. Furthermore, the National Department of Mineral Research (DNPM) may also close *garimpos* for reasons of 'public order' or due to destruction of the mineral site (Baxter 1975 p. 12). The success of *garimpeiros* in resisting government actions in favour of the companies has been mixed.

The best known case was that of Rondônia, where a tin rush occurred during the end of the 1950s and the 1960s. Rondônia's deposits of cassiterite (the ore from which tin is made) are of very high quality and account for the vast majority of Brazil's tin production. By 1968, at the peak of the rush, there were an estimated 45 000 *garimpeiros*, many of them former rubber collectors from Rondônia and neighbouring Acre and Amazonas (Monte-Mor 1980 p. 79). The companies argued that the *garimpeiros* were spoiling the deposits, and that their crude manual methods allowed only about 30 per cent of the ore's value to be extracted, whereas 95 per cent could be taken out by mechanical means. As a result, in 1970 the federal Ministry of Mines and Energy prohibited further activities by *garimpeiros* in the areas, conceding exploitation rights to a few big companies (Monte-Mor 1980 p. 79). The *garimpeiros* were evicted in a military operation, creating large-scale unemployment and rural to urban migration, and accompanied by great social tension. Despite these actions and massive investments by the government, tin ore production initially fell after the introduction of mechanised extraction. Several companies went too heavily into debt, and they encountered difficulties in transferring technologies borrowed from Bolivia and Malaysia to Rondônia (*Minérios*, September 1977, p. 20). Rising costs led to a constant process of decapitalisation of Brazil's tin companies during the mid-1970s (*Minérios* op. cit. p. 16). Nevertheless, tin ore production recovered and has gradually increased since the early 1970s.

The so-called '*garimpo* controversy' which began in Rondônia passed later to other states such as Goiás and Pará. Some tin-producing companies argued that there could be no role for *garimpeiros* in rational, planned tin production. Others noted the important role *garimpeiros* could play in reducing costs during the initial stages of discovery, and in exploitation of deposits near the surface (*Minérios* op. cit. p. 21). Some argue that with minimal assistance in technological improvements the *garimpo* system could greatly increase its productivity (Dall Agnol 1982; Salomão 1982).

The experience in Rondônia had provoked mixed feelings about the proposition of evicting *garimpeiros*, en masse, from other areas. In December of 1976, a government decree prohibited *garimpo* activities in areas where legitimate companies had legal licence. In September of 1977 this dispensation was changed to allow their functioning by concession of the licensed company. These changes led to uncertainty on the part of both company and *garimpeiro* (*Minérios* op. cit. p. 21). In the tin fields of Pará, a middle-course solution was found, granting licensed companies exclusive buying rights, but not demanding the immediate expulsion of the *garimpeiros*. Nevertheless, the imposition of the companies severely disrupted social relations in these *garimpos*, as the following case study material illustrates.

Cassiterite deposits in southern Pará were first noted by a team of geologists from DOCEGEO, a research subsidiary of the state-owned Companhia Vale do Rio Doce, in 1971. Since the researchers were looking for lead deposits, they paid little attention to cassiterite they encountered. However the word passed quickly among *garimpeiros*, perhaps originating with the employees of the research team. Actual extraction of ore in the area began when a landing strip was constructed in 1976. By this time, Brazil's largest tin-producing company, Estanífera, held a research licence for the area.

It was this company that financed construction of the airstrip, advancing Cr$ 500 000 (roughly US$ 50 000) to the *garimpeiro* who built it. This individual had made a business of opening up *garimpos*, was a pilot and owned two small single-engined planes. During the initial months the role played by Estanífera was limited to this financing, and to buying the ore from the airstrip owner, who operated a 'closed' *garimpo* through this monopoly over transportation and commercial activities. In July of 1976, there were about 200 *garimpeiros* in the area. The ore was of relatively low quality and mixed with impurities that added to its weight and decreased its value. The price paid to the *garimpeiros* oscillated from Cr$ 9 to Cr$ 18 per kilo.

Within the next year, about 3000 *garimpeiros* invaded the area and several new airstrips were constructed. Some of the new areas contained higher quality ore for which research licences were held by the Vale do Rio Doce company or by CIA (another large tin producer in Brazil). By 1977 *garimpeiros* were reportedly receiving Cr$ 40 to Cr$ 55 for a kilo of ore, and were able to make more than Cr$ 1000 per month. The short hand-hewn airstrips were insufficient to allow planes to take off with full loads of ore; instead they took half-loads to the town of São Felix do Xingu about 50 km distant, then took off from that excellent new airstrip for Redenção (300 km away) and thence to Santarém, Manaus or southern Brazil.

While larger companies held official research rights, giving them a legal foothold in the area, the 'rush' of *garimpeiros* was difficult to control. Furthermore, the 'opening' of the cassiterite areas from the monopoly control of one owner tied to one company had also meant the invasion by smaller companies buying ore. This meant that prices were bid up, ultimately benefiting the producer. At the same time, it was a threat to the larger companies who held legal licence to research the areas, and who were not as free as the smaller buyers (who more frequently evaded payment of taxes and labour benefits) to manipulate prices. The loss of government tax money, and the loss of control over the areas by the large companies, made the tin rush a threat to dominant economic interests.

In response, an interministerial directive introduced in 1978 conceded exclusive buying rights to DOCEGEO and to Mamoré, a subsidiary of Paranapanema and one of Brazil's largest producers. By this time there were about 8–10 000 *garimpeiros* working in five active airstrips. Since the *garimpeiros* were to be permitted to remain, the directive effectively amounted to an eviction of the other buyers who were operating in the area. These had large investments sunk into the *garimpo* and its supply system, and therefore stood to lose substantially from the change. They therefore rallied the *garimpeiros* to their cause in resisting the takeover by the two companies.

The largest single *garimpo* at the time of the takeover was Pista Nova, with approximately 4000 *garimpeiros* working eight or nine different streambeds accessed by the same airstrip. This area passed into the hands of Mamoré, and the company expected its competitors to leave the area immediately. One smaller company had made the initial investment to open the area, and still had many debts to collect from merchants and suppliers. This company, reportedly founded by a prospector, cultivates its image as being 'of' *garimpeiros* and as understanding their needs. When its interests were threatened, this claim to *garimpeiro* solidarity, combined with more direct measures, allowed the company to recover some potentially heavy losses.

Before Mamoré took over, buyers had controlled the transport of both ore and supplies to and from the *garimpo*, cooperating with merchants operating on the airstrip. Generally, for each kilo of ore merchants sold to the company, they were entitled to bring in one kilo of supplies on the planes which would otherwise be flying empty into the area. This agreement helped to ensure provisions to underwrite production, saving on the cost of freight to merchants and thereby keeping the cost of provisions down. Moreover, the arrangement was maintained even during periods of low production, such as the rainy season. On these occasions, buyers provided merchants with advances to cover the freight of provisions. To the *garimpeiros*, this system provided the certainty that they would not starve, whether production at that moment was high or low. The *garimpeiros* also profited from the price competition among buyers. On the other hand, the buyers sometimes ran short of cash with which to purchase, and were suspected of cheating the *garimpeiros* in the process of evaluating ore quality (a factor in price determination).

With the takeover by Mamoré, this system immediately broke down. Merchants were now suddenly without credit, and the few larger ones who had sold ore directly in southern Brazil at higher prices now had this option cut off. Their response was to simply stop providing supplies. The *garimpeiros*, their lifeline suddenly cut, descended en masse on the Mamoré headquarters on the airstrip demanding a solution. Faced with an incipient riot, Mamoré made some concessions. The main buyer was given an additional 90 days to continue to buy ore (and sell it to Mamoré) and to collect on its debts. Merchants selling ore to Mamoré at the official price were granted a Cr$ 2–3 commission on each kilo. This measure, in the absence of credit advances, helped to reduce risks and stimulated production.

This solution soon created its own problems. Mamoré now purchased ore at a fixed price from anyone in the *garimpeiro* social system. Miners therefore had the option of selling either to their supplier, or directly to Mamoré. The latter option provided a means of avoiding repayment of debts to the supplier. The merchants again threatened to stop supplying the *garimpo*. At this point Mamoré agreed to buy ore only from the merchants, at the official minimum price. At the same time, the company began stockpiling supplies in a warehouse nearby in case of a similar emergency. Although they had no interest in becoming merchant-suppliers, they needed a back-up system in order to bargain with the merchants. Their ultimate objective was not to support the *garimpo* system, but rather to see it slowly decline, leaving them in a position to explore the possibilities for mechanised production.

Similar conflicts occurred at the other airstrips where DOCEGEO took over. Entering a few months after Mamoré, the company took the precaution of permitting a grace period to the companies previously in the area. Rumours flew that with their entry the price of ore would drop, and that, as in Rondônia, the army would come in and close down the *garimpo*. The buyers raised the price being paid for cassiterite to Cr$ 100 per kilo, hoping to bring in enough ore to pay off their outstanding debts in the short time left to them. They also encouraged the threatening rumours as a further stimulus. The result was a rush on the extraction of the easily exploitable ore in the area, which was sold off at an artificially high price. The *garimpeiros* obviously benefited from this strategy.

When the first representatives of DOCEGEO arrived, the *garimpeiros* viewed them suspiciously as disguised military men who would soon close down the *garimpo*. The price of ore, now determined at the official rate based on the latest London Metal Exchange price, fell drastically to Cr$ 70 per kilo. Due to the uncertainty of the future of the *garimpo*, merchants were reluctant to supply the *garimpeiros*. Production declined brusquely as a result of the earlier rush, the decrease in price, the lack of supplies, and the general uncertainty.

On a third airstrip, the first one opened in 1976 by Estanifera, different problems arose. With the takeover by DOCEGEO, the airstrip's owner encouraged a return to his *garimpo* by suspending the payment of his 'royalties' for use of the airstrip. (In other DOCEGEO areas, Cr$ 2 per kilo was still paid to the airstrip owner based on tradition, not legal right.) *Garimpeiros* began to pour into the area. However, since the ore there was particularly impure, DOCEGEO refused to purchase it. This meant there were many newly arrived miners needing provisioning, there was as yet no production, and the ore being produced was unsaleable. Furthermore, the work crews had many men but few pumps, which contributed to the demand for food and kept productivity low. Faced with this crisis, DOCEGEO had granted Cr$ 300 000 in credit for one of the airstrip's merchants so that he could supply the *garimpeiros*. Since he was unable to sell the low-quality ore, he was still unable to pay off the debt, and provisioning came to a standstill. DOCEGEO was hurrying to install an electromagnetic separator which would purify the ore (for a fee) and resolve this bottleneck. This would facilitate the purchase of the ore already produced, favouring DOCEGEO, the merchants and suppliers, and the owner of the airstrip. But the *garimpeiros* now had to produce a greater volume of ore than formerly when the other companies had bought lower quality ore at a lower price.

Despite these complications, and the efforts by buyers, merchants, suppliers and *garimpeiros* to disrupt the transition, the tin-ore prospecting areas eventually came under the control of the two licensed companies. Their lack of interest in supporting the *garimpo* system, and the exploitation of the most readily accessible ore, led to the virtual abandonment of the *garimpos* by the end of 1978. Neither were the companies successful in moving to mechanised production, at least by 1981. The *garimpeiros* themselves moved on to other employment in the frontier area or to other strikes nearby. Many would end up taking part in the massive gold rush that took place two years later in the same part of southern Pará. It was this rush that inaugurated a new phase in state intervention in the *garimpo*.

## The state-controlled *garimpo*

The tin rush that took place in southern Pará from 1976 to 1978 was dwarfed by the massive gold rush that followed it two years later in the same general area. As in the case of tin, the *garimpeiros* proved to be better prospectors than the specialised geologists in the government employ. DOCEGEO explored the area now known as Serra Pelada in 1979, looking for iron; they overlooked the rich gold deposits there. These were found by *garimpeiros* in January of 1980, and rumours quickly spread during February, triggering a rush which would attract 20 000 *garimpeiros* by May (*Veja* 11 June 1980). As the richness of these deposits became known, Brazil's Amazon jungle once again became the focus of extensive international media attention.

The Brazilian government quickly took steps to extend its control over the rapidly expanding gold extraction. If a desire to minimise tax evasion had motivated state intervention in the tin areas on behalf of the licensed companies, the potential loss through gold smuggling was far greater. In the first few months of 1980, an agent of the National Intelligence Service (SNI), linked directly to the Presidential Palace and the military National Security Council investigated the situation in Serra Pelada (*Veja* op. cit.). On 21 May of that year, the government took the unprecedented step of directly taking control of the *garimpo*. By that time an estimated ton of gold had already been extracted (*Veja* op. cit.). An inter-agency coordination was put in place to take charge of the purchase of ore, commerce, medical assistance, entertainment, and control over entry to the area. The owner of the land was no longer permitted to receive his traditional 10 per cent of production, and he turned over $14\frac{1}{2}$ kilos of gold to the authorities. The owner of the airstrip was similarly denied rights to the 8 grams of gold he had been charging as a landing fee. Certain parts of the area were closed off to the *garimpeiros* altogether. The *garimpeiros* were given documents, and 3000 people were evicted because of illegal activities (gamblers, gunslingers, and drug dealers) (*Veja* op. cit.). Foreigners were not permitted to work the claims. Arms, women, gambling, and liquor were prohibited in the *garimpo*. The Federal Police controlled both the road and the airstrip, and barred entry to newcomers.

The *garimpo* thereafter was ruled by a military–technical–bureaucratic corps of 120 persons, at whose head was the flamboyant 'Major Curió'. Curió, whose real name is Sebastião Rodrigues de Moura, is a lieutenant-colonel linked to the SNI and the National Security Council. He has been a trouble-shooter for the government during diverse crisis situations in the past, including the anti-guerilla operations in the nearby Araguaia region in the 1970s (*Informe Amazônico* 5, 16–31 November 1980). His trademark is his populist style. Upon arrival in the *garimpo*, he was reportedly carried from his helicopter on the shoulders of *garimpeiros*. Firing his Magnum into the air, he reminded them that 'the revolver that shoots the loudest is mine' (*Parade* 29 March 1981).

Aside from the practical measures of control described above, Curió moved to establish a pro-government political base through the imposition of rituals alien to the traditional *garimpo*. At early-morning ceremonies miners sang the national anthem as the flag was raised, and woke up with some regimented calisthenics. The training required for the latter was reported to be one method by which to spot *furões* (*garimpeiros* who have infiltrated without permission). *Garimpeiros* were also treated to talks on such topics as the importance to the nation of work in mining. As a result, they frequently make reference to their role in paying off the national debt. Such forms of political orientation helped to prepare the *garimpeiros* for the well organised visit by President Figueiredo to Serra Pelada in November of 1980. It was the largest popular demonstration of support for the President since his taking office (*Informe Amazônico* op. cit.). Curió himself ran for Federal Deputy from the State of Pará, in the elections of November 1982. The tens of thousands of *garimpeiros* in that state who received legal documents and political orientation through his populist policies provided an important base of power for the pro-government party (PDS). Curió was elected, although most of the ballots from Serra Pelada were later invalidated.

Serra Pelada is not the only area where gold is to be found in southern Pará, and its discovery soon stimulated others. Later in 1980 another rich area called Cumaru was opened up by *garimpeiros*. In February and March of 1981, Cumaru filled up with miners, many of whom moved to this more spread-out area from Serra Pelada.

Part of the gold deposits lie within the bounds of the reserve of the Gorotire Indians, and conflicts between this group and the *garimpeiros* soon arose. In March a federal presence was established there via a project similar to that in Serra Pelada. Its head was a more discreet but no less mysterious military man than Curió. In addition to the measures introduced in Serra Pelada, the Cumaru administration settled the Indian question by allowing the *garimpeiros* to work that area, and turning over to the Gorotire the full amount of federal taxes collected from that ore. By July of 1981, 26 000 *garimpeiro* work cards had been issued in Cumaru, and an estimated 18 000 *garimpeiros* were still in the area. The federal bank was purchasing an average of 6 kilos of gold per day. Estimates for Serra Pelada, in June of 1980, placed its production at 26 kilos per day (*Veja* op. cit.).

Authorities involved in the control of the gold-mining areas insist that these interventions are ad hoc and loosely structured 'coordinations' rather than formalised entities. They are described as special-case interventions, since in general the government prefers to support exploitation by private companies (*Latin American Regional Report on Brazil*, 8 August 1980). Although the precise nature of these *garimpo* projects and of the identity of their leaders remains somewhat mysterious, the reasons for the actions are relatively clear. The head of the Cumaru project defined these as twofold: 'social problems' or 'economic expression'. The latter by itself is clearly cause for concern, given the great value of the deposits and the ease with which gold may be smuggled through the jungle. If this were the only concern, a more rational strategy would be to ban prospecting outright and to reserve the deposits for exploitation by DOCEGEO. But the social question is also increasingly important in the frontier context where tensions related to land conflicts are high. We will return to this point in the concluding section.

As might be expected, conditions within the government-controlled *garimpos* are quite different from those in the traditional prospecting areas. In place of the figure of the traditional merchant with his ties to mineral buyers and to suppliers, the *garimpeiros* are ministered to by an array of at least fifteen government agencies (Salomão 1982 p. 20). Gold is sold to the state mining company, payment is received at a window of the Central Bank, and supplies are purchased with cash at a government store (COBAL). Under these circumstances claim owners must rely on their own resources, and most were therefore an elite group far removed from the traditional figure of the supplier in the *garimpo*. The *meia-praça* arrangement was still in use, but owners preferred to pay day workers on productive claims (*Isto É*, 28 May 1980). By November of 1980 the number of *garimpeiros* in Serra Pelada had fallen from 25 000 to 15 000, of which an estimated two-thirds worked under a wage system (*Informe Amazônico* op. cit.). Traditional social relations in the government-controlled *garimpos* were thus being replaced by more typically capitalist systems of work relations. The *garimpo* population was increasingly dominated by elites who had the capital to work claims, on the one hand, and inexperienced or *bravo* (wild) *garimpeiros* (as opposed to *manso* or tame), on the other.

With these modifications in *garimpo* social relations, changes can also be expected in the traditional redistributive ethic and practices of the *garimpo*. Many functions formerly carried out by the *garimpeiros* themselves have been coopted by the authorities. Even the smallest *garimpos* now have some form of military presence, with its prohibitions of arms, liquor, gambling and prostitution. With the penetration of these external forms of control, however, *garimpeiros* complain that the traditional forms of social control in the *garimpo* have broken down. Tasks of expelling a criminal or caring for a victim have been usurped by the police and military. Especially in the gold areas, theft is a new form of criminality in the *garimpo*.

Even traditional forms of garimpeiro generosity have been coopted. The *regue*, the practice of granting rights to re-wash already worked gravel, was formerly a gift from one *garimpeiro* to another to provide a minimal beginning stake. In Serra Pelada, Curió used the *regue* system as one more populist tactic, granting licence to some 3500 miners to re-clean *cascalho* that had been worked during 1980. The re-cleaning process improved the efficiency of mining in Serra Pelada, reducing the gold found in rejected gravel to only 0.4 to 0.7 grams per ton (Guimarães *et al.* 1981, cited in Salomão 1982 p. 17). Although DOCEGEO had hoped to mechanise this operation. Curió preferred to make the 'filet mignon' his gift to the *garimpeiros* (*Informe Amazônico* op. cit.).

## The *garimpo* in the frontier context

The cases of the tin- and gold-prospecting areas provide concrete examples of the process by which the character of the traditional *garimpo* is changed with interventions by the state. Concessions to large mining companies in the tin areas broke down the traditional labour and supply system, replacing these with capitalist social relations and paving the way for mechanised production. Resistance to this takeover by the *garimpeiros* and buyers operating under the *garimpo* system was effective only in retarding the process of explusion of *garimpeiros*. With the gold rush in Serra Pelada and Cumaru, more effective measures of immediate intervention were used. The power of the authorities involved in these takeovers was such that resistance was impossible. Federal intervention sought to replace the traditional *garimpo* socio-economic system and to impose its own pro-government ideologies through populist cooptation of *garimpo* traditions.

These extreme measures of military control are justified not only by the economic importance of the goldfields, but also by the frontier context in which they are located. Federal intervention in the *garimpo* in southern Pará is consistent with the government's strategy of defusing political tensions while seeking to build political support in the area (Martins nd; Schmink 1982). Social tensions centre on widespread and persistent disputes over land between large landowners and would-be small farmers, *posseiros* (Pinto 1982).

In this context relations between landowners and *garimpeiros* may also become strained, despite the fact that the latter's activities in extracting ore do not provide the basis for claims to land. Traditionally, landowners have encouraged mining on their lands as a source of additional revenue (Baxter 1975 p. 344). In the Tapajós region there is little interest in pressing claims to land, a factor Salomão (1981 p. 40) finds to be important in maintaining conditions for the traditional *garimpo* system. By contrast, in southern Pará invasions by *garimpeiros* of private lands are often carried out by massive collectives due to the fear of violent expulsion by ranch guards, known as *jagunços*. These notoriously violent characters, whose primary job is to keep their employers' land clear of *posseiros*, are also typically charged with controlling those *garimpos* that are established on the property. Under these circumstances, the traditionally cordial relations between *garimpeiros* and landowners are replaced by mutual distrust and dislike (Equipes Pastorais 1982 pp. 51–4).

*Garimpeiros* are in fact often indistinguishable from the general population of small farmers and rural workers. While some work solely in mining, moving throughout their lifetime from one *garimpo* to another, these 'professional' *garimpeiros* are probably a minority. In his survey of *garimpeiros* in Poxoréo in Mato Grosso, Baxter (1975 pp. 193, 211) found only 15 per cent who cited mining as their sole occupation; the large majority, like their fathers, combined the activity with work in agriculture. In southern Pará, the gold rush attracted migrants from the surrounding area who had been employed as wage labourers on ranches or in urban areas, as well as farmers with their own small plots of land (Equipes Pastorais 1982 pp. 62–3; Esterci 1982 pp. 81–3). The vast majority of these were migrants who had come to the area with the hope of gaining their own piece of land, only to find most of the territory claimed by large landowners (Pinto 1982; Schmink 1981).

The attraction of the *garimpo* for these migrants was in part the possibility of attaining real wealth. Certainly some astronomical fortunes have been made, as in the case of the famous seven-kilo gold nugget, and have been well publicised by the media. Of the tens of thousands of *garimpeiros* in the area, however, these are a very small proportion. Still, even the more modest earnings to be had in the *garimpo* represent an attractive alternative for populations with few resources (Baxter 1975 pp. 232, 354). Daily wages in Serra Pelada were high compared to other employment. A *garimpeiro* skilled in washing or cleaning ore might earn Cr$ 2–3000 per day, while an unskilled *formiga* (who carried sacks of mud) was paid Cr$ 1500 per day. Working a seven-day week could therefore yield a monthly income of Cr$ 45 000 even for unskilled workers, far above their earning power in urban areas (*Informe Amazônico* op. cit.). For those working as *meia-praças*, *garimpagem* offered work that virtually eliminated living expenses. Furthermore, *garimpagem* is relatively free from supervision, in contrast to work as a *peão* in forest clearing for ranches, with the *jagunço* as overseer. Control over their own labour process, and freedom from debt, have both material and symbolic value for *garimpeiros* (Equipes Pastorais 1982 p. 72; Esterci 1982 p. 75). These motivations for joining Brazil's latter-day gold rush parallel those found in a survey of gold miners in the United States during the Great Depression (Merrill, Henderson and Kiessling 1937).

In allowing the *garimpeiros* to remain in the goldfields, the government hoped to reduce the social tensions present in southern Pará by diluting the increasingly aggressive pressures by *posseiros* for access to land. At the same time, political indoctrination and Curió's populist tactics were designed to forge a pro-government political base to counter the growing opposition forces in the region. Curió's victory in the 1982 elections is one indication of the success of these actions, but opposition candidates won in most of southern Pará. Furthermore, organised *posseiro* invasions have continued unabated. Some *posseiros* who went to the *garimpo* left relatives or others on their land in order to retain their rights, even if they failed to plant crops that season. The *garimpo* represented a transitory means of earning some monetary income to allow them to hold on longer and continue their struggle for land (Esterci 1982). A great many *garimpeiros* were drawn not from *posseiro* populations involved in land struggles, but from landless workers in both rural and urban areas. Their absence created a labour shortage in the area that had a positive impact on wage rates (Equipes Pastorais 1982 p. 73).

Military intervention in the *garimpo* has therefore probably been more successful in transforming the traditional social and ideological systems of the *garimpo* itself than in achieving a significant impact on the broader political struggles in the region. *Garimpeiros* share a common social position with other resource-poor migrants whose material interests are threatened by powerful economic interests and by military control. At an ideological level, their traditions embodied in the law of the *garimpeiro* are fundamentally opposed to the new forms of social relations being imposed on the frontier. They are therefore in a position to construct an 'anti-capitalist critique' of the dominant socio-economic structure that seeks to transform their way of life (Taussig 1980). In this way their resistance contributes to the more general and growing opposition among dispossessed social groups on the frontier, to government policies that favour the interests of powerful capitalist groups.

## Acknowledgements

Except where otherwise noted, the material presented here is taken from field reports based on visits to prospecting areas and on interviews with those involved in this activity. In most cases the author was directly involved, but some reports were written by other members of the CEDEPLAR research team. The author is greatful to her colleagues for their collaboration in collecting and sharing field data. Appreciation is also due to José de Souza Martins for useful comments on an earlier version of this paper. The responsibility for the analysis presented, however, lies with the author. Dr Schmink is Executive Director of the Amazon Research and Training Program, Center for Latin American Studies, University of Florida, Gainesville.

1 The term comes from '*grimpeiro*', referring to miners who hid in higher elevations to warn of the approach of royal soldiers (Saint-Hilaire 1941 pp. 17–18).
2 This analysis draws on material collected during fieldwork in 1976, 1978, 1980, and 1981 carried out in conjunction with CEDEPLAR (Centro de Desenvolvimento e Planejamento Regional), Federal University of Minas Gerais. Research has been financed at different times by SUDAM (Superintendência do Desenvolvimento da Amazônia), Brazil; IDRC (International Development Research Centre), Canada; The Tinker Foundation, New York; and the University of Florida.

# 11 Land grants for indigenous communities in the Ecuadorian Amazon

JORGE E. UQUILLAS

## Introduction

The Ecuadorian Amazon is at present a vast tropical rainforest of about 83 700 square miles. Its estimated population in 1982 was almost 300 000 inhabitants, 40% of whom were natives and the rest either new settlers or descendants of settlers. Although its oil is the principal source of Ecuador's national income, the region's economy generally depends on farming and cattle ranching; in fact, about 70% of the economically active population works on the land.

Although the non-indigenous occupation of the region began a few years after the Spanish Conquest, only after the 1970s has there been an accelerating process of colonisation that has attracted thousands of people from other parts of Ecuador (Uquillas 1982a). This process has been the harbinger of other significant events, many with negative consequences for the native inhabitants as well as for the environment, particularly in the oil-producing Northeast. One consequence of these phenomena has been a growing concern among indigenous communities about the need to protect their territorial rights and thus avoid further damage to their physical and cultural integrity.

The dominant trend at national level is to ignore or underestimate the native lands issue and to advocate new and far-reaching colonisation schemes. But there is also an opposite current, inspired by native organisations – such as the Shuar Federation and other associations of Quechua-speaking communities – as well as parties committed to their cause, that are seeking official recognition of the territorial rights of the indigenous peoples.

The present study analyses data on land tenure among indigenous communities of the Ecuadorian Amazon and describes some new efforts to deal appropriately with the problem, particularly the Project for the Delimitation of Native Territories, in which the author of this report has played an active role.

## Who controls the land in Amazonia?

The indigenous people of the Amazon region have usually resorted to non-violent resistance when entrepreneurs or settlers advanced and took over their ancestral lands. However, there have been times when their reaction has been violent, as illustrated by the 1578 rebellion of the Quijos-Quechua under the leadership of Cacique Jumandi (Oberem 1980) and a similar uprising of the Shuar in 1599, under Quirrube (Harner 1973). In both cases the natives fought against foreign domination, as represented by either the Spanish colonial administration or the Roman Catholic missions. In relatively recent times, the Waorani have also adopted violent methods to keep missionaries, oil-exploration parties and other intruders out of their territorial domains (Muratorio 1982 pp. 48–69).

In contrast, the last decade has witnessed a significant change of tactics as the different native ethnic groups, and especially the most numerous and organised ones, have learned to use the dominant system to achieve their objectives. In the particular issue of land rights, the indigenous communities have not only requested but demanded that their traditionally held territories be granted legally to them, usually with global or communal titles.

The State has been responsive and has consequently acted on many of those requests. Thus, from 1964 to mid-1982, out of a total of 874 741 hectares granted in the Amazon region, the indigenous communities have received 345 677 or approximately 40% of the total, allocated to 4343 families (see Table 1). The rest has gone to colonists and to agricultural and cattle-ranching companies. Most of the land given to indigenous people has benefited Shuar and Quechua communities in the province of Morona Santiago and Napo, respectively (see Table 2). Also, according to the agrarian reform and colonisation institute (IERAC), by mid-1982 there were a further 210 772 hectares demarcated and in the process of adjudication (IERAC nd).

Significantly, the Shuar people had received titles to lands located not only in their traditionally held areas of Morona Santiago and Zamora Chinchipe but also in other provinces of Ecuador's Amazonia. This is a result both of a demographic increase and of the Shuars' ability to exert political pressure. They have thus been able to obtain legal rights to land in other areas of the country.

Some small ethnic groups of the Northeast have also been granted plots of land with communal title. The Cofan of Dureno and Dovino as well as the Siona-Secoya

Table 1   Land titles granted in the Amazon Region, Ecuador, 1964 to mid–1982

| | Hectares | % | Number of Families | % |
|---|---|---|---|---|
| Amazon Region | 874 741 | 100.0 | 17 181 | 100.0 |
| Colonists and companies | 529 064 | 60.5 | 12 838 | 74.7 |
| Indigenous communities | 345 677 | 39.5 | 4 343 | 25.3 |

Source: Compiled and computed by the author from data in IERAC (nd).

Table 2  Land granted to indigenous communities of the Amazon Region, by province, Ecuador, 1964 to mid-1982. (Areas in hectares.)

| | Communities | | | |
|---|---|---|---|---|
| Province | Shuar and Achuar | Quechua | Cofan | Siona and Secoya |
| Total | 198 520 | 125 937[a] | 13 435 | 7 787 |
| Napo | 10 653 | | 13 435 | 7 787 |
| | | 125 935[a] | | |
| Pastaza | 8 884 | | | |
| Morona Santiago | 174 975 | | | |
| Zamora Chinchipe | 4 008 | | | |

Source: Compiled and computed by the author from data in IERAC (nd).
Note: a Estimated number; it includes Canelos Quechua and Quijos Quechua.

of San Pablo and Cuyabeno, numbering about 500 in each ethnic group, have received extensions of 13 435 and 787 hectares, respectively. It is very significant to note that, according to reports to the author by Cofan and Siona-Secoya leaders, the sites were selected by their own people with the assistance of personnel from the Summer Institute of Linguistics, rather than arbitrarily by other parties. Undoubtedly, the Government of Ecuador has made great efforts to recognise the Amazon natives' right to hold their traditional territories legally. However, those efforts have been only partial. There are still innumerable communities whose lands have not yet been delimited, much less granted titles. The most dramatic example is that of the Waorani, who do not have legal title to any of the very ample territories they have occupied for generations.

Official policies favouring the formation of new settlements and greater farm and cattle production, plus the pioneers' greater cunning and ability, have determined that the best lands, both in terms of location and soil type have been given to individual and corporated colonists. These settlers therefore predominate in areas with easy access to the provincial capitals and main roads as well as in the more fertile lands of the Upano and Alto Napo river basins and in the Shushufindi sector. Most of the colonists' cooperatives and pre-cooperatives[1] as well as the larger cattle-ranching, palm and tea-producing concerns are found in the above-mentioned areas. De-facto possession of land is also much greater among new settlers than among natives, especially in the Northeast.

## The land-granting process

The official process of land delimitation and adjudication continues normally, but its progress is rather slow. As stated previously, there are hundreds of thousands of hectares delimited but without titles duly granted, and of course greater areas have not yet even been surveyed. According to verbal reports by IERAC officials to the author, this serious situation is due to an acute lack of human and financial resources as the Institution's Amazon branches. Such deficiencies have obliged some native organisations to adopt other measures to obtain land titles. Thus, the Quechua-speaking communities of UNAE (Unión de Nativos de la Amazonía Ecuatoriana) have delimited their territories themselves, to the despair of local public officials and colonists who would prefer to see those lands without a declared proprietor. Similarly, the Shuar Federation had to seek help from outside institutions such as the United States Peace Corps in order to organise land-surveying teams that measured and delimited communal lands under a special agreement with IERAC.

Apart from the slowness of the process, a much more serious and complex problem is that the criteria used to allocate land are directed more to the needs of colonists than of indigenous people, and more to intensive-agriculture practices and market-oriented production than to the patterns of forest resource utilisation and management characteristic of native ethnic groups.

Indigenous land-use patterns, although not homogeneous, are very different from the colonists'. Briefly stated, they range from a combination of shifting cultivation, hunting, fishing and collecting forest products, to sedentary subsistence agriculture, and even to incipient farm and cattle production oriented towards local markets.

Prevailing official criteria have established, as a general rule, grants of 40–50 hectares to individual families in the Amazon region. In recent times, indigenous communities have been given larger extensions of land which result in greater averages per family, but they have been awarded with communal titles. Unfortunately, in IERAC as well as in other public institutions there is still much inflexibility and resistance to criteria that maintain that for many indigenous communities the average area per family must be greater than 80 to 100 hectares. This tendency is even worse if one argues that, instead of computing averages as is usually done, decisions should be based on other parameters such as the social and cultural needs of the native people or the prevailing patterns of resource utilisation.

## The Project for the Delimitation of Native Territories

### Policy making

A relatively novel approach to the land problem affecting various Ecuadorian native groups has been applied since 1979. The Project for the Delimitation of Native Territories, started as a joint initiative of the Amazon Colonisation Institute (INCRAE) and Cultural Survival, is developing an appropriate methodology to determine what constitutes a sufficient land base for the physical and cultural survival as well as the self-determination of native ethnic groups of the Amazon region. Officially the Project is in the hands of an inter-institutional commission, created by the Minister of Agriculture on 11 September 1980, and composed of INCRAE, IERAC and three other departments of the Ministry. Unofficially, this initiative counts on the direct participation of indigenous communities and leaders interested in the land issue. It has, in addition, received support from individual social scientists and naturalists as well as from some public and private organisations.

Besides the necessary fieldwork to determine delimitation criteria, the Project's methodology has involved the active participation of researchers and some native leaders in the national policy-making process. Technical and political considerations have usually gone hand-in-hand at every stage of the work, particularly in the final and crucial stages of making decisions. As a consequence, by the end of 1982 the Project has completed its field research, which obviously included close consultations with the ethnic groups: Cofan, Siona-Secoya and Waorani. There has been concerted action to make public officials more aware of the problem and, on the basis of the research reports (Uquillas 1982b) several recommended solutions to the land problem have been considered and partially approved. However, these deicisions have not yet been officially announced as there are a few issues still under study.

The policy-making process has been long and arduous. At the start, the objective proposed by the Project (to determine the most pressing problems affecting the indigenous people of the Amazon region and, particularly, to secure for them extensions of land considered sufficient and adequate for each community or ethnic group, according to appropriate criteria or parameters) were approved enthusiastically by the directors of the participating institutions. Furthermore, official delegates who went into the field and learned first-hand the plight of the ethnic groups under study, became acutely aware of the importance of finding adequate solutions to the problems they found. Their individual reports closely reflected the needs and aspirations of the native peoples. In general they argued in favour of granting each community fairly extensive territories, including (in some cases) extra land as buffer zones (see Macdonald 1982, Vickers 1982, and Yost 1982). At the final stages of the Project, the land issue had to be dealt with at the director's level because of the political implications involved. The only exception was the participation of the present author, who acted as secretary of the commission. It is significant that at the beginning, the Project was heavily influenced by the people who inspired it as well as by the field workers, among whom were four anthropologists and a sociologist. However, at the final stages the influence of the heads of the participating public institutions, most of whom were agricultural technicians with political considerations uppermost in their minds, tended to predominate. In any case, some important decisions are still under consideration. These will provide acceptable solutions to the pressing territorial needs of the ethnic groups considered so far.

**Methodology**

The Delimitation Project has not pretended to find a formula to compute the exact land area which should be allocated to an indigenous family or community in Amazonia. It has, rather, sought to identify factors that should be given priority consideration in order to delimit sufficient and adequate territories to allow the physical and cultural continuity of native ethnic groups of the region, particularly those most threatened by the advance of colonists and entrepreneurs. This complex work is described briefly below, with some illustrations from the Waorani case.

The first stage of the Project involved a historical overview of each ethnic group, including its social and cultural transformations, settlement patterns and the extent of its traditionally held territories. This work relied heavily on previous studies and field research carried on by William Vickers and James Yost, anthropologists who covered the Siona-Secoya and Waorani respectively and collaborated actively on this Project. (Some of their earlier work can be found in Yost 1978, 1979 and 1981 as well as in Vickers 1976.) Thus the Waorani, who for generations exerted territorial control over an area of nearly 20 000 square kilometres on the south side of the Napo river, have in the past 25 years gradually moved into the Protectorate, a sort of reserve of 1600 square kilometres established by IERAC in 1969. This process of resettlement has occurred because of a combination of factors, such as the pressure of oil interests, colonist and Quechua groups, all of which competed with the Waorani for the soil and subsoil resources of this territory. Similarly, it has been the direct consequence of action taken by the Summer Institute of Linguistics, whose aim was precisely to concentrate the Waorani into a specific land area in order to facilitate its work among this unique ethnic group of Ecuador's Amazonia.

The second stage of the study depended largely on field research, including meetings with all the native communities involved. Values that these indigenous people assigned to different natural resources as well as their actual patterns of utilisation were analysed. It was established that, despite the growing influence of Hispanic culture, all the ethnic groups studied were still highly dependent on the tropical forests: their local economy, social structure and value systems were intimately related to their jungle habitat. For instance, the Waorani's daily diet depended largely not only on the protein they obtained from their hunting and fishing but also on the wild fruits collected in the forest and on the products of their shifting subsistence agriculture.

Population growth and the reduction of their traditional habitat have produced a greater demand for game meat among the Waorani. They have therefore become increasingly aware of the need to have alternative land areas to which they could turn before resources are depleted. In addition, the well known low soil fertility of Amazon land has led the Waorani to adopt special management practices such as planting alternative gardens, often at intervals of several miles. This gives them a continuous supply of cultivated products, because when the returns of the nearest gardens are low others will be at the harvest stage, and when they in turn become unproductive new distant plots will be ready.

In cases when the resources of a given extended land area have become scarce and not been sufficient for the subsistence needs of a community, the Waorani have turned to resettlement. (This happened with some frequency in the past but in recent times has been increasingly difficult, owing to their larger population, dependency on air flights that makes them stay close to the landing strips, and reduction of traditional territory, among other things.)

Finally, the commission evaluated phenomena affecting the Amazon as a whole, such as the rapid advance of spontaneous settlement and the increasing exploitation of natural resources, particularly wood and oil. In the case of the Waorani, it was found that their previously isolated communities are presently under great pressure and that a large portion of their traditionally held territory is now occupied by colonists. (For more detail on the variables affecting land needs of the Waorani, see Yost 1978.)

## Concluding remarks

The present analysis of land tenure in the Ecuadorian Amazon has shown that nearly 40% of the legally granted area belongs to indigenous communities. This fact reflects public policies favourable to the plight of native ethnic groups regarding their land rights. However, there are still hundreds of thousands of hectares without a defined legal status, most of which have for centuries been occupied by indigenous peoples. There is an urgent need to tackle this problem and find solutions, using not only routine methods but also the application of new and appropriate criteria for delimitation.

One of these new approaches described here is the Project for the Delimitation of Native Territories in Ecuador's Amazonia, presently being carried out by a commission made up of representatives of several institutions dependent on the Ministry of Agriculture. The commission's work has been guided by the criteria that the physical integrity, self-determination and cultural continuity of native ethnic groups should be guaranteed. Also, additional violent change should not be imposed on indigenous communities who are already under the overpowering influence of events which it is almost impossible to control in present conditions, such as oil exploitation and the influx of spontaneous settlers. To achieve these goals it is essential that natives of Ecuador's Amazonia be fully granted the right to ample land extensions in their ancestral territories.

This Project, which could become a model for the solution of similar problems in other areas of the world, is a joint enterprise of Amazon native peoples and involved individuals and institutions who believe that man and nature should live in harmony and that existing problems must be studied in depth in order to find appropriate solutions.

1 Literally, a cooperative in the process of formation. Settlers organised pre-cooperatives in order to claim land; this enables them to apply for titles and official loans.

# 12 Indigenous communities and Peru's conquest of the Amazon: the distribution of land and resources in the Pichis-Palcazu

RICHARD CHASE SMITH

In May 1981 the Peruvian Prime Minister and Minister of Finance, Dr Manuel Ulloa, presented a package of proposed projects to representatives of the international banking community and the multi- and bilateral lending institutions gathered in Paris. These projects, representing a total of US$ 8 thousand million, will require at least US$ 4.6 thousand million from external sources. The largest investments are planned for projects to develop Peru's mining, petroleum, and hydroelectric potential. The second priority is the development of Peru's eastern lowlands. The Belaúnde government plans to invest about US$ 850 million in roads, colonisation, and rural development. This represents 72% of the total investments in the agricultural/rural development sector.

The target areas in the eastern lowlands are the Pichis-Palcazu, Oxapampa-Satipo, Alto Mayo, Jaén-Bagua-San Ignacio, Alto Huallaga, Huallaga Central, and Madre de Dios. A Special Project Office will be established under the Prime Minister for each project, purportedly permitting greater administrative autonomy. A Special Project Office was established for the Pichis-Palcazu project in November 1980; one for the Madre de Dios project was established in late 1981; and others are expected to open soon.

Though the 1974–8 Native Communities Law guarantees each indigenous settlement an adequate resource base, development plans for the Peruvian Amazon raise serious doubts about the government's intention to respect the rights of the region's 300 000 Indians. As many as 10 000 Aguaruna will be affected by the Alto Mayo and Jaén-Bagua-San Ignacio projects; as many as 20 000 Campa, Amuesha, and Cashibo Indians will be affected by the Pichis-Palcazu and Oxapampa projects; and perhaps 4000 Amarakaeri, Sapiteri, Huachipaeri, Ese'ejja, and Amahuaca will be affected by the Madre de Dios project.

To date, the Peruvian government has focused most of its attention on the Pichis-Palcazu project, for which it originally projected an investment of US$ 250 million in road construction, colonisation, and forestry development. Optimistic cabinet members talked of plans to resettle 150 000 people into this area. Plans are now being drawn up for the construction of a new city at the intersection of the Marginal Highway and the Palcazu river. President Belaúnde, the project's staunchest supporter, envisions a future commercial centre at this site which will rival Pucallpa in size and scope.

Thus far USAID, CIDA of Canada, the Federal Republic of Germany and the Inter-American Development Bank have made commitments to fund the Pichis-Palcazu project with far less than the Peruvian officials were counting on. USAID and the Peruvian government are currently working out the details of the Palcazu Natural Resource Management project for which US$ 22 million have been made available.

Meanwhile, the Peruvian government has moved ahead to create a large Special Project Office in Lima and two regional offices, one in the Palcazu and one in the Pachitea. Four more regional offices are planned for the near future. Construction is proceeding on the San Alejandro–Puerto Bermudez section of the Marginal Highway. Construction of the 115 km branch road through the Palcazu valley, which began in 1981 with funds from the US PL480 programme, has apparently been halted due to a funding dispute between USAID and the Peruvian government. The Ministry of Agriculture has been commissioned to prepare a plan to settle existing land claims and to resettle an unknown number of new families into the area. The Forestry Department of the National Agrarian University has been contracted to prepare a plan for forestry and lumber development in the same region.

During a USAID-sponsored environmental assessment of the Palcazu valley, three key problems surfaced concerning the project. They were the poor land-use potential of the valley, the high social and economic cost of the branch road, and the inadequate and poorly protected land and resource base of the indigenous Amuesha population. Though all three problems are closely interrelated, I want to examine the last in more detail at this time.

The Amuesha are an indigenous group who have inhabited the central Peruvian *montaña* for several millennia. Today the 5000 Amuesha are organised into 29 Native Communities which were legally established in 1974 by the Law of Native Communities. These 29 communities are located in the Departments of Pasco, Junín, and Huánuco. Under the 1974 Law and its 1978 revised version, the Peruvian Government has extended communal land titles to 17 of the 29 Amuesha communities for a total of approximately 40 000 hectares. By law, community lands are inalienable, whether through sale, rent, mortgage or by any other arrangement. Though in most cases the lands are worked by individual families, they are administered and defended collectively by the community assembly. The 1978 version of the law distinguishes between lands with a capacity for agriculture, production forestry, and protection. Lands designated for production forestry under this law cannot be titled to a community, but only ceded in usufruct. No Amuesha community has received a land title since 1978.

Fourteen of the 29 Amuesha communities are located in the Palcazu drainage area. The current population of Amuesha in this area is about 3000. Nine of these 14 communities in the Palcazu area have legal title to a total of 28 226 hectares of land. Since 1976 these communities have petitioned the Peruvian government to extend land titles to all 14 communities and to additional land needed to create a continuous territory of about 60 000 hectares. The most recent petition was presented to the Minister of Agriculture in February 1981, after the Pichis-Palcazu project had been established (Chase Smith 1982b Appendix D).

Partially in response to public outcry and to pressure from the US Congress (Chase Smith 1982b Appendices E and F). USAID attached a land-titling condition to their funding commitment: no funds would be forthcoming until Indian lands were demarcated and titled. By July of 1981 the Special Project Office, by special arrangements with the Ministry of Agriculture had sent teams to the Palcazu area to begin demarcating Indian lands. However the project officer made it clear that Indian communities which already had clear title would not receive more land, despite the existence in most cases of unsettled state-owned land contiguous to the community. The project said that all state-owned lands were reserved for colonisation projects. The project director justified this policy by saying that Peru's tribal peoples must be incorporated into the market economy. Additional land grants to the Amuesha, he argued, would only encourage them to continue their primitive nomadism and subsistence agriculture.

In order for an indigenous population to successfully participate in the market economy, and retain their distinctive social organisation and cultural identity, they must be assured an adequate land and resource base, sufficient technical capacity, and capital to organise, develop and administer their own productive forces in such a way as to maximise a sustained-yield economy capable of maintaining the community over many generations. Although the Amuesha have been participating in the market economy for over a century through wage labour, coffee production, and cattle raising, the great majority remain extremely poor. This is so because the conditions under which they participate in the market economy have always been extremely unfavourable, and, as I will demonstrate here, their reduced resource base, while adequate in most cases for shifting subsistence agriculture, is not adequate for commercially productive activities.

An analysis was made of the land-use suitability of areas within the landholdings of 10 to 14 native communities in the Palcazu drainage area (Chase Smith 1981). Three kinds of data were used in this study: the semi-detailed ONERN soil and land-use classification maps for the Palcazu valley at a scale of 1/25 000, later revised by Tosi of the USAID environmental evaluation team;[1] the original land-survey maps for each titled community at a scale of 1/20 000; and current population censuses for the same communities. The procedure was simple: the community boundaries were transposed to the land-use classification maps and a polar planimeter was used to ascertain the area in hectares of the different land-use classes within each community. Then the total area of each land-use class was divided by the number of families living in each community to give an accurate land/family ratio. The results are shown in Table 1.

As might be expected, there is a wide range in the quantity and quality of lands available in the ten communities under study. Agricultural lands range from a high of 40% of the total community area to a low of 6%. Land for production forestry ranges from a high of 78% of total area to a low, in three communities, of 6%. There is clearly an unequal distribution of usable lands amongst these communities. The five communities located on the alluvial plains of the Palcazu river and its tributaries have more better-quality lands than those located in the mountainous headwaters.

A comparison of the ratios of agricultural land per family points at this inequality more clearly (Table 2). The ten communities fall into three ranges: one community with a ratio of 30 hectares per family is clearly in a class by itself; the second group of four floodplain communities ranges from 12 to 19 hectares per family; and the third group of five upland communities ranges from 7 to 8 hectares per family. A comparison of production forest lands demonstrates a similar range (Table 3). One floodplain community has a high of 77 hectares per family; a second group of

Table 1    Land-use capability class areas as percentage of total area

| Native Community | Class A+C+P | Class F1+F2 | Total usable area |
|---|---|---|---|
| 1  7 de Junio | 39.5 | 50 | 89.5 |
| 2  Santa Rosa Chuchurras | 19.8 | 78 | 97.8 |
| 3  Buenos Aires | 21.5 | 51.5 | 73 |
| 4  Alto Iscozacin | 16.2 | 28 | 44.2 |
| 5  Shiringamazu | 19 | 42 | 61 |
| 6  Loma Linda – P. Laguna | 12.5 | 5.5 | 18 |
| 7  Santa Rosa de Pichanas | 7 | 6 | 13 |
| 8  San Pedro de Pichanas | 6 | 6 | 12 |
| 9  Alto Lagarto | 7 | 6 | 13 |

Table 2    Ratio of agricultural lands per family (class A, class P, class C)

| Native Community | Hectares/family 1980 | Hectares/family 1990 |
|---|---|---|
| 7 de Junio | 29.5 | 19.6 |
| Santa Rosa Chuchurras | 19.4 | 12.8 |
| Buenos Aires | 17.5 | 11.7 |
| Alto Iscozacin | 15.5 | 10.2 |
| Shiringamazu | 12.2 | 8 |
| Loma Linda – P. Laguna | 8 | 5.2 |
| Santa Rosa de Pichanas | 8 | 5.2 |
| San Pedro de Pichanas | 8.1 | 5.3 |
| Alto Lagarto | 7 | 4.6 |

Table 3    Ratio of production forestry lands per family (class F1 and F2)

| Native Community | Hectares/family 1980 | Hectares/family 1990 |
|---|---|---|
| Santa Rosa Chuchurras | 77 | 50.8 |
| Buenos Aires | 38.5 | 25.4 |
| 7 de Junio | 37.8 | 25 |
| Shiringamazu | 27.2 | 17.9 |
| Alto Iscozacin | 26.9 | 17.7 |
| San Pedro de Pichanas | 8.1 | 5.3 |
| Santa Rosa de Pichanas | 6.9 | 4.5 |
| Alto Lagarto | 6 | 3.9 |
| Loma Linda – P. Laguna | 3.5 | 2.3 |

floodplain communities ranges from 27 to 37 hectares per family; and five upland communities range from 3.5 to 8 hectares per family.

These land/family ratios were then compared with the calculated land needs of an average-size family for different economic activities. Subsistence agriculture, commercial agriculture, cattle raising, and production forestry were considered. The Amuesha, like the non-indigenous colonists of the Palcazu valley, practise a variety of slash-and-burn subsistence agriculture, in which they cut an area of forest, burn it, and plant their food crops. When depleted soil fertility and the invasion of weeds make the garden production dwindle, the site is abandoned and the forest is allowed to regenerate itself.

If we assume an average-size garden of 1.5 hectares per year and an average fallow time of 10 years, then a minimum of 15 hectares of agricultural land is needed to supply the vegetable food intake of an individual Amuesha family. A brief comparison of this minimum with the current holdings (Table 2) demonstrates that 6 of the 10 communities studied did not have sufficient agricultural land to provide each family with the minimum needed for subsistence. Three others could provide a small margin beyond that needed for subsistence.

Because commercial agriculture is not an important activity in the Palcazu valley, it is difficult to estimate with precision the minimum amount of land which is necessary for a viable agricultural enterprise. A study commissioned by the Special Project Office concluded that a minimum of 10 hectares of Class A land for intensive annual crop production or 30 hectares of Class C land for traditional shifting cultivation with permanent crops was necessary to provide a family with a minimum standard of living. The USAID evaluation team concurred with those estimates and added data to show that a minimum of 50 hectares of Class P land for cattle production was required to provide the same standard of living (Pool 1981; Staver 1981). In this way, we can establish a simple formula of equivalents: 1 hectare of Class A land is roughly equivalent to 3 hectares of Class C land or to 5 ha of Class P land.

*Table 4    Ratio of unit-equivalents of agricultural land per family (1 ha A land=3 ha; C land=5 ha; P land)*

| Native Community | Unit-equivalent 1980 | Unit-equivalent 1990 |
|---|---|---|
| 1  7 de Junio | 10.4 | 6.8 |
| 2  Santa Rosa Chuchurras | 8.7 | 5.7 |
| 3  Buenos Aires | 5.4 | 3.5 |
| 4  Alto Iscozacin | 5.8 | 3.8 |
| 5  Shiringamazu | 3.8 | 2.8 |
| 6  San Pedro de Pichanas | 2.3 | 1.6 |
| 7  Loma Linda – P. Laguna | 2.4 | 1.5 |
| 8  Santa Rosa de Pichanas | 2.3 | 1.5 |
| 9  Alto Lagarto | 2 | 1.3 |

By converting the land available to the communities to Class A land-unit equivalents, it is possible to establish the current ratio of agricultural land unit-equivalents per family for each community (Table 4). By comparing this figure with the minimum 10 unit-equivalents necessary to support a family, a fair estimate of the adequacy of the current landholdings for commercial agricultural activities can be established.

This analysis shows that only one community currently has sufficient agricultural land to provide the minimum of 10 unit-equivalents per family. Six communities have less than half the minimum required. With the exception of one community, the current landholdings of the Palcazu Indians are not even minimally sufficient to provide a cash income from either agriculture or cattle raising.

Because of the severe land limitations, cattle raising is not an alternative that is both economically viable and ecologically sound (Staver 1981). However, the Amuesha in all the Palcazu communities are actively engaged in cattle raising; the current cattle population in these communities is about 2500 head and growing. In 8 of the 10 communities, areas currently cleared and in pasture far exceed the area classified for that activity. In 2 communities the total area under pasture exceeds the total area classified for agricultural use. Clearly in these communities lands suitable only for forestry activities or for protection is being cleared for agricultural use primarily because of the lack of suitable lands.

The Special Project Office has made two different calculations of the parcel size for the forestry colonisation project within the Von Humboldt National Forest (Proyecto Especial Pichis-Palcazu 1981). One established a minimum parcel size of 400 hectares per family with a yearly exploitation of 20 ha; the other 235 ha with a yearly exploitation of 12 ha. In each case the colonist would presumably combine some subsistence agriculture with his forestry activities in order to provide food for his family.

Judging from this basis, no community in the Palcazu area has sufficient forest lands to make timber extraction a viable economic alternative on a long-term sustained-yield basis. By combining production forestry with subsistence and commercial agriculture, two of the Palcazu communities may have an adequate resource base to support their populations. The five communities with less than 10 ha of production forestry land per family cannot count on sustained-yield lumbering to support any portion of their population. At best the lumber from these communities could provide an initial capital for investing in other more productive activities.

If one were to rate the Palcazu native communities in terms of the capacity of their current land and resource base to sustain long-range economic development and to permit the Amuesha residents to participate successfully in the market economy, one community would receive a good rating; four communities a fair to poor rating; and five communities a critically poor rating.

This last group are so poorly endowed with agricultural and forest lands that their situation is already critical. Serious problems have so far been avoided only because the residents of these communities have been relatively isolated and therefore minimally dependent on the market economy. As the Palcazu branch road will shortly pass through three of these five communities, their needs for consumer goods will rapidly increase as will the pressure on their land and resources to produce greater cash incomes to pay for these goods. Within the decade, the resources of these communities will be under severe pressure, provoking serious overall environmental degradation and possible food shortages.

Given this extremely poor resource base, the forced incorporation of the Palcazu Amuesha into the market economy through the construction of the branch road, the influx of large numbers of colonists, and the development of large cattle and lumber enterprises, will have serious long-range effects on the Amuesha population.

1    The Amuesha will become poorer. Increasing population, decreasing soil fertility, and resource depletion will combine to reduce productivity and income per capita. Individual families will become less able to sustain their own basic needs for food, clothing and shelter from local resources and thus more dependent on the market to supply them.

2    The Amuesha who can no longer satisfy their increasing needs for cash will:

(a)  continue to live and practise subsistence agriculture in their community, but form part of a marginally employed labour pool for the large cattle ranches and the growing lumber industry of the Palcazu valley;

(b)  migrate to other better-endowed communities, increasing the pressure on their resources;

(c)  or migrate to urban areas in search of higher-paying jobs, thus adding to the ranks of the urban unemployed.

3    The current situation will create a marked inequality in land distribution in the valley with individual colonists holding up to 50 times the amount of land available to individual Amuesha families. This will increase both social resentment and potential conflict between different socio-economic groups.

4    As the land/family ratio decreases, the control over the communities' land and resources will become more individualised, and their distribution more unequal. As competition for these scarce resources increases, promoted by the exigencies of the market economy, social conflict will increase within the community, straining the community structure and the whole web of ties which holds the Amuesha together as a distinct social and ethnic group.

Many members of the development community claim that the government's attitude toward the indigenous population in the project area is based on ignorance. They say that if only enough of the right information could be put into the right hands, then mistaken policies would be corrected. No doubt there is a great need for correct information and solid analysis for the development process to benefit all segments of society, especially, in this case, the indigenous peoples.

However, when presented with the results of this study and with specific recommendations to improve the Amuesha situation, government officials, though visibly uncomfortable, refuted the conclusions. They reiterated their policy that the government would not recognise any new native communities nor expand the existing ones within the project area. Some time later the project director announced that the project would give individual family parcels to the current 'excess population' of the communities, provided the families leave their home communities.

This announcement was followed some time later by an article in a prominent Lima newspaper in which a project official was quoted as questioning the validity of the Native Community structure. 'If the natives have always been nomads, why is it that now they can be settled on an established land base? Are they really accustomed to living in "Community"? Or would a policy of giving an individual parcel of land to each family be the best alternative?'

While the government is not likely to challenge the Constitution by directly eliminating the Native Community in the Pichis-Palcazu area, its policies will weaken the community organisation by luring away individual community members, who are already suffering the effects of land shortage, with the promise of their own private parcel of land (Chase Smith 1982a). In all likelihood, credit and technical assistance will flow to those with private parcels while the communities will be ignored. It has been a common pattern in the history of Indian–State relations in Peru.

Information alone then is not sufficient. Government policies towards the indigenous peoples of the Amazon are not based on ignorance, they are based largely on the political interests of the ruling elites. Information and analysis must be combined with direct political action on the part of indigenous peoples and organisations who support them in order to bring about changes in the current policies.

1 The land-use classification used here includes the following classes: agricultural land (Class A, clean tillage; Class P, pasture; Class C, permanent crops); production forest (Class F1, intensive production; Class F2, less intensive production); and protection land, Class X (Tosi 1981).

# 13 The political dimension of intertribal relations: an ethnohistorical approach

## ALONSO ZARZAR

## Abstract

A historical reconstruction and the ethnological analysis of intertribal relations between six ethnic groups in the southern part of the Peruvian Amazon Basin from prehistoric times until the turn of this century leads us to propose the existence of an indigenous social and political structure in which the central characteristic is determined by the evident asymmetry of the inter-ethnic system.

This case study classifies and analyses the different types of relations which, depending on the pattern, combined hostility with trade and war with exchange of women. Here the emphasis is put on the nature of such relations and the differences are stated according to their characteristics: equality, hierarchy and/or domination.

The result is a general picture of an indigenous political system, mainly hierarchical, combining a series of institutionalised tribal relations where the cultural assimilation by means of temporal servility and the trade between the tropical forest and highlands played main roles in its constitution and its maintenance.

## Introduction

By organising historical data from diverse sources we wish to present here a first approach to what seems to have been a system of traditional intertribal relations. In so doing we have followed Cardoso de Oliveira's methodological approach (1976). Originally conceived for analysing current situations, we have arranged it in order to clarify the history of relations between six ethnic groups of the southern Peruvian Amazon Basin.

According to Cardoso de Oliveira, four types of inter-ethnic systems can be established theoretically combining two pairs of variables: the symmetry and asymmetry of relations between tribal groups, and between these groups and sectors of the greater society. This gives the following results:

1 Egalitarian and symmetrical relations between tribal groups.
2 Hierarchic or asymmetrical relations between tribal groups.

Table 1

| Riparian groups | Linguistic classification | River |
|---|---|---|
| Piro | Arawak | Lower Urubamba and upper Ucayali |
| Conibo | Pano | Upper Ucayali |

| Groups from the affluents | Linguistic classification | River |
|---|---|---|
| Amahuaca | Pano | Right margin of the upper Ucayali, lower Urubamba and upper Purús |
| Yaminahua | Pano | As above |
| Machiguenga | Pano | Right margin of lower and upper Urubamba |
| Campa (Ashaninka) | Arawak | Tambo and affluents |

Note: Due to the currently wide dispersion of the groups, the settlements described here cannot claim to be complete. Nevertheless they account for the settlement of most of these populations since early times. Similarly, with the Campa we are only referring to a segment of this extensive and dispersed ethnic group.
Here and throughout the chapter, the terms 'riparian' and 'riverside' refer to the people who live along the main rivers of the region (lower Urubamba and upper Ucayali).

3    Relations of subordination–domination (asymmetric) between tribal groups and regional segments of the greater society.
4    Egalitarian or symmetrical relations between these two latter.

This last possibility is only theoretical and in any case it implies a utopian social state since it does not describe any known real situation.

Although this classification, which has attained a high level of abstraction, through the use of ideal types, shows us the nature of the relationship, it can say little about the character and contents of it, whether it be egalitarian or hierarchical; for in each case the relation may be friendly or hostile and furthermore may imply war, slavery or trade. On the other hand, the sharp division between the hierarchical relation and one of subordination–domination (retained for the formula: tribal groups–regional segments of the greater society) denies the possibility of speaking about a tribal relationship of the latter type. As will be made clear in the following pages these critiques can be applied to the ethnohistory of the region and, possibly, to the rest of Peruvian Amazonia.

Rather than classifying the groups linguistically we have classified according to their ecological distribution, this being of vital significance in the development of intertribal relations (see Table 1 and Figure 1). Here, and throughout the chapter, the terms 'riparian' and 'riverside' refer to the people who live along the main rivers of the region (lower Urubamba and upper Ucayali).

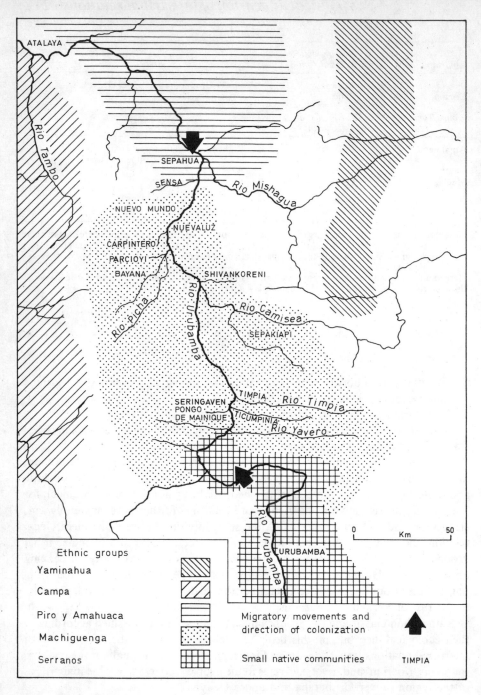

ATALAYA

Rio Tambo

SEPAHUA

SENSA

Rio Mishagua

NUEVO MUNDO

NUEVALUZ

CARPINTERO

PARCIOYI

BAYANA

SHIVANKORENI

Rio Picha

Rio Urubamba

Rio Camisea

SEPAKIAPI

TIMPIA

Rio Timpia

SERINGAVEN

PONGO
DE MAINIQUE

TICUMPINIA

Rio Yavero

Rio Urubamba

URUBAMBA

0          Km          50

Ethnic groups

Yaminahua

Campa

Piro y Amahuaca

Machiguenga

Serranos

Migratory movements and
direction of colonization

Small native communities

TIMPIA

Fig. 1 Ethnic boundaries in the lower Urubamba (source Stuart White)

## Relationships between riverside groups

First evidence of the hostilities among the riparian groups Cocama, Conibo and Piro is the large territorial distances found between each ethnic group during the sixteenth century. This hostile behaviour seems to have its origin in the rivalry for land control, for the domain over groups inhabiting the tributaries and for access to the natural resources controlled by the latter (Myers 1974). See Figure 2.

Due to the similar social and political organisation of these ethnic groups one is tempted to describe the existence of a relationship in neat equal terms. Nevertheless, this is difficult to prove; we would be more inclined to think that this equality, so clear in some of the sources; was merely an apparent one. Behind it an ambiguous, shadowy but important hierarchy can be found, neither as evident nor as extreme as the one present between the riparian groups and those settled on the affluents.

From early documents it can be deduced that at least between the Conibo and the Piro there were power differences that made an equal relationship impossible. In 1685 we read in P. Biedma's diary that:

> ... the Piro from River Tambo had a spiteful grudge against the Conibo since these captured them to work in their fields. The Conibo treated the conquered with ease and they ended up marrying Conibo women (Izaguirre 1922 I p. 252).

Thus we see how the 'equal relationship' is, in this case, a mere consequence of cultural assimilation by a more powerful ethnic group, arising from a hierarchial relationship.

This quotation does not refer to an isolated case. Ortiz (1947 p. 92) informs us that in P. Biedma's report there is reference to a Conibo chief who told the missionary that on several occasions they had raided areas around the river now named Urubamba, the land of the Piro. On the other hand, Beidma's death at the hands of the Piro is in itself evidence of this rivalry. 'It was a revenge taken by the Piro for the death of eight Piro caused by the Conibo ... when they sailed up river accompanied by P. Biedma' (Ortiz 1974, p. 105). Another reference which could seem a linguistic trait but is in fact a proof of our contention is the ancient name of the present Ucayali river: 'The name Ucayali comes from Ucayle or Ucallale which in Pano language means confluence and, according to others: river of enemies' (Heras 1978 p. 204).

However, it is not certain that the term is Pano, for, according to Stiglich (1904, p. 167) the toponymic is Campa. Although both meanings are clearly accurate: on one hand it could refer to the springs of this river at the *confluence* of the Tambo river and the Urubamba, traditionally a Piro territory; on the other hand and in Campa − according to Stiglich (idem) − it means 'river of enemies' which would obviously be the Piro who have been settled there since early times.

In 1806, almost 39 years after P. Biedma's expedition, another Franciscan reports on the stability of the hostilities between the Piro and Conibo: 'Conibos: their rivals are the Piros, but they rarely take up arms because they fear each other'

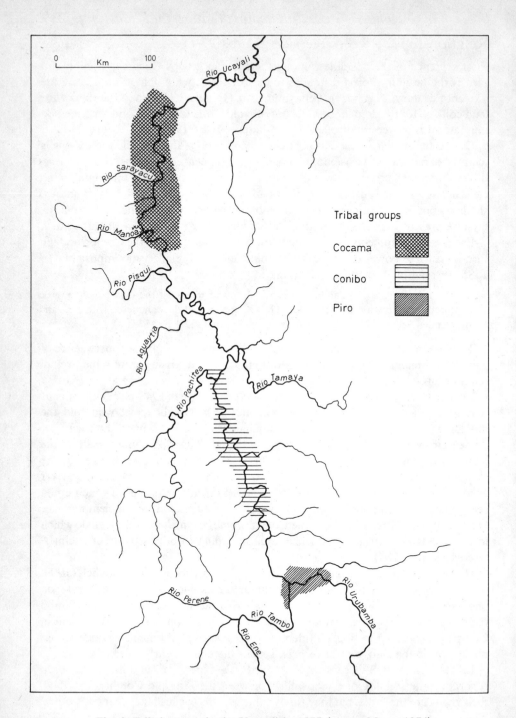

**Fig. 2 Tribal groups in the Ucuyali in 1577 (source Myers 1974)**

(P. Bousquet in Raimondi 1897 III, p. 62). We thus see there have been some changes, and the mutual feuds seem to have diminished. Forty years later, in 1846, Marcoy (1875 p 514) says: 'We were received here (Paruitcha, Conibo village and border of the Piro territory) with a frank hospitality, which event extended itself to our rowers (Piros) notwithstanding a certain antipathy which existed between the two nations.'

After that, at the turn of this century, in the middle of the rubber boom, Stiglich (1904 p. 344) corroborates that same information: '(The Conibo) are resentful of the Piro but as these have already moved further up the Mirari River, there is no opportunity for skirmishing.'

These sources account for a long-term tendency towards the pacification of the riparian groups or to the ending of hostilities between them, although there were times in which the rivalry between Piros and Conibos seems to have sharpened. Near the end of 1873 P. Sabate describes the arrival of a Piro commission at the city of Cuzco, which '. . . in name of the tribe of the Piro asked for *protection* from the Government . . .' (Izaguirre 1922 X, p. 22, my emphasis). That claim for protection can be understood only as a consequence of a highly conflicting situation; once in the Ucayali the same informant describes: 'We suddenly saw many canoes coming towards us which the Piro thought to be Conibos with whom they were at war. In those rivers everything is *fear, dread* . . .' (Izaguirre 1922 X, p. 23, my emphasis). Otherwise it would be difficult to explain the arrival of the Piro in the city of Cuzco, when the usual point of arrival for exchange with the Quechua was many days' travel from this site.

Thus, relations between Piro and Conibo were predominantly asymmetrical, faintly hierarchical and hostile; such a relationship combined the exchange of goods – precious metals obtained by the Piro from the Quechua with Conibo pottery – with raids and '*correrias*', with Conibo pre-eminence, which were aimed at increasing the labour force and its ultimate assimilation into the more powerful group's culture. This would enlarge the ethnic group, allow it more control over the territory and therefore more power.

## Relations between riparian groups and those from the affluents

In contrast, the relations between the riverside groups and the inhabitants of the streams were much more straightforward. Their nature was obviously asymmetrical and clearly hierarchical, but character and content varied according to the groups involved. As Steward and Metraux point out (1948 III p. 582): 'Slaves, captured from the weaker Panoan tribes of the hinterland, were evidently an important element in the communities of the stronger Ucayali river peoples. The Pano used to capture Mayoruna, Panatahua, Amahuaca and Shipibo.'

We can claim a similar type of relationship, with slight differences, between the Conibo and the Amahuaca as that between the Piro and these others. The same can be said about the relation between Conibo/Piro and Campa.

(a) In 1791 the Franciscan Missionary, Father Leceta, related that both Piros and Conibos capture Amahuaca (Izaguirre 1922 IX, p. 41). Half a century later Paul Marcoy wrote: 'The Remos, the Amahuacas and the Cucayas ... are victimized by the greed of the Conibos, Shipibos and Shetibos ...' (1875 II, p. 52). Just before the first rubber decade Izaguirre mentions (1922 X, p. 125), through the missionaries of that time, the existence of armed Conibo raids into Amahuaca land. Ten years later the Peruvian Carlos Fry (1886, p. 474) wrote, almost euphemistically, that in their '*correrias*' the Conibo seek to civilise the Amahuaca 'to whom they give tools in exchange for boys' in a sort of 'pacific' conquest:

> The Conibo families possess Campa and Amahuaca servants ... the children of these that are born in the house of their Conibo patrons and who have their heads flattened in the usual (Conibo) way, speak Conibo language, are circumcised, learn their (Conibo) manners and are Conibo, are now allowed to marry any member of the main family; at the 'father's' or patron's death the servant is free and may leave; but they do not do so, preferring to stay among the Conibo.

This detailed account shows what might have been a traditional strategy of assimilation which continued until the turn of the century: 'Every Conibo has a shotgun and many own Winchesters. These are used for hunting and for 'correrias' of Amahuacas whom they capture to use as servants.' (Stiglich 1904, p. 344).

Just to have an idea of how widespread this practice was: 'Almost all the Conibo, adult men and youngsters, own one or more Amahuaca servants. (idem).

Although these sources show an increase in the power of the riparian groups over those settled on the tributaries, they also hide the causes which are exogenous to the relationships between the groups and which partially explain this increased dominion. This was the setting up of an indigenous slave commerce by the first white traders of the region, a process that intensified with the coming of rubber extraction.

On the other hand, and simultaneously, the Piro practised a different type of control over the Amahuaca, consisting basically of the raiding of objects.

> A canoe of Piro indians caught up with us. They were heading towards Sepahua with the intention of doing a 'correria' into the Ipetineris (Amahuaca), from whom these people are used to steal and destroy as much as they can ... (Fray Buenaventura 1875, in Izaguirre 1922 X, p. 239).

These relationships were also paralleled in attitude:

> The inoffensive character of these natives is proverbial among the river-tribes of the Ucayali, who treat them roughly, and commonly use the expression 'stupid as an Amahuaca' ... (Marcoy 1875 II, p. 213).

We can therefore conclude that the relations between the riparian groups (Conibo and Piro) and the Amahuaca were clearly asymmetrical, deeply hierarchical and, rather than hostile they implied domination–subordination and assimilation into the culture of the riparian groups under conditions of temporal servility. This occurred despite the fact that the Piro exchange goods with the Amahuaca; a fact that does not seem to have affected the existing inequalities.

In this illustration we find a combination of what Cardoso de Oliveira considers two different types of inter-ethnic systems – asymmetrical hierarchical and the asymmetry of domination–subordination – although for this author the last category is characteristic of the relationship between Indians and whites or '*mestizos*'.

(b) The relationship between Conibos/Piros and Campas belongs to the same type of intertribal system but with certain variations.

The early historical sources mention the existence of Piro subgroups inhabiting Campa lands, more specifically some affluents of the Tambo river. This data and the fact that nowadays marriage alliances are forged between families of both groups may lead us to think of the existence of a traditional friendly or equal relationship.

In 1816 one of the greatest missionary expeditions, led by P. Plaza and made up of 326 Conibo and Piro armed with arrows and 30 men armed with shotguns in 66 canoes (Ortiz 1974, p. 258), aimed at pacifying and 'convincing' the groups still hostile to evangelisation. The Franciscans, well acquainted with the traditional political system existing among the ethnic groups, mastered this knowledge, as any conqueror would, of subduing the rebel groups to their own interests. Thus, the same story mentions the feud between a part of the convoy and the Campa groups inhabiting the Tambo river (idem p. 259).

Seventy years later Fry (1886, p. 474) compares the way the Piro treated the Campa with the relations between Conibo and Amahuaca:

> Their 'correrias' (cf. Conibo) reach mainly the Amahuaca settled on the right margin of the Ucayali River, *but are not as hostile as the Piro to the Amahuaca* [my italics].

Again, Fry points out the Conibo–Campa relationship: 'The Conibo families own Campa servants . . .' (idem). Nowadays, as part of their ethnic ideology and their belief about the origin of their illnesses, the Piro often blame the Campa when they fall ill.

We can conclude that the Conibo–Campa relationship was similar to the one between the Conibo and the Amahuaca, although unlike the former the latter share a linguistic system. Even though the Piro–Campa relationship appears more ambiguous and difficult to classify into one of the types proposed by Cardoso de Oliveira, from the sources quoted above we can be sure that hostility sharpened due to the Franciscan evangelisation.

With the information handled so far we may affirm that the traditional Piro–Campa relationship was asymmetric though oscillating between hostility and alliance; and that it was shaped though the exchange of goods and women as well as through occasional feuds.

(c) Within the links between riparian groups and inhabitants of the tributaries there existed a relationship with peculiar characteristics which was important for the trade between the jungle and the highlands. The Piro obtained their exchange goods not only as a product of work, nor exclusively from pacific trade with other groups. Among their main suppliers, forced and involuntary, were the Machiguenga; the traditional relationship between them and the Piro could not be thought of outside that context.

The earliest historical source that mentions the existence of continuous conflicts between the Manaries (Machiguenga) and the Pilcozones (Piro) is dated 1671 (Ocampo Conejeros 1955). As Camino says in his exhaustive article (1977, p. 128): '... in order to trade with the Quechua they crossed the lengthy territory of the Machiguenga, robbing, attacking and enslaving them.'

According to oral tradition compiled by Durand (1923) this pillage seems to have started many years before the conquest of the Inca Empire, and lasted until the beginning of this century. Its impact upon the Machiguenga was such that, as Camino points out, it not only altered its settlement patterns – from their original Urubamba environment they moved to its tributaries – but also altered its social and political organisation and its economy.

One of the devices employed by the Machiguenga to avoid the Piro raids was the preparation of big clearings near the mouths of the tributaries in order to provide the invaders with plenty of food.

The major change in the social organisation of the Machiguenga was the transformation of shamans into '*curacas*' (chiefs) who shifted to a redistributive role:

> To stop the Piro-Chontaquiro from robbing Machiguenga households on the tributaries, the local curacas settled on the mouths of the rivers received from their kin women and children under their control and protection. These were peacefuly given to the Piro-Chontaquiro in exchange for metal tools, fine pottery and other manufactured goods. (Camino 1977, p. 135).

In turn, these goods were redistributed by the *curacas* among the inhabitants of the tributaries.

This exchange between both ethnic groups was not exactly equal: for the Machiguenga it was more a means of avoiding pillage and raiding rather than a trade. This inequality was reflected in different spheres of their social life; Marcoy (1875 I, p. 473) illustrates this by describing the way some Piro treated a Machiguenga:

> If an Antis (Machiguenga) was by chance in their way, they (the Piro) brushed past him and even elbowed him; but without affection, as one might treat a being or a thing of no importance. From this manner of proceeding it was easy to recognize, besides the inherent foppery of the individual, the preponderance of the one nation over the other.

To conclude, we may point out that the traditional Piro–Machiguenga relationship, like the one between the Conibo and the Amahuaca, was clearly asymmetric, highly hierarchical, of dominance and subordination, but without aiming at assimilation; moreover its intention was the exchange or pillage of goods, not human beings.

## Relationships between groups from the tributaries

Unfortunately there is no early data on the relationship between Amahuaca and Yaminahua – both inhabiting major and minor affluents – but from documents of this century an old relationship can be inferred. Early this century Farabee (1922, p. 108) reports that among the Amahuaca: 'The common cause of warfare are the 'correrias'' aimed at kidnapping women.' During our visit to Sepahua on the lower Urubamba, we were able to verify not only the existence of marriage links between both groups (Zarzar and Montenegro 1977) but also the Amahuaca marriages outside their own ethnic group were almost exclusively to Yaminahua women. In 1952 Kietzman (p. 228) found a scarcity of adult men among the Amahuaca on the Sepahua river, a condition which he explained by referring to the constant skirmishes with the Yaminahua from the east (Purús river region) and the fact that the men had more contact with whites, thus being more exposed to foreign illnesses fatal to them. Another fact that favours the existence of an old relationship is in the locations both groups have had, nearly always as neighbours, being on the Purús or Yuruá rivers or in Brazil, near the Embira Basin. To all this one must add a similar vocabulary and pronunciation which makes them linguistically related.

A document which carefully illustrates the traditional relationship between the groups is the story of two battles held seventeen years ago on the Cujar and Sepahua rivers (Alvarez 1964). The first clash took place on the Cujar river, a tributary of the upper Purús inhabited by both groups. The Amahuaca on the Cujar and Curiuja rivers attacked by surprise the Yaminahua settlement on the border of the Curiuja river. The small village was composed of 37 Yaminahua 'friends of the same Amahuaca'. That day most of them were either away hunting or on excursion. Those who had stayed behind were massacred and two women were kidnapped by the Amahuaca (idem, p. 21); later the Amahuaca fled to the Curiuja river leading an errant life and fearing probable revenge from their victims.

The surviving Yaminahua abandoned their habitat and headed towards the Sepahua river where a few of their relatives were already living with some Amahuaca. There they were welcome and thus started their new settlement. But they could not forget their dead. One night a Yaminahua man mixed into a bowl leaves, ashes, water, hammock threads and other ingredients; he brought the bowl close to his mouth and sang over it. The Amahuaca who were watching thought this was a curse: 'It was the defiant cry which announced the Amahuaca's death' (idem, p. 23). Dreading this challenge the Amahuaca decided to annihilate the Yaminahua. By means of alibis and excuses to avoid resistance they made the Yaminahua men spread downstream and led the women upstream. The men were ambushed and hanged while the women and children waited in the Amahuaca village. They too would suffer the same fate or even worse. Only two women survived as a reward for joining the Amahuaca who since that moment

> ... found themselves in the same situation as their fellows of the Cujar and Curiuja rivers ... they live errant ... with the constant anxiety of one who is persecuted. (idem, p. 24).

This summary is quite self-explanatory and will not need major commentary. However, we must point out that the relationship between Yaminahua and Amahuaca, outlined by a combination of hostile behaviour and marriage alliance, is enriched by an ideological dimension present in all groups, the importance of which we have been able to evaluate: sorcery and magic beliefs shape social conduct and generate patterns of group behaviour which may sometimes be crucial to the configuration of intertribal relations.

Let us mention that the Amahuaca–Yaminahua relationship is the only one hitherto studied that gives evidence of a symmetrical nature, though with some Amahuaca superiority, where exchange of women through institutionalised kidnapping, and the ideological dimension, expressed in sorcery and the ethnic awareness of the 'other', lead to a number of skirmishes between sections of each group that combine hostility with alliance (intermarriage).

## Conclusions

To conclude we will refer to some of the probable causes which helped not only the formation of the traditional political context but the sharpening of hostile relations and servility among ethnic groups.

In the second half of the nineteenth century Raimondi (1862) explained the existing hostility between riparian groups and those inhabiting the tributaries by referring to the type of marriage among the former. According to this author the scarcity of women, due to a predominant polygamy, would have developed a need for renewed supplies of women who could only be found among the weaker ethnic groups on the tributaries.

Although this might have been an original motivation for the '*correrias*', Raimondi himself reports that children were captured for sale. It is a fact that with the arrival of the first traders and pioneers in about 1860 a slave-trade was started in that area. This lasted well into the 1950s. This new and terrible commerce, serving as a source of a labour force for '*caucheros*' (rubber men), landowners and later timber traders, radically emphasised the existing hostilities and '*correrias*' between the groups. In 1868 P. Sáenz describes:

> ... the abuse through correrias which some tribes of the Ucayali put upon others such as the Campa, Casibo, Remo, Amahuaca, which are gradually being destroyed. If the Government does not strongly commit itself to forbid the *buying and selling of indian youngsters*, the Ucayali infidels will not cease their hostilities against other tribes because

through this exercise they assure themselves of what they lack for attending their needs. (Ortiz 1974, p. 26; my italics).

But the government did not pay any attention to these claims; nearly twenty years later Samanez Ocampo (1883, p. 328) comments about *correrias* by the Conibo: 'Once back home they sell the prisoners if they do not wish to keep them as servants.'

Thus slavery, in the form of Indian sale to white patrons, was added to the temporal traditional servility which existed prior to contact. Therefore the causes for hostile intertribal relations were: (1) the search for women in order to enlarge the group through adding prestige and power to extended families; (2) the traditional temporal servile system existing between the riparian groups and those inhabiting the tributaries; (3) the inter-regional trade that led the Piro into pillage and raiding of Machiguenga as a means of supplying themselves with goods for exchange with the Quechua; (4) the usage of the traditional system of relations by the early missionaries to subdue the rebel groups into their evangelising and pacifying plans; and (5) the slave-trade of young Indians set up by regional segments of the wider society to obtain a labour force.

Although we have mentioned the presence of this last cause in the region until the 1950s, it is also true that the traditional servility also lasted until the same decade:

Apart, however, from the actual contacts with individuals, the attitude of the Piro towards surrounding tribes has not been friendly *until within the last three or four years*. There are Campa, Machiguenga and Amahuaca slaves who were stolen in raids. Some are still little children, indicating that the practice has not been long discontinued. These slaves are actually treated as members of the family. They apparently are taken by men who lack children of their own. When they grow up they marry members of the tribe and are entirely free. (Matteson 1954, p. 92; my italics).

As can be inferred from the last part of this quotation, traditional servility can in no way be compared to the slavery held by trade patrons, *caucheros*, landowners and timber traders. The first phenomenon was a temporal servility aimed at cultural assimilation, while the second was a definite slavery subject to the impersonal market laws and to an overexploitation solely intended to benefit the patron.

# 14 Why one culture stays put: a case of resistance to change in authority and economic structure in an indigenous community in the northwest Amazon

JANET M. CHERNELA

Only recently have anthropologists begun to examine the effects of missionary activity on indigenous cultures. In 1970, Elmer S. Miller described a 'breakdown' in Toba traditional ideology as a result of mission influence. A decade later, Schieffelin (1981) documented the dramatic reorientation of Kaluli social and economic organisation as a result of missionary activity; this change, despite its pervasive nature, took place in merely eight years. These papers, along with those of Beidelman (1974), Shapiro (1981), Wright (1981) and others, form the important groundwork from which a body of literature on missionisation is now developing.

This paper[1] focuses less on missionary efforts *per se*, than on the resilience and creativity with which indigenous peoples respond to evangelisation and its attempts to appropriate traditional authority. In the case related below, missionary intervention disrupted political and social existence at a settlement in Brazil's Uaupés Basin: the attempt to revise a traditional system failed. In short, kinship and rank remained the source of legitimate authority, and missionary efforts to install as chief a trader middleman were thwarted. The indigenous system was neither as passive nor as fragile as such systems are often represented.

The following case occured among the Kotiria (known also by the names Wanana, Uanano, and Anana),[2] a linguistically distinguished group of the Eastern Tukanoan family, inhabiting the Uaupés Basin in Brazil and Colombia. With a population of 1600, the Kotiria are one of 15 to 20 linguistically exogamous[3] fishing and horticultural peoples who form an integrated, intermarrying system in the northwest Amazon.[4] The group is divided into sibs, or named descent groups, inhabiting riverine settlements.

White contact has proceeded intermittently in the Uaupés area since the eighteenth century. The Indians of the Uaupés were subject to enslavement from the early eighteenth century; this practice culminated in the slave raids associated with the rising market for rubber between 1870 and 1912.

Salesian missionaries entered the upper Rio Negro Basin in 1915, offering the promise that slaving would be curtailed so long as they were present. The order established missions on the Uaupés river at Taracuá in 1924, at Iauaretê in 1929, and in Pari Cachoeira in 1945. The Indians chose to stave off the conquering and dividing power of the white slavers by relying on the mission and their promises. In this way, mutual interest promoted the Kotiria–Salesian relationship. Aside from protection from slavers, the Salesians have also furnished manufactured goods and medicines. In turn, the Salesians hope to induce more production from the Kotiria. While fostering dependency on the mission for survival and basic economic needs, the Salesians want to instil western language, values, and culture. To this end, the Salesians' intervention in the life of a settlement is generally designed to undermine the traditional culture.

Among the missionaries' principal goals was to intensify agricultural labour in order to integrate the region into the national economy. The missionaries encouraged surplus production of food crops to be sold at the mission in order to: support the high number of mission personnel; increase missionary activities; and reorient the area's economy from a subsistence to a cash-crop basis, linking it to larger market systems. To this end, the missionaries encouraged males to spend less time fishing, and to contribute to the production of export crops such as cacao and coffee.

Replacing traditional leaders with younger men schooled in the mission's ideas was one means of realising their goals. Ideally, the younger mission-educated leader would motivate villagers to cultivate cash crops and to manufacture marketable products, such as modified traditional crafts. When the old chief of Curideri died, the Salesians attempted to install such a young man in his place. A crisis ensued.

## Kotiria system of authority, rank, and redistribution

Before we examine the case in which the Salesians attempted to usurp local power in a Kotiria village it is important to understand the traditional system of rank and redistribution among the Kotiria.

The chieftancy or headmanship of any Kotiria village is held by its highest-ranked male. His authority rests on his position as the senior living descendant of the founding ancestor of the local senior sib; he is the 'oldest brother' in his generation, known as *Mahsa Wami*, 'the People's Oldest Brother'. He is also called *Dahpu* or 'Head', a term which refers not only to his leadership role, but also to the anatomical head, which 'leads', 'organises', and 'speaks for' the human body. These functions of the anatomical head attach to the Head of the Kotiria village. More specifically, the terms refers to the head of the ancestral anaconda, from whose body the exogamous language groups of the Uaupés originated. The highest-ranked male is also called *Putoro*, which has been translated both as 'First' and 'Chief'. I will refer to the highest-ranked male as *Mahsa Wami*.

Kotiria chieftainship entails control over three major aspects of village life:

fishing resources, labour, and ritual. A *Mahsa Wami* must hold sway over all three areas to lead effectively. Inability to harvest and redistribute fish, for example, will make it difficult for the *Mahsa Wami* to mobilise and coordinate labour. Control, then, implies the obligation to redistribute.

### Fishing resources

In every settlement, prime fishing sites are controlled by the senior sib member. These sites are designated because weir traps installed there are particularly productive in terms of yield per man-hour. The *Mahsa Wami* may allocate these territories on a usufruct basis, or he may retain his prerogative of priority access, and organise the collective installation, maintenance, the harvest of the traps. Fish harvested from the regulated traps are shared by all village members in communal meals. Whenever there is surplus fish, the chief is expected to assemble the community to eat. Shared meals are also expected to precede any communal work.

### Labour

The chief mobilises communal labour and coordinates collective work. Any individual who desires community participation in a project, such as the gathering of roof thatch, submits a request to the chief, who determines the project's priority. The chief then coordinates communal labour, carefully balancing collective projects against individual work such as gardening, so that collective and individual labour do not conflict.

I observed several kinds of community projects in Kotiria villages, including: the construction and maintenance of houses; the clearing and burning of gardens; and the intensive preparations for inter-sib exchange of gifts, known as the *po?oa* ceremony.

### Ritual

The *Mahsa Wami* is spokesman for the sib and the community. He must command leadership etiquette, display diplomacy in representing his sib to outsiders, and receive visitors with graciousness and eloquence. The *Mahsa Wami* receives and redistributes the gifts presented by other chiefs at *po?oa* ceremonies held in the chief's residence, a spacious dance house. His skilful display of oratory and ritual language reflects on the entire sib, and manifests high rank.

### Language

Among the possessions exchanged between groups is language, which holds special importance in the Uaupés. Received from ancestors, language is a key symbol of identity, uniting a named group. When two affinal groups come together, as they do to give or receive wives, or to exchange goods at subsequent ceremonies, they are also seen as exchanging their distinct languages. Each group's *Mahsa Wami* presides over these sib interactions. During such ritual gatherings, the chief must perform the specialised litanies which only the seniors know. This knowledge is the patrimony of ancestral inheritance. The litanies belong to the sib, but only the chief, who personifies its 'Head', may perform them. The litanies are complex and their correct performance requires elaborate training.

## The Curideri case

### Missionary intervention

The Kotiria village of Curideri (Turtle Egg Village),[5] with a population of 77, is a five-day canoe trip from the Salesian Mission of Iauareté. Curideri is occupied by two sibs: the senior Macaw-Eye sib and the junior Opossum-Ear sib.

In 1975, the aged chief of Curideri, Bati Diani, died. His younger brother, Dahsiro, would traditionally have succeeded him; however, the Salesian fathers saw Bati Diani's death as an opportunity to exert their influence. A missionary arrived at Curideri and proposed as chief Pedro, a Portuguese-speaking member of the lower-ranked Opossum-Ear sib. Raised partly in São Gabriel, the governmental post at the outskirts of the Uaupés region, Pedro was closely acquainted with national values.

Dahsiro, the senior Macaw-Eye in line to become chief, was outraged. He openly challenged the missionary, threatening to go to Iauareté to tear down the Brazilian flag. In response, the missionary ordered an open election, with Pedro as one of several candidates. At the election, Dahsiro announced, 'The chief will be my nephew, Edu.' As the son of Dahsiro's deceased younger brother, Edu was a member of the Macaw-Eye, the higher-ranking sib at Curideri. He spoke some Portuguese, but had not been educated in the mission.

When the Salesian father called for a vote, Edu won: the lower-ranking sib had declined to vote, deferring to the higher-ranking sib's choice. The outcome suggested the strength of the traditional hierarchy.

After Edu won the election, it soon became clear that the power structure at Curideri was far from settled. People complained that Edu was not a satisfactory leader. The former chief, Bati Diani, was frequently eulogised and praised for the 'succulence' he had exhibited by: providing abundant fish, hosting many exchange dances to show the sib's prosperity and generosity, acquiring in return imported goods and specialised utensils for the community, representing the group eloquently with his memorable oratory, and receiving visitors graciously.

Unable to fulfil these obligations, Edu was said to be 'dry'. Edu had neither the desire nor the preparation to lead, but had accepted the role at his uncle's insistence. Without a dance house, without control over a productive fishing installation, he was not the sib head and therefore could not speak on behalf of the sibs. As a result, Dahsiro was designated *Mahsa Wami*, and assumed this role in greeting all visitors. Furthermore, Dahsiro held dances and communal meals in the large dance house which he had shared with his deceased brother, the previous chief. It began to appear that the election had been a ploy to placate the missionaries.

The crisis was not soon resolved, however. Over the next two years, the chieftancy continued to be divided. As senior sib member, Dahsiro retained the ceremonial functions and prime resources of a chief: he held control of the principal fish weir and the dance house; he hosted dances and communal fish feasts. To appease the missionaries – who were mainly concerned with the allocation of labour – he relegated to Edu, his puppet, the unappealing executive function of inducing and organising the villagers' labour.

### Work stoppage

Without the full spectrum of leadership roles, Edu had not the leverage to compel villagers to follow his initiative. He planned numerous work projects, including the construction of a large canoe to facilitate trade (of artifacts for manufactured goods) with the missionaries. But between 1978 and 1979 attendance at collective projects declined until only three people responded to Edu's calls to work: (his own younger brother and two visiting client sons-in-law) in service to the community. Edu was obliged to solicit people's participation in a house-by-house round of visits. At last, a sorcery threat and an overt breach of authority precipitated open confrontation between Edu and the villagers.

As tensions mounted, an in-law Baniwa shaman walked through the jungle from the distant Aiari river to advise Edu of a hallucinogenic vision. The shaman said that a near relative was planning to assassinate Edu through sorcery.

Two days later, Edu learned that a member of the lower-ranking Opossum-Ear sib had planned to lead villagers in an open challenge to his authority by thatching a roof at the moment when Edu had scheduled work on the trading canoe. The action was intended to be non-violent but decisive disobedience. Edu heard of the conspiracy at the morning communal meal on the day the canoe was to be built.

In Kotiria society, to shout, to address a complaint directly, or to show any emotion is considered not only inappropriate but shameful. As a consequence, the quiet is seldom broken. Conversation, although frequent, is kept at a discreet, low pitch; facial expressions and gestures are deliberately understated. To an unfamiliar observer, villagers' faces may often seem frozen – reminiscent of the unnatural formality of a daguerrotype portrait.

Despite these conventions Edu broadcast his anger and fear at the communal meal. He shouted in a tremulous voice:

> You didn't go through me! You didn't come to me first! None of you works. I work alone. Now one of you is going to kill me. I do not sleep with your wives. I am not the proper chief. I was made chief by the mission. I am not the real chief. You are telling me this. Now one of you is going to kill me. I haven't slept with your wives.

A few days later, Edu called a meeting. Continuing in a similar vein, he told the villagers:

> I have something important to tell you. One of you is wanting to put holes in me. One of you is wanting to give me poison. One of you is envious of the work that I am doing. But I am not speaking behind your backs and I am not sleeping with my relatives' women. I never go with other women for this reason: not to be poisoned, not to be killed. I am

telling all of this to you. One of you wants to kill me. This is what a shaman told me.

The sorcery threat obviously worried Edu. It was a dramatic materialisation of his greatest fear – a direct challenge to his role. Since the threat and the villagers' confrontation occurred within days of each other, it is difficult to say which, if either, incited Edu to action. In any case, he finally undertook an effective course of action, asserting his authority. He made the rounds of houses, sitting in each to make the appropriate, ritualised but affectionate small talk. Furthermore, he announced that he was sponsoring a very large dance at which his son and other boys would receive life-breath names.

Then Edu set off on a fishing expedition which lasted four and a half days. When he returned in the evening of the fifth day, his wife smoked fish until the following morning. In the morning she visited each household with offerings of fish. Villagers commented with approval: several said, '*This*, at last, was chief's behaviour.'

In contrast, Dahsiro was dour. He complained that if 'everyone' held dances in his house, he would be exposed to menstruating women and other elements which pose danger to a shaman. Dahsiro, aside from being in line for the chieftancy, also happened to be a powerful shaman. Nevertheless, Edu's naming ceremony – three days of uninterrupted hospitality – was considered a great success. In the weeks before I left Curideri, complaints about Edu had abated. On another visit several months later, I saw that Edu had expanded his house.

Though the power struggle between Dahsiro and Edu continued, the younger man had clearly established a measure of legitimacy. Ironically, while Salesian intervention had hoisted him to chieftancy, he began to assume that role in fact as well as in name only when he reverted to traditional styles of authority.

**Implications of the leadership crisis**

Missionaries in the Uaupés are attempting to shift authority from descent, its traditional locus, to a power configuration which has, as its authoritative and economic centre, the mission. To this end, they introduce new status positions that undermine the hereditary basis of chieftancy, and attempt to use their candidate for chief as a link between the village and the mission. The mediating chief is expected to encourage villagers to produce surplus agricultural products to be traded, on an individual basis, for manufactured goods at the mission.

At Curideri, the Kotiria did not accept the authority of the individual chosen in the election instigated by the missionaries. In Kotiria society, traditional authority is legitimised not by consensus, but by descent and concomitant control over redistribution. Rather than allow the mission to usurp the traditional power structure, the hereditary successor to the chieftancy named a figurehead. In effect, the traditional system, with the hereditary successor as *Mahsa Wami*, went underground. The missionaries nevertheless viewed the figurehead as chief: they failed to see that the hereditary successor assumed leadership and all of its reponsibilities, except mobilisation of labour. The Kotiria in this way resisted the challenge to their political integrity, and retained the principle of chiefly succession within the primogeniture line.

Although the ruse deceived the missionaries and to some degree thwarted their goal, instability resulted due to the wrenching apart of the traditional *Mahsa Wami* functions: mobilising labour, redistributing resources, and presiding over ritual. Partial resolution came only when the elected, compromise chief asserted his legitimacy by fulfilling the chief's traditional obligations.

Several symbols demonstrate that the leadership system at Curideri, and indeed the Kotiria concept of authority, remained intact despite Edu's election. First, Edu defended his limited authority by stating, 'I do not sleep with your wives. I am not the proper chief. I was made chief.' He makes these statements in the context of a plea to the villagers to forgive his incapacity to lead properly. In so doing, he hoped to communicate his political impotence in the hope that sympathetic listeners would forgive him his wrongs. A traditional symbol of usurpation, the appropriation of others' wives, is denied. An agnatic dilemma, namely chiefly succession within the sib, is inverted and expressed through a powerful affinal metaphor.

A second symbol shows that Edu worries not only about his power, but his life. According to Sahlins, ' "Every chief acts as conqueror when he comes to power," Hawaiians say. And even if he has not actually killed his predecessor, he is presumed to have poisoned him . . .' (1981 p. 24). At first, Edu makes no effort to seize Dahsiro's power. All power bestowed upon Edu emanates from Dahsiro. He has not threatened or poisoned Dahsiro; rather, Edu learns from the Baniwa shaman that he himself is the target of an assassination plot. Again, a traditional symbol of usurpation and power is inverted. 'One of you is wanting to give me poison,' Edu cries, fearing that his own authority and person are endangered. Communication of this threat by an in-law may also be seen as the result of Edu's agnatic dilemma.

Poison as symbolic means of usurpation figures again in the episode when Edu asserts traditional authority, but now Edu is the poisoner. When Edu finally presides over a successful naming ceremony, a ritual previously in Dahsiro's province as *Mahsa Wami*, Dahsiro claims that Edu has brought him into the polluting presence of menstruating women. This exposure threatens his shamanic powers. With this poison – menstruating females – the pretender usurps his uncle's authority, and symbolically reverses his former impotence.

Edu prevails, but legitimation of his chieftancy hardly introduces the new system of leadership intended by the mission. Indeed, it represents a reassertion of the old. In his writings on 'Deviance and Social Control', Murphy writes about a Mundurucu chief who finds himself in much the same position as Edu:

> The contemporary Mundurucu chief is in a dilemma. If we look upon a boundary role as one in which both ends have to be played against the middle, we see the chief caught between the interests of the trader and those of his followers; these interests rarely coincide. It is a difficult position, but one that can be maintained by maximal adherence

to the traditional behavior expected of chiefs and minimal acquiescence to the demands of the traders [1961 p. 58].

After considerable difficulty, Edu learns to take the route of 'maximal adherence to the traditional behavior expected of chiefs'. Initially, he lacked the resources and knowledge to emulate the style of leadership which is traditional at Curideri. The period of upheaval tests Edu, forcing him to learn and then implement the traditional forms of authority, and compelling him to acquire the resources needed to gain recognition as a leader.

Lacking control of a fixed fishing facility which might yield a substantial harvest with minimal labour, Edu resorts to strenuous, single-handed physical labour. The fishing trip satisfies the villagers' expectations. At the same time, it suggests the leverage of the work force, which can move chiefs to distribute goods by witholding labour and recognition of the chief's political authority.

Edu's dilemma was that though a nominal chief, he could not be the 'Head' since he was not the highest-ranked sib member. The resulting disjuncture between 'Head' and chief is not customary in Kotiria society; normally, as we have seen, the *Mahsa Wami* controls fishing resources, labour, and ritual. Because he was not 'Head', Edu could not for some time redistribute goods obtained from fishing and exchange ceremonies. He was therefore, 'dry'.

The 'succulence' which the past chief was said to have embodied might appear to be a personal attribute. However, this quality refers not to the person, but rather to the structure of redistribution. That is to say, 'succulence' is the equivalent of maximal redistribution, and 'dryness' the equivalent of minimal redistribution. In such a system, even charisma cannot replace redistributive capacity as a basis for leadership.

## Conclusion

By presiding over the redistributive system of ritual exchange, the *Mahsa Wami* recycles surplus within the community, and in this way undermines the mission's effort to accumulate surplus for export. When the young chief installed as a result of the mission's intervention reverts to traditional leadership behaviour, he therefore defeats the purpose of his election.

In the final analysis, the mission failed in its attempt to become the centre of economic and political action at Curideri. As Dahsiro's puppet, Edu could not induce labour so long as he could not fulfil other chiefly functions, including redistribution and hospitality. The case indicates that unless he fulfils these expectations, a leader will not be recognised.

In summary, the Kotiria tradition of redistribution prevents the accumulation of surplus goods for export. The mission's effort to change this practice by introducing a new leader was doomed to eventual failure, since only through redistribution will a leader's authority be recognised by the Kotiria.

## Acknowledgements

Dr Chernela was formerly with INPA, Manaus.

## Notes

1 The fieldwork on which this paper is based was carried out in approximately 24 months between 1978 and 1981.

2 While this group has been referred to in the literature by the *lingua geral* term Uanano (and its spelling variants), I have chosen to call them Kotiria, since it is the name which they call themselves and by which they are known to other Uaupés groups.

3 The Cubeo (Goldman 1963) and the Makuna (Arhem 1981) are exceptions to the rule of linguistic exogamy.

4 The number of groups estimated to be within this field depends upon definitions of group boundaries and the size of geographic area considered.

5 All proper names (of places or people) are fictitious.

# 15 Nutritional status and cultural change in Venezuela's Amazon territory

REBECCA HOLMES

## Introduction

Nutritional deficiency has a direct impact on the health of individuals throughout the world, its effects being especially evident in the developing or Third World areas. A World Health Organisation study of over 35 000 Latin American and Caribbean children who died before the age of 5, 'implicates nutritional deficiency as the most important contributor to excessive mortality in 13 projects of the Investigation in Latin America' (Puffer and Serrano 1973 p 161).

If nutritional deficiency is the greatest contributor to mortality in these children, one may ask, what is the nature and cause of these nutritional deficiencies? The answer is complicated. Broadly speaking, economic and environmental pressures which exceed the ability of the population to adjust, either biologically or culturally, produce malnutrition. The process of culture change observed in the developing nations today is thought by many to produce overwhelming nutritional problems for traditional peoples; the link between cultural change and malnutrition is direct. This research, through the investigation of eight Amerindian villages[1] in Venezuela's Amazon Territory, challenges this assumption.

This analysis of culture change and nutrition in the Amazon Basin is concerned with accurately documenting the nutritional status of the groups under study and exploring the ways in which these groups have adjusted to their traditional and modern environments. The approach is anthropological, drawing on the work of both biological and cultural anthropologists. Hopefully this study will reflect the unique contributions that anthropologists can make to the study of health and nutrition, on both the basic and applied levels.

## Methods

In order to explore the relationship between culture change and nutritional status, research was first begun in the upper Río Negro under the direction of the ecology and anthropology departments of the Instituto Venezolano de Investigaciones Científicas (IVIC). This study was designed and carried out to complement the data gathered in a much larger investigation of the ecology of the Río Negro region of

Venezuela: a UNESCO Man in the Biosphere (MAB) 1 Pilot Project under the classification 'Ecological effects of increasing human activities in tropical and subtropical forest ecosystems'. Partial financial support for my work was given by the Centro de Estudios (IVIC). The duration of the study was approximately 18 months, from the first visit to San Carlos de Río Negro (field headquarters of the UNESCO:MAB project) in January 1980 to the completion of the data analysis and report in July 1981 (Holmes 1981). This included three and a half months of fieldwork during the rainy season (July–October 1980).

A second phase of the research was begun in March 1982 with fieldwork among the Yanomama Indians and a return visit, this time in the dry season, to San Carlos de Río Negro. An additional field investigation took place in July 1982 in two Amerindian villages in the upper Orinoco near San Fernando de Atabapo. Research in this second phase is under the direction of the Programa de Investigación y Control de Enfermedades Tropicales – PROICET Amazonas, funded by Venezuela's Amazon territorial government and the National Council for Scientific and Technological Research (CONICIT). Fieldwork during the second phase has been one and a half months; the research is still in progress.

## Fieldwork locations

All eight study villages are located in the Venezuelan Amazon Territory. This is the most southern and isolated territory in the country, bordering on the south and west with Brazil and Colombia, respectively. The territory as a whole has less than one person per square kilometre (MARNR 1979) making this one of the world's least populated regions.

Six of the eight villages (four in the upper Río Negro and two in the upper Orinoco) are riverine settlements surrounded by tropical rainforest. This forest, some of which becomes flooded during the months when the river level is highest, covers flat or slightly rolling terrain. Due to the villages' proximity to the Equator (between 2° and 2° N), and to their low altitude (119 m above sea level at San Carlos de Río Negro), they experience high mean annual temperatures (26 °C), rainfall (▷3000 mm) and humidity (▷80%). The remaining two villages are located in the Parima Mountains on the southeast border with Brazil. They are inhabited by Yanomama Indians, the least acculturated of the study groups, and are situated in high (950 m) natural savanna areas within the tropical forest. Rainfall and humidity are high in this area but temperatures are somewhat lower due to the increased altitude.

The study villages may be reached by light aircraft from the Territorial capital, Puerto Ayacucho. Although there are daily commercial flights from Caracas to Puerto Ayacucho, the Amazon Territory is isolated, by lack of roads, from Venezuela's main population centres in the north. The six riverine villages may also be reached by boat during most of the year while the Yanomama study area is accessible only by plane or overland foot travel.

# The problem

Numerous authors have postulated that the health and nutritional status of traditional peoples is better than that of more 'civilised' or 'modern' groups; furthermore, these traditional peoples suffer from worsening health and nutrition in the process of cultural change. The reasons for these beliefs are many, any include the following:

1 Certain degenerative diseases appear to be less frequent in traditional groups, e.g. ischemic heart disease (localised tissue hypoxia), obesity, diabetes and cancer (Robson and Wadsworth 1977 p. 187).

2 The change in diet from natural to altered or refined foods has contributed to malnutrition, dental disease and nutrition-related disorders (Price 1945; Bodley 1975 p. 156; Robson and Wadsworth 1977 p. 187).

3 Breast-feeding is not as frequent or prolonged in modern or recently modernised groups, due to social custom and new work demands on the mother; thus the infant and weanling are exposed to more severe nutritional stress than they were traditionally (Hegstead 1978 p. 64; Robson and Wadsworth 1977 p. 193).

4 The size of traditional populations is controlled so as not to exceed the ability of the environment, both physical and cultural, to maintain these groups in a healthy condition (Seijas and Arvelo-Jiménez 1978 p. 259; Neel 1977 p. 156; Robson and Wadsworth 1977 p. 196).

5 Through culture contact traditional groups are exposed to exogenous diseases which seriously affect their health, and as a result, their nutritional status (Dubos 1977 pp. 31–40, Seijas and Arvelo-Jiménez 1978 p. 259).

6 The desire to become more 'civilised' encourages traditional people to choose symbols of modern life – such as baby bottles and canned foods – which are nutritionally inferior to their native diet (Bodley 1975; Wood 1979 p. 62).

The underlying assumption of all those authors, either stated or implied, is that traditional peoples have adapted successfully to their environments, both biologically and culturally, in a manner which favours good health and nutrition. In the process of abandoning this mode of existence, modern man, and the newly acculturated indigenous populations, have suffered deteriorating health and nutrition due to their inability to adapt to a quickly changing environment.

This investigation, then, examines the assumption the acculturation produces lower health and nutritional status through maladaptation, by a systematic study of eight Amazonian villages in the process of acculturation.

# Upper Río Negro study

Four villages in the upper Río Negro area were chosen for study. These settlements are located in an area of low biological productivity associated with blackwater rivers and were studied during the rain-season 'lean months' when wild food availability was at its yearly low point. It was assumed that these conditions would make adaptive responses to nutritional problems more evident than they would be under favourable environmental conditions. In addition, the villages were chosen to reflect different levels of acculturation. San Carlos de Río Negro (population 600), the village with longest and most intense contact with 'modern' people and their technology, was the base of investigation. It is located on the Río Negro, a blackwater tributary of the Amazon, just south of the confluence of the Guainia and Casiquiare rivers (late. 1.56 N, long. 67.03 W). Three other villages, increasingly isolated from San Carlos, were chosen on the assumption that the greater the isolation, the more traditional would be the village. Fieldwork data tended to confirm this relationship, although it was considerably more complex than originally envisioned. A stratified sample subpopulation (66 individuals, eight households) was selected for study from a larger randomly chosen household study. The three upriver villages, in order of increasing distance from San Carlos, were: Chivacoa (67 persons, ten households), Garrapata (41 persons, seven households) and La Nigua (20 persons, three households). These figures represent the total population of each upriver settlement.

**Nutritional status**

Anthropometric measurements are the prime indicators used in this study to determine individual nutritional status. Measurements of weight, height, sitting height and left upper arm circumference were taken of 194 individuals of all ages in the four villages. Fatfold thickness was not measured during this phase of the study but it was added to the group of measurements taken on some 400 individuals studied in the second phase.

Community-level indicators of nutritional status, including a dietary study and an analysis of birthweights in San Carlos for the last 10 years were included to support the anthropometric evidence. Clinical signs of malnutrition were few so they have not been included in this report (Holmes 1981 pp. 117–22).

The analyses of the above-mentioned measurements are made in several ways using both age-dependent and age-independent (e.g. weight for height) methods. Since the degree to which an individual suffers from malnutrition is determined by comparing his measurements with those of some reference population, the choice of this population is extremely important. For this study I have chosen both international standards (Jelliffe 1966:Annex; WHO 1978; Keller *et al.* 1976) and Venezuelan standards (Fundacredesa 1981) of reference, although both, as will be shown below, are somewhat inadequate for a precise classification of Venezuelan Indians. Age groupings for this study are 0–5 years (young children), 6–17 years (schoolchildren), 18 years and older (adults).

*(a) Birthweights*

Low birthweight ($<2.5$ or $3.0$ kg) is associated with undernutrition, low socio-economic status and poor health of the mother. Inasmuch as the mother's condition reflects the environment in which she lives, the change in mean

birthweight over time in a given community, and the percentage of low birthweights
have been used as indices of the nutritional status of the community (Keller *et al.*
1976 p. 592).

The birthweights of 175 San Carlos infants compared with those of populations
under moderate: Delhi, 1968 (Banik *et al.* 1968), and severe: Leningrad, 1942
(Antonov 1947) nutritional stress, as well as those of a well nourished population:
Boston, 1959 (Stewart and Stevenson 1959) are shown in Figure 1. The San Carlos
infant birthweights are remarkably close in distribution to the Boston birthweights.
Although they consistently run slightly below this standard in each weight category,
the mean overall birthweight for the San Carlos population of 3.257 kg compares
favourably with the mean Boston birthweight of 3.400 kg. This is especially
significant when one considers that the adult stature of the San Carlos inhabitants is
substantially lower than that of the Boston (North American) population.

The assessment, then, of the San Carlos community, using birthweights as an
indicator, reveals the community to be adequately nourished (that is, not suffering
from undernutrition). One must assume, with this kind of indirect assessment, that
the indicator reflects accurately the status of segments of the population not
actually measured. The birthweights of San Carlos infants reveal not only the
adequate nutrition received by the foetus, but also the good nutritional status of the
mother who was able to produce a child of this birthweight. Since I have no
indication from my own observations that pregnant women in San Carlos receive
more food than other family members (in fact, they may receive slightly less food
due to pregnancy food restrictions) I assume that men and children are at least as
well nourished as the women.

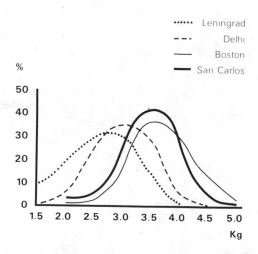

Fig. 1 Distribution of birthweights in four populations

### (b) Children's growth curves

In Venezuela, the National Nutrition Institute (INN) uses international growth charts (WHO 1978) as references in the nutritional assessment of its child population. These growth charts are presented separately for boys and girls, and for the pre-school and school-age child. An assessment of 142 San Carlos area children (69 boys and 73 girls) was made using the INN charts.

These charts revealed an average of 80% (63%–94%) of the San Carlos area children to be malnourished or borderline malnourished using height for age as a measure. This means that they fall below the 10th percentile of the reference population.

In contrast to height for age, the study children fared much better when considering weight for age. In fact, the majority of the children (60%) fall within the normal range.

Using school-age boys as an example, we can see in Figure 2 that only two boys are found in the normal range in height for age, while the remainder are classified as first, or even second- and third-degree malnourished. The distribution changes in weight for age, when about one-half of the individuals fall within the normal range and one-half are classified as first-degree malnourished.

What are we to make of this difference in relative classification? Since the great majority of children observed did not have clinical signs of malnutrition, and were

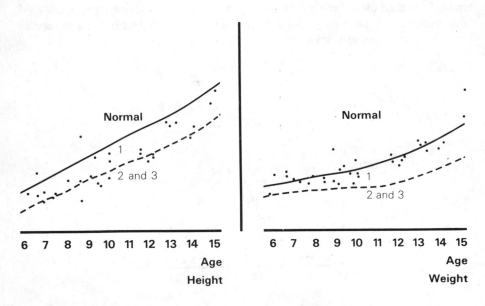

Fig. 2 Height/age and weight/age curves for school-age boys in San Carlos area

indeed sturdy, energetic individuals, one must look for another, possibly more appropriate method for classifying these children.

The solution to this problem appears to be found by choosing an age-independent variable, the most obvious of which is weight for height. If we plot weight for height of the same school-age boys (Figure 3), we find that they are not only classified as normal, but are actually above standard (100) as determined by international standards (Jelliffe 1966).

Weight for height, then, as an indicator of nutritional status may be used to assess the present condition of nutritional health of the individual since it reflects the individual's body proportions, or degree of thinness (Keller *et al.* 1976 p. 596). Low body weight for height indicates wasting, or a condition of acute malnutrition presently exhibited by the individual. In populations where ages are unknown, this measure is especially useful. Even in populations where ages are fairly accurately known, this indicator is useful in correcting for the reference population bias toward tall individuals which may be inappropriate, as it is in the case of the San Carlos area study population, for populations of unusually short people[2] who apparently are not suffering from chronic malnutrition.

*(c) Arm circumference for age and weight for height: total population*
Arm circumference has been used in many studies to determine the presence of malnutrition (Shakir and Morley 1974; Horner *et al.* 1977; Dowler *et al.* 1980; Berlin and Markell 1977) as it measures the degree of muscle wasting, due to undernutrition, exhibited by the individual. This indicator depends on age classifications.

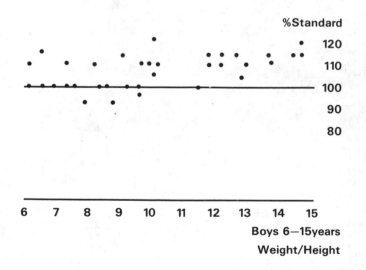

Fig. 3 Weight/height plots for school-age boys in San Carlos area

A summary of the arm circumference for age and weight for height in the total population, ages and sexes combined, revealed that the means for these measurements were all close to 100% standard, most even surpassing this figure:

| Community | Arm circumference | % Standard Weight/height | Combined mean |
|---|---|---|---|
| La Nigua | 101.18 | 108.13 | 104.65 |
| Garrapata | 97.13 | 106.97 | 102.05 |
| San Carlos | 97.18 | 104.52 | 100.85 |
| Chivacoa | 95.07 | 102.58 | 98.83 |

A most interesting comparison using these two indicators and the three age groupings may be made between the upriver villages (excluding San Carlos) and the Aguaruna Jívaro community studied by Berlin and Markell (1977). Environmental and dietary characteristics of the two groups are very similar, yet the San Carlos area indigenous communities show much higher percentages of individuals in the 90% standard or above category (Table 1).

Table 1  Comparison of San Carlos area and Aguaruna Jívaro populations

| % standard | Weight for height | | Arm circumference for age | |
|---|---|---|---|---|
| | Percentage of the population | | | |
| | Aguaruna | San Carlos area | Aguaruna | San Carlos area |
| Young Children | | | | |
| | (0–5 years) | | | |
| =90 | 33 | 90 | 71 | 72 |
| 80–99 | 32 | 10 | 29 | 26 |
| 70–79 | 29 | – | – | 2 |
| 60–69 | 3 | – | – | – |
| 50–59 | – | – | – | – |
| 40–49 | 3 | – | – | – |
| n= | 35 | 59 | 35 | 58 |
| School children | | | | |
| | (6–19 years) | (6–17 years) | | |
| =90 | 59 | 94 | 63 | 78 |
| 80–89 | 29 | 6 | 37 | 22 |
| 70–79 | 6 | – | – | – |
| 60–69 | 6 | – | – | – |
| 50–59 | – | – | – | – |
| n= | 32 | 52 | 32 | 51 |
| Adults | | | | |
| | (20 years+) | (18 years+) | | |
| =90 | 54 | 96 | 22 | 85 |
| 80–89 | 35.5 | 4 | 62 | 15 |
| 70–79 | 6.5 | – | 16 | – |
| 60–69 | 4 | – | 1 | – |
| 50–59 | – | – | – | – |
| n= | 50 | 47 | 50 | 47 |

It is evident from both the general assessment of the San Carlos area, as well as the specific inter-village comparisons, that the population of this area does not suffer serious malnutrition. Indeed by most indicators it can be considered an area with well nourished village and town populations.

*Culture contact and change*

The history of culture contact between the peoples indigenous to the Río Negro-Guainia and the Spanish, Portuguese and 'modern' Venezuelans is a long one. For more than 200 years soldiers, missionaries, traders, explorers, rubber workers, boat-builders and government functionaries have travelled and settled in these rivers.[3] Their influence on indigenous cultures has caused significant modification in housing, religion, language, social structure and kinship relations, but rather insignificant changes in village subsistence strategies.[4]

The study communities as we see them today reflect different adjustments to, and assimilation of, these foreign influences. All of the study communities have replaced the traditional *maloca* with single-family dwellings of mud walls and zinc or palm-thatch roofs. Except for the addition of the zinc roofs in San Carlos and Chivacoa, and some cement floors in San Carlos, native materials and methods are still used in construction. Electricity has had little apparent impact on the upriver villages, being absent in La Nigua, and of use only for lighting in the evening in the other two. Even in San Carlos, where electricity is sometimes supplied on a 24-hour basis from the new gas-oil generating plant, electric power may be unavailable for weeks at a time due to lack of fuel for the generator.

Medical facilities and a doctor are available only in San Carlos, and even these facilities are not used by all of the local inhabitants. Schooling is available in all communities but La Nigua, however few of the members of the adult populations in the upriver villages have attended. San Carlos is set apart from the other communities in the amount of formal education of its adults and in the much greater *per capita* income available to purchased food and imported non-food items such as gasoline, outboard motors, clothing and even tape recorders and refrigerators.

A close examination of Table 2 makes it evident that there is a difference in the level of acculturation between the study villages, especially the upriver villages as a group and San Carlos. Since there is no substantial difference in nutritional status among the villages, we can state for the Río Negro study region that the anthropometric measurements show no significant association between acculturation and nutritional status.[5] Dietary data, discussed below, confirm this conclusion.

**Diet composition**

An adequate diet is the basis for the maintenance of good nutritional status in the individual. However, the use of dietary measures to determine nutritional status is problematical since nutritional status is the end product of the interaction of diet, health and the specific nutritional needs of the individual. Therefore, for the purposes of this investigation, anthropometric measurements are used to determine

Table 2    Levels of acculturation among the study villages

| Characteristic | San Carlos (66)* | Chivacoá (67)* | Garrapata (41)* | La Nigua (20)* |
|---|---|---|---|---|
| 1 Electricity | 24-hour | 2 hours–evening | 2 hours–evening | None |
| 2 Medical clinic with doctor | In community | None – must travel 2 hrs. by canoe paddling | None – must travel ½ day by canoe paddling | None – must travel full day by canoe paddling |
| 3 Distance to trader with food/gasoline | In community | 1 hour by canoe paddling | 1–2 hours by canoe paddling | 6 hours by canoe paddling |
| 4 School | In community elementary and two years high school | In community: 3 years | None – some children studied at Catholic Mission in La Esmeralda | None – some children studied in govt. school on Guainia in Colombia |
| 5 Housing | All but one had mud walls covered with cement, cement floors, and zinc roofs – the exception had palm roof and stick walls | Walls: 7 mud, 4 palm Roofs: 6 zinc, 5 palm Floors: Dirt all | Walls: Mud all Roofs: Palm all Floors: Dirt all | Walls: Mud all Roofs: Palm all Floors: Dirt all |
| 6 Water for cooking and bathing | Piped into homes – one study home obtains water from neighbour | Directly from river | Directly from river at head of island or on west side | Directly from river |
| 7 Disposition of faeces | Toilet 1 Latrines 3 In woods 4 | All use woods (*monte*) | Directly in river – east side of island or in woods | In woods (*monte*) |
| 8 Domestic animals/person dogs chickens pigs | 0.17 0.94 0.11 | 0.22 0.23 0.00 | 0.20 0.34 0.36 | 0.45 0.40 0.35 |
| 9 Years of schooling completed by adult average men women | 5.60 4.29 | 0.58 0.36 | 1.10 0.89 | 0.00 0.00 |
| 10 Income/person /month | Bs. 277.50 range: 200 to 5200 per household | Bs. 46.00 range: 40 to 700 per household | Bs. 18.00 range: 0 to 200 per household | Bs. 25.00 range: about Bs. 125 per household |
| 11 Predominant Language % of persons: | Spanish 74.6 | Lingua Geral 38.3 | Caropaco 37.8 | Curripaco 70.6 |

*Table 2 continued*

| Characteristic | San Carlos (66)% | Chivacoá (67)* | Garrapata (41)* | La Nigua (20)* |
|---|---|---|---|---|
| bilingual | 13.6 | 33.3 | 40.5 | 29.4 |
| trilingual | 10.2 | 26.7 | 13.5 | 0 |
| | 1.6 | 1.7 | 8.2 | 0 |
| Secondary lan- | Lingua Geral | Español | Lingua Geral | Español |
| guages in order | Caropaco | Curripaco | Español | |
| of predominance | Portuguese | Piapoco | Portuguese | |
| | Bare | Portuguese | Ye'cuana | |

* Figures in parentheses are the numbers of persons in the stratified subpopulation sample for each village; for explanation see text (p. 000).

nutritional status and dietary information is analysed to clarify the relationship between acculturation and nutritional status. Specifically, this section on diet shows the most acculturated community, San Carlos, to have (a) an increased dependence on purchased foods, and (b) to have abandoned the practice of communal meals for individual household consumption of food.

**Protein and starch consumption in San Carlos and Chivacoa**

Since anthropometric data revealed that the study populations were not underweight for their height and did not suffer from oedema, it was almost certain that they did not have a lack of calories in their diets. It was unclear, however, whether they were receiving sufficient protein, although clinical signs of protein deficiencies were not apparent. To assess the relative protein intake at the community level and to ascertain how this protein was procured, I compared data on protein availability for San Carlos with that for one of the upriver villages, Chivacoa, during the same time period, 15 August to 21 September, 1980. During this time period Kathleen Clark surveyed the study households in San Carlos five times, asking for the fish, meat, eggs or other protein consumed by that household during the previous 24 hour period. From her data I calculated the average daily protein consumption for the eight study households and compared it with the protein needs of the population adjusted for age and sex. Hunting and fishing data from Chivacoa were collected during this time period by an indigenous worker and analysed in like manner.[6] The results of the analysis are as follows:

| | 15 August to 21 September 1980 | |
|---|---|---|
| | San Carlos | Chivacoa |
| Daily protein needs for population (grams) | 1864 | 1809 |
| Actual protein intake for population (grams) | 2147 | 2458 |
| Percentage of protein needs met | 115.2 | 135.9 |

| | | |
|---|---|---|
| Adults (18 or over) | Men | 51 |
| | Women | 53 |
| Children (17 and under) | Boys | 72 |
| | Girls | 66 |

All protein consumed in Chivacoa was obtained by hunting and fishing, the former activity done exclusively by the men and boys, and the latter by both sexes and all ages, with women procuring the least amount of protein.

In contrast to the completely self-sufficient food production in Chivacoa and the upriver villages, San Carlos residents purchased more than half their protein. The findings of the San Carlos protein study revealed that:

1 Nutritional status, as measured anthropometrically, did not correlate with protein intake in each household. This was not unpredictable since average nutritional status was above 90% standard for all households. In addition, there was no particular nutritional advantage to ingesting more than the required amount of protein.

2 Protein obtained from canned or packaged foods varied widely (from 3.9% of the total protein intake to 58.1%) but averaged less than 20% of the total.

3 Over 80% of the total protein intake came from fresh fish, game or domestic meat, and of these sources local fish and game supplied the most protein consumed (46.9% of total protein intake).

4 There was no apparent correlation between protein intake and *per capita* household income, although the two households with the highest incomes had the highest percentage of protein in the diet (203% and 146% of the requirement).

5 Approximately 60% of the protein consumed by the study households was purchased. In order of quantity purchased, the sources were: (a) game and fish from local hunters and fishermen (including upriver villagers) 25%, (b) canned or packaged products principally from the government store 18%, and (c) imported domestic animal fresh meats sold by local businessmen 17%. The remaining 40% of the protein consumed was obtained in hunting and fishing by the household members.

Manioc flour (*mañoco*) and garden produce is consumed in both the upriver villages and San Carlos. Inasmuch as the daily diet consists of meat or fish soups with an added starch such as *mañoco* or *casabe* bread (made from manioc flour), we can say that the diet in San Carlos is essentially traditional.

Only half of the San Carlos study households maintained their own *conucos*. The average nutritional status of the households with *conucos* was 100.2% standard and the average for those without *conucos* was 100.0% standard, showing no particular advantage in nutritional status for those who had their own source of food. Apparently additional income is one of the main factors in determining whether a *conuco* is to be maintained. The average income *per capita* for households without *conuco* was Bs. 357.80 per month while that for households with conucos was Bs. 278.30 per month. Increased income then, allows the household to make up for the lack of auto-produced foods by the purchase of these foods from local hunters, fishermen and businessmen.

Inasmuch as the success of the San Carlos inhabitants in maintaining good nutritional status appears to be dependent on their continuing to eat a traditional diet, their good nutritional status is maintained in spite of, rather than because of, acculturating influences.

## Yanomama and upper Orinoco studies

The second phase of the nutritional assessment of the Amazon Territory residents included the study of two Yanomama community areas (Parimas A and B) and two villages, one Curripaco and one Piapoco, in the upper Orinoco near San Fernando de Atabapo.

The Yanomama communities, located in the Parima mountains, are in different phases of contact with the 'modern world'. The residents of Parima B have experienced the presence of protestant missionaries in their midst for the past eleven years. Although the process of cultural change is underway, it may not have affected greatly the subsistence patterns of these Indians. The missionaries have brought modern medicine in the form of vaccinations, and an Indian nurse (from the Ye'cuana tribe) administers simplified medical treatment. Occasionally a critically-ill patient is flown to the territorial capital by government or missionary plane. Basically, though, the residents of Parima B live a traditional existence as far as the obtention of food is concerned. They hunt, fish and tend their *conucos*, consuming plantains as their basic starch, supplemented by wild game, fish, insects, fruit and honey. Neither the missionaries nor the nurse have sold or traded canned or non-traditional foods to these people. They still practise warfare with neighbouring villages (*shabonos*). Raids resulting in serious wounds and death occur several times a year in spite of missionary pressure to restrict warfare. About 20 warriors from Parima A, a two-day walk through the jungle from Parima B, raided one of the settlements in Parima B during our fieldwork. There were no injuries, although a study of the nurse's recent medical records indicates that these raids not uncommonly result in wounds from poison arrows.

In contrast to the residents of Parima B, who have the constant presence of missionaries within a ten-minute walk from their village, the Yanomama of Parima A are more isolated, living a virtually traditional existence. A natural grassy area near their complex of *shabonos* allowed us to land with a small plane and set up a field clinic. While the Proicet medical team was treating this population for river blindness (hyperendemic onchocerciasis affects some 90% of the population), I collected the nutritional anthropometric measurements, including weight, height, arm circumference and fatfold thickness.

A total of 242 Yanomama were measured in both Parima settlements. The breakdown according to age and sex was as follows:

| | | |
|---|---|---|
| Adults (18 or over) | Men | 51 |
| | Women | 53 |
| Children (17 and under) | Boys | 72 |
| | Girls | 66 |

Since the Yanomama are very short people, adult men average 145.3 cm and adult women 136.2 cm, it is most appropriate to continue the use of weight for height as the indicator of nutritional status, since age-dependent measurements would considerably overestimate community malnutrition.

Using Yanomama children as a data base, we may compare their weight for height with reference populations – from both England and Caracas (Castellano *et al.* 1981). As can be seen in Figure 4, Yanomama boys as well as girls fall below the 50th percentile for these reference populations of well fed children when they are in the younger age groups. Interestingly, though, as they reach puberty they surpass the 50th percentil. In other words, most Yanomama children from 1 to 12 years old are relatively thin, many falling in the moderate to severely malnourished categories, while in contrast, all teenagers are relatively heavy, indicating stocky body proportions.

Measurements of arm circumference (Figure 5) as well as fatfold thickness for the Yanomama child population confirm the impression that these children are considerably below standard by international measurement, although the teenagers fare much better than do the younger children.

Since all individuals in this community are under the same biological stresses imposed by the physical environment as well as the acculturative stresses that may

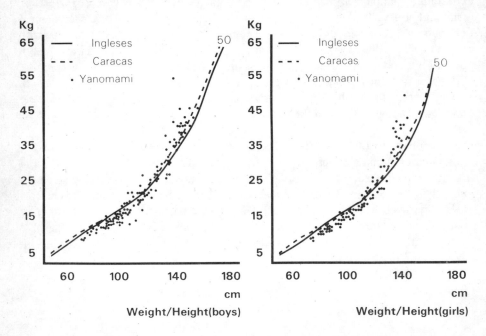

Fig. 4 Weight/height curves comparing Yanomama children against reference populations

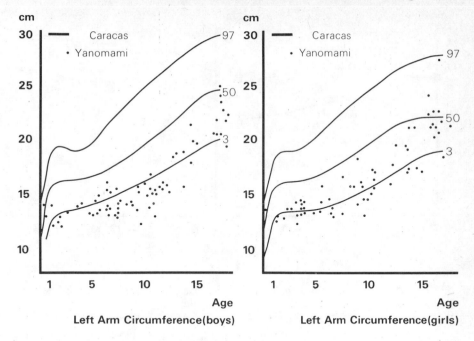

Fig. 5 Arm circumference measurements of Yanomama children compared against reference populations

be present, one must assume that there is a selective process at work in these traditional communities which produces healthy, well nourished young adults entering the reproductive period.

The harsh process by which nature controls this most traditional Yanomama population may indeed show us that the least acculturated people on earth, as a population, may not be as well nourished as we imagine. Rather, healthy young adults who have survived the trials of childhood, give us the impression that primitive man, eating the natural fruits of the jungle, is healthy and fit. However, these populations as a whole, including young children and older adults, do not show community-wide good nutritional status.

In addition to the Yanomama research, the second phase of this investigation into the relationship between culture change and nutrition in the Amazon included the study, in July 1982, of two communities near San Fernando de Atabapo in the upper Orinoco. Approximately 200 Amerindians, 100 from each village, were studied intensively. Besides the nutritional measurements, a complete history was taken for each individual. This included demographic information, migration history, language affiliation and physical and economic indicators of the community as well as a complete physical examination by Proicet doctors, medical

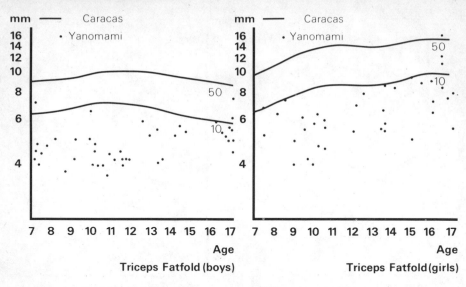

Fig. 6 Fatfold thickness measurements of Yanomama children compared against reference populations

history, blood, urine and faecal exams and a skin biopsy for the presence of microfilariae. Processing of this data is now in progress.

Preliminary results of the nutritional status of children in one of the communities reveals these children to be in good nutritional health. A comparison of weight for height in both boys and girls (Figure 7) indicates that both groups, but especially the boys, fall close to the 50th percentile of the reference populations. Of the two communities studied, this was the relatively more acculturated one. The population was totally of Curripaco ancestry. Although Curripaco was spoken among all community members, all men and most women and children had a knowledge of Spanish. Their community had been established for some 25 years, the residents having migrated to the upper Orinoco from the area of the upper Vaupés, Içana and Guainia rivers. Most members of the community had been converted to evangelical protestantism. They held two communal meals daily, the evening one being followed by a church service. This pattern was virtually identical to that of the upriver villagers in the San Carlos study. The community had a government school, a simple medical dispensary attended by a local resident nurse, and an electric generating plant for illumination in the evenings. Three heads of households received small government salaries (the nurse, sheriff and electric plant operator). As with the upriver communities in the Río Negro, all food consumed in the community was obtained from hunting, fishing and garden produce.

In contrast to this stable, well nourished community in the process of cultural change, was the other community, of similar size, located in a similar setting some

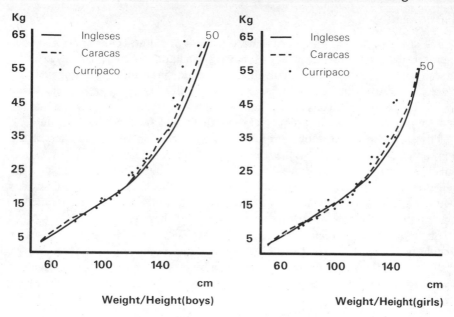

Fig. 7 Weight/height curves comparing Curripaco children against reference populations

four hours by dugout canoe downriver from the first village. Here we encountered a newly forming community of Piapoco Indians who had migrated from various locations in the upper Orinoco as well as from the Meta and Inirida rivers in Colombia. Most residents had settled in the community within the previous two years. Although all members spoke Piapoco, the community had little feeling of cohesiveness. Homes were in the process of construction and *conucos* were being established in the forest; however, the homes usually lacked walls and the *conucos* were being harvested before the crops were mature. The village had no school, medical dispensary or electric generating plant. None of the heads of households received any salary. A small proportion of the men, and virtually none of the women and children could speak Spanish. Although the adults seemed to be in a reasonably good nutritional health, the children showed some signs of malnutrition, especially in the under-five-years-old age cohort. Medical records showed a very high rate of infant mortality and morbidity.

The completed analysis of the data of these communities should give an accurate picture of the determinants of nutritional status. It appears at this stage in the analysis that the newness and instability of the community as well as the lack of medical services, are important factors contributing to the generally poorer health and nutritional status of the individuals.

## Conclusions

Many investigators have assumed that the process of cultural change brings about increasingly poor nutritional status among traditional peoples. A systematic investigation of some 700 individuals in eight indigenous communities in Venezuela's Amazon Territory does not support this assumption. Rather, it was found that community stability and access to modern medical care were among the most important factors in producing good nutritional status in the community.

The least acculturated of the groups studied, the Yanomama Indians of the Parima mountains, were also the least well nourished. Their traditional system of subsistence produced a few well nourished young adults, but at the cost of the selective removal from the community of undernourished children. Constant warfare and village instability, as well as isolation from modern medical treatment, contributed to the low overall nutritional status of these communities.

Six villages in the upper Orinoco and Río Negro areas, in various stages of acculturation, were generally experiencing good nutritional and health status, even during times of nutritional stress during the rainy season. Except for one village, the least acculturated and most unstable community, the settlements were stable and had some contact with government medical treatment clinics. The initial stages of integration into the broader Venezuelan economy experienced by the upper Río Negro villagers, especially the residents of San Carlos, revealed that as traditional subsistence strategies were abandoned in favour of wage earning, local fish, game and garden produce were purchased to make up for the deficit produced as *conucos* were given up and household hunting and fishing time decreased. The purchase of fresh food was preferred over that of canned or packaged foods. In this way the traditional diet was maintained in the face of acculturating influences.

The detrimental effects produced in these individuals through the introduction of exogenous diseases and refined foods appeared to be mediated or completely offset by the availability of modern medical and dental treatment.

The impact of cultural change on these traditional Amazonian communities must be viewed within the broad framework of the biological and cultural stresses the community must face. Against the backdrop of seasonal fluctuations in food availability, the least acculturated communities responded most dramatically, while the more acculturated communities did not show such wide fluctuations. However, both groups of communities experience better nutritional health in the dry season reflecting the dependence, even of the acculturated community, on the food-production activities of the less acculturated neighbouring communities.

## Acknowledgements

Of the many people who supported and contributed to this research I would like to especially thank Dr Rafael Herrera, IVIC; Dr Luis Yarzabal, Proicet; Drs Leslie Sponsel and David Holmes, and Kathleen Clark.

## Notes

1 About 700 individuals are included in the total study population.
2 In the San Carlos area study population the average adult male height was 157.3 cm and the average adult female height was 144.3 cm.
3 See Wright (1981), Gonzalez Ñañez (1977) and Pérez (1981) for detailed historical accounts of the region. My comparative data is based on Matos Arvelo (1912) and Wallace (1889).
4 Probably because traditional subsistence strategies are successful and difficult to replace with modern agriculture or raising domestic animals.
5 There is some indication that nutritional status may be deteriorating with acculturation if the incidence of obesity and rising blood pressures is taken into account.
6 See Holmes (1981, p. 174 and Appendix XI) for details on protein calculations by species of wild game and fish and for the human protein requirements.

# 16 The Missions and the acculturation of the Shuar

## FR. JUAN BOTTASSO

The Shuar, part of the Jívaro group, together with the Awajún, Wampis, Shiwiar (Mainas?), and Achuar, are at present in an historic period of rapid cultural change. Many factors have contributed to the development of this situation; our concern here is to consider the role played in this process by the Missions. This study will deal principally, indeed almost exclusively, with the Shuar of the Amazonian region of Ecuador.

The Untsuri Shuar, as they describe themselves, had their first contact with Western civilisation with the arrival of the Conquistadors in their territories. The first account of this people was furnished by Captain Hernán de Benavente, in a letter addressed to the Audiencia at Lima on 25 March 1550, on the occasion of his journey to the Macas region (Bottasso p. 16). As well as the Conquistadors, who came with their weapons in their hands, there appeared Franciscan, Dominican and Jesuit missionaries. Whilst these rude military adventurers, attracted by cinnamon and gold, wanted the riches and the lands of the Indians, the desire of the missionaries was to 'convert' and 'save' the Shuar. But both groups were deeply steeped in the ethnocentric attitudes which prevailed at that time, and which unquestionably survived until very recently. It was their impregnable conviction that Western civilisation was the only truly human mode of existence upon this planet, and that any other culture was barbarous, savage, or aberrant. To exert oneself in order to change such cultures was, therefore, a duty and an act of humanity towards those peoples who had not yet approached the threshold of decent civilisation. For the missionaries, to dedicate oneself to transforming peoples so backward that they could scarcely be considered human communities, came to be regarded as a work of mercy. It is astonishing to us today to learn that, at an early stage, there was actually theological debate over whether the Indians had a rational soul, such was the amazement that their existence had caused among the Europeans.

The psychological and sociological reasons for these attitudes are well known. Different human groups do not accept one another because there exists a fear of the unfamiliar; he who is different must disappear, and for this there are only these alternatives: to destroy him, to subjugate him keeping him in a state of dependence, or to assimilate him in order to transform him into someone like ourselves. The people of the Iberian Peninsula came to America fresh from a lengthy struggle against the Moors in their own country, in which national identity and unity in the Catholic faith had come to be identified with each other. To be a Christian, to be a subject of the King, to be civilised, and to be a human being worth considering as a person, were all one and the same thing. It is within this climate of opinion that one must understand, if not justify, the thoughts and actions of the missionaries who came to America.

Whilst the missionary can reasonably be considered as a deliberate agent of change in so far as he is 'sent to convert and to save' in accordance with the commandment 'Go ye and preach, make all the nations my disciples', with this outlook and in this historical context he became a specific agent of acculturation who, without consciously wishing to, could lead to ethnocide and, as we shall see, in some cases to genocide.

Until the Second Vatican Council, this mentality remained practically intact, at least in Church circles, despite the advance in the science of anthropology. The Missions set themselves the task of civilising and Christianising the Shuar, and thus became the biggest organised attempt at their acculturation. Whilst in North America the arriving Europeans wanted to destroy the Indian to take over his territory, and whilst the Spanish Conquestadors wanted to dominate him so that he should work in their mines and manufactures as a slave, the missionaries did their utmost to make of the Indian a man who no longer led a 'savage' existence, and made desperate attempts to bring him into some lifestyle similar to that of the European nations. What has varied, over the years, has been not so much the mentality underlying this effort, as certain aspects of this point of view and above all the methods by which it has been put into effect.

## The colonial period

During the colonial period, it was hoped to Christianise the Indians, civilising them or at least pacifying them, with the following aims:

1   To incorporate them into the community of Christendom and the Hispanic empire. The existence of savages was an affront to a civilised people who lived alongside them, and an irritation to their Christian sensibilities. In the seventeenth century, the Jesuits were to begin a comprehensive attempt to resolve the problem along the lines already tried in a positive way by their brethren among the Guaraní of Paraguay (op. cit. p. 119).

2   To make them into a productive group, always useful to the interests of the Crown, because, moreover, it was a common conviction that idleness was what contributed most to their degeneration: '. . . idleness is the most disastrous inheritance which the Jívaros pass on to one another down the centuries and for this reason a programme to civilise them must especially attempt to remove them from this state of indolence' (Fr. Elias Brito, *D. Bosco en el Ecuador*, III, p. 473).

3    To prevent their becoming an obstacle to the Mainas Missions, which were the Spanish bulwark against the advance of the Portuguese along the navigable rivers of Brazil.

The following methods were employed:

1    Fr. Juan Lorenzo Lucero attempted preaching, but without achieving much. In a document from Quito dated 16 April 1689, we read '. . . Fr. Juan Lorenzo Lucero did not overcome them, for although at first they came saying they wished to be friends, once they received axes they showed their perverse inclinations by using them to kill many Indians and even some Spaniards.'

2    In 1690 Fr. Francisco Viva obtained the consent of the Bishop of Quito, the Rev. Dr Sancho Andrade y Figueroa, and of the Royal Audiencia of that city, to undertake a comprehensive project with more drastic and energetic methods. 'With this zeal to hand over Christians to the Crown, he proposed to attack the Jívaros from the four points of the compass and to this end prepared with care his armed squadrons which were to assail them with weapons and violence from Mainas, Loja, Cuenca and Macas alike.' The aim of Fr. Viva was to drive the Indians downriver and establish them in a supervised settlement. But after half a decade of fighting, he was obliged to desist, and commented sadly: 'The orders cannot be carried out, seeing at first hand the present state of the Missions, so disturbed, exhausted, and ruined, worn out by the Jívaros . . . In five years we have succeeded in bringing 1360 Jívaros out of their hiding-places, but what spiritual benefit has been gained? Many of these captives despair and hang themselves, others in desperation die by refusing food and drink, other stuff sticks in their throats and choke themselves.' (A true case of genocide was occurring, although intentions had been very different!) Fr. Viva concluded: 'When all is said and done, the Jívaros are like brute animals.'

Reading these lines, one captures all the bitterness of the failure of a project which had been planned on grandiose lines, but what this confession reveals about the mentality of the period is astonishing. At no time were these men struck by the notion that it was they who were the aggressors (op. cit. p. 17).

During this colonial period, the Shuar resisted all attempts at conquest, whether by soldiers or by missionaries, by passive resistance, refusing to live other than in their natural manner, or by open hostilities, as in 1599, when, in the celebrated rising chronicled by Juan de Velasco, they destroyed the mining town of Logroño and killed the Governor, pouring molten gold into his mouth. From this was born the myth that the Shuar were resistant to a civilisation and were brutes lacking in spiritual attributes.

Again, on 19 July 1720, Fr. Juan Bautista Sánchez de Orellana, judge of the Audiencia at Quito, wrote to the King, requesting decisive support to resolve the problem once and for all, and recalling that 'more than thirty expeditions have been made, but without effect on account of apparently insuperable difficulties which are encountered'. But he too failed to put an end to the resistance of this people. That the Shuar should maintain their liberty continued to be seen as a misfortune for them, although in passing no attempt was made to hide the loss and damage which this entailed for the Crown: 'This people is the most unfortunate of all among the Indians' (because it refused the light of the Gospel), but it was also noted that 'they have caused and continue to cause much damage, killing captains and soldiers and obstructing the route to the mines which belonged to His Majesty . . .' (op. cit. p. 30 note).

## The republican period

During the republican period the struggles for independence and the internecine strife which followed brought about an almost total lack of interest in the territory of the Jívaros, but not even at this time was there a halt to attempts at penetration. It was, however, now a question of sporadic attempts of little importance.

The Jesuits attempted to convert them for religious reasons, but with almost no effects at all. Fr. J. Jounen reports the words of the Jesuit Superior in Ecuador, Fr. Francisco Javier Hernández, written in 1863: 'Three centuries have now passed since the conquest, and these wretches are still, with little exception, as barbarous and as heathen as when the Conquistadors came to these lands.'

Here are some of the reasons which lay behind the withdrawal of the Jesuits from Gualaquiza: 'I saw afterwards that the two (missionaries) who were in Gualaquiza were wasting their time . . . and that is why I withdrew them from that isolation and lack of support in which they languished' (letter from the Visitor of the Jesuits, Augustín Delgado, to the Bishop of Loja in 1869). 'They hate the white men and consider them to be their enemies. They do not love the Missionary Fathers, nor do they invite them to their homes nor their villages, as do the people of Macas. The customs of these Jívaros are appalling' (letter from Fr. Luis Pozzi, 21 February 1870).

The abandonment of Macas came somewhat later, but for the same reasons: '. . . Since several dangerous attempts have confirmed that these bloody tribes of Jívaros . . . obstinately refuse the light, in order not to have to improve their corrupted customs' (Lorenzo López Sanvicente, *La misión del Napo*. Quito, 1894, p. 16), (op. cit. p. 33).

It was to be García Moreno, President of the Republic of Ecuador, whose preoccupation with the unification of the nation's territory would lead once again to an interest in the lands of the Shuar and their evangelisation, and to a willingness to take drastic measures; but his sudden disappearance cut short this project (op. cit. p. 19). To accomplish his objectives he had not hesitated to envisage the use of force.

The plan to entrust the eastern region of Ecuador to various religious organisations (Apostolic Vicarships apportioned among various religious orders) arose from the National Congress of Ecuador rather than from the Church.

Conversion and civilisation were advanced as the reasons, but it must not be forgotten that the rubber boom was beginning and that Ecuador saw her eastern territories threatened. Now, as before, the Church would not be able to keep her involvement from turning into an instrument of the civil power.

In 1888 Dr Antonio Flores became President of the Republic. The Congress requested him to write to the Pope to ask for the constitution of four Apostolic Vicarships in the east: El Napo (Jesuits), Canelos (Dominicans), Méndez and Gualaquiza (Salesians), and Zamora (Franciscans). Leo XIII replied on 30 January 1889 that he would take note of the proposal. In the years which followed, the Vicarships were established, and from that time the Shuar were divided among the Vicarships of Canelos, Méndez-Gualaquiza, and Zamora. The number of missionaries in their territory began to multiply from then on, but once again they succeeded in disheartening them all, at least in the initial phase. The Dominicans soon withdrew from Macas. The Franciscans went into Zamora in 1892, and left it in confusion four years later; the liberal revolution had left them without official support, and in the judgement of their Superior, Fr. Luis Torra, without the backing of the army any initiatives in that area would have failed. The Salesians, too, who were the last to come into Gualaquiza in 1893–4, were on the point of coming out for good. In 1912 Fr. Joaquín Spinelli, who had been the pioneer of the Salesians in the Vicarship, wrote in a highly confidential report to the Inspector at Lima: 'Missionaries have now been working amongst them for so many years . . . and little result is to be seen . . . Would it not be better to betake our tents elsewhere, and to shake off the dust from our feet? Let our superiors consider this matter carefully and not continue to sacrifice our personnel.'

The remark attributed to the Apostolic Vicar Mgr. Domingo Comín in a report to Pope Benedict XV has become historic; referring to the fruitlessness of missionary work among the Shuar, he observed 'We are watering a dead stick.'

We may conclude that until well into this century the Shuar people rejected almost totally anything which appeared likely to change them. Contacts which were at first almost friendly, with the aim of obtaining gifts, soon became indifferent and then immediately hostile when the gifts ceased. Fr. Torra, whom we have already mentioned, indeed writes: '. . . about a year ago twelve or so Jívaros from Logroño came to visit us. . . . and since they had a warm welcome in our village, and we gave them such gifts as we were able to, they offered to return in larger numbers, I believe with the sole aim of obtaining further presents. I have already said this was about a year ago, and up to the present time they have not reappeared.'

In the twentieth century, liberal governments supported the Missions not because they were projects leading to Christianisation, but because they tamed the ferocity of the Jívaros and made colonisation possible. Ironically, it is in this very period that the missionaries began to view their task with somewhat greater optimism. What was happening? In the 1920s the flow of immigration by white and mixed-race (*mestizo*) colonists from the mountains towards Amazonia was increasing, and creating a new situation in the Shuar territory. It would be ingenuous to believe that colonisation had been planned with the aim of bringing about the acculturation of the Shuar. What happened was that expansion to the east became even more inevitable, and the acculturation of the Shuar was still considered necessary. Since the colonists were 'civilised', it is easy to understand why their presence should have been seen as a means of transforming the Shuar (op. cit. p. 103).

There were also proposals and plans for foreign colonisation. Fr. Joaquín Spinelli wrote: 'All the South American Republics which have savages in their territory have a great interest in attracting them to civilisation through Catholic Missions, opening lines of communication and favouring colonisation by settlers from home and abroad.' Fr. Miguel Allioni and Fr. Carlos Crespi also declared themselves in favour of immigration from abroad. Steps were taken, including some at government level, to put these proposals into effect, but they never came to anything.

It was in fact immigration from within the country itself which opened the way and came to impose itself, because it answered the needs of thousands of impoverished Ecuadorians from the mountains who had no prospect of improving their economic situation, and who were constrained by the exploitative structure of the big estates. This cause was taken up as a priority by various missionaries, including Fr. Albino del Curto, who dedicated his entire life from 1917 onwards to constructing the horse track from the mountains to Méndez.

The ever-nearer and more numerous presence of the colonists in their lands aroused the interest of the Shuar in 'Christianity'. The missionaries were delighted at this new attitude, which they believed to arise from an interest in religion; but in reality the Shuar came closer to the missionary above all for economic reasons and for security. In this respect, the observation of one Shuar is revealing: 'Christian being rich, got everything, Jívaro being poor, got nothing, got no shirt, got no gunpowder.' Surely this judgement was not the personal opinion of the individual who gave voice to it, but rather revealed the general feeling of the Shuar, who were drawn by the material wealth of the poor colonists, relative though this certainly was.

The Shuar deduced that in order to have the goods of the white man it was necessary to become Christian and civilised like him, and the missionary became the natural intermediary for this objective: he knew the world of the colonist and was at the side of the Shuar, since he had come for them. The *úunt* (leaders, chieftains) felt more secure against the power and numbers of the whites because of their good relations with the Fathers, and at the same time they became the axis and important links in a commercial system consisting of the chain of trading partners (*amikru*) who could ensure the supply of certain products which the technology of the forests cannot produce, such as gunpowder, knives, machetes, and clothing. A very interesting analysis of this phenomenon can be found in the work of M. J. Harner, *The Jívaro, People of the Sacred Waterfalls* (1973).

In addition, the Shuar began to realise that in order to receive these goods, the missionaries expected them to accept preaching, take part in acts of worship, and adopt new norms of behaviour such as abandoning polygamy and their pagan rituals. It would be foolish to take for granted sincerity and genuine conviction in this new moral code, but at the level of visible external behaviour it gradually created a new mode of existence for the Shuar.

Another price exacted by the missionary was that they should send their children to school. Some of the Shuar, for example their leader Timias de Yukipa, guessed from the outset that in the ability to read and write there must be found the secret of the knowledge and prosperity of the westerners. Thus the school, which was at first entirely in the hands of the missionaries, was another factor which had profoud consequences in the process of acculturation. It brought new knowledge and new values, which often tended to alienate; it distanced the new generations from their parents, undermined the strength of their culture, and their appreciation of what was their own. In books, they learned to read in Spanish that the Shuar are savages, that their language is not worthy of Christians, and that their homes are the receptacles of every kind of vice.

But for a people who live in so dispersed a fashion as do the Shuar, the school brought with it another institution: the school residence, in which the children and young people had to stay all the time in order to attend classes with any regularity. The Mission-cum-residential-school structure was to become increasingly the norm in the Vicarship of Méndez, especially from the 1940s until its greatest vogue in the 1960s. A very high percentage both of males and females spent some years in the Mission, and perhaps between eighty and ninety per cent of the entire population spent at least a short spell there.

In the mind of many missionaries, a stay in the school residence also had the aim of preserving the young people from the corruption of native living and of accustoming them to methodical work, the basis of a future 'wellbeing' according to western criteria. As a factor in their acculturation, the school residence was extremely important: it isolated the young person, often for a number of years, from contact with his family and clan, abruptly cutting the essential channel of socialisation; it created conditions in which marriage links could be forged in an atmosphere which perhaps left greater scope for freedom of choice in the matter of a partner, but which destabilised the solid bonds of the tribal marriage laws; it created ludicrous aspirations in the pupil, and produced in him alienation from his own group, his world, and its customs.

If the arrival of the colonists was at first greeted as something positive by the missionaries and even by the Shuar, it very soon began to arouse concern about the ownership of the land. In 1935 Fr. Juan Vigna demanded legal measures from the government on this question. The Missions were awarded trusteeship over the lands of the Shuar people, a task which the Mission accomplished with many sacrifices. But in the meanwhile the Shuar had now learned that land could be divided into lots, that land could be sold and bought, that the government requires, in order to recognise ownership, that the greater part of the land should be worked, and that the boundaries of their territory were shrinking. In short, there had been created a new relationship with the land which left the Shuar people very shaken and traumatised, and an indirect, but very profound, kind of acculturation had been accomplished.

To sum up. The missionaries have always wished to 'convert' the Shuar. Products of their age, they shared in the different periods of history the ideas of their contemporaries, and because of this they were unable to make a distinction between the work of evangelisation and that of civilisation, but often rather did they consider the latter to be a precondition for preaching the Gospel. They consented to be the instruments of the civil power in the defence of empires and national territories, with a totally uncritical conviction that the good of the empire or the recently created South American nation must also be what was best for the Indian people. For this reason they felt it deeply when, in their obstinate desire to maintain their freedom, the Indians refused to accept these 'advantages'. But it was not after all their preaching, nor those moves most directly concerned with evangelisation, which had the greatest influence for change. Other factors which modified the general context were those which have made the Shuar people of today so different from that people which the first Conquistadors had encountered.

## The present situation

The Shuar of today are a people exhibiting a greater or a lesser degree of acculturation according to their region. The process of change is accelerating year by year, and it is certainly not the Mission which has had the greatest influence in all this. The society which surrounds the Shuar has reached them and is assailing them from all sides.

The climate of ideas has changed greatly. The anthropological sciences have progressed and have succeeded in sowing doubts even within the Church, especially since the Second Vatican Council. Some dialogue has begun between theology, pastoral practice, and anthropology.

What, then, is the role of the Missions today?

The anthropologists have already declared themselves in an extremely peremptory tone: '. . . the best thing for the Indian peoples, and for the preservation of the moral integrity of the Churches themselves, is to put an end to all missionary activity' (Declaration of Barbados, 1971).

What do the Shuar expect from the Missions today? There are no studies on this topic, nor any scientific investigations which would enable a reply to be given, but listening to what the Shuar say in their meetings and assemblies it seems to me that we can claim that two tendencies may be observed. Some (not the majority), at least in their speeches, are demanding the departure of all foreigners, including the missionaries, in order to remain free of what they consider to be an inappropriate tutelage. Others, without being ignorant of the limitations and errors of the missionaries, accept and even desire their presence, since in the critical situation of cultural shock in which they find themselves, they realise that they need intermediaries and supporters upon whom they can rely. Among the various people who are interested in the Shuar (politicians, bureaucrats, academics, the curious, folklorists, etc.) the missionaries seem to them to be those who offer the best guarantees of loyalty to the people because of their lifetime commitment.

What do the missionaries think?

After not a few internal wrangles, nearly all have arrived at a new attitude with regard to the missionary's work. The dialogue with anthropology has opened to them new horizons and new problems. To accompany the people in the defence of their rights, their identity, and their values is what they feel their fundamental task to be today.

What of achievements? In 1964, at the urging of one of the missionaries, Fr. Juan Shutka, supported by others and with the active involvement of the community leaders, there was founded the Federation of Shuar Centres, with its headquarters in Sucúa. It is a native organisation, with its roots in the entire people, directed by natives, which seeks the good of the people in many fields: the defence of their lands (obtaining from the State the legal title to the whole land allotments of the more than two hundred communities), education (with the Bilingual and Bicultural Shuar Radio network, with Shuar teachers and appropriate programmes to infuse new vigour into their culture), the means of social communication (especially the Federation radio transmitter through which the language and music of the Shuar find an authentic means of diffusion), the recognition of civil rights (through the Shuar Group for Civil Registration), health (with the training of medical auxiliaries and campaigns against the diseases of the Amazon region), craft (not allowing the traditional techniques to be lost). In the Federation the missionaries are present as advisors, but the responsibility and the decisions remain in the hands of the Shuar.

It would be ingenuous to deny that the Federation, with its structure modelled upon western organisations, is a means of acculturation; but faced with the challenge of the present time it is a positive response for a people which wishes to survive and go forward: the alternatives are to organise or to perish.

We must also bear in mind the extensive work of 'recovering memory' which has been carried out for almost ten years through the 'Shuar World' publications, a collection of booklets and books covering all aspects of this people, from hunting techniques to myths and ethnohistory. All this material is today widely used for teaching in schools and bilingual colleges (in Shuar and Spanish), and has also contributed greatly towards making Shuar culture known beyond its boundaries.

As a missionary, I should also like to say a word about 'spreading the Gospel'. This primary reason for our prescence among the Shuar has not been abandoned. Following Vatican II, we are trying to make the Gospel present through specific works of promoting and defending human rights, this being the first form of salvation the Gospel wants, without denying the other which the Gospel also preaches.

In the specifically religious field, new methods have been attempted which take respect and esteem for the culture as their first consideration. In the same vein there is also the extensive work of the '*etserin*' or native religious leaders of natural communities. There is also a programme of consciousness-raising, with the conviction that the values of Christianity (dignity of the person: each man is the image of God), human fraternity (we are all brothers), and hope in the future, are not only not prejudicial to the Shuar people, but will provide them with a solid foundation and frame of reference on which to orient themselves securely for the future.

As missionaries we recognise our limitations and errors, and we perceive the risk of new mistakes; but only he who does not risk his life and does nothing can keep his hands clean in the business of history.

## Acknowledgements

Fr. Bottasso is with Mundo Shuar (an organisation to help the Shuar or Jívaro Indians) in Quito, Ecuador. This paper was translated by Dr David Hook of the Department of Spanish, King's College, University of London.

## Notes

1 Bottasso, Juan, *Los Shuar y las misiones. Entre la hostilidad y el diálogo (The Shuar and the Missions. From Hostility to Dialogue)*, p. 16.
2 Op. cit., p. 119.
3 Op. cit., p. 17.
4 Op. cit., p. 30, note.
5 Op. cit., p. 33.
6 Op. cit., p. 19.
7 Op. cit., p. 103.

# 17 The present policy of developing Peruvian Amazonia and its social and ecological impact

ALBERTO CHIRIF

Different Peruvian governments have regarded Amazonia as a region that is uninhabited, is scarcely exploited, possesses inherent natural resources, and is a food larder for the country.

They therefore saw it as capable of absorbing large contingents of the unemployed population, and as an attractive region for investment of national and foreign capital. Indigenous populations are being increasingly affected by this policy of occupation of Amazonia. Many native groups have lost a large part of their traditional territories. Those indigenous groups who had kept themselves relatively safe from extractive greed now see their existence threatened in proportion to the advance of new roads and the promotion of colonisation projects.

The present government is about to deny them their rights in a new manner: it has undertaken to carry out a programme of parcelling out the Indians' lands. This means a programme that denies them the right to own their land collectively as social groups: land titles will be granted only on an individual basis. Should this take place, it will destroy any possibility of indigenous groups organising themselves to give a response to the present historical momentum based on their own cultural tradition.

To understand and evaluate the impact suffered by the native population, by natural resources and by the regional economy, it is important to place the present policy of development within the crisis that Peru has been experiencing since the mid-1970s. We must also analyse the following aspects:

1 present Peruvian legislation about land and resources in Amazonia (which, among other things, makes it possible to reimpose the system of *latifundio* land holding in the region), and the concrete expression that this legislation is taking;

2 the 'special projects' that the present government is planning and executing in various parts of Amazonia, and their implications for the indigenous population and for migrant rural workers;

3 the road-building programme that supports both realisation of those 'special projects' and the general exploitation of Amazonia's natural resources.

# 18 Amazonia and foreign aid: the regression of development

STEPHEN NUGENT

The main purpose of this paper is to discuss some of the domains within which anthropological studies of non-indigenous Amazonian societies are located. By domains I am referring to types of social science practice differentiated according to the unit of analysis. What is notable in Amazonian studies is that outside of ethnographic treatments of Amerindians – for whom the concept 'tribe' is still rather uncritically applied – anthropological models have tended to be adjuncts of models derived from ecologically-oriented work. A consequence of this is that Amazonian peasantries – on which relatively little research has been focused – are most frequently depicted as contingent societies, that is societies for which the determination of structure and process is, in the last analysis, a function of the natural landscape.

A second purpose of the paper is to consider the relationship between the astructural depiction of Amazonian peasantries and the political implications of Amazonian development planning.

The detachment of anthropological practice from the broader political process has long been disputed and controversy about the role of social scientists in the political process has largely centred around the realisation of overt imperial aims. With few exceptions, issues relating to the major political shifts which have derived from post-WW II imperial and neo-imperial ventures have not featured prominently in anthropological discourse in spite of the fact that anthropologists have been actively publishing the results of research undertaken in precisely those areas of the world where the incursions of metropolitan states are most marked.

# 19 The state and the reproduction of the social structure on the frontier: Ariquêmes/Rondônia

JEAN HÉBETTE and ROSA ACEVEDO M.

This paper discusses the various interests and aspirations of capitalist centres towards Amazonia, over a period since the 1960s. The interests of national and foreign capital in Amazonia are met by the Policy of National Security, created by the state to facilitate the occupation of Amazonia. This is the framework within which government policies were launched in Rondônia. It was a priority area for state action during the 1970s, particularly in the implantation of colonisation projects.

This paper argues that this area was organised by the Instituto Brasileiro de Colonização e Reforma Agrária (and later by the Instituto Nacional de Colonização e Reforma Agrária) in a manner that catered to the interests of capital.

An analysis of the landholding structure and its recent transformationS constituted a model for consideration and demonstrated a tendency and mechanisms for concentrating the land in the interests of mining companies, private groups, colonisation developers, and traditional large landowners; whereas Indians, small settlers, rubber gatherers and squatters were attacked in a violent process of expropriation.

Our fieldwork was concentrated on the Ariquêmes local authority. Ariquêmes demonstrated how these categories are regarded within INCRA's colonisation policy, in relation to distribution of land, access to plots of land, financial credit, and technical assistance. On the basis of bank registers it shows how credit is concentrated according to agricultural activity and type of producer. A similar examination was made on the basis of technical assistance. The revival of land conflicts in the Territory is the result of this process of monopolising land under these new norms.

## 20 Some aspects of the process of change in northeast Pará
### LOURDES GONÇALVES FURTADO

This paper focuses on some aspects of change in northeast Pará. It is a vast area that lives under the influence of two ecological zones: the coastal fringe and the inland *terra firme*. The populations of these zones have their economies based respectively on fishing and agriculture, in which subsistence peasant farming predominates. This region is being affected by the expansion of an economic frontier represented by agro-ranching and extractive projects. These particularly result from a policy of financial incentives generated by SUDAM (Superintendência do Desenvolvimento da Amazônia). Apart from these frontiers, the expansion of the road network into the area is another factor helping to alter the way of life of its inhabitants.

On the basis of these preliminary facts, the paper seeks to establish how the social sectors of northeast Pará are reacting to these factors. In other words: what are the effects of the expanding frontiers on their social organisation in the productive process and the relationship between man and his environment.

# Bibliography

Alvarez, Ricardo (1964) Icaros: Crimen y Venganza. In *Revista de Misiones Dominicanas del Perú*, XLV, 267 20–5, May–Jun.

Alvim, P. de T. (1980) Agricultural production potential in the Amazon Region. In Barbira–Scazzocchio, F. (ed.) *Land, People and Planning in Contemporary Amazonia* (pp. 27–36). Centre of Latin American Studies, Occasional Paper 3, Cambridge.

Antonov, A. N. (1947) Children born during the siege of Leningrad in 1942. *Journal of Pediatrics* **30**: 250–9.

Aragón, Luis Eduardo (1978) *Migration to Northern Goiás: Geographical and occupational mobility in Southeastern Amazonia, Brazil*. Ph.D. dissertation, Michigan State University.

Arhem, Kaj (1981) *Makuna Social Organization*, Uppsala, Sweden.

Banik, N. D. D. *et al.* (1968) *A longitudinal study on morbidity and mortality and growth and development of preschool children in Delhi*, Indian Council of Medical Research: New Delhi.

Barbira-Scazzocchio, F. (ed.) (1980) *Land, People and Planning in Contemporary Amazonia*. Centre for Latin American Studies, University of Cambridge.

Barraclough, Solon L. and Domike, Arthur L. (1960) Agrarian structure in seven Latin American countries. *Land economics* **42**(4) (November): 391–424.

Bates, Henry Walter (1864) *The Naturalist on the River Amazons*. Reprinted from the second edition by the University of California Press; Berkeley & Los Angeles, 1962.

Batista, Djalma (1976) *O complexo da Amazônia: análise do processo de desenvolvimento*. Conquista: Rio de Janeiro.

Baxter, Michael W. P. (1975) *Garimpeiros of Poxoréo: small scale diamond miners and their environment in Brazil*. Ph.D. dissertation, University of California, Berkeley.

Becker, Olga Maria Schild, *et al.* (1978) Áreas de atração e evasão populacional no Brasil no período 1960–70. paper presented at *3° Encontro Nacional de Geógrafos* (AGB), Fortaleza, July 1978. (Mimeo.).

Beidelman, Thomas O. (1974) Social theory and the study of Christian missions in Africa *Africa* XLIV(3): 235–49.

Beier, George, Churchill, Anthony, Cohen, Michael and Renaud, Bertrand (1976) The task ahead for the cities of the developing world. *World Development* **4**(5) (May): 363–4.

Berlin, Elois Ann and Markell, Edward K. (1977) An assessment of the nutritional and health status of the Aguaruna Jívaro Community, Amazonas, Peru, *Ecology of Food and Nutrition*, **6**: 69–81.

Berquó, Elza S. (nd) *Anais do primeiro encontro nacional de estudos populacionais*. Associação Brasileira de Estudos Populacionais (ABEP): São Paulo.

Bishop, J. P. (1979) *Development and transfer of technology for small farms in the Ecuadorian Amazonic Region*. In CATIE, *Agroforestry Systems in Latin America* (pp. 145–50), Turrialba, Costa Rica.

Bodley, John H. (1975) *Victims of Progress*, Cummings: Menlo Park, California.

Bourne, R. (1978) *Assault on the Amazon*, Gollancz: London.

Brazil (1964) *Estatuto da Terra: Lei no. 4504*. INCRA: Brasília.

—— (1965) *Ordenação no. 56795*. Diario da União: Brasília.

—— (1966) *Ordenação no. 54428*. Diario da União: Brasília.

Brazil, Departamento Nacional de Pesquisa Mineral (1981) *Anuário Mineral Brasileiro, 1981* (preliminary). Brasília.

Brazil, Ministério da Agricultura (1972) *Altamira I*. INCRA: Brasília.

Brazil, Ministério do Interior (1975) *II Plano nacional de desenvolvimento: programa de ação do governo para a Amazônia*. MINTER/SUDAM: Belém.

—— (1976) (ed.) *Mudanças na composição do emprego e na distribuição da renda: efeitos sôbre as migrações internas*. Organização Internacional do Trabalho (OIT)/Banco Nacional da Habitação (BNH): Brasília.

Briscoe, C. (1979) Agroforestry at Jari. In CATIE *Agroforestry Systems in Latin America* (pp. 122–6). CATIE: Turrialba, Costa Rica.

Brookfield, Harold (1979) *Interdependent Development*. (First published 1965) Methuen: London.

Brooks, E. (1974) Frontiers of ethnic conflict in the Brazilian Amazon. *International Journal of Environmental Studies* 7(1): 63–74.

Brown, Lawrence A. and Gilliard, Rickie S. (1981) On the interrelationships between development and migration processes. In Martinson, Tom L. and Elbow, Gary S. (eds.) *Geographical Research on Latin America: Benchmark 1980* (pp. 357–73). Conference of Latin Americanist Geographers – CLAG, Muncie, Indiana.

Bunker, Stephen G. (1979) Power structures and exchange between government agencies in the expansion of the agricultural sector. *Studies in Comparative International Development*. XIV, I: 56–76.

—— (1980) Forces of destruction in Amazonia. *Environment* 22(7), (September): 14–20, 34–43.

—— (1981) The impact of deforestation on peasant communities in the Medio Amazonas of Brazil. *Studies in Third World Societies*, 13: 45–60.

—— (1982) The cost of modernity: Inappropriate bureaucracy, inequality, and development program failure in the Brazilian Amazon. *Journal of Developing Areas*, 16(4): 573–96.

—— (1983) Policy implementation in an authoritarian state: A case from Brazil. *Latin American Research Review*, 18(1): 33–58.

—— (1984) *Underdeveloping the Amazon: Extraction, Unequal Exchange, and the Failure of the Modern State*. University of Illinois: Urbana.

Butland, Gilbert J. (1966) Frontiers of settlement in South America. *Revista Geográfica* 65 (December): 93–108.

Camargo, José Geraldo da Cunha (1973) *Urbanismo Rural*. INCRA: Brasília.

—— (1973) *Urbanismo Rural*. Ministério da Agricultura (MA)/Instituto Nacional de Colonização e Reforma Agrária (INCRA): Brasília.

Camino, Alejandro (1977) Trueque, Correrías e Intercambios entre los Quechuas Andinos y los Piro y Machiguenga de la Montaña Peruana. *Amazonía Peruana*. 1(2) Ed. CAAAP: Lima.

Cardoso, Fernando H. and Müller, Geraldo (1977) *Amazônia: expansão do capitalismo*. Editora Brasiliense: São Paulo.

Cardoso de Oliveira, Roberto (1976) *Identidade, Entnía y Estrutura Social*. Editorial São

Paulo.

Carlstein, T. (1973) *Population, Activities and Settlement as a System: The Case of Shifting Cultivation*. Geography, Lund (mimeo.).

—— (1978) Innovation, time allocation and time-space packing. In Carlstein, T., Parkes, D. and Thrift, N. (eds.), *Timing space and spacing time* 1, Edward Arnold: London.

Carvalho, José Alberto Magno de (1973) *Analysis of Regional Trends in Fertility, Mortality and Migration in Brazil, 1940–70*. Ph.D. dissertation, University of London.

Carvalho, José Alberto Magno de and Moreira, Morvan de Mello (1976) *Migrações internas na Região Norte*. I. Belém: Ministério do Interior (MINTER)/Superintendência do Desenvolvimento da Amazônia (SUDAM).

Carvalho, José Alberto Magno de *et al*. (1979a) Migrações internas na Amazônia. In Costa, José Marcelino Monteiro da (ed.) *Amazônia: desenvolvimento e ocupação*, (pp. 193–243). Instituto de Planejamento Econômico e Social (IPEA)/Instituto de Pesquisas (INPES): Rio de Janeiro.

—— (1979b) *Migração interna na Região Norte: estudo de campo da região de Marabá*. Belo Horizonte (mimeo.).

Carvalho Filho, R. and Peixoto, E. S. (1976) Solos do Projeto Ouro Prêto: área de expansão 111, *Cacau Atualidades* **14**(3): 3–9.

Castro, Antonio Ferreira de (nd) *A Selva* (22nd edn.). Livraria Editôra Guimarães: Lisbon.

CATIE (Centro Agronómico Tropical de Investigación y Enseñanza) (1979) *Agroforestry Systems in Latin America*. Turrialba, Costa Rica.

CETR (Coordenadoria Especial do Território de Rondônia) (1980) *Areas de tensão social no Território de Rondônia: Coordenadoria Especial de Rondônia/INCRA*, Relatório circulação interna 16.6.80, Pôrto Velho.

Chambers, R. (1979) *Rural Health Planning: Why Seasons Matter*. Working Paper Draft, Institute of Development Studies, Sussex.

Chambers, R., Longhurst, R., Bradley, D. and Feachem, R. (1979) *Seasonal Dimensions to Rural Poverty: Analysis and Practical Implications*. Discussion Paper 142, Institute of Development Studies, University of Sussex, Brighton.

Chambers, R., Longhurst, R., Pacey, A. (eds. (1981) *Seasonal Dimensions to Rural Poverty*, Frances Pinter: London; Allanheld: Osmun, New Jersey.

Chase Smith, Richard (1981) *Land, Natural Resources, and Economic Development of the Amuesha Native Communities in the Palcazu Valley*. Central Selva Resource Management 2: L1–L38; Lima: JRB Associates.

—— (1982a) Liberal ideology and indigenous communities in post-independence Peru. *Journal of International Affairs* **36**, 1.

—— (1982b) *The Dialectics of Domination: Native Communities and the Myth of the Vast Amazonian Emptiness*. Occasional Paper 8, Cultural Survival, Inc. Cambridge, Mass.

Chossudovsky, Michel (1981) Capitalist development and agriculture in Latin America. In Alschuler, Lawrence A. (ed.) *Dependent Agricultural Development and Agrarian Reform in Latin America* (pp. 13–28). University of Ottawa Press.

Clark, Kathleen E. (1980) Indigenous fisheries at San Carlos de Río Negro, Venezuela, *Annual Meeting of the American Society of Ichthyologists & Herpetologists*, Fort Worth, Texas.

Costa, José Marcelino Monteiro da (ed.) (1979) *Amazônia: desenvolvimento e ocupação*. Instituto de Planejamento Econômico e Social (IPEA)/Instituto de Pesquisas (INPES):

Rio de Janeiro.

Couto e Silva, G. do (1957) *Aspectos Geopolíticos do Brasil*. Biblioteca do Exército: Rio de Janeiro.

Crist, R. and Nissly, C. (1973) *East from the Andes*. University of Florida Press: Gainesville.

Crossley, J. C. (1961) Santa Cruz at the cross-roads. A study of development in Eastern Bolivia, *Tijdschrift voor Economische en Sociale Geografie*, **52** (1961), 187–206.

—— (1977) *Spatial Variations in Bolivian Agricultural Marketing Behaviour in Areas of Recent Colonization*. Report to the Social Sciences Research Council (Leicester University, mimeo.).

Crossley, J. C. and Johnson, C. E. (1977) *The Work of the British Tropical Agricultural Mission in Bolivia 1963–1972. An Evaluation* Ministry of Overseas Development: London.

Daland, Robert T. (1969) Urbanization policy and poltical development in Latin America. *American Behavioral Scientist* **12**(5) (May–June): 22–33.

Dall'Agno, Roberto (1982) *Tecnologias de exploração mineral na Amazônia*. Presented at the 34th annual meeting of the Sociedade Brasileira para o Progresso da Ciência, Campinas, São Paulo, July.

d'Apole, Vincenzo, *et al.* (1972) *Bases para uma politica de colonização e reforma agrária no Nordeste do Brasil*. Ministério do Interior (MINTER)/Superintendência do Desenvolvimento do Nordeste (SUDENE)/DAA: Recife.

Davis, Shelton H. (1977) *Victims of the Miracle*. Cambridge University Press.

Declaration of Barbados for the Liberation of the Indians (1971). Conference 'The Situation of the Indian in South America' Bridgetown, Barbados 25–30 January 1971. Dorstal, W. (ed.) (p. 376). World Council of Churches: Geneva.

de Janvry, A. and Ground, L. (1978) Types and consequences of land reform in Latin America. *Latin American Perspectives* **19**(4).

Denevan, W. M. (1966) *The Aboriginal Cultural Geography of the Llanos de Mojos de Bolivia* University of California: Berkeley.

—— (1978) *The Role of Geographic Research in Latin America*. Conference of Latin Americanist Geographers (CLAG) 1978: Muncie, Indiana.

—— (1980) Latin America. In Klee, G. A. (ed.) *World Systems of Traditional Resource Management* (pp. 217–44). Arnold: London.

Denevan, W. M. and Bergman, R. W. (1975) Karinya Indian swamp cultivation in the Venezuelan Llanos. *Yearbook of the Association of Pacific Coast Geographers* **37**: 23–37.

Dias, A. C. C. P. and Melo, A. A. O. (1976) Solos de Projeto Ouro Preto; área de expansão 11, *Bol-téc*. 45, *Centro de Pesquisas do Cacau*, Itabuna, Bahia.

D.N.P.M. (Departamento Nacional da Produção Mineral) (1976) *Levantamento de recursos naturais, Folha SC 19 Rio Branco*, Projeto Radambrasil, Rio de Janeiro.

—— (1978) *Levantamento de recursos naturais, Folha SC 20 Pôrto Velho*, Projeto Radambrasil, Rio de Janeiro.

—— (1979) *Levantamento de recursos naturais, Folha SD 20 Guaporé*, Projeto Radambrasil, Rio de Janeiro.

Dowler, E. A., Luck, B. M., Robson, V. A. and Kigeme, E. A. R. (1980) An anthropometric survey of 1,074 preschool children in Southern Rwanda, Central Equatorial Africa.

*Journal of Tropical Pediatrics* **26**: 134–8.

Dubos, Rene (1977) Determinants of health and disease. In Landy, David (ed.) *Culture, Disease and Healing: Studies in Medical Anthropology* (pp. 31–40). Macmillan: New York.

Dupon, Jean-François and Vant, André (1979) Contrastes et changements dans l'agriculture du Goiás central. *Les Cahiers d'Outre-Mer* **32**(127) (July–September): 217–52.

Durand, Juan E. (1923) *Leyendas Incaicas, Kore.* Antofagasta, Chile.

Dutra, Manoel (1981) Desnutrição – as primeiras revelações de uma tragédia amazônica. *O Liberal,* 20 caderno (02/08/81): 22–3.

Equipes Pastorais da Prelazia de São Felix do Araguaia e da Diocese de Conceição do Araguaia (1982) *O fogo do ouro.* (Unpublished).

Esterci, Neide (1982) *A questão da terra.* (Unpublished).

Evans, Peter (1979) *Dependent Development: The Alliance of Multinational State, and Local Capital in Brazil.* Princeton University Press.

Falesi, I. (1974) Soils of the Amazon Basin. In Wagley, C. (ed.) *Man in the Amazon* (pp. 201–29). University of Florida Press.

—— (1976) Ecosistemas de pastagem cultivada na Amazônia Brasileira, *Bol. Téc. 1 CPATU (Centro de Pesquisa Agropecuária do Trópico Úmido),* Belém, Pará.

Farabee, William Curtis (1922) *Indian Tribes of Eastern Peru.* Harvard University.

Faria, Vilmar E. (1976) *Occupational Marginality, Employment and Poverty in Urban Brazil.* Ph.D. dissertation, Harvard University.

Fearnside, P. M. (1978) *Estimation of Carrying Capacity for Human Populations in a Part of the Transamazon Highway Colonization Area of Brazil.* Ph.D. dissertation, University of Michigan, Ann Arbor.

—— (1979) Cattle yield prediction for the Transamazon highway of Brazil. *Interciencia,* **4**(4): 220–6.

—— (1980) Land use allocation of the Transamazon highway colonists of Brazil and its relation to human carrying capacity. In Barbira–Scazzocchio, F. (ed.) *Land, People and Planning in Contemporary Amazonia* (pp. 114–38). Centre for Latin American Studies, Cambridge University.

Feder, Ernest (1971) *The Rape of the Peasantry: Latin America's Landholding System.* Doubleday: Garden City, New York.

—— (1979) *Lean Cows – Fat Ranchers. The International Ramifactions of Mexico's Beef Cattle Industry* Distributed by America Latina, London. (Mimeo.).

Ferreira, Roberto da Costa (1981) Setor industrial no estado do Pará. Paper presented at *Seminário Ciência e Tecnologia na Amazônia* (CNPq/NAEA/UFPa.) Belém, September 1981. (Mimeo.).

Fleming-Moran, Millicent and Moran, Emilio (1978) O Surgimento de Clases Sociais numa Comunidade Planejada para ser Igualitária. *Boletím do Museo Paraense Emílio Goeldi.* Nova Série. Antropologia **69**: 1–38.

Fonseca, Manoel Pinto da (1980) *Padrões de colonização e o desenvolvimento regional – o caso paranaense e o caso matogrossense (Análise comparativa).* Tese de mestrado, Universidade Federal de Minas Gerais.

Forman, Shepard (1975) *The Brazilian Peasantry.* Columbia University Press: New York.

Foweraker, J. (1981) *The Struggle for Land,* Cambridge Latin American Studies 39.

Cambridge University Press.

Fox, Robert, W. (1975) *Urban Population Growth Trends in Latin America*. Inter-American Development Bank: Washington DC.

Fraenkel, Lêda Maria and Souza, Mário Duayer de (1976) Diferenças na composição do emprêgo, distribuição da renda e migrações internas. In *Mudanças na composição do emprêgo e na distribuição da renda: efeitos sôbre as migrações internas* (pp. 33–67). Edited by Brasil, Ministério do Interior (MINTER). Brasília, D.F.: Organização Internacional do Trabalho (OIT)/Banco Nacional da Habitação (BNH).

Fry, Carlos (1886) Diario de los Viajes i Exploración de los Ríos Urubamba, Ucayali, Amazonas, Pachitea i Palcazu. In *Colección de Leyes, Decretos, Resoluciones y Otros Documentos Oficiales Referentes al Departamento de Loreto*, Vol. XI. Larrabure y Correa, Carlos: 1911, 18 vols. Ministerio de Relaciones Exteriores, Lima.

Fundação de Assistência aos Garimpeiros (FAG) (1973) *Relação dos municípios ou localidades aonde existem garimpeiros*. Brasília: unpublished.

Fundação Nacional de Arte (FUNARTE) (1981) *Museu Paraense Emílio Goeldi*. Rio de Janeiro.

Fundacredesa (1981) *Estudio Transversal – Area Metropolitana de Caracas 1981* Patrones de Referencia: Caracas.

Furley, P. A. (1979) Solos e aptidão agricola, Setor Ecológica, Diagnóstico e estudo de perspectivas para o Território Federal de Rondônia, *Convênio FUB/SUDDECO*, Universidade de Brasília.

—— (1980) Development planning in Rondonia based on naturally renewable resource surveys. In Barbira–Scazzocchio, F. (ed.) *Land, People and Planning in Contemporary Amazonia*, Centre of Latin American Studies, Cambridge.

Gall, N. (1977) *Letter from Rondônia; a Report on the Brazilian Frontier*, International Fact Finding Center, Carnegie Endowment for International Peace (draft copy) New York.

Gifford, D. R. (1981) *Report on the Environmental Protection sub-project of the World Bank, Appraisal Mission to North-East Brazil* (Jan–Feb), draft copy.

Gilbert, Alan (1974) *Latin American Development – A Geographical Perspective*. Penguin Books: Harmondsworth, Middlesex.

Goldman, Irving (1963) *The Cubeo: Indians of the Northwest Amazon*. Illinois Studies in Anthropology No. 2, The University of Illinois Press.

Gonzales, Elbio Neris and Bastos, Maria Inês (1976) Migração rural e o trabalho volante na agricultura brasileira. In *Encontro brasileiro de estudos populacionais: contribuições apresentadas* (pp. 240–61). Edited by Instituto Brasileiro de Geografia e Estatística (IBGE): Rio de Janeiro.

Gonzalez Nañez, Omar (1977) *Los Indígenas de las Riberas del Guainia-Río Negro: Etapas de un Proceso de Aculturación en la Amazonía Venezolana*, Caracas: UCV, Department of Anthropology, manuscript.

Goodland, R. J. A. (1980) Environmental ranking of Amazonian development. In Barbira–Scazzocchio, F. B. (ed.) *Land, People and Planning in Contemporary Amazonia*, Centre of Latin American Studies, Cambridge.

Goodland, R. J. A. and Irwin, H. S. (1974) An ecological discussion of the environmental impact of the highway constructional program in the Amazon Basin. *Landscape Planning* 1: 123–254.

Goulding, M. (1980) *The Fishes and the Forest*. University of California Press, Berkeley.
—— (1981) *Man and Fisheries on an Amazon Frontier*. Junk Publ.: The Hague.
—— (1982) Amazonian fisheries. In Moran, E. (ed.) *The Dilemma of Amazonian Development*. Westview Press: Boulder, Colorado.
Graber, K. (1976) *Comparación de gastos entre distintos tipos de mecanización en la zona de Santa Cruz, Bolivia* Methodist Church: Cochabamba.
Gros, Christian (1977) La fin d'une autonomie indienne: le cas des indiens Tatuyo du Pira-Paraná. *Cahiers des Amériques Latines* 15: 113–46.
Guillet, D. (1981) Agrarian ecology and peasant production in the central Andes. *Mountain Research and Development* 1(1): 19–28.
Guimarães, G. *et al.* (1981) *Garimpos brasileiros: da história aos fatos atuais*. Presented at symposium on '*Mineralizações auríferas no estado da Bahia*' Sociedade Brasileira de Geologia, Salvador, Bahia.
Guimarães Neto, Leonardo (1976) *O emprêgo urbano no Nordeste: situação atual e evolução recente 1950–70*. Ministério do Interior MINTER/Banco do Nordeste do Brasil BNB: Fortaleza.
Halberg, F. and Katinas, G. (1973) Chronobiologic glossary *International Journal of Chronobiology* 1, 31–63.
Hall, A. L. (1978) *Drought and Irrigation in North-East Brazil* Cambridge Latin American Studies 29 Cambridge University Press.
Hames, R. and Vickers, W. (eds.) (in press) *Adaptive Strategies of Native Amazonians*. Academic Press: New York.
Hardesty, D. L. (1975) The niche concept. *Human Ecology* 3(2): 71–85.
Harner, Michael J. (1973) *The Jívaro: People of the Sacred Waterfalls*. Anchor: Garden City, New York.
Haswell, M. (1981) *Energy for Subsistence* Macmillan: London.
Hébette, Jean and Acevedo Marin, Rosa (1979) Colonização espontânea, política agrária e grupos sociais. In Costa, José Marcelino Monteiro da (ed.) *Amazônia: desenvolvimento e ocupação* (pp. 141–91). Instituto de Planejamento Econômico e Social (IPEA)/Instituto de Pesquisas (INPES): Rio de Janeiro.
Hecht, S. B. (1982) Deforestation in the Amazon Basin: magnitude, dynamics and soil resource effects. In *Regional development alternatives in the Third World, Latin American Regional Conference*, Fundação João Pineiro and International Geographical Union, Belo Horizonte.
—— (ed.) (1983) *Amazonia: Agriculture and Land-use Research*. Centro Internacional de Agricultura Tropical.
Hegstead, D. M. (1978) Protein–calorie malnutrition, *American Scientist*, 66(1): 61–5.
Hennessy, Alistair (1978) *The Frontier in Latin American History*. University of New Mexico: Albuquerque.
Heras, Julian (1978) Los Franciscanos en el Pagoa, Tambo y alto Ucayali a fines del Siglo XVII. In *Amazonía Peruana*, Vol. II, no. 3 Ed. CAAAP: Lima.
Herrera, R., Jordan, C. F., Klinge, H. and Medina, E. (1978) Amazon ecosystems: their structure and functioning with particular emphasis on nutrients. *Interciencia* 3(4): 223–32.
Hiraoka, Mario (1977) Landscape change in a pioneer region: The East Bolivian example. In Eidt, R. C. *et al.* (eds.) *Man, Culture and Settlement* (pp. 69–81). National

Geographical Society of India: Varanasi.

—— (1978) Settlement and development of the Upper Amazon: The East Bolivian example. In Denevan, William M. (ed.) *The Role of Geographic Research in Latin America* (pp. 165–7). Conference of Latin Americanist Geographers (CLAG): Muncie, Indiana.

Holmes, Rebecca (1981) *Estado Nutritional en Cuatro Aldeas de la Selva Amazonica, Venezuela: Un Estudio de Adaptación y Aculturación*, Centro de Estudios Avanzados: Caracas.

Horner, M. R., Harris, W. S., Brown-Lee, B. J., Goldstein, R. S. and Taylor, A. K. (1977) Anthropometric and dietary study of Miskito Indian children in rural Nicaragua, *Ecology of Food and Nutrition*, **6**: 137–46.

Ianni, O. (1978) *A Luta pela Terra*. Vozes: Petrópolis.

—— (1979) *Ditadura e agricultura*. Civilização Brasileira: Rio de Janeiro.

IBGE (nd) *VII Recenseamento geral do Brasil. Censo agrícola de 1960*, série regional II/I–II, 10 parte. Rio de Janeiro.

—— (nd) *Brasil – divisão municipal: situação vigente em 30 – VI – 1967*. Rio de Janeiro.

—— (1972) *Divisão do Brasil em regiões funcionais urbanas*. Rio de Janeiro.

—— (1974) *VIII Recenseamento geral. Censo agropecuário de 1970*, série regional III/I/IV. Rio de Janeiro.

—— (1976) (ed.) *Encontro brasileiro de estudos populacionais: contribuições apresentadas*. Rio de Janeiro.

—— (1977a) *Geografia do Brasil – Vo. 1 Região Norte*. Rio de Janeiro.

—— (1977b) *Atlas de Rondônia* 2e, Rio de Janeiro.

—— (1979a) *A organização do espaço na faixa da Transamaẑonica*, Vol. 1 Rio de Janeiro.

—— (1979b) *Censos econômicos de 1975. Censo agropecuário*, série regional I/1–2—3–4. Rio de Janeiro.

—— (1979c) Indicadores sociais – tabelas selecionadas. Rio de Janeiro

INC/BID (1969) Programa de colonización. *Informe semestral* No 21. La Paz.

INC/CIU (1981) *Evaluación del programa de orientación para nuevos colones en San Julián*: Tomo II. Resultados de las encuestas y escrutinio de los documentos, Tomo III. Conclusiones y recomendaciones. Santa Cruz.

INCRA (1971) *Metodologia para programação operacional dos projetos de assentamento*. Brasília.

—— (1973) *INCRA – Altamira – 1*. Ministério da Agricultura (MA): Brasília.

—— (1974) *Projeto técnico do Projeto Integrado de Colonização de Sagarana; Co-ordenadoria Regional de Minas Gerais* (MA/INCRA/CR.006). Belo Horizonte.

—— (1976a) *Sistema nacional de cadastro rural. Cadastro de imóveis rurais – 1972. Estatísticas cadastrais. Base recadastramento 1972*, vols. 1 and 2. Ministério da Agricultura (MA): Brasília.

—— (1976b) *Programação do Projeto Ouro Prêto/76*, Brasília.

—— (1979) *Programação Operacional do Projeto Ouro Prêto/79*, Brasília.

—— (1980) *Os 10 anos do INCRA*, Brasília.

Izaguirre, Fray Bernardino (1922–9) *Historia de las Misiones Franciscanas y Narración de los Progresos de la Geografía en el Oriente del Perú*, 14 Volumes. Tipografía San Antonio: Cajamarca.

Janzen, Daniel H. (1973) Tropical agroecosystems. *Science*, **182**: 1212–19.

Jelliffe, Derrick B. (1966) *The Assessment of the Nutritional Status of the Community*,

World Health Organization Monograph Series, No. 53, Geneva.

Jerez, P., Padre José Antonio (1765, 1768) Viaje por el Orinoco y el Río Negro, reprinted in Cesáreo de Armellada, *Por la Venezuela Indígena de Ayer y Hoy: Relatos de Misioneros Capuchinos en Viaje por la Venezuela Indígena durante los siglos XVII, XVIII, XIX*, Sociedad de Ciencias Naturales La Salle, Caracas.

Jones, Richard C. (1980) Behavioral causes and consequences of rural–urban migration: special reference to Venezuela. In Thomas, Robert N. and Hunter, John M. (eds.) *Internal Migration Systems in the Developing World With Special Reference to Latin America* (pp. 26–50). Schenkman Publishing Company: Cambridge, Mass.

—— (1981) The impact of perception on urban migration in Latin America. In Martinson, Tom L. and Elbow, Gary S. (eds.) *Geographic Research on Latin America: Benchmark 1980* (pp. 119–27). Conference of Latin Americanist Geographers (CLAG): Muncie, Indiana.

Katzman, Martin T. (1975) Regional development policy in Brazil: The role of growth poles and development highways in Goiás. *Economic Development and Cultural Change* **24**(1) (October 1975): 75–107.

—— (1977) *Cities and Frontiers in Brazil: Regional Dimensions of Economic Development*. Harvard University Press: Cambridge, Mass.

Kay, C. (1980) The hacienda system; proletarianization and agrarian reform. In *El Sector Agrario en América Latina* (pp. 23–38). Publicaciones del Instituto de Estudios Latino Americanos 4, 4: Stockholm.

Keller, Elza C. de Souza (1977) População. In *Geografia do Brasil – Região Norte* (pp. 167–271). Edited by Instituto Brasileiro de Geografia e Estatística (IBGE): Rio de Janeiro.

Keller, W., Donoso, G. and DeMaeyer, E. M. (1976) Anthropometry in nutritional surveillance: A review based on results of the WHO collaborative study on nutritional anthropometry, *Nutrition Abstracts and Reviews*, **46**(8): 591–609.

Kietzman, Dale (1952) Afinidades Culturales de los Amahuacas del Perú. In *Perú Indígena*, Vol. II n°5, 6. Lima.

Kirby, John M. (1976) Agricultural land use and the settlement of Amazonia. *Pacific Viewpoint* **17**(2) (October): 105–32.

Kleinpenning, J. M. G. (1975) *The Integration and Colonization of the Brazilian Portion of the Amazon Basin*. Institute of Geography and Planning: Nijmegen, Holland.

—— (1977) An evaluation of the Brazilian Policy for the Integration of the Amazon Region (1964–1974). *Tijdschrift voor Economische en Sociale Geografie* LXVIII(5): 297–311.

—— (1978) A further evaluation of the Policy for the Integration of the Amazon Region (1974–1976). *Tijdschrift voor Economische en Sociale Geografie* LXIX (1–2): 78–86.

Kowarick, Lúcio (1977) *Capitalismo e marginalidade na América latina*. Paz e Terra: Rio de Janeiro.

Kondratieff, N. D. (1935) The long waves in economic life. *Lloyds Bank Review* **129**: 41–60. (Translated by W. F. Stolper 1935 and abbreviated 1978.)

Kunstadter, P., Chapman, E. C. and Sabhasri, S. (eds.) (1978) *Farmers in the Forest*. Hawaii University Press.

Latin American Regional Report on Brazil. 8 August 1980. Latin American Newsletters: London.

Lee, Everitt S. (1966) A theory of migration. *Demography* **3**(1) (February): 47–57.

## 278 · Bibliography

Leite, L. L. (1982) *The relative importance of land quality to the success of three colonization projects in Brasil*, Ph.D. thesis, University of Edinburgh.

Leite, L. L. and Furley, P. A. (1982) *An appraisal of the success of the land development objectives in the Sagarana Integrated Colonization Project.* Paper given to the Symposium on '*Land Development in the tropics*', I.G.U., Belo Horizonte, Minas Gerais.

Lewis, W. A. (1954) Thoughts on land settlement. *Journal of Agricultural Economics* **11**(1): 3–11.

Leys, Colin (1975) *Underdevelopment in Kenya.* Heinemann: London.

Lieth, H. (1970) Phenology in productivity studies. In Reichle, D. *Analysis of Temperate Forest Ecosystems* (p. 29) Springer-Verlag: Heidelberg.

—— (1974) Purposes of a phenology book. In Lieth, H. (ed.) *Phenology and Seasonality Modelling* (p. 5) Ecological Studies 8. Chapman and Hall Ltd: London.

Linares, O. F. (1976) Garden hunting in the American Tropics. *Human Ecology* **4**(4): 331–50.

Lipset, Seymour M. and Solari, Aldo (eds.) (1967) *Elites in Latin America.* Oxford University Press: New York.

Lisansky, Judith (1979) Women in the Brazilian Frontier. *Latin Americanist* **15**(1) (December 1): 1–2.

—— (1980) *Santa Terezinha: Life in a Brazilian Frontier Town.* Ph.D. dissertation, University of Florida.

Macdonald, Theodore, Jr. (1982) Teoría y metodología para la delimitación de territorios nativos en el Ecuador. In Uquillas, Jorge E. (ed.) *Informe para la Delimitación de Territorios Nativos.* INCRAE: Quito.

Mahar, Dennis J. (1978) *Desenvolvimento econômico da Amazônia: uma análise das políticas governamentais.* Instituto de Planejamento Econômico e Social (IPEA)/Instituto de pesquisas (INPES): Rio de Janeiro.

—— (1979) *Frontier Development Policy in Brazil: A Study of Amazonia.* Praeger: New York.

Maia, Maria Elisabeth C. de Sá Távora (1977) Atividade agrária. In *Geografia do Brasil — Região Norte* (pp. 341–93). Edited by Instituto de Geografia e Estatistica (IBGE): Rio de Janeiro.

Marcoy, Paul (1875) *Travels in South America from the Pacific Ocean to the Atlantic Ocean*, 2 volumes. London.

MARNR (1979) *Atlas de Venezuela*, Dirección de Cartografía Nacional, Caracas.

Martine, George (1976) Adaptação de Migrantes ou Sobrevivência dos Mais Fortes? *Projeto de Planejamento de Recursos Humanos BRA/70/550*, Relatório técnico 30 (September): 1–31.

—— (nd) Migrações internas e alternativas de fixação produtiva: experiências recentes de colonização no Brasil. In Berquó, Elza S. *Anais do primeiro encontro nacional de estudos populacionais* (pp. 51–85). Associação Brasileira de Estudos Populacionais (ABEP): São Paulo.

Martine, George and Peliano, José Carlos, P. (1978) *Migrantes no mercado de trabalho metropolitano.* Instituto de Planejamento Econômico e Social (IPEA)/Instituto de Planejamento (IPLAN): Brasília.

Martins, José de Souza (1980) *Expropriação e violência: a questão política no campo.*

Editora de Humanismo, Ciência e Tecnologia (HUCITEC): São Paulo.

—— (nd) The state and the militarization of the agrarian question in Amazonia. In Schmink, Marianne and Wood, Charles H. (eds.) *Frontier Expansion in Amazonia*. University Presses of Florida: Gainesville (forthcoming).

Martinson, Tom L. and Elbow, Gary S. (eds.) (1981) *Geographical Research on Latin America: Benchmark 1980*. Conference of Latin Americanist Geographers (CLAG): Muncie, Indiana.

Matos Arvelo, Martín (1912) *Vida Indiana*, Casa Editorial Maucci: Barcelona.

Matteson, Esther (1954) The Piro of the Urubamba, *Kroeber Anthropological Society Papers*. Berkeley.

Maxwell, S. (1980) Marginalised colonists to the north of Santa Cruz. Avenues of escape from the *barbecho* crisis. In Barbira-Scazzocchio, F. (ed.) *Land, People and Planning in Contemporary Amazonia* (pp. 162–70). Cambridge, Centre of Latin American Studies Occasional Publication No. 3.

Meier, G. M. (1976) *Leading Issues in Economic Development* (3rd edn.) Oxford University Press: New York.

Mendes, Armando D. (1971) *Estradas para o desenvolvimento*, Cadernos Paraenses IDESP 6. Governo do Estado do Pará: Belém.

Merrick, Thomas W. and Moran, Ricardo (1979) Annex I – Population. In *Brazil – Human Resources Special Report*, (pp. 1–85). Edited by Latin American and the Caribbean Regional Office, The World Bank. Washington D.C.: The World Bank/The International Bank for Reconstruction and Development (IBRD).

Merrill, Charles W., Henderson, Charles W. and Kiessling, O. E. (1937) *Small-Scale Placer Mining as a Source of Gold, Employment, and Livelihood in 1935*. Philadelphia: U.S. Works Progress Administration National Research Project and Bureau of Mines, Department of the Interior.

Miller, Darrel (1979) *Transamazon Town: Transformation of a Brazilian Riverine Community*. Ph.D. dissertation, University of Florida.

—— (1982) Entrepreneurs and bureaucrats: The rise of an urban middle class. In Moran, Emilio (ed.) *The Dilemma of Amazonian Development*. Westview Press: Boulder, Colorado.

Miller, Elmer S. (1970) The Christian missionary, agent of secularization, *Anthropological Quarterly*, **43**(1): pp. 14–22.

Miller, Linda (1981) *Patrons, Politics, and Schools: An Arena for Brazilian Women*. Studies in Third World Societies **15**: 67–90.

Monte-Mor, Roberto Luis de (1980) *Espaço e Planejamento Urbano: Considerações sobre o Caso de Rondônia*. M.Sc. Thesis. Federal University of Rio de Janeiro.

Moore, W. M. (1968) *A Dictionary of Geography*. Penguin: Harmondsworth, Middlesex.

Moran, Emilio F. (1975) *Pioneer Farmers of the Transamazon Highway: Adaptation and Agricultural Production in the Lowland Tropics*. Ph.D. dissertation, University of Florida: Gainesville.

—— (1976) *Agricultural Development on the Transamazon Highway*. Latin American Studies Working Papers. Indiana University, Bloomington.

—— (1977) Estrategias de Sobrevivência: O Uso de Recursos ao Longo da Rodovia Transamazônica. *Acta Amazônica* **7**(3): 363–79.

—— (1979) Criteria for choosing homesteaders in Brazil. *Research in Economic*

## 280 · Bibliography

*Anthropology* **3**: 339–59.

—— (1981) *Developing the Amazon.* Indiana University Press: Bloomington.

—— (1982) Ecological, anthropological, and agronomic research in the Amazon Basin. *Latin American Research Review* **17**: 3–41.

—— (1982a) Colonization in the Transamazon and Rondonia. In Schmink, M. and Wood, C. (eds.) *Frontier Expansion in Amazonia.*

—— (1981b) (ed.) *The Dilemma of Amazonian Development.* Westview Press: Boulder, Colorado.

Moran, E. F. and Hill, J. (in press) Adaptive strategies of Wakuenai peoples to an oligotrophic environment, Rio Negro, Venezuelan Amazon. In Salisbury, R. (ed.) *Affluence and Cultural Survival. Proceedings of the 1981 Meeting of American Ethnological Society.* West Publishing Co.: St Paul, Minnesota.

Moreira, Morvan de Mello and Carvalho, José Alberto Magno de (1976) *Migrações internas na Região Norte, II.* Belém Ministério do Interior (MINTER)/ Superintendência do Desenvolvimento da Amazônia (SUDAM).

Morin, Claude (1977) Les rapports de production dans l'agriculture latino-américaine: le 'problème agraire' devant l'histoire. *Notes de Recherche des Ateliers de Recherche Latino-américaine*, série G, n⁰ 2. Institut de Coopération Internationale de l'Université d'Ottawa.

Mougeot, Luc J. A. (1976) De la marginalité à l'intégration: les migrants du bidonville Siloé, Cali, Colombie. Thèse de maîtrise, Université d'Ottawa.

—— (1978) Seletividade e retenção migratória nas cidades pequenas das frentes de expansão amazônica. Paper presented at *3⁰ Encontro Nacional de Geógrafos* (AGB), Fortaleza, July 1978. (mimeo.).

—— (1980a) *City-ward Migration and Migrant Retention During Frontier Development in Brazil's North Region.* Ph.D. dissertation, Michigan State University.

—— (1980b) Frontier population absorption and migrant socio-economic mobility: evidence from Brazilian Amazonia. In Martinson, Tom L. and Elbow, Gary S. (eds.) *Geographic Research on Latin America: Benchmark 1980* (pp. 150–61). Muncie: Conference of Latin Americanist Geographers CLAG, 1981. Original version presented at *Xth Meeting of the Conference of Latin Americanist Geographers* (CLAG), Muncie, April 1980. (mimeo.).

Mougeot, Luc J. A. and Aragón, Luis E. (1981) Introdução. In *O despovoamento do território amazônico: contribuições para a sua interpretação.* Cadernos NAEA n⁰ 6, pp. 19–31. Organised by idem. Belém: Serviço de Imprensa Universitária.

Mueller, C. C. (1980) Frontier-based agricultural expansion: the case of Rondônia. In Barbira-Scazzocchio, F. (ed.) *Land, People and Planning in contemporary Amazonia*, (pp. 141–53). Centre for Latin American Studies, Cambridge University.

Muratorio, Blanca (1982) *Etnicidad, Evangelización y Protesta en el Ecuador.* CIESE: Quito.

Murphy, Robert (1960) *Headhunters' Heritage.* University of California Press: Berkeley.

—— (1961) Deviance and social control I: What makes Waru run? *Kroeber Anthropological Society Papers*, Number 24, pp. 55–61.

Murra, J. V. (1960) Rite and crop in the Inca state. In Diamond, S. (ed.) *Culture in History: Essays in Honour of Paul Radin* (pp. 393–407). Columbia University Press: New York.

—— (1972) El control vertical de un máximo de pisos ecológicas en la economia de las sociedades Andinas. In *Visita a la Provincia León de Huánuco – 1562*. Huánuco.

—— (1975) *Formaciones Económicas y Políticas del Mundo Andino*. Instituto de Estudios Peruanos, Serie Historia 3, Lima.

Myers, Thomas P. (1974) Spanish contacts and social change on the Ucayali River, Perú. *Ethnohistory*, **21**(2) Spring, pp. 35–158.

Neel, James V. (1977) *Health and disease in unacculturated Amerindian populations*, CIBA Foundation Symposium 49 (New Series): 155–77. New York.

Nelson, Joan M. (1976) Sojourners versus new urbanites: Causes and consequences of temporary versus permanent city-ward migration in developing countries. *Economic Development and Cultural Change* **24**(4) (July): 721–58.

Nelson, M. (1973) *The Development of Tropical Lands*. The Johns Hopkins University Press: Baltimore.

Nicholaides, J. *et al.* (1982) Cropping systems in the Amazon. In Moran, E. F. (ed.) *The Dilemma of Amazonian Development*. Westview Press: Boulder, Colorado.

Norgaard, R. (1979) *The Economics of Agricultural Technology and Environmental Transformation in the Amazon*. Paper presented at seminar at UFMg. (mimeo.).

Norman, M. J. T. (1978) Energy inputs and outputs of subsistence systems in the tropics *Agro-Ecosystems* **4**: 355–66.

Oberem, Udo (1980) *Los Quijos: Historia de la Transculturación de un Grupo Indígena en el Oriente Ecuatoriano*. Otavalo: IOA.

Ocampo Conejeros, Baltazar (1955) Descripción y sucesos históricos de la Provincia de Vilcabamba. In *Revista del Archivo Histórico del Cuzco*. VI, nº 6.

O'Donnell, Guillermo (1978) Reflections on the patterns of change in the bureaucratic-authoritarian state, *Latin American Research Review* **1**(78): 3–39.

Ortiz, Dionisio OFM. (1974) *Alto Ucayali y Pachitea*, 2 Volumes. Lima.

Oxaal, Ivar, Barnett, Tony and Booth, David (1975) *Beyond the Sociology of Development*. Routledge and Kegan Paul: London.

Pacheco, L. M. T. (1979) *Colonização dirigida: estrategia de acumulação e legitimação de um estado autoritário*, Tese de mestrado, Depto. de Ciências Sociais: Brasília.

Paget, Ernest (1960) Comments on the adjustment of settlement in marginal areas. *Geografiska Annaler* **42**(4): 324.

Panagides, S. and Magalhães, V. L. (1974) Amazon economic policy and prospects. In Wagley, C. (ed.) *Man in the Amazon*. University of Florida Press: Gainesville.

Parsons, J. J. (1976) Forest to pasture: development or destruction? *Rev. Biologia Tropical* **24** (Supl. 1) 121–38.

Pastore, José (1979) *Desigualdade e mobilidade social no Brasil*. T. A. Queiroz: São Paulo.

Pérez, Antonio (1981) Los Baré. In Coppens, W. (ed.) *Aborígenes de Venezuela*, Fundación La Salle: Caracas.

Pickersgill, B. and Heisen, C. (1977) Origins and distribution of plants domesticated in the New World tropics. In Reed, C. A. (ed.) *Origins of Agriculture* (pp. 803–35). Mouton: The Hague.

Pimentel, Lourdes, (1973–4) A Transamazônica e o problema da integração social. *A Amazônia Brasileira em Foco* **9** (junho 1973–junho 1974): 24–60.

Pinto, Lúcio Flávio (1982) Conflitos de terras no sul do Pará. *Reforma Agrária* **12**(2): 3–12.

Poleman, Thomas (1964) *The Papaloapan Project: Agricultural Development in the Mexican Tropics*. Stanford University Press.

Pool, Douglas (1981) *Agricultural Potential and Natural Resource Management of the Palcazu Valley, Peru*. Central Selva Resource Management 2: K1–K38; JRB Associates: Lima.

Posey, D. (1982) Indigenous ecological knowledge and development of the Amazon. In Moran, E. F. (ed.) *The Dilemma of Amazonian Development*. Westview Press: Boulder, Colorado.

Price, Weston Andrew (1945) *Nutrition and Physical Degeneration: A Comparison of Primitive and Modern Diets and Their Effects*, Redlands, Calif., published by the author.

Proyecto Especial Pichis-Palcazu (1981a) *Proyecto Forestal Dentro del Bosque Nacional Alexander Von Humboldt*. (mimeo.) Lima.

—— (1981b) *Documento sin título sobre el evaluación del potencial forestal del área del Proyecto*. (mimeo.) Lima.

Puffer, R. R. and Serrano, C. V. (1973) *Patterns of Mortality in Childhood*. Pan American Health Organization, Publ. no. 262: Washington, DC.

Raimondi, Antonio (1862) Informe sobre la Provincia Litoral de Loreto Vol. VII. In *Colección de Leyes* . . . Larrabure y Correa, 1911, 18 volumes.

—— (1879) *El Perú*, 3 volumes. Imprenta del Estado: Lima.

Ribeiro, Darcy (1977) *Os índios e a civilização: a integração das populações indígenas no Brasil moderno*. 2nd ed. Editora Vozes: Petrópolis.

Rios, R. (1979) *Development of integrated agricultural, livestock and forestry production systems in rural Peru*. In CATIE *Agroforestry Systems in Latin America* (pp. 91–106). Turrialba, Costa Rica.

Riviere, P. G. (1972) *The Forgotten Frontier: Ranchers of North Brazil*. Holt, Rinehart & Winston: New York.

Rivière d'Arc, Hélène (1977) Le Nord du Mato Grosso: colonisation et nouveau 'bandeirismo'. *Annales de Géographie* 86(475) May–June: 279–308.

Rivière d'Arc, Hélène and Apestéguy, Christine (1978) Les nouvelles franges pionnières en Amazonie brésilienne – La vallée de l'Araguaia. *Etudes Rurales* 69 (January–March): 81–100.

Roberts, Bryan (1978) *Cities of Peasants: The Political Economy of Urbanization in the Third World*. Sage Publications: Beverley Hills, California.

Robson, J. R. K. and Wadsworth, G. R. (1977) The health and nutritional status of primitive populations. *Ecology of Food and Nutrition*, 6: 187–202.

Roett, Riordan (1978) *Brazil: Politics in a Patrimonial Society*. Praeger: New York.

Ross, Eric (1978) The evolution of the Amazon peasantry. *Journal of Latin American Studies* 10(2): 193–218.

Ruddle, K. (1974) The Yukpa cultivation system. *Ibero-Americana 52*. University of California Press: Berkeley.

Sahlins, Marshall (1981) *Historical Metaphors and Mythical Realities: Structure in the Early History of the Sandwich Islands Kingdom*. Association for Social Anthropology in Oceania, The University of Michigan Press.

Saint-Hilaire, Auguste (1941) *Viagens pelo Distrito dos Diamantes e Litoral do Brasil*. Nacional: São Paulo.

Sales, Herberto (1955) *Garimpos de Bahia*. Ministério da Agricultura, Serviço de Informação, Documentário da Vida Rural, No. 8, Rio de Janeiro.

Salomão, Elmer Prata (1981) Garimpos do Tapajós. *Ciências da Terra* 1 (Nov./Dec.): 38–45.

—— (1982) A Força do Garimpo. *Rev. Bras. Tecnol.* **13**(2) (April/May): 13–20.

Samanez Ocampo, José B. (1883) Exploración de los Ríos Apurímac, Ene, Tambo, Urubamba i Ucayali. In Vol. XI de la *Colección de Leyes* . . . Larrabure y Correa; 1911, 18 volumes.

Sánchez, P. A. (1976) *Properties and Management of Soils in the Tropics.* Wiley-Interscience: New York.

Sánchez, P. A., Bandy, D. E., Villachica, J. H. and Nicholaides, J. J. III (1982) Amazon Basin soils: management for continuous crop production *Science* **216**, 821–7.

Sanders, John H. and Bein, Frederick, L. (1976) Agricultural development on the Brazilian frontier: Southern Mato Grosso. *Economic Development and Cultural Change* **24**(3) (April): 593–610.

Santos, Roberto (1979) Sistema de propriedade e relacões de trabalho no meio rural paraense. In da Costa, José Marcelino Monteiro (ed.) *Amazônia: desenvolvimento e ocupação,* (pp. 103–40). Instituto de Planejamento Econômico e Social (IPEA)/Instituto de Pesquisas (INPES): Rio de Janeiro.

Santos, Roberto Araújo de Oliveira (1980) *História econômica da Amazônia: 1800–1920.* T. A. Queiroz: São Paulo.

Saunders, J. (1974) The population of the Brazilian Amazon today. In Wagley, C. (ed.) *Man in the Amazon* (pp. 160–80). University of Florida Press: Gainesville.

Sawyer, Donald R. *et al.* (1979) *Ocupação agrícola da Amazônia: primeiros estudos para a fixação de diretrizes. vol. II.* Ministério da Agricultura (MA)/Centro de Desenvolvimento e Planejamento Regional (CEDEPLAR), UFMG: Brasília and Belo Horizonte.

Schieffelin, Edward L. (1981) Evangelical rhetoric and the transformation of traditional culture in Papua New Guinea, *Society for Comparative Study of Society and History*, pp 150–6.

Schmink, Marianne (1977) *Frontier expansion and land conflicts in the Brazilian Amazon: Contradictions in policy and process.* Paper presented at American Anthropological Association meeting, Houston.

—— (1981) *A Case Study of the Closing Frontier in Brazil.* Amazon Research Paper Series, Center for Latin American Studies, University of Florida, Gainesville.

—— (1982) Land conflicts in Amazonia. *American Ethnologist* **9**(2) (May): 341–57.

Schmink, M. and Wood, C. H. (eds.) (in press) *Frontier Expansion in Amazonia.*

Schofield, S. (1979) *Development and the Problems of Village Nutrition.* Croom Helm: London.

Schuurman, F. (1981) The Amazon Region in national regional development planning. In Banck, G. *et al.* (eds.) *State and Region in Latin America: A Workshop.* CEDLA: Amsterdam.

SEAC (1980) *Rondônia rural development project: farm models* Secretaria de Agricultura e Colonização do Territorio de Rondônia (preliminary version), Pôrto Velho.

Secretaria de Planejamento da Presidência da República (SEPLAN)/Fundação Instituto Brasileiro de Geografia e Estatística (FIBGE) (1981) *IX Recenseamento geral do Brasil – 1980. Sinopse preliminar do censo demográfico,* 1/1, nº 1, 6, 23, 24. IBGE: Rio de Janeiro.

Seijas, Haydée and Arvelo-Jiménez, Nelly (1978) Factores condicionantes de los niveles de salud en grupos indígenas venezolanos, estudio preliminar (1), in Wagner, Erika and Zucci, Alberta (eds.), *Unidad y Variedad: Ensayos Antropológicos en Homenaje a José M. Cruxent*, Ediciones CEA: IVIC.

Seligson, M. (1979) The impact of agrarian reform: A study of Costa Rica. *J. Developing Areas* 13, 161–74.

Shakir, A. and Morley, D. (1974) *Lancet* 1: 758.

Shapiro, Judith (1981) Ideologies of Catholic missionary practice in a postcolonial era, *Society for Comparative Study of Society and History*, pp. 130–49.

Shoemaker, R. (1981) *Peasants of El Dorado: Conflict and Contradiction in a Peruvian Frontier Settlement*. Cornell University Press: Ithaca, New York.

Silva, L. F. and Carvalho Filho, R. and Santana, M. B. M. (1973) Solos do Projeto Ouro Prêto, *Bol. Téc.* 23 Centro de Pesquisas do Cacau, Itabuna, Bahia.

Silva, Nelson do Valle (1973) *Posição social das ocupações*. IBGE: Rio de Janeiro. (mimeo.).

Silva, Renato Nunes da (1981) *Migrações internas no estado do Acre: Rio Branco, um caso de urbanização precoce*. Tese de mestrado, Universidade Federal do Pará.

Sioli, H. (1973) Recent human activities in the Brazilian Amazon region and their ecological effects. Meggers, Betty L., Ayensu, Edward S. and Duckworth, W. Donald (eds.) *Tropical Forest Ecosystems in Africa and South America: a comparative review.* Smithsonian Institution: Washington DC.

Smith, Nigel J. (1976a) *Transamazon Highway: A Cultural Ecological Analysis of Settlement in the Lowland Tropics*. Ph.D. dissertation, University of California, Berkeley.

—— (1976b) Utilization of game along Brazil's Transamazon Highway *Acta Amazonica* 7(1): 23–38.

—— (1978) Agricultural productivity along Brazil's Transamazon Highway. *Agroecosystems* 4: 415–32.

—— (1980) Anthrosols and human carrying capacity *Annals of the Association of American Geographers* 70(4): 553–66.

—— (1981) *Man, Fishes and the Amazon*, Columbia University Press: New York.

Smole, W. J. (1976) *The Yanoama Indians: a Cultural Geography*. University of Texas Press: Austin.

—— (1982) *Rainforest Corridors*. University of California Press: Berkeley.

Souza Martins, J. (1980) *Fighting for Land: Indians and Posseiros in Legal Amazonia* in Barbira-Scazzocchio pp. 95–105.

Spielmann, H. O. (1974) Problems of agricultural development in Costa Rica *Applied Sciences and Development* 1: 97–118.

Spruce, Richard (1908) *Notes of a Botanist on the Amazon and Andes*. Volumes I and II, London: reprinted by Johnson Reprint Corp.

Staver, Charles (1981) *Annual Production Systems in the Palcazu Valley and Means for their Expansion and Intensification*. Central Selva Resource Management 2: M1–M53; JRB Associates: Lima.

Steward, Julian, ed. (1948) *Handbook of South American Indians*, 6 volumes, Washington.

Stewart, H. C. and Stevenson, S. S. (1959) Physical growth and development. In Nelson, W. (ed.) *Textbook of Pediatrics*, 7th edn.

Stiglich, Germán (1904) *Últimas Exploraciones de le Junta de Vías Fluviales*, Oficina Tipográfica de la 'Opinión Nacional' Lima.

Stoddart, D. R. and Walsh, R. (1982) Environmental variability and environmental extremes in an island ecosystem. *Proceedings of the 13th Pacific Science Congress.*

Tambs, L. (1974) Geopolitics of the Amazon. In Wagley, C. (ed.) *Man in the Amazon.* University of Florida Press: Gainesville.

Taussig, Michael T. (1980) *The Devil and Commodity Fetishism in South America.* University of North Carolina Press: Chapel Hill.

Teruel, J. R., Gomes, U. A. and Nogueira, J. L. (1973) Seasonal distribution of deaths caused by diarrhoea and malnutrition in childhood. *Rev. Inst. Med. Trop. São Paulo*, 15: 289–97.

Thompson, Stephen I. (1975) The contemporary Latin American frontier. *Comparative Frontier Studies* I (Fall): 7.

Tocantins, Antonio M. G. (1877) Estudo sobre a tribu Mundurucú. *Revista Trimensal do Institutuo Histórico, Geográfico e Ethnográfico do Brasil.* XL: 73–161.

Tosi, Joseph, (1981) *Land Use Capability and Recommended Land Use for the Palcazu Valley.* Central Selva Resource Management 2: N1–N70; JRB Associates: Lima.

Tosi, J. A. and Voertman, R. F. (1964) Some environmental factors in the economic development of the tropics. *Economic Geography* 40(3): 189–205.

Townsend, J. G. (1976) *Land and Society in the Middle Magdalena Valley*, Colombia, Unpublished D.Phil. thesis, Oxford.

—— (1977) Perceived worlds of the colonists of tropical rainforest, Colombia. *Transactions, Institute of British Geographers*, New Series 2(4): 430–57.

Tupiassú, Amilcar A. and Jatene, Simão R. (1978) *Evolução e situação atual da agricultura na Amazônia: contribuição para o estudo.* NAEA/UFPa: Belém. (mimeo.).

Uhl, C. and Murphy, P. (1981) A comparison of energy values and productivities between successional vegetation and agricultural crops after cutting and burning a terra firme rain forest in the Amazon Basin. *Agroecosystems* 7: 63–83.

Unikel, Luis (1975) Urbanism and urbanization in Mexico: situation and prospects. In Hardoy, Jorge (ed.) *Urbanization in Latin America: Approaches and Issues* (pp. 391–434). Anchor: Garden City, New York.

Uquillas, Jorge E. (1982a) *Colonization and spontaneous settlement in Ecuador.* Paper presented at the 31st Latin American Conference on Frontier Expansion in Amazonia. University of Florida, Gainesville.

—— (1982b) (ed.) *Informe para la Delimitación de Territorios Nativos Siona-Secoya, Cofán y Huaorani.* INCRAE: Quito.

Van Wambeke, A. (1978) Properties and potentials of soils in the Amazon Basin, *Interciencia* 3(4): 223–47.

Velho, Otavio Guilherme (1972) *Frentes de Expansão e Estrutura Agrária: Estudo do Processo de Penetração numa Área da Transamazônica.* Zahar Editores: Rio de Janeiro.

—— (1976) *Capitalismo Autoritario e Campesinato.* Difel: São Paulo.

Vickers, William T. (1972) Indians, oil and colonists: contrasting systems of man-land relations in the Aguarico river valley of Eastern Ecuador. *Latinamericanist* 8(2): December 20.

—— (1976) *Cultural Adaptation to Amazonian Habitats: the Siona-Secoya of Eastern*

*Ecuador*. University Microfilms International: Ann Arbor.

—— (1982) Informe preliminar sobre las culturas Siona-Secoya y Cofán y su situación de tenencia de la tierra. In Uquillas, Jorge E. (ed.) *Informe para la Delimitación de Territorios Nativos*. INCRAE: Quito.

Volbeda, S. (1982a) *Bevolkingsontwikkelingen in Amazônia Legal. Een identificatie van frontiers*. 41 pp. Publikatie 32, Vakgroep Sociale Geografie van de Ontwikkelingslanden: Nijmegen.

—— (1982b) *Urbanisatie in Amazônia Legal. Een identificatie van pionierssteden, hun ontstaan en hun rol in het integratieproces van Amazônia*. 34 pp. Publikatie 33, Vakgroep Sociale Geografie van de Ontwikkelingslanden: Nijmegen.

Wagley, Charles W. (1953) *Amazon Town: A Study of Man in the Tropics*. Macmillan: London, (reprinted 1976 Oxford University Press: New York).

—— (ed.) (1974) *Man in the Amazon*. University of Florida Press: Gainesville.

—— (1977) *Welcome of Tears: The Tapirapé Indians of Central Brazil*. Oxford University Press: New York.

Wallace, Alfred Russell (1889) *A Narrative of Travels on the Amazon and Rio Negro*, New York: reprinted from the second edition, Dover Publications, 1972.

Walsh, R. (1980) *Drainage Density and Process in a Humid Tropical Environment*. Ph.D. thesis, University of Cambridge.

—— (1981) The nature of climatic seasonality. In Chambers, R. *et al.* (eds.) *Seasonal Dimensions to Rural Poverty*, Frances Pinter: London; Allanheld: Osmun, New Jersey.

Webb, K. E. (1974) *The Changing Face of North-East Brazil*, Columbia University Press: New York.

Wesche, Rolf (1978) A moderna ocupação agricola em Rondônia, *Revista Bras. Geogr.* **40**, 3, 4: 233–47.

—— (1981) Amazonic colonization: a solution for Brazil's land tenure problems? In Alschuler, Lawrence R. (ed.) *Dependent Agricultural Development and Agrarian Reform in Latin America* (pp. 103–33). University of Ottawa Press.

Wilken, G. C. (1977) Integrating forest and small-scale farm systems in Middle America *Agroecosystems* **3**: 291–302.

Wilkie, Richard W. (1981) The dynamics of human settlement and migration. In Martinson, Tom L. and Elbow, Gary S. (eds.) *Geographical Research on Latin America: Benchmark 1980* (pp. 66–89). Conference of Latin Americanist Geographers (CLAG), Muncie, Indiana.

Winterhalder, B. P. and Thomas, R. B. (1978) *Geoecology of Southern Highland Peru*. Institute of Arctic and Alpine Research, Occasional paper 27, University of Colorado, Boulder.

Wolpe, H. (1978) *The Articulation of Modes of Production*. University of Essex, Colchester (mimeo.).

Wood, Charles H. (1977) Infant mortality trends and capitalist development in Brazil: the case of São Paulo and Belo Horizonte. *Latin American Perspectives* **4**: 56–65.

Wood, Charles, and Schmink, Marianne (1979) Blaming the Victim: Small Farmer Production in an Amazon Colonization Project. *Studies in Third World Societies* **7**: 77–93. Washington DC. (Previously presented at the Annual Meeting of the American Association for the Advancement of Science, Washington DC, 1978.)

Wood, Charles, and Wilson J. (1982) *The Role of the Amazon Frontier in the Demography of Rural Brazil.* Paper presented at the Conference on Frontier Expansion in Amazonia. University of Florida, Gainesville Feb. 7–11, 1982.

Wood, Corrine Shear (1979) Nutrition, anthropology and human health, Ch. 3 in *Human Sickness and Health: A Biocultural View*, Mayfield Publishing Co.: Palo Alto, California.

World Bank (1979) *An integrated development of Brazil's north west frontier*, Rept. No. 3042aBR Washington DC.

World Health Organisation (1978) *A Growth Chart for International Use in Maternal and Child Health Care*, Geneva.

Wright, Robin (1981) *History and Religion of the Baniwa Peoples of the Upper Rio Negro Valley*, Stanford University Ph.D. Dissertation, University Microfilms International.

Yost, James A. (1978) Variables affecting land requirements for tropical forest horticulturalists: some policy implications. Paper read at the symposium *Amazonia: Extinction or Survival?* University of Wisconsin, Madison.

—— (1979) El Desarrollo Comunitario y la Supervivencia Etnica: el caso de los Huaorani, Amazonía Ecuatoriana. *Cuadernos Etnolingüísticos* No. 6, ILV: Quito.

—— (1981) Veinte Años de Contacto: los Mecanismos de Cambio en la Cultura Huao (Auca). *Cuadernos Etnolingüísticos* No 9. ILV: Quito.

—— (1982) Informe y recomendaciones para solucionar el problema de tierras del grupo étnico nativo Huaorani. In Uquillas, Jorge E. (ed.) *Informe para la Delimitación de Territorios Nativos*. INCRAE: Quito.

Zarzar, Alonso and Montenegro, Carlos (1977) *Informe del Trabajo de Campo en Sepahua*, 76 pp. Typed.

# Index